Out On Stage

out on stage

Lesbian and Gay Theatre in the Twentieth Century

Alan Sinfield

Yale University Press
New Haven and London

for Gowan

Set in Walbaum MT and ITC Officina Sans
Printed in Great Britain by The Bath Press, Bath

Library of Congress Cataloging in Publication Data

Sinfield, Alan.
    Out on stage: lesbian and gay theatre in the twentieth century/Alan Sinfield
    Includes bibliographical references and index.
    ISBN 0–300–08102–2 (hbk: alk. paper)
    1. English drama—20th century—History and criticism. 2. Homosexuality and
literature—Great Britain—History—20th century. 3. Homosexuality and literature—
United States—History—20th century. 4. Gays' writings, American—history and criticism.
5. Gays' writings, English—History and criticism. 6. Lesbians in literature. 7. Gay men in
literature. I. Title.
PR739.H65S56 1999
820.9'3520664—dc21   99–28103
                                                                          CIP

A catalogue record for this book is available from the British Library.

10   9   8   7   6   5   4   3   2   1

Contents

Contents · vi

Acknowledgements

Many people have been very generous with suggestions, materials, reminiscences. I am specially indebted to Neil Bartlett, Peter Burton, Sue-Ellen Case, Robin Dashwood, Jonathan Dollimore, the late David Elwyn-Jones, Linda Fitzsimmons, the late Jackie Forster, Christine Fox, Sandra Freeman, Lynda Hart, Gowan Hewlett, John Holmstrom (Roger Gellert), Michael Jamieson, Karen Leick, Stephen Maddison, Susan Manning, Ben May, Joel Pfister, Vincent Quinn, Dan Rebellato, Brian Roberts, Stephen Rooney, Simon Shepherd, Mark Sinfield, Colin Spencer, Mick Wallis, Lois Weaver, Gregory Woods.

I have benefited greatly from the libraries of the University of Sussex (which has scoured the world for me to supplement its own holdings), the Theatre Museum (London), Northwestern University (Evanston), the Drama Association of Wales (Cardiff), and the Theater Instituut Nederland (Amsterdam).

Ultimately this book is about working out new ways to be human — though not, of course, in conditions of our own choosing. The people who have most helped me to do that lately are Gowan Hewlett and Vincent Quinn.

Note on Indexes and Citations

In the text, the name of a play is followed by the date (in brackets); page references are to the edition listed in the Index of Plays. Plays are indexed there alphabetically by title; the date following the title (in brackets) is normally the date of first performance. Then the edition cited in the text is specified; and figures in bold type index references to the play in the text. I make no attempt to give production histories as such; they would not mean much to most readers without considerable explanation, so it would be an immense project. However, this is not a work of textual criticism, and circumstances of production are often adduced.

A few musicals are listed in the Index of Plays because they came specially to attention, but generally this index is limited to plays. Other citations are in the endnotes. Playwrights appear alphabetically in the Index of Names and Topics.

In several plays quoted from typescripts, references follow the conventions of such scripts: they are to act, scene and page, with the pagination starting at one at the beginning of each act.

Plays by W. Somerset Maugham (with the exception of *The Letter*) are referenced to the three-volume *Collected Plays*, in which each volume contains two parts, each starting at page one. The first part is referenced as 'a' and the second part as 'b'.

Three dots, except when credited to an author, indicate my streamlining of a quotation. When quoting stage directions I have not maintained the conventional uses of italics, except when they are counterposed with dialogue or other material in roman type.

1

Introduction

The Project

Theatre and homosexuality are explored together here for two reasons. First, theatre has been a powerful institution. It has afforded the legitimacy that accompanies presentation in public; that is why it has often attracted censorship and sponsorship from the State, the Church, political organisations and big business. Stage representations of lesbians and gay men are influential. Second, theatre and theatricality have been experienced throughout the twentieth century as queer – though not simply so, since until recently almost nowhere has been that. 'Male homosexuality has long been associated in the public mind with Bohemian artistic and theatrical circles', D.J. West declared in 1955.[1] Theatre has been a particular site for the formation of dissident sexual identities.

Both theatre and homosexuality are presented here in their histories; changes in theatre as an institution interact with shifts in ideologies of gender and sexuality. My engagement is with the period between the end of the nineteenth century, when Oscar Wilde was celebrated and vilified, and the end of the twentieth century, when the conditions for explicit lesbian and gay theatre have been achieved – to the point where gay presence in the mainstream can be complained of as disproportionate. This period begins with the rapid spread of the modern idea of the homosexual (through the notoriety of Wilde and Radclyffe Hall in particular), continues with his and her discreet but tantalising presence (in plays and in the world), pivots upon the decisive arrival of the gay man and the lesbian (out of the Stonewall riot of 1969 and

1

the women's movement), and concludes with 'queer' challenges to him and her as (allegedly) complacent. I adduce historical studies and autobiographical and fictive texts to give shape and density to the social experience which is both the context for and the consequence of theatre images.

The shape of theatre for much of this period, like society generally, was dominated by assumptions about good manners, respectability and keeping up appearances. No wonder representations of gayness in theatre were generally oblique and/or hostile. For the modern student this produces fascinating problems of interpretation, as we observe matters which are initially hard even to conceive working their way into utterance, through diverse kinds of textual indirection and institutional opportunism. What, then, have Wilde's or Somerset Maugham's plays to do with gayness? Or John Osborne's or Lorraine Hansberry's? When do fussy bachelors and mannish spinsters get to be perceived as homosexuals? How can Noël Coward and Tennessee Williams be queer icons at the same time as being (respectively) a matinee idol and the great American tragedian? How come queerness figures in such a 'safe' playwright as Agatha Christie? Which audience members heard which nuances − who, for instance, was shocked by Joe Orton and upset by Edward Albee? What did the break-out that we call 'The Sixties' do for sexual dissidents? What were male writers such as Tennessee Williams, Ronald Duncan, David Mercer, Frank Marcus, David Pinner, Ed Bullins, Edward Bond and John Bowen trying to do with lesbian characters?

Much of the existing work in this field centres around censorship − spurred on in the 1990s by the availability of the Lord Chamberlain's papers in Britain. This emphasis produces a story of harassment and repression, and certainly there was a good deal of that. But a key part of my argument is that there was a lot more sexual dissidence in theatre than has been properly registered. It is to be found in such unsuspected places as mysteries by Patrick Hamilton and Philip King; comedies by Harry Wagstaff Gribble, Dodie Smith, John van Druten and Hugh and Margaret Williams; historical dramas by Gordon Daviot and Jean Anouilh. We have tended to suppose that such instances betray individual moments of peculiar blindness on the part of the censor, or miraculous breakthroughs on the part of playwrights, or specially neat manoeuvres on the part of directors. We need a more complex and systematic account − one that will discover, in an admittedly familiar Foucauldian manoeuvre, a *production* of certain kinds of sexual dissidence. We will find both resistance by lesbians and gay men, and complicity between them and their persecutors.

My concluding chapters bring the story up to the time of writing, addressing a period when activists assert theatre as a major site upon which to constitute, and challenge, lesbian and gay identities. At this point it becomes no longer relevant, let alone possible, to show the extent of queer representation by attempting some kind of coverage. I aim, rather, to show how new options for subcultural theatre work were installed during the 1970s, and to comment on the continuing scope for those options. The plays discussed in these later chapters signal institutional changes and illustrate arguments about realism and stylisation, butch/femme and camp, and venues and audiences – avant-garde, fringe, mainstream and subcultural.

The point is not to decide who is a lesbian or gay writer. My focus is on *representation.* I am concerned mainly with the production and circulation of concepts and images, and with the sense of possible lives that they create. As Richard Dyer observes, 'how anything is represented is the means by which we think and feel about that thing, by which we apprehend it'.[2] It is interesting, therefore, but not crucial, to say which authors are or were 'gay'. In fact, to do so with any precision would be contradictory, since my themes include the emergence of the concept 'gay'. I do not need, therefore, to enter into the question of which writing can truly be termed lesbian and gay, or to wrestle with the fact that, even when the playwright was queer, some among the producers, performers, directors and designers were certainly not. Indeed, many significant representations derive from people whom we regard as straight identified, and others betoken the interests of the director rather than the author.

For there is no correlation between the (reported) sexuality of the writer, director or performer and the way he or she represents homosexuality. On the one hand, lesbians and gay men have produced hostile representations, because that was how they saw themselves, or that was the best they could manage in those conditions, or they needed to work. On the other, *The Killing of Sister George* (1965), which was written by a man, influenced ideas of what lesbians are like, including those held by some lesbians. Queer history is not just that which we have made for ourselves and it is not composed only of positive images. We might chart the situation on two axes: in/visibility and un/friendliness. Very often, representations scoring high on visibility would score low on friendliness; in fact, until recently there was a distinct correlation: the more hostile a representation, the easier for it to claim visibility.

Nor is it just a matter of deciding that this or that character 'is gay', or 'is really gay'. We need to investigate characters who appear gay in one version of a story but not in another, or who were perceived as gay by some commentators and not by others, or who look as if they might be shaping up to be gay and then turn out not to be. The near miss displays both the conditions in which queerness filters into discourse and the processes of negotiation and denial through which it is controlled. In early chapters particularly, we will be looking at where gayness would be if it were there.

I fear that these explanations of my purposes do not entirely answer James Gardiner's reported objection to 'definitions of gay theatre which restrict the field to gay-themed theatre'.[3] It is indeed central to my argument that *theatre generally* has been shot through with images and practices of queerness. It has been a place for both disclosure and subterfuge; like sexuality, it straddles the fuzzy line where we imagine a public realm to end and our private subjectivities to begin. However, my concern with queer representation is attempting a particular task. It is often asserted that lesbians and gay men were unspeakable, invisible, in the larger part of the twentieth century. I mean to show that this was not so, though the ways in which they appear require careful analysis. Representations in theatre helped to establish, consolidate and challenge notions of lesbians and gay men which were held both by them and in society at large. For my purposes, then, I don't need a 'definition of gay theatre', but I am specially interested in 'gay themes'.

In earlier work, I suggested that theatre was a distinctively male homosexual space and that the roles of lesbians would require separate attention. This proposition has been disputed by Terry Castle, who argues that Noël Coward and Radclyffe Hall exercised considerable influence over each other.[4] The evidence she adduces does, I believe, show that there were both lesbians and gay men in their overlapping milieux — high society, the cultural establishment, the bohemian avant-garde. These people knew each other, worked together, and loved each other, and there was considerable convergence in their lifestyles and assumptions. I accept that lesbian and gay theatre representations need to be considered together, and that is part of the project of this book.

At the same time, Castle is one of those who have noted a danger: 'As soon as the lesbian is lumped in — for better or for worse — with her male counterpart, the singularity of her experience (sexual and otherwise) tends to become obscured. We "forget" about the lesbian by focusing instead upon gay men.'[5] It is true that this book has more to say about gay men, because I have been able to find more material about them. However, I have tried to maintain the specificity of lesbian situations, and I unearth many more lesbian representations than we have been led to expect.

I thought initially that the United Kingdom and the United States would require separate consideration. In practice, the overwhelming proportion of plays has been produced both in London and New York — mainly for the structural reason that success in the one was taken as a reason to invest in the other. There are large differences in the two milieux, but I have found it instructive to place them side by side, and only sometimes in separate chapters and sections. If I had been able to consider much theatre outside London and New York, more variation might have emerged, but I have been able to do that only occasionally. This focus may be defended, however: the cultural prominence of metropolitan theatre has made it a key place where dominant values may be brought into jeopardy and faultlines exposed, at least until the cunningly contrived resolution; and hence a specially sensitive place for registering sexual dissidence. The great traditions of continental Europe, on the other hand, strike me as generally separate; I refer to plays from them when they enter Anglo-American orbits.

Britain and the United States belong together also in the development of lesbian and gay concepts and subcultures. The Wilde trials and the Stonewall riot, for instance, are crucial subcultural myths in both countries. However, we will encounter intriguing differences as well, particularly in attitudes to manliness and nation.

It has not been easy to draw a boundary around 'theatre' — which on some definitions includes any kind of performance before an audience. I do think it would be splendid to discuss opera and the musical; I don't believe these function independently of 'straight' theatre. The problem is, that would be true also of pantomime, ballet, music hall, rock concerts and stand-up comedy. Or, indeed, Punch and Judy. I do talk about musicals and revues when they specially impinge on plays. But for the most part I have just drawn a line, hoping that other people will be inspired to handle adjacent topics.

I need to explain my deployment of several words and phrases. 'Same-sex passion' is a recent coinage, whose advantage is that it avoids the assumptions that follow from choosing one of the pre-existing terms. 'Sexual dissidence' invokes a wider range of practices and a degree of purposeful opposition. But mostly I have used the less-offensive of the historical terms. Up to the 1960s, 'queer' is appropriate because it includes that obscure sense of something 'not quite right' which so often accompanied dawning or partial awareness of same-sex passion. That runs alongside the more formal term 'homosexual'. 'Gay' comes in gradually (I will show) as a more self-conscious and eventually campaigning word. Sometimes I use these terms to refer to women as well as men, but usually women are specified as 'lesbian'. In the 1980s 'queer' returns, as 'gay' and 'lesbian' come to seem inadequate to the aspirations of sexual dissidents.

On such sensitive and intricate matters nothing can be taken for granted. Provocatively, for it was the 1940s, the playwright Rodney Ackland and his partner Arthur Boys, a successful interior decorator, would walk down the street hand in hand. One day Ackland was by himself, climbing onto a bus, and an old lady asked: 'And how is your poor dear blind friend?'[6]

Queer Space

The association of theatre and queerness is longstanding. In Ben Jonson's *Poetaster* (1601) Ovid Senior is alarmed that his son is going to write for the theatre: 'What! Shall I have my son a stager now? An engle for players? A gull, a rook, a shot-clog to make suppers, and be laughed at?'.[7] 'Engle' means 'catamite'. The point is not laboured – evidently same-sex practices are common among theatre people and are just one of the degrading prospects that await young Ovid.

In London's West End, since the late nineteenth century at least, theatre bars and adjacent public houses and coffee shops have been known as places for same-sex encounters. In the Wilde trials his co-defendant, Alfred Taylor, was asked how he met the Parker brothers: he was having a drink after the theatre.[8] It wasn't just queerness. For Jocelyn Brooke, in the 1920s, theatre had 'an aura of wickedness derived, I suppose, from my nurse who, being a Strict Baptist, had been brought up to believe that playhouses were Sinks of Iniquity'.[9]

The (supposed) infiltration of theatre by queers was sufficiently notorious to form the basis for Noël Langley's novel, *There's a Porpoise Close Behind Us*; it was published in 1936 and reprinted three times that year. Robin and Diana, a nice young couple at drama school, are warned by Christopher (who, it turns out at the end, has written the book):

> I've had jobs whipped away from under my nose by funny little creatures belonging to the leading man or the management more times than I like to remember . . . half the young men in the theatre slide into their jobs on their stomachs, and the frightening thing is, that they're not booed by the gallery the moment they open their mouths on a first night. There's a sort of dry rot in the theatre, or they'd never be able to get away with it. They're so strong that nothing short of a Pogrom à la Hitler'll ever clean 'em out.[10]

Robin accepts backing from Middleton to produce a play, but Middleton makes a pass; 'Robin's first reaction was disbelief, and then the conviction that he was being dragged down into black slimy water by something evil in a nightmare.' Behind his 'dazzling veneer of irresistible charm' Middleton is obsessive, hysterical and spiteful (211, 132). He sabotages the rehearsals in quite intricate ways (the sense of how theatre works is strong); people are paid to barrack on the opening night. Robin copes with it all, losing his cool only when Middleton calls out 'Kept boy!' However, the scandal gets Robin a film contract; Diana abandons her career and marries him.

Arthur, an oral history respondent, read *There's a Porpoise Close Behind Us* when he was a student in New Zealand, trying to work out his sexuality. 'My stepmother told me not to read it, so of course I did. My friends and I heard rumours about Noël Coward. So my perceptions were confused, and remained confused for a very long time.'[11]

In the 1950s it was received wisdom that queers congregate in sinister ways in theatres. The 'Evil Men' series of articles published by the *Sunday Pictorial* in 1952 specifies the stage as one of the typically 'unvirile' occupations – 'Homosexuality is rife in the theatrical profession.'[12] *The Heart in Exile* (1953), a novel by Rodney Garland which aims to display the scope of queer subculture in the 1950s, depicts the protagonist attending a party given by a famous dramatist and remarks rumours that 'popping into bed' with someone, straight or gay, was the usual way of getting work in an overcrowded profession.[13] An actor interviewed by Richard Hauser reports an uproar over an alleged gay casting couch in Australia: 'When I came over here I found it was worse than in Sydney.'[14] An article by John Deane Potter in the *Daily Express* in 1959 attacked the 'unpleasant free-masonry' whereby homosexual producers favoured homosexual actors; they were 'evil men' and should be 'driven from their positions of theatrical power'.[15]

These ideas were still active in 1973, when Noël Coward and the powerful impresario Hugh 'Binkie' Beaumont died. A columnist (Will Waspe) remarked in the *Spectator*: 'It cannot, of course, be said that with the deaths of Hugh (Binkie) Beaumont and Sir Noël Coward the whole edifice of homosexual domination of the British theatre will come tumbling down, but with the loss of these two pillars the structure begins, inevitably, to look a little less secure.' These were still sensitive topics. Waspe noted 'the absence of conjecture along these lines in the obituary columns'; even he felt 'constrained to proceed delicately'.[16]

Similar preoccupations abound in the USA. Kaier Curtin quotes a newspaper article about the production of Mae West's *The Pleasure Man*

(1928), averring that West 'didn't have to work hard to complete the homosexual cast. The nature of these creatures is such that they will snap at a chance of appearing in public. And, when they are offered a chance to appear on the stage in gowns, dearie, real gowns; well — woops!'[17] In 1956 *Tip-Off* magazine explained 'Why They Call Broadway the "GAY" White Way': 'Homosexuals have gained such a stranglehold on the theater, those in the know contend, that quite a few big stars on Broadway and in Hollywood have at one stage or another in their career, been forced to "play the game" in order to get work.' As Martin Duberman observes, this was hardly news; what is notable is the 'exaggerated description' and 'ugly tone'.[18] 'On Broadway, it would be difficult to find a production without homosexuals playing important parts, either on-stage or off', *Time* magazine declared in 1966. 'The notion that the arts are dominated by a kind of homosexual mafia — or "Homintern", as it has been called — is sometimes exaggerated, particularly by spiteful failures looking for scapegoats. But in the theater, dance and music world, deviates are so widespread that they sometimes seem to be running a closed shop.' And it's not as if they were really gifted; 'For the most part, thinks Los Angeles Psychiatrist Edward Stainbrook, homosexuals are failed artists, and their special creative gift a myth'.[19]

Our (supposed) theatricality has often been assimilated by theorists into their speculations about our natures. It seems that we have a special sensitivity, though one that is not altogether healthy. It is not just a matter of having to live a lie, says the sexologist Albert Moll; 'the capacity and the inclination to conceive situations and to represent them in a masterly manner corresponds to an abnormal predisposition of the nervous system'. Havelock Ellis quotes this in *Sexual Inversion* in 1897, and glosses:

> the congenitally inverted may, I believe, be looked upon as a class of individuals exhibiting nervous characters [*sic*] which to some extent approximate them to persons of artistic genius. The dramatic and artistic aptitudes of inverts are, therefore, partly due to the circumstances of the invert's life, which render him necessarily an actor — and in some few cases lead him into a love of deception comparable with that of a hysterical woman — and partly, it is probable, to a congenital nervous predisposition allied to the predisposition to inversion.

At the start of that paragraph we seem close to genius; by the end we have sunk to 'a love of deception comparable with that of a hysterical woman'. Ellis thought gay men tend also to exhibit 'vanity and the love of applause'.[20]

John Addington Symonds, who 'had long been struck by the frequency of inversion among actors and actresses', reported the opinions of 'an inverted actor' who was inclined to seek a more pragmatic explanation — 'less in the original sexual constitution than in the exercise of sympathetic, assimilative emotional qualities, powerfully stimulated and acted on by the conditions of the individual's life'.[21] In other words, the actor's work requires emotional flexibility and queers are used to pretending to be someone else. Kenneth Plummer suggests that while all people play social roles, homosexuals are likely to be aware of 'passing', 'presenting a self', 'keeping up an act'; hence they have 'dramaturgical consciousness'.[22] John Lahr believes that 'Coward's acute awareness (and insistence) on the performing self comes out of a homosexual world where disguise is crucial for survival.'[23]

Freudians found theatre happily apposite to their theory. 'Concerning *acting*, there is no doubt about the nature of the underlying partial instinct: it is *exhibitionism*,' declared Otto Fenichel. Women don't do this much because they don't have a penis to exhibit, and hence it is felt that all '"sublimation" of exhibitionism is somehow feminine'. Understandably, therefore, 'the art of acting is generally looked upon as a feminine art, and — although one should be careful of making hasty generalizations [!] — the percentage of homosexuals seems to be higher among actors than in most other professions'.[24] In 1959 Yoti Lane thought he had located the 'obvious' reasons why 'the theatrical life has a strong attraction for the homosexual':

> The stage offers an opportunity for the homosexual to obtain power and authority which he would fear to fight for in real life. He can, as far as his audiences are concerned, appear to be a potent and fascinating lover in romantic roles which his immature emotional development would prevent his undertaking in the outside world. Also he is in an environment where a love of fantasy, and a delight in dressing up, is approved.[25]

In short, the man who exhibits emotions is suspected of femininity; if he does it habitually he is less than a man.

Overall, these theories fall into two groups: gays are theatrical (a) because they are flamboyant, affected, hysterical and feminine; (b) because they are disguised, covert, discreet and feminine. A contradiction is evident: if one was (b) — and that would apply, anyway, only to closeted gays — one would presumably not want to be (a). These theories are confused and homophobic; also, they suppose rather limited notions of theatre.

In *The 'Sissy Boy Syndrome' and the Development of Homosexuality* (1987) Richard Green describes research which showed a strong correlation between 'feminine' boys, 'masculine' boys, and vocational aspirations at ages thirteen to fifteen. All sixteen boys who wanted to become actors had already been distinguished as feminine. So were five of the eight boys who wanted to be doctors. But all the boys who wanted to be lawyers, athletes, engineers or pilots were masculine. In the event, eight of the boys who had wanted to be actors 'emerged as homosexual or bisexual, as did one of the aspiring doctors'.[26] What Green has demonstrated is that some kind of association with theatre may be helpful as a way of dealing with some of the consequences of stigma for 'feminine' boys. 'These boys find approval in drama classes and acting schools, where they can share their interests with others, a commonality previously denied them because of their aversion to rough-and-tumble play and sports' (57). What is not reported is whether they achieved any success in a stage career. We can all camp around in a theatre foyer, but the disciplined and demanding work of an actor is another matter.

The point to grasp is that, while queerness and theatre are certainly internalised by individuals as components in their identities, both are social formations. In practice, because gay men are said to congregate in and around theatres, that becomes a good way for them to feel at home and meet other gays. Gordon Westwood's research, published in England in 1960, did not find homosexuals disproportionately in theatrical and artistic occupations. But he did find that the interests of homosexuals were often 'cultural', and 'ability to gossip knowledgeably about the theatre' might be 'a very important asset'.[27] Martin Hoffman notes in the USA in 1968 'more interest in and knowledge about opera, ballet and theatre in homosexual groups' than among 'hetero-sexual groups of comparable age and socio-economic level'.[28]

Further, theatre and illicit sexual activity tend to occupy the same inner-city territory. The arrest of the transvestites Boulton and Park in 1870 occurred as they left the Strand Theatre, and they were said in court to have frequented diverse theatres.[29] A gay Londoner attests, of the 1930s:

> There were places people used to go in those days, for example the Criterion [Theatre], in Piccadilly Circus where there was a bar and tables. Enormous place downstairs, you could sit there all night with a beer. There was a circle bar at the Palladium, I remember the barmaid, her name was Julie or something. You could get a Rover ticket at the Palladium. People used to stand along the back of the circle and there about.

I think that's a joke — a Rover ticket entitled you to travel anywhere on London Transport. Other oral history reports offer similar descriptions.[30] Peter Burton describes clubs, pubs and theatres in close geographical conjunction in the 1960s.[31]

The stereotypes read differently for women. While the female actor makes a public exhibition of herself and is therefore likely to be perceived as getting above her station, and hence as disreputable, most of the roles available to her are cravenly heterosexist. On the eighteenth century London stage women such as Margaret Woffington and Charlotte Charke played the 'breeches part'; Kristina Straub discovers unease, in contemporary accounts of this, that same-sex passions may be aroused.[32] In the nineteenth century women such as Sarah Siddons, Sarah Bernhardt, Charlotte Cushman and Alice Marriott played male Shakespearean parts but, according to Marjorie Garber, 'reviews commended the excellence of their portrayals, without any reference to gender cross-casting' and 'no one apparently thought it strange or inappropriate'.[33] We may suppose nonetheless that some women and some men found it intriguing and exciting.

Havelock Ellis prints a note from a friend — presumably Edith Ellis, a lesbian, his wife and a playwright (see chapter 3):

> Passionate friendships among girls, from the most innocent to the most elaborate excursions in the direction of Lesbos, are extremely common in theatres, both among actresses and, even more, among chorus and ballet girls. Here the pell-mell of the dressing rooms, the wait of perhaps two hours between the performances, during which all the girls are cooped up, in a state of inaction and excitement, in a few crowded dressing-rooms, affords every opportunity for the growth of this particular kind of sentiment.[34]

For Mark, in Blair Niles' novel *Strange Brother* (1931), Broadway is queer territory for women as well as men: 'A certain actress, he had heard, was well-known for her preference for women, and thus belonged to the feminine half of his world. Such and such an actor, he would declare, belonged also to that world.'[35]

Feminists colonised theatre as a platform for political and social ideas. Edith Craig, for instance, who lived with the writer Chris St John, produced plays for the Actresses' Franchise League and the Women Writers' Suffrage League from 1908; between 1911 and 1921 the two women founded and managed the Pioneer Players, presenting plays dealing with current social, political and moral ideas. Probably this militantly feminist work translated, for some women, into a sense that these theatres were lesbian space.[36]

In the heyday of Coward, when, I will show, Society and bohemia became tangled together, (John) Radclyffe Hall and Una Troubridge were prominent first-nighters: 'John's appearance in high stiff collar, man's stock, and black military cloak, invariably caused a stir'; in the 1920s they were attending three or four openings in a week.[37] Castle mentions among their lesbian friends the playwrights Gabrielle Enthoven and Clemence Dane, the actresses Teddie Gerard and Tallulah Bankhead, and the designer Gladys Calthrop; among Coward's collaborators she lists additionally Mercedes de Acosta, Blyth Daly, Eva Le Gallienne, Katharine Cornell, Estelle Winwood, Elsa Maxwell, Beatrice Lillie, Marlene Dietrich, Mary Martin and Gertrude Lawrence.[38]

Nonetheless, in the present state of research, I do not find that lesbians, until the rise of feminist troupes in the 1970s, have claimed theatre in quite the same way as gay men. There are lesbians in *There's a Porpoise Close Behind Us* – Sadia (who is like a sergeant major) and Doodoo (the little woman) – but they aren't connected with the theatre plot. Women in oral histories mention theatre only rarely and in passing. Myrtle Solomon persuaded her parents to let her leave school by saying she was going on the stage, but she offers no further indication of a link between sexuality and theatre; Sharley McLean and her girlfriend 'went to concerts and plays. We did a lot of things together' – there is no sense that theatre was specially queer for them; Elsa Beckett enjoyed taking a man's part in a school play, but it didn't lead anywhere – 'If I had done more acting like this I think I would have done something about being a lesbian a lot earlier.' She went to Southern Rhodesia, where there was a drama group 'and apparently they all knew what homosexuality was', but she didn't find out about it until later.[39] Lesbians in Buffalo in the 1950s were 'pushing beyond the limitations of socializing in their own houses', Elizabeth Lapovsky Kennedy and Madeline D. Davis report, and 'highly motivated to go out', but even upper-class women did not report an interest in theatre.[40] The question is not whether lesbians went to the theatre or worked in theatre; of course they did. And, I will show, they were significantly represented there. But I don't find women developing their experience of themselves as lesbians specially through their experience of theatre.

Even so, they may well have contributed to and felt at home in the general aura of queerness. For what is striking is the weight of public attention to what is alleged to be a secret practice. An element of queerness, so long as it is kept more or less out of sight, has been a price that society pays to have theatre as we have known it. For sexual dissidents, the price has been a tacit admission that we are by definition indecent and that a degree of discretion is only proper.

Hearing Things

When Coward's *Present Laughter* (1942) reaches a peak of interpersonal confusion, the door-bell rings: is it a rescue? 'With any luck it's the Lord Chamberlain' (237). He, it is implied, would put a stop to such irregular goings-on. Like the homosexual, theatre is subject to the ominous official ring on the door-bell. However, the knowledge that theatre was under surveillance and operating at the boundary of the speakable was itself part of its fascination. If censorship was designed to suppress homosexuality in theatre, then it was remarkably unsuccessful. It would be more true to say that it helped to give theatre the status of a thoroughly queer space.

The regulations governing the UK stage up until 1968 derived from the Theatres Act of 1843. This placed theatre censorship under the supervision of the head of the Royal Household, the Lord Chamberlain. A script had to be submitted to his office before a performance was permitted; changes might be demanded, or a play might be banned altogether. Difficult cases would be determined by the Chamberlain himself, and even, on occasion, by the King. The forbidden territories were to do with slander, religion, sex, royal and political figures at home and abroad. Homosexuality was not the only sexual taboo. Frivolous pieces were banned where adultery, bedroom scenes or some detail of expression or undress was objected to, and so were earnest crusading projects on birth control and free love. However, it was believed that the Chamberlain's writ did not cover performances in private, for instance in a theatre club.

In the United States there was no pre-censorship, but the police, incited by pressure groups, newspapers and politicians, might close a production arbitrarily, and did so in several notorious instances. Production on Broadway was expensive, so managements generally were very conservative anyway. The little theatre movement (from the early years of the century), Off-Broadway (from the late 1950s), and then Off Off-Broadway, afforded privileged yet precarious spaces for experimentation of various kinds.

Theatre was controlled in this way because extraordinary powers were ascribed to it. The critic Wolcott Gibbs got someone at the *New Yorker* to phone round a group of ministers to ask why they had condemned Dorothy and

Howard Baker's Broadway play *Trio* (1944), in which a marriageable young woman is drawn away from her fascinating woman friend by a marriageable young man. Most of them hadn't seen the play but thought it disgusting. One added: 'it's terrible when youngsters are permitted to see this sort of thing. Why, a teen-aged girl in Bonnell's parish went to see one of these plays six times; the whole course of her life is now warped.'[41]

Defenders of censorship in the UK claimed that they were protecting the moral fabric of the nation. However, it is apparent that censorship was doing at least two other things. One was protecting conservative ideas from radical challenge – which is why trivial and hostile representations of sexual dissidents were more likely to be allowed than serious and sympathetic treatments. A whole range of topics in religion and politics was ruled out – neither anti-God nor anti-Nazi plays were allowed. The other was protecting conventional notions of good taste and decency. Violet Bonham Carter, one of the independent minds and a very rare woman on the Lord Chamberlain's Advisory Board, pondered in 1935 a play by J. Baxter Somerville in which a man speculates through diary dates whether he might be the father of an infant: 'This play could not possibly be a threat to anybody's morals, but it must, I should think, be an offense to other people's taste. It raises again the problem as to whether we have the right to act as arbiters of taste or only as protectors of public morality.'[42]

The Lord Chamberlain's reader admitted that he was trying to prevent public acknowledgement of matters which people might well know about, when he objected to Aimée and Philip Stuart's *Love of Women* (1934). This play, in which two devoted women may be regarded either as intense friends or as lesbian lovers, 'does introduce perversion as a factor in the plot and this gives an advertisement, in the emotional atmosphere of the Theatre, to a fact of life which it would seem undesirable should be discussed in public'.[43] Ivor Brown made the point in relation to *Mrs Warren's Profession* (1894) by George Bernard Shaw, which was banned between 1894 and 1925: 'The patrons of the fashionable London theatres were well aware of the Mrs Warrens and their professional activities. . . . But what was gossiped about and even gloated over was not to be exposed on the stage. The Censor was there to prevent such unmannerly candour and veracity.'[44]

Even those who wanted a change in the censorship regime held that theatre was a uniquely dangerous medium. In 1909 a UK parliamentary committee recommended that licensing continue, but that plays might be produced without it – running the risk of prosecution (this was not enacted). The Committee declared:

Ideas or situations which, when described on a printed page may work little mischief, when represented through the human personality of actors may have a more powerful and deleterious effect. The existence of an audience, moved by the same emotions, its members conscious of one another's presence, intensifies the influence of what is done and spoken on the stage . . . . The performance, day after day, in the presence of numbers of people, of plays containing one or other of these [dangerous] elements, would have cumulative effects to which the conveyance of similar ideas by print offers no analogy.[45]

John van Druten, while calling in 1929 for at least the partial removal of stage censorship, also granted that the public nature of theatre made it special:

How are our audiences to be educated not to be shocked by the public expression of what they must have read or thought or discussed in private? The fault lies in part only with the censorship; it lies also (but again only in part) in the aforesaid nature of the drama which, by being performed to an entirely unselected audience by living men and women, takes on an additional reality that is apt to make embarrassing on the stage what would not be so in print.[46]

Van Druten was upset because his *Young Woodley* (1925), which shows how a sensitive boy may be harassed by hearty boys and masters but rescued for heterosexuality by the love of his housemaster's wife, had been banned in London. Generally, though, van Druten was not at odds with the censor. *Young Woodley* was successful on Broadway, and was licensed in the UK in 1928. In the interim van Druten rewrote the story as a novel but, so far from taking an opportunity to reveal the truly queer nature of such matters, the novel strengthens innocently homosocial aspects.[47] In fact, as Richard Findlater points out, the major dramatists of the period 1918–56 – Maugham, Lonsdale, Rattigan, Emlyn Williams, Priestley, Coward – were hardly troubled by the Chamberlain. This was because, by and large, they shared his view of what was suitable for stage presentation. Discretion in the theatre was only mirroring the discretion that was required generally in Society.[48] Notwithstanding, they did all have performed plays containing somewhat queer characters.

The specially permitted spaces – the theatre club in Britain and the little theatres and Off-Broadway in the US – indicate that the idea was not to prevent improper performances altogether, but to limit them to controlled circumstances. Also, British censorship applied only to new plays. With classic texts directors might go much further. In 1956 Tyrone Guthrie's production of Shakespeare's *Troilus and Cressida* (1601–2) presented Achilles and Patroclus hugging and kissing, the former, reported Brian Inglis, a body-builder in a dressing gown, the latter 'a cringing, squirming pathic'.[49]

Because censorship operated with such specificity in theatre, and because its abolition was such a tidy liberal cause in the 1960s, the Lord Chamberlain's papers have been intensively studied.[50] However, as I have indicated, this should not draw us into the idea of theatre as a place where queerness wells up through the creative organs of the playwright, only to be suppressed by the foolish, philistine and oppressive State – with the fate of Oscar Wilde hanging over it all. By controlling irregular sexuality the Chamberlain did not eliminate it; on the contrary, he implied that it was always about to irrupt into visibility. He was helping to make theatre a place where sexuality lurked in forbidden forms.

Third Person (1951) by Andrew Rosenthal illustrates the games that writers and producers played in the heyday of the censor's office. It was written and is set in the United States, but New York managements refused it. It was presented at the Arts Theatre Club in London in 1951 and transferred to the West End in 1952. It concerns the threat to the marriage of Hank and Jean when the wealthy Hank returns from the War in the (romantic) Pacific with his attractive, plausible and penniless young buddy, Kip – he is the 'third person'. Eventually Kip is found to have lied about his past, in which he made his way through the patronage of an affluent but disreputable painter. He is expelled from the household and the marriage of Hank and Jean is affirmed.

The *Plays of the Year* edition prints the Arts version of *Third Person* and the cuts required for the West End transfer. In the Arts text queerness is already quite hard to hear: the most direct indication is when it is said that Kip and the painter once 'lived together'. For the West End this had to be changed to 'He knew Eric very well' (409). Again, instead of 'Kip was also a guest of Eric's, for two years', they had to say 'They knew one another *very* well. For several years' (386). These changes are weird, for the same implication is there, only you have to work a bit harder for it; otherwise you miss the point of the play. At the Arts Hank swore to his wife: 'Christ, one of these seconds you're going to come right out and accuse me of having something to do with him! I've done a lot of things in my life, Jean, but that doesn't happen to be one of them.' But in the West End Hank said only: 'Look, just what in the Hell are you trying to say?' (412). Hank was not allowed to declare that he had not 'had something to do' with Kip, because that would imply that he might have done. Yet the audience was still expected to make some sense of what Jean was 'trying to say'. Even the censored text invites the audience to understand queerness. D.J. West, pondering the diversity of human sexuality, mentions the play as a place where a *ménage à trois* had been 'hinted at'.[51]

What is striking here is the slightness of the required changes. On the one hand, this shows that Rosenthal had not taken the opportunity of club production to present explicitly gay dialogue. He was ready to operate within social expectations which were actually quite close to what the censor was prepared to admit. On the other, it shows that the Lord Chamberlain did not seek to suppress queerness altogether, but to ensure that it appeared only in contexts where its disgraceful nature was acknowledged through manifest indirection. Stephen Rooney points out that *Third Person* was licensed 'on the understanding that the part of Kip must not be played in an effeminate manner', implying 'a recognition on the part of the Chamberlain's office that the play's homosexuality is teetering on the brink of visibility'.[52]

It is interesting to compare Rosenthal's later reworking of *Third Person* as a novel: *The Extra Man* (1977). In this version Kip has explicit homosexual relations, though not with Hank, before and during his sojourn in the household of Hank and Jean, and Hank finally confesses that he has frequently thought of Kip sexually but was 'too fucking yellow ever to do anything about it'.[53] It is unclear what Hank will do with this self-knowledge; there is no adequate reconciliation with Jean. But this was in another genre and another decade.

That the effect of censorship was not to suppress queerness, but to maintain a surface of decency, was widely understood. Coward complained that 'an "unpleasant" subject is something that everyone knows about, but shrinks from the belief that other people know about it too'.[54] When people asked Michael Hill, author of the banned play *Queer People* (1932), why he had chosen such an 'unsavoury' subject, he would ask: And what is that? 'I have had no satisfactory reply, and have been forced to the conclusion that an "unsavoury" subject is something that you and I know about, but of which each of us fervently hopes the other to be blissfully ignorant.' Hill wrote this in his preface to a new version, titled *Tragedy in Jermyn Street* (1934, 10); despite slanting the argument further against homosexuality it too was banned. In *The Children's Hour* by Lillian Hellman (1934) Mary whispers her teachers' alleged misdeeds into the ear of her grandmother: the child's discretion enables Hellman neatly to avoid explicitness on the stage. Nonetheless, lesbian sexuality is signalled, and the hesitation and indirection are part of the meaning.

The half-heard character of queerness in discreet discourse has been theorised in terms afforded by D.A. Miller's suggestion that homosexuality is an *open secret*. It must not be allowed fully into the open, for that would grant it public status; yet it must not disappear altogether, for then it would be beyond control and would no longer contribute to a general surveillance of aberrant desire. It lurks on the margins of awareness as the almost-unthinkable alternative – so awful that it can be envisaged only as private, yet always obscurely present as a warning against the public consequences of deviance. The function of the secret, Miller observes, 'is not to conceal knowledge, so much as to conceal the knowledge of the knowledge'.[55]

Miller develops this argument in relation to Alfred Hitchcock's film, *Rope* (1948 – based on the play by Patrick Hamilton, which I discuss in chapter 9). Because the representation of homosexuality (in American popular culture, as elsewhere) 'appertained exclusively to the shadow kingdom of connotation, where insinuations could be at once developed and denied . . . one couldn't be sure whether homosexuality was being meant at all, but on the chance it was, one also learned, along with the codes that might be conveying it, the silence necessary to keep about their deployment'.[56] As Robin Wood puts it, the film could not answer a question (about the gayness of the characters) because it couldn't even broach it: 'It's not simply that *Rope* cannot tell us that the two men sleep together; it also cannot tell us clearly that they *don't*, since that would imply that they might.'[57] Such representations, Miller adds, helped to 'construct a homosexuality held definitionally in suspense on no less a question than that of its own existence', producing thereby 'homosexual subjects doubtful of the validity and even the reality of their desire, which *may only be, does not necessarily mean*, and all the rest'.

In Somerset Maugham's play *Caesar's Wife* (1919), Arthur knows that his young wife is in love with someone else, but he tries to stop her saying so out loud. 'I don't want to have any secrets from you', she says. 'Oh, my dear, don't you see that things said can never be taken back. We may both know something', he says. 'But so long as we don't tell one another we can ignore it. If certain words pass our lips the situation is entirely changed.'[58] Arthur's discretion mimics the way Society, accustomed to the preservation of respectability, preferred not to register meanings of which it was, at least subliminally, aware. Today, this is likely to appear hypocritical, though of course we have our own areas of reticence. For Maugham, his characters, the Lord Chamberlain and most audiences, it was necessary for the running of Society.

The idea of an open secret helps us to think about queerness on the mid-century stage. However, in other times and places same-sex passion has been a secret but not open; or open but not a secret; or inconceivable altogether. Not to remark this would encourage an inference that gay people are trapped eternally by their sexuality as such (that might be a psychoanalytic perspective). Also, same-sex passion is not open and secret in the same ways to different groups at any one time, even in the one audience.

Audiences

Lytton Strachey saw *A Woman of No Importance* revived by Beerbohm Tree in 1907:

> Mr Tree is a wicked Lord, staying in a country house, who has made up his mind to bugger one of the other guests — a handsome young man of twenty. The handsome young man is delighted; when his mother enters, sees his Lordship and recognises him as having copulated with her twenty years before, the result of which was — the handsome young man. She appeals to Lord Tree not to bugger his own son. He replies that that's an additional reason for doing it (oh! he's a very wicked Lord!). . . . The audience was of course charmed.[59]

If the play had been read generally in this way, the audience would not have been charmed and the play would not have been performed on the West End stage, in 1907 or initially in 1893.

Theatre folk say, rightly, that a play only reaches its full potential when it is performed. It is not adequate, therefore, to offer a reading: one must consider the response of the audience. However, the experience of performance is not captured when we say: The audience is moved by her speech; or The audience realises that he is a pervert. We cannot assume that all the audience, even on the same night, will think the same.

'The audience' is comparable to 'the reader' in literary criticism which, until recently, hardly addressed the complexity of the historical conditions in which texts are actually decoded. Sub-literary texts were assumed to be read, listened to or watched by 'the masses', who were supposed to accept naively what they were told, so the question of interpretation did not arise there. And the literary text, it was believed, was written from the position of Man, so the task of the critic was to align himself (or sometimes herself) with that position. If the literary reader seemed to be coming from a more particular stance, that was regarded as a failure of sensibility; he or she should try harder to expunge partiality and achieve the position of Man. Such an effacement of the specificity of reading positions is specially coercive for subordinated groups who might read differently, and who have a weaker claim on Man and other normative constructs.

Absolutising reading processes tends also to obscure the actuality of contest in cultural production. Change in the social organisation is registered and effected partly through cultural contest, in which rival formulations strive to substantiate claims to superior explanatory power. To prefer one reading to another is to take a side in an argument. When we say what and how the text signifies, therefore, we should also say *for whom*. If Strachey hears *A Woman of No Importance* as about a wicked Lord 'who has made up his mind to bugger one of the other guests', while 'the audience was of course charmed', then they were probably hearing different things.

Strachey's reading is neither incidental nor merely personal. He has an upper-class, leisured, aesthetical, educated, Bloomsbury knowledge and awareness; he is an intellectual and a bohemian; he cultivates Wildean manners, he is queer. This is his *reading formation*: it was shared with and supported by many other people, including Duncan Grant, to whom he was writing. It is the availability of this reading formation that enables Strachey to decode *A Woman of No Importance* in a non-mainstream way – indeed, in defiance of what he knows to be mainstream assumptions. It does not *cause* him to do this; it makes it possible.

Sara Mills develops Judith Fetterley's concept of the 'resisting reader', as a way of theorising 'the process whereby readers can refuse to take up the position offered them by the text'. We should envisage reading as a process of negotiation: 'the reader may locate and recognise a set of specific inflections which would lead to the dominant reading; then those inflections might be "translated" into a different discursive framework, to make them "mean" differently'.[60] Susan Gledhill, with women and popular film in mind, also calls for an understanding of culture as *negotiation*: 'Meaning is neither imposed, nor passively imbibed, but arises out of a struggle or negotiation between competing frames of reference, motivation or experience.'[61] I will be trying to locate the frames of reference that were available to audiences, and the ways in which sexual dissidents sought to establish and cultivate their concerns. Strachey in his way, and other parts of the audience in theirs, negotiate between 'competing frames of reference'.

I am not proposing a simple alignment of text, sexuality and reading. It cannot be assumed that queer people hear queer messages. At the age of seventeen, in 1948, Robin Wood was fascinated by the film *Rope*. But, 'despite the fact that I knew I was gay myself, it never occurred to me for a moment that the characters in the film might be: it was, at that time, literally *unthinkable*. If I couldn't believe, emotionally, in the existence of other homosexuals in real life, how could I believe in their existence within a Hollywood film?'[62] Conversely, gay people are adroit at deriving their own meanings from ostensibly mainstream texts. Teresa de Lauretis quotes Elizabeth Ellsworth's findings in respect of the film *Personal Best* (1982). While the film seems determined to disavow love between women, lesbian feminist viewers redefined the protagonist, ignored sections focused on heterosexual romance, disregarded the actual ending, and discovered apparently unintended erotic moments. Such contest over interpretation, de Lauretis observes, 'is a constitutive process for marginal subjectivities, as well as an important form of resistance'.[63]

People working in theatre between the wars were entirely self-conscious about how they might address their different audiences, as we will see further in discussion of Coward in chapter 5. In Dodie Smith's West End comedy *Call It a Day* (1935), the delightful family of Dorothy and Roger is falling suddenly into disarray. The older daughter, Catherine, is in love with a married, middle-aged painter; the younger daughter, Ann, is very romantic and excessively involved with the Rossettis; Dorothy and Roger, to their surprise, have opportunities to embark on affairs. Fortunately they are all so nice and so amusing that nothing very dreadful can happen; and the servants maintain steadily benevolent support. But what about Martin, the son (aged seventeen)? Why is his father so keen to put a stop to his friendship with Alistair (aged twenty)? Dorothy thinks Alistair 'a charming boy' — not 'rough and wild' (44). His attractions include use of his mother's car; he wants Martin to go walking with him at Easter; he invites him to the cinema; he wants to start up in business with him — *interior decoration*. So that's it! 'Designing people's rooms - working out colour schemes — finding lovely things to sell' (108). What's more, Martin appears susceptible - he comes to breakfast in his dressing gown — 'trying to be Noël Coward', Catherine says (24). Fortunately, it is a false alarm. Martin is taken up by the daughter of the new neighbours , who has a car of her own. He forgets the cinema date with Alistair to go out with her, and decides to spend Easter with her. As with the other threats to the family, danger is averted.

Despite this happy ending Beaumont, the producer, was anxious about whether Alistair would pass the censor. The answer, Beaumont believed, was to get the right actor: 'somebody really attractive and virile, and you won't hear a squeak from anybody'. And so they did, and 'in the whole of the long run there wasn't a single complaint or murmur'.[64] So what did audiences hear? Some people, we may suppose, did not notice a queer aspect; they may have wondered why Alistair was a problem. Others noticed it, and divided into those who disliked it on principle and those who accepted it as an interesting topic. Of the latter, some would be appeased by the conventional masculinity in the casting and by Martin's default to heterosexuality, while a few sexual dissidents (probably) might be disappointed that Alistair gains so little gratification. Others might fall between, half hearing something more than they had expected, perhaps more than they could cope with. The scope for reading queerness ranged from conservatives who didn't want to be disturbed, to lesbians and gay men who were contriving to construct their subculture in the margins of the mainstream.

Richard of Bordeaux (1932) by Gordon Daviot − the pseudonym of Elizabeth MacKintosh − was an interpretation of the life of Richard II, and the first major success for John Gielgud (who produced the play, initially at the Arts Theatre Club). Pictures outside the theatre told the story, Emlyn Williams recalls: 'With the crown to which he had been born set on the long blond hair, the robes flowing, the etched mouth sensitive and fired with the defiance of spoilt youth, the nobly androgynous figure struck a new note in the theatre.'[65] In the opening scene the kingdom is already in political turmoil, but the focus is on two page boys, whom Richard engages in friendly banter. He does love his wife, Anne − he responds to the beautiful velvet material of her dress and they develop together a 'feminine' anti-war policy; he is distraught when she dies. But, also, Richard is accused of giving money to a page, so his 'name stands for everything that is wanton and contemptible'; his secretary is called 'a disgusting little fop'; and he enters from his inner chamber with his hand on the arm of 'a girlish youth, very pretty' (44, 64, 69). Richard's final calamity is his separation from his secretary. His interest in feminine matters is linked by hostile barons with his anti-war policy: 'Richard would rather stay at home and buy clothes than take an army into France like his father!' (11−12). He is 'That fool! That scented fop! A man who takes an hour to choose a pair of gloves! . . .

that silken packet of whims and fancies' (68). The fate of his great-grandfather, Edward II, is recalled.

Many reviewers were discreet about all this; Desmond MacCarthy thought Richard very well characterised as 'the victim and beneficiary of an artistic temperament – running in his case too much in the direction of finery and display'.[66] But James Agate, in his review in the *Sunday Times*, was ready to acknowledge a queer reading. He compares the account of Richard in the *Encyclopaedia Britannica*: 'Having looked the effeminate King full in his beardless face, this respectable authority [the encyclopaedia] then declares that his character must remain an enigma to the historian. J'ever hear such hypocrisy? . . . none are so blind as those who will not see.' Shakespeare, though he diverted Richard's 'effeminacy' into 'preciosity and aestheticism which are effeminacy's co-ordinates', knew better. For he

certainly knew about his friend's play of *Edward II*, a King whose character has never presented any riddle even to a historian. From which we may take it that Shakespeare was perfectly well aware how many abnormal beans make five. . . . Something of the foregoing must be in the mind of any spectator who is not going to find Miss Daviot's Richard wholly enigmatic, and all of it was obviously in the author's mind since she has created a Richard who, in this light, at once becomes wholly understandable.[67]

It doesn't matter here that Agate was himself homosexual. His point is that some people at least know what the riddle is about, and that they will be using this knowledge when they watch the play, even if they choose not to talk about it.

Conversely, plays on sensitive topics such as schools had to work hard to head off awkward inferences. The popular farcical comedy *Housemaster* (1937) by Ian Hay opens with a boy kneeling over a chair with his bottom toward us: he has just been caned. 'Do you think I enjoy doing this?' Donkin asks. 'Yes, sir', Bimbo [Bimbo?!] replies – 'The fellows in the house think you do, sir.' Donkin is a bachelor, though he is credited with a long-lost love, and resists any hint of effeminacy. 'And don't mess that paper about like a woman!' he tells a colleague. Opening windows 'is entirely a feminine foible', he tells another. 'We're both bachelors; sit down, and be thankful' (8–11). Somewhat implausibly, four females are introduced as objects of erotic attention – including Button, the twin of Bimbo – also cute and charming, but more legitimately so than the boy. After many complications the women become engaged to the men around Donkin and he, escaping such involvements, supersedes the unsuitable headmaster. In its construction, *Housemaster* works hard not to be a play about homosexuality. Yet it cannot but share some of the same territory, and cannot prevent audiences from reading against the grain. The most illuminating comment on Donkin is offered by Ellen, the housemaid: 'That's only his way of talking, miss. You know — queer! An old bachelor! I don't think he always understands what he's saying' (35).

Why is it that Beckett's intensely symbiotic couples rarely strike commentators as queer? Why, in *Waiting for Godot* (1952, *En Attendant Godot*; Arts Theatre Club, 1955) should not the bickering but affectionate Gogo be played as a camp item, with Didi as his straight-acting partner? And Pozzo and Lucky as an S/M routine — the master/slave dialetical duo? Might not Hamm in *Endgame* (1957, *Fin de partie*; Royal Court) be the Wildean gent and Clov his bit of rough (an erstwhile telegraph boy, perhaps) — a pattern destined to be repeated at the end with the boy who has appeared outside? The answer is, first, that language and structure persuade audiences to interpret these plays on a metaphysical plane where they enact 'Man' (gayness could only be an impertinent intrusion on such a lofty topic). Second, Beckett or his estate refuse permission for productions that deviate from his prescriptive stage directions.[68] We might begin to ponder, though, what dangerous interpretations are trying to break through. 'We're not beginning to . . . to . . . mean something?' Hamm muses. 'Imagine if a rational being came back to earth, wouldn't he be liable to get ideas into his head if he observed us long enough[?]' (*Endgame*, 27, Beckett's pauses).

Privilege

It is not a matter, then, of deciding that this or that character is 'really', 'underneath', gay; to say that would be to override the ambiguity which at the time was crucial. During those decades of discretion we should not imagine homosexuality as *there*, fully formed but hidden in the closet, like a statue shrouded by a sheet until ready for exhibition. The closet (as discreet homosexuality was named when it came under scrutiny in the 1960s) did not obscure queerness: in the form that dominated for the first two-thirds of the century, it *created* it. Freud proposes a similar approach when he disputes that one should expect to find 'the essence of dreams in their latent content': the important thing is the dream-*work* which produces such images.[69] It is not so much that same-sex passion was silenced, as that it was on a wavelength that is difficult for us to reach. The task for cultural commentary is to retrace the *processes* of representation and decoding, and the social determinants that construct such processes.

There is also a political difficulty. Our central concept of queerness today privileges openness and equality, whereas the mid-century world was furtive and hierarchical. I discuss in chapter 8 representations of the lower-class man taken up by the leisure-class man. Rightly, we have seen that world as something to be repudiated, as much as celebrated. The butch/femme model in the history of lesbianism is comparably problematic; chapter 7 is partly about this. Here again, there is an aspect of history which some women want to define themselves against, while others want to cultivate a more positive or a more thoughtful relation to it.

Upper-class people, while they were notably vulnerable to scandal, could organise their personal lives more or less as they wished. They had the resources and glamour to attract partners, and the relative privacy to pursue liaisons. Part of the centrality of the Wildean queer gent derives from the fact that he was able to cultivate opportunities in places other than toilets, alleyways and waste-land. Much of the public circulation of ideas about homosexuality occurred through gossipy rumours about his behaviour. The gay private party, Broadway and Hollywood writer Leonard Spigelgass reports, was prestigious: 'it was a club into which you couldn't get . . . I mean, no ordinary certified public accountant could get in the Larry Hart, Cole Porter, George Cukor world. That was *the* world. That was Somerset Maugham. That was Cole Porter. That was Noël Coward'.[70] Even in the English small town, in the 1940s and 1950s, the most likely queer venues were 'some corner of a bar, usually in the "best" hotel', or in cities perhaps 'behind the facade of some "gentleman's club"'.[71]

Such affluent queers had the money and cachet to force social change. However, in the manner of the privileged, they often collaborated with a system which, by and large, they could manipulate. Maugham, Coward and Rattigan did nothing to advance the situation of most lesbian and gay people, and became conservative as they became wealthy. Even dramatists whom we associate with the overthrow of that hegemony − writers such as Tennessee Williams, John Osborne and Edward Albee − found discretion convenient. Joe Orton was far from candid.

To be sure, it is unhistorical to suppose that such writers could have been significantly more frank, and pointless to lambast them from a post-Stonewall stance. It is quite hard now to re-envisage the extent to which our predecessors emerged into a sexuality that was not just reviled, as it still often is, but supposed not even to exist. That is why the fact that most of the representations of queerness that we shall consider are hostile, partial and oblique doesn't make them less significant. Those were the terms on which lesbian and gay subcultural formation occurred. On the other hand, it is naive to suppose that these people could live a life of partly clandestine relations without it affecting those relations and everything else. Finally, discretion always colludes with oppression, because it acknowledges the unspeakability of homosexuality where that acknowledgement must be most damaging: among homosexuals.

While it is right that gays and lesbians should want to separate themselves from the exploitation recorded in this past, we need also to recognise its enduring significance. For it is premature to suppose that we have become simply candid and egalitarian. Contact ads still often promise and require discretion. The class system, and its accompanying snobberies and prejudices, have not changed all that much. Indeed, they reverted during the 1980s to the haves-and-have-nots pattern of the 1930s — as is witnessed, among other things, by the immense growth in prostitution. In a context where the market is offered as the appropriate structure for all relations, the libertarian and egalitarian ideals of the Gay Liberation Front seem almost as remote as Coward's posh gent and his bit of rough. We are the outcomes of our histories, so far.

2

Society and its Others: Scandal

Bunburying

In *The Importance of Being Earnest* (1895) Algernon has invented Bunbury, a permanent invalid, as a pretext for going down into the country when he wishes. Surely, modern commentators suppose, 'Bunburying' must be queer. The Lord Chamberlain failed to notice 'Wilde's bawdy humor in devising a name that contains a slang expression for the buttocks', Kaier Curtin believes. Bunburying 'blatantly calls forth the image of a promiscuous sodomite and foreshadows the epithet "somdomite" [*sic*] applied to Wilde' by Lord Queensberry, Patricia Flanagan Behrendt declares. Bunbury was 'the term for a homosexual pickup', says Linda Gertner Zatlin. It 'was not only British slang for a male brothel, but is also a collection of signifiers that straightforwardly express their desire to bury in the bun', Joel Fineman asserts.[1]

I can discover no historical ground for any of these assertions. According to Eric Partridge's *Dictionary of Slang*, from the first edition (1937) to the eighth (1984), *bun* does not mean 'buttock'. It means women's sexual parts – and that is the gloss in John Farmer's dictionary of 1890 (it's to do with squirrels and rabbits).[2] So, if anything, Bunburying is heterosexual. According to the *Oxford Dictionary of Modern Slang*, the meaning 'male buttock' appears in the United States from around 1960; in my view it enters the British Isles from there.[3] (Sometimes the Cheshire village of Bunbury is said to be so remote as to be suitably nowhere, but it is less than ten miles from Crewe and hence very accessible by rail from London.)

Some of the effect these commentators proclaim may be obtained by invoking the similar sound of the old English word 'bum', but still we don't have anything about brothels or pick-ups. The arresting point here is the conviction of these modern commentators that homosexuality must be discoverable, somehow, in *The Importance of Being Earnest*. For how could Wilde, the apogee of queerness, not be manifesting it in his best-known play?

What turned out to be a book, *The Wilde Century* (1994), began as my attempt to write a chapter for the present project. I was struck by the extent to which, although Wilde made an exhibition of himself for fourteen years, looking and sounding first like an aesthete and then like a dandy, most of his contemporaries did not 'recognise' these 'effeminate' manners as signs of 'homosexuality' − even when the trials had begun. To us, Wilde looks like the ultimate instance of the queer man, but that is because the trials established him, and his image, as this − in English-speaking countries at least − until the 1970s. Of course, Wilde didn't do this by himself or out of nothing, and other concepts of same-sex passion certainly coexisted in the early and mid-twentieth century. But at the trials the entire, vaguely disconcerting nexus of effeminacy, leisure, idleness, immorality, luxury, insouciance, decadence and aestheticism, which Wilde was perceived as instantiating, was transformed into a brilliantly precise image: the queer. As with Radclyffe Hall's *The Well of Loneliness* and the manly lesbian, the parts were there already, and were being combined, diversely, by various people. But a distinctive possibility cohered, far more clearly, and for far more people than hitherto.[4] Now effeminacy signified both queerness and the leisure class − to the point where, even today, it is sometimes unclear which is in play. This ambiguity facilitated both boldness and evasion.

Among the privileged set who set much of the tone at Broadway and West End theatres, Wildean influence is well-documented. In New York, as early as World War I when Malcolm Cowley was at Harvard, it was the thing to cultivate the 'aesthetic' decadence of the 1890s. They read the *Yellow Book*, Pater, Beardsley, Swinburne and Dowson, 'displayed crucifixes in their bedroom and declared that they found the Church "voluptuous"'.[5] In London in the 1920s Ronald Firbank and Harold Acton listened eagerly to Reggie Turner's stories of Wilde.[6] When Michael Davidson arrived in 1924 he found, to his great relief, 'what today would be called a "queer set"' − mainly people who maintained a 'decadent' stance − Christopher Millard (who had a large collection of Wildean material and under the name Stuart Mason had published a bibliography of Wilde), Robbie Ross, Charles Kains-Jackson. This wasn't how Davidson saw himself: 'They were feminine, aesthetical, fussily elegant; my only womanish traits, I suppose, were the invisible femininity

implicit in phallic worship and a pronounced talent for materalism.'[7]
Nevertheless, they gave him a base.

After an initial hesitation, Wilde's comedies were performed widely — though, so far as I know, without encouraging queer inferences. *Salomé* (1891) was another matter. Herod offers Salomé half his kingdom if she will dance for him, but she doesn't want the kingdom, she wants the death of the man who has rejected her. For men it is a troubling story: the woman in power is dangerous (initial reviewers compared Ibsen's strong female characters). *Salomé* was refused a licence between 1891 and 1931, but performed privately in 1905 and 1906. A private production in 1918 featuring Maud Allan provoked an accusation of lesbianism in *The Vigilante*, a right-wing newspaper edited by Noel Pemberton Billing (the article was called 'The Cult of the Clitoris'). Allan had made a career as an exotic-erotic dancer and was rumoured to have a relationship with Margot Asquith, but, as Jane Marcus observes, there was no justification in the text or the performance for an imputation of lesbianism. 'Nothing overt in the play indicates that Salomé was a lover of her own sex. She kills a man, therefore she must be a lesbian, runs the reasoning of the trial.'[8] Billing said also that the list of subscribers to the performance would largely coincide with the 'Black Book' of 47,000 names, male and female, which German Intelligence was alleged to have compiled with a view to blackmailing notable British sexual dissidents.

Allan sued for defamation (as Wilde had done). Billing's case was that Wilde personified all kinds of sexual dissidence: 'this social leper, Oscar Wilde, had founded a cult of sodomy in this country, and travelled from end to end of it perverting youth wherever he could. He was not satisfied even that his evil influence should die with him; he left behind his works, so that his crimes may be perpetuated even after he was dead'.[9]

The Wilde trials had established queerness not just generally, but at the heart of theatre. Paul Bailey recalls how he announced that he meant to study at the Central School of Speech and Drama in the 1950s:

'The theatre is a breeding-ground for pansies', a concerned relation warned me. 'And they say most actresses are prostitutes'. . . . 'Pansy' was the word my family used whenever the 'love that dare not speak its name' was spoken of, derisively. Oscar Wilde was mentioned, too: 'He looks like an Oscar Wilde to me'; 'He's the Oscar Wilde type'; 'I know an Oscar Wilde when I see one'. These Oscar Wilde's were invariably famous, with their photographs in the papers — actors, principally; ballet dancers, painters, composers.[10]

Theatre sought to comment on this element in its own constitution. The play *Oscar Wilde* (1936), by Leslie and Sewell Stokes, received club productions in England at the Gate Theatre in 1936 and the Boltons in 1948 and 1957; it was shown successfully on Broadway in 1938 and 1957. The account of Wilde's life is fairly full and straightforward; it is taken for granted from the start that he is engaged in illicit sexual relations with a number of boys, mainly for money, and that he asks for trouble by being reckless — we see him dining at a fashionable restaurant with the young cockney Charles Parker. The trial verdict turns upon why Wilde didn't kiss Walter Grainger (he was extremely ugly). Further signs of homosexuality are that Wilde makes camp aphorisms all the time, and is surrounded mainly by effeminate queers, of his own and of lower classes, who quote him and seem to derive much of their manner from him. By way of contrast we have Wilde's blunt, vigorous and straight friend, Frank Harris.

Wilde's speech on 'The love that dare not speak its name' is made to conclude the trial scene, and is followed immediately by the judge's condemnation: 'That you, Wilde, have been the centre of a circle of extensive corruption of the most hideous kind among young men, it is impossible to doubt' (79). From what we have seen, that is not an unfair assessment: male homosexuality does appear to centre upon and proceed from Wilde. He ends up duly drunk, dishonest and demoralised. 'Scandals used to lend charm, or at least interest, to a man', Wilde avers as he leaves prison. 'Now they crush him' (83). Some critics welcomed this display, others regretted it, but none disputed that it was indeed what Wilde was like, and what homosexuality was like.[11]

In 1960, the year of Wilde films starring Robert Morley and Peter Finch, Micheál macLiammóir presented in Dublin, London, New York and around the world his one-man show, *The Importance of Being Oscar*. This is a far more timid telling of the story, and it wasn't censored. MacLiammóir declares that Wilde was in love (successively) with Lily Langtry and with his wife; in 1895, still, he has him as a happy husband, with Queensberry protesting against the friendship of his son; the words on Queensberry's insulting card ('posing as a somdomite') are not quoted ('on the card his Lordship had scribbled a few libellous and, incidentally, wrongly spelt words': 44–5). The entire trials occur during the interval, so there is no indictment, no witnesses, and no defence of the love that dare not speak its name. Part two begins with the judge's sentence for a crime which is at no point mentioned, and dwells upon Wilde's religious fervour in *De Profundis* and 'The Ballad of Reading Gaol'.

For the tragedy, we are told, is that 'to so many thousands of people today, the name of Oscar Wilde merely conjures up an immediate image of shame and scandal. It is time not to forget the scandal or the shame but to place them in their correct relationship with his subsequent development as an artist and a human soul' (48). If Wilde is to be redeemed, it is through art and suffering; there is no sympathy, let alone justification, for sexual deviancy — which, as I have noted, is scarcely mentioned. MacLiammóir wondered whether audiences picked up all the references: when Wilde's letter comparing Douglas to Hyacinth, Jonquil and Narcissus was quoted, they 'might be wondering if he were referring to Woolworth's catalogues of spring bulbs'.[12] Very likely. Indeed, unless they knew about Wilde already, they wouldn't understand any of it. But then, of course, they did know. They knew that Wilde was *the homosexual*. And, surely, this was transmitted also by macLiammóir's notoriously queeny presence.

Wilde remains a stage figure through whom we are invited to redefine our identities. Donald Sinden presented *Diversions and Delights* (1990) by John Gay, an uninspired monologue stressing Wilde's suffering. Terry Eagleton in *Saint Oscar* (1989) explores Wilde as a generally marginal figure — in nation, class and political allegiances, as well as sexuality. Refreshingly, rather than piecing the dialogue together out of Wilde's sayings, Eagleton writes original pastiche, shifting lightly from one register to another. 'No Surrender', Carson pronounces, in true Unionist manner (60); an allusion to Shakespeare deftly points an equivalence between Wilde and Bosie and Falstaff and Prince Hal. Less happily, *Saint Oscar* encourages the Freudian inference that queerness is a failure of manhood deriving from a castrating mother. 'You speak up for women, mother; I've learnt from you there. I've laid aside my manhood: that ought to please you. Instead it's the very weakness you can't abide' (17–18). And, more seriously for his project of recovering Wilde's Irishness, Eagleton allows the inference that queerness is specially English. 'Homosexual behaviour is as English as morris dancing, if somewhat less tedious. To try a man in this country for homosexuality is as illogical as trying him for foxhunting', Wilde avers (40). What remains to be attempted is an articulation of Wilde's sexuality with his Irishness.

Neil Bartlett doesn't present Wilde himself in his adaptation of *The Picture of Dorian Gray* (1994), but he makes his text almost entirely out of Wilde's words, as they are redeployed by members of his circle who meet in 1924 to perform a version of the novella. As they move between the worlds of Wilde, Dorian Gray and the 1920s, Bartlett says, they manifest Wilde's influence: 'right up until the 1930s, some people still not only carried in their conversation traces of Wilde's distinctive manner and rhythms of speech, but would also still, consciously or unconsciously, repeat, parody, or claim as their own his aphorisms, adjectives and catch phrases'.[13] One might hope that all this cultural work on Wilde would help us put his spirit to rest, but it rarely turns out that way. Generally, the more someone is written about, the more it seems necessary to write about them. *Dorian*, a musical by David Reeve (1997), *Gross Indecency: The Three Trials of Oscar Wilde* (1997) by Moises Kaufman, *The Invention of Love* (1997) by Tom Stoppard and *The Judas Kiss* (1998) by David Hare betray no loss of appetite.

Wildean Dandies

If the queer man as we know him is a consequence of the Wilde trials, it must be a question whether there can be any homosexuals in the plays. If he and his dandies look suspect to us, that is because they furnished, after the event, the central model for pre-Stonewall queerness. In their initial context, they show something more interesting: the point at which this model was getting constituted. The interpretive challenge is to recover the moment of indeterminacy – when Wilde and his errant lords are on the brink of manifesting a new concept.

Before Wilde, the effeminate dandy, typically, was a heterosexual philanderer. During the eighteenth century effeminacy had come to function as a broad signal of the leisure class. Eve Sedgwick writes of 'the feminisation of the aristocracy as a whole', whereby 'the abstract image of the entire class, came to be seen as ethereal, decorative, and otiose in relation to the vigorous and productive values of the middle class'.[14] The newly dominant middle class justified itself by claiming manly purpose and purity, and invested the leisure class with effeminate idleness and immorality. In the face of this manoeuvre, there were two alternatives for the wealthy and those who sought to appear wealthy. One was to attempt to appear useful and good; Sir Robert Chiltern does this in *An Ideal Husband* (1895). The other was to repudiate the hegemony of middle-class values by displaying conspicuous idleness and immorality – the 'feminine', dandy manners. From Beau Brummell (1788–1840) through 'profligate young lords in Victorian novels', Sedgwick adds, 'almost *all* share the traits of the Sporus-like aristocratic homosexual "type", and it is impossible to predict from their feckless, "effeminate" behavior whether their final ruin will be the work of male favorites, female favorites, the racecourse, or the bottle; waste and wastage is the presiding category of scandal' (174–5).

Mademoiselle de Maupin by Théophile Gautier, published in 1835, figures in Lillian Hellman's play *The Children's Hour*: it is where the girls get their knowledge of sex. D'Albert in this novel is a youthful idealist voluptuary, renowned for his explicitly erotic affairs with women. Falling in love with Théodore, a young man, does not much dismay him. 'Sometimes I try to persuade myself that this love is abominable, and I say this to myself as sternly as possible; but the words lie no deeper than my lips; it is an argument which I produce but do not believe. Actually it seems to me the simplest thing in the world, and that everyone else would do the same in my place.'[15] There is no question of d'Albert finding that he is in fact *a homosexual*; indeed, he takes a new mistress. (It turns out that 'Théodore' is a young woman; in a further gender-bending twist, she allows him to perceive this while playing Rosalind to his Orlando in *As You Like It*.)

Gautier's d'Albert is effeminate, but it is rivals for the attention of women who criticise him: 'They say that I dress too effeminately, that my hair is curled and glossed with over much care and that this, taken with my beardless face, makes me look most ridiculously foppish. . . . But all this only adds to my favour; the ladies think I have the loveliest hair and that my careful elegance is in the best taste' (41). When commentators see queerness in *The Importance of Being Earnest* because Algernon and Jack appear effeminate, therefore, they are precisely wrong. Patricia Behrendt quotes Gwendolen: 'Once a man begins to neglect his domestic duties he becomes painfully effeminate, does he not? And I don't like that. It makes men so very attractive', she says (65). Behrendt comments: 'the attraction that the effeminate man would hold for Gwendolyn [*sic*] would be his lack of interest in her': she is 'attracted specifically to men of questionable sexual preferences'.[16] But the effeminate dandy is dangerously attractive because, despising responsible, middle-class domesticity (earnestness) and having nothing better to do, he spends his time flirting. That is what Gwendolen likes.

Wilde's dandies are generally heterosexually passionate, and/or philanderers. Lord Darlington in *Lady Windermere's Fan* (1892) tries to persuade Lady Windermere to run away with him. Lord Augustus, in the same play, is especially effeminate. He has been married and divorced several times, and is infatuated with Mrs Erlynne despite evidence of her unreliability. He falls too easily for female charms; he is flabby; men insult him. 'Tuppy', they call him, mocking his ram-ish proclivities. Even in *The Picture of Dorian Gray*, where the plot springs from the response of Lord Wotton, the dandy, to the attractions of Dorian, Wotton's other involvements seem to be with women. He reflects with wonderment upon Basil Hallward's infatuation with Dorian: 'He remembered something like it in history. Was it not Plato, that artist in thought, who had first analyzed it?'[17] Hallward is the homosexual in *Dorian Gray*, if anyone is, but he is not a dandy; he is earnest — moral and hard-working.

At the same time, the dissolute aristocrat might indulge in any kind of debauchery; so while same-sex passion was not ruled in, *neither was it ruled out*. In *Lady Windermere's Fan* Cecil Graham is a dandy and unattached. He becomes very appreciative of Mrs Erlynne: she looked very handsome tonight, he has become one of her admirers. Graham, here, could be the heterosexual philanderer. But he appears to have no personal attachments to women, and could equally be admiring the style with which the stigmatised Mrs Erlynne is managing her re-entry into Society (rather like Judy Garland making a come-back). Asked how long he could love a woman who didn't love him, Graham replies: 'Oh, all my life!' (66). This might indicate either boundless passionate devotion to women, or a preference for relations that never get anywhere. This ambivalence lurks around all Wilde's dandy figures. The task is not to decode them as really queer, but to study the indeterminacy.

The closest we come to a queer scandal in Wilde's plays is in *A Woman of No Importance* (1893). Lord Illingworth is very prominent, and apparently able to get away with scandalous behaviour; only he, Mrs Arbuthnot and the audience know that he once seduced her and that Gerald is his son. At the end he is exposed for forcing his attentions on the puritanical American, Hester Worsley. Nonetheless, Illingworth's approach to Gerald is Wilde's most dangerous flirtation with same-sex passion in the plays. For a young man in Gerald's position — a bank clerk — Illingworth is plainly a bad influence. Going to church, as Gerald's mother does, is not modern:

> You want to be modern, don't you, Gerald? You want to know life as it really is. Not to be put off with any old-fashioned theories about life. Well, what you have to do at present is simply to fit yourself for the best society. A man who can dominate a London dinner-table can dominate the world. The future belongs to the dandy. It is the exquisites who are going to rule. (75)

Illingworth's aggressive heterosexuality distracts attention from any thought that he is trying to develop a same-sex relationship with Gerald — who is, after all, his son (which in heteronormative ideology means that sexual attraction may not occur between them). Illingworth would seem to have the perfect cover. Furthermore, other characters see no impropriety, even though they don't know of the father–son connection. Lady Hunstanton has no misgivings: 'It means a very brilliant future in store for you. Your dear mother will be delighted.' Wilde risks some amorous language: 'Lord Illingworth seems to have taken quite a fancy to him', Lady Caroline observes, without any evident awareness of sexual innuendo (15–17). 'I took a great fancy to young Arbuthnot the moment I met him', Illingworth says (23).

Mrs Arbuthnot's anxiety at the enticement of her son is paradoxical, as Illingworth remarks: 'if I were a perfect stranger, you would allow Gerald to go away with me, but as he is my own flesh and blood you won't. How utterly illogical you are!' (69). And yet, are her fears altogether illogical? Illingworth got the idea that Gerald should become his secretary *before* knowing that he is his son. He sees him simply as a 'Charming fellow' when he says: 'It is because I like you so much that I want to have you with me' (35). And the more explicitly heterosexual he appears, the more he is a selfish cad – having seduced and abandoned Mrs Arbuthnot; and hence the less likely, suddenly, to be drawn to his son by wholesome familial ties. This makes critics uneasy: Illingworth discovers 'paternal feelings he never even suspected he had', says one recent reviewer; 'The basis of this change of heart is never dramatized', notes Kerry Powell.[18] The more Illingworth claims paternal devotion, the more he may seem to manifest a strange excess of male-to-male attachment. 'You have missed not having a father, I suppose, Gerald?' he asks, placing his hand on his son's shoulder (74).

Leisure-class men did have intimate secretaries, and usually they didn't turn out to be their offspring. In 1894, Lord Alfred Douglas' twenty-five-year-old brother, Francis, Viscount Drumlanrig, was found dead from a gunshot wound. Drumlanrig was assistant private secretary to Lord Rosebery, then Foreign Minister, and the Douglas family were convinced that his death was caused by the pressures of a same-sex relationship with Rosebery.[19] 'The world will know him merely as my private secretary', Illingworth tells Mrs Arbuthnot, 'but to me he will be something very near, and very dear' (66).

Illingworth's amorousness is stronger in drafts of the play, and in some cancelled dialogue the knowing Mrs Allonby seems to have twigged something. 'How you delight in disciples!' she teases. 'What is their charm?' Illingworth replies: 'It is always pleasant to have a slave to whisper in one's ear that, after all, one is immortal. But young Arbuthnot is not a disciple . . . as yet. He is simply one of the most delightful young men I have ever met' (272,

Wilde's pause). When Lady Hunstanton reiterates how Illingworth has 'taken such a fancy' to Gerald, Mrs Allonby comments: 'Lord Illingworth would talk about nothing else but Mr Arbuthnot, the whole of yesterday afternoon. He looks on him as his most promising disciple. I believe he intends him to be an exact replica of himself, for the use of schools' (281). None of this amounts to queerness, but Wilde prudently deleted it.

If homosexuality was hardly to be specified when Wilde was writing, it tends nonetheless to lurk around when scandal of any kind is in the air. My central thought in this chapter is that queerness should be understood, from Wilde through to the 1920s, as one among a bundle of transgressions that provoked, and was evoked by, scandal.

Society and Scandal

MRS CHEVELEY: It is nearly six years since I have been in London for the season, and I must say Society has become dreadfully mixed. One sees the oddest people everywhere.

LADY MARKBY: That is quite true dear. But one needn't know them. I'm sure I don't know half the people who come to my house. Indeed, from all I hear, I shouldn't like to. (*An Ideal Husband*, 200)

Wilde's plays are obsessed with the boundaries of Society. Miss Worsley in *A Woman of No Importance* and Mr Hopper in *Lady Windermere's Fan* are mocked as outsiders (American, Australian) but, whatever the sources of their income, they are rich and the mockery is part of the process whereby they are being accommodated. Other would-be entrants are more dangerous. In *Lady Windermere's Fan* and *An Ideal Husband* a doubtful woman wanting to get back into Society is the catalyst for the unearthing and perpetrating of various scandalous doings, with consequent danger to people who have believed themselves to be secure.

If you were 'in Society' you would leave cards and exchange visits with other people in good standing; you would attend receptions, balls, parties and dinners at the residences of aristocrats and the royal family, and be acknowledged on public occasions such as the Ascot and Derby horse races and the Henley Regatta. If you tried to aspire above your station by claiming an inappropriate acquaintance you would be 'cut' − publicly snubbed. A principal concern, as we see in Wilde's plays, was to secure appropriate spouses for the young people. Marriage, C. Wright Mills notes, was the central process serving 'to keep a propertied class intact and unscattered; by monopoly of sons and daughters, anchoring the class in the legalities of blood lines'.[20]

The ideology of Society proclaimed a stable and settled system of social ranking, founded in family lineage, private virtue and public responsibility. Actually it was the means for a negotiation between established hierarchy and new wealth. It was important not as the transmitter of coherent social relations, but as a way of handling instability. Old names and new money were united, and unknown South Africans, Europeans, Jews and Americans were filtered into acceptable positions, in order to provide the wealth from business that more established families were unable to make, either out of ineptitude or because direct involvement in market operations (other than landed estates) was distasteful to them. The actuality was continual improvisation and compromise. Beatrice Webb records: 'There were no fixed caste barriers; there seemed to be, in fact, no recognised types of exclusiveness based on birth or breeding, on personal riches or on personal charm; there was no fastidiousness about manners or morals or intellectual gifts.' The implicit test of membership was 'the possession of some form of power over other people'.[21]

To be sure, most people were untouched by Society, though all classes were influenced by notions of respectability and good-standing, but the press reported its glittering occasions. 'The pageant of splendour impressed the populace while whetting the appetite of the ambitious', Davidoff observes.[22] 'The aristocracy was irresistibly fascinating to a historically- and hierarchically-minded, socially ambitious and envious society, because its members seemed to be heroic', Geoffrey Best says — more handsome and passionate, apparently because of their noble breeding.[23] The idea, the conservative Walter Bagehot cheerfully admitted, was to foster popular reverence and submission: 'The office of an order of nobility is to impose on the common people — not necessarily to impose on them what is untrue, yet less what is hurtful; but still to impose on their quiescent imaginations what would not otherwise be there.'[24] George Bernard Shaw was not impressed: 'There is no doubt that these glimpses of expensive receptions in Park Lane, with the servants announcing titles *ad libitum*, are enormously attractive to social outsiders (say ninety-nine hundredths of us); but the stage reproduction is not convincing: everybody has an outrageous air of being at a party; of not being used to it.'[25]

All this was policed by the threat of scandal. The drawback with Society's use of the media was that these powerful people forfeited some control over their own situation, and even the most privileged were vulnerable, If, as

Bagehot said, the masses were deferring to 'the *theatrical show* of society',[26] a corollary was another kind of theatre: the fall of great men. Mrs Cheveley in *An Ideal Husband* has a letter incriminating a government minister in a financial swindle:

> Suppose that when I leave this house I drive down to some newspaper office, and give them this scandal and the proofs of it! Think of their loathsome joy, of the delight they would have in dragging you down, of the mud and mire they would plunge you in. Think of the hypocrite with his greasy smile penning his leading article, and arranging the foulness of the public placard. (162)

Exposures – such as that of Wilde – complemented the brilliant pageantry. Partly, perhaps, they reassured the public that standards were being maintained; just as likely, they spoke to an underlying grudging sense that these glittering stars were probably no better than they should be.

If Society was theatrical, West End theatres such as the Haymarket and the St James' were places where Society recognised and exhibited itself. In 1893 the first night of Wilde's *A Woman of No Importance*, following the success of *Lady Windermere's Fan*, attracted the most prominent members of Society – aristocratic, political and artistic; the Prince of Wales attended a few nights later. 'The costume on stage and off filled the women's columns in subsequent weeks', Regenia Gagnier notes.[27] George Augustus Sala observed in 1894 how the Lyceum Theatre was organised to reflect divisions in society:

> The fact is, that the 'classes' are divided into innumerable sections, and that certain sections make it a point of honour not to know other sections . . . ; and even if they knew them by sight it would clearly never do for the Duchess of Beaurivage to bestow even a nod on a lady in mauve velvet and diamonds, who might turn out to be Mrs Stockyard, the wife of a pork-butcher from Chicago.[28]

Joel H. Kaplan and Sheila Stowell observe: 'by the century's end, a select group of West End theatres had themselves become part of the London Season, perpetuating in their very architecture some of the tension between public space and privileged enclosure that helped to define late Victorian society'.[29] It was altogether appropriate that theatre censorship was operated by the Lord Chamberlain, whose other tasks included organising royal garden parties, administering royal homes, and examining the credentials of people who wished to be presented at Court or admitted to the royal enclosure at Ascot. On occasions the Chamberlain appealed to the King for his opinion about a playtext: he was at the head of Society.

Major scandalous matters were to do with mental illness, race (anti-Semitism was rife), and alcohol and drug abuse; but mainly there was money and sex. Insolvency was far more disgraceful than it is today, and, partly for this reason, people were prepared to lend huge sums to those of good social standing because it was supposed they could not afford to default. Very many people lived under the threat that large debts might be called in; writing cheques that could not be cashed was fraud (see, for instance, the cancelled Gribsby episode in *The Importance of Being Earnest*).

The sex-and-gender scandals were illegitimacy, marital discord, adultery, bigamy, homosexuality. They too were ultimately about money − conventional transmission of property through the legitimate male line not only regulated the distribution of wealth; it appeared to justify it. If inheritance passed smoothly, in accord with law and tradition, many people were persuaded to believe that the social order was working properly. A custom which served the interests of the rich was perceived, widely, as in accord with nature, religion, and even biology. As William A. Cohen points out, the typical Victorian novel depends on loss and recovery of fortune, benefactor, child, sibling or spouse; and this typically necessitates disclosure of a secret which is in some way immoral or illegal − mostly adultery or illegitimacy. Once this is revealed, 'the goods (property, family) are redistributed, now more justly, among those who survive'.[30]

The anxieties that clustered around these social processes were all immensely exacerbated if racial mixing was involved. In Somerset Maugham's play *The Letter* (1927) it is Leslie's discovery that her lover has a Chinese mistress that precipitates the exposure of her own scandalous behaviour; in *East of Suez* (1922) Maugham's premise is that a Eurasian mistress must be a disaster. This intense phobia correlates with the flourishing of the British empire and the need to repudiate anything that might threaten imperial domination. Scandal protected the property not just of the family, but ultimately of the tribe.

Same-sex passion did not directly interfere with the transmission of property; as I have argued elsewhere, it might be for that reason *relatively unimportant*. In the sixteenth, seventeenth and eighteenth centuries in England, as in many parts of the world at the present time, same-sex practices did not loom large as an ideological phenomenon − so long as the priorities of marriage, family, gender hierarchy, property and inheritance were maintained. Individual expressions of dissident sexuality became dangerous if they were allowed to interfere with the system — which, of course, they might do if pursued with sufficient passion (as, for instance, in Christopher Marlowe's *Edward II*, 1591).

Even so, same-sex passion may call into question the alleged inevitability of heterosexual relations, implying a penumbra of forbidden fruits around the allegedly precise kernel of a biological imperative to procreate. Indeed, in the public imagining of the late Victorians and through to the 1950s, the main visibility of homosexuality must have been as Society scandal; that is how it got into public discourse. The Boulton and Park trial of 1870 involved Lord Arthur Clinton, MP; the Cleveland Street scandal of 1889 featured Lord Arthur Somerset, the Earl of Euston, and a rumoured member of the royal family. From Wilde to Lord Montagu in 1954, public notice of homosexuality consists mainly of a sequence of prosecutions, exiles and suicides of notable figures. 'I thought men like that shot themselves', said George V.[31]

It is tempting to suppose that queerness is 'really' at the back of all scandal. Neil Bartlett remarks the range of perils in Wilde's plays — 'a poisonous philosophy or prophesy, a professional or marital scandal, a concealed parentage'. He believes they 'give spurious fictional shape to the source of their terror' — the revelation of queerness.[32] But rather than one of these terrors underlying all the others, I think they all imply each other — in the sense that scandal generally involved dark suspicions and, once 'beyond the pale', the scandalous person would be thought liable to diverse infringements, amounting to a general overthrow of morality and propriety. This is how Wilde was regarded. 'Before he broke the law of his country and outraged human decency', the *Evening News* asserted, Wilde was

> one of the high priests of a school which attacks all the wholesome, manly, simple ideals of English life, and sets up false gods of decadent culture and intellectual debauchery. . . . these abominable vices, which were the natural outcome of his diseased intellectual condition, will be a salutary warning to the unhealthy boys who posed as sharers of his culture.[33]

We have seen the persistence of this attitude in the Maud Allan trial. Homosexuality appears, characteristically, as one among a sheaf of scandalous behaviours, all of which tend to implicate each other.

These processes are displayed in *The Blackmailers* (1894), by John Gray and Marc-André Raffalovich, which received a single matinée performance at the Prince of Wales theatre. Gray had attracted Wilde's attention in 1889, and some thought he was the inspiration for Dorian Gray. Raffalovich disapproved of Wilde and of explicit homosexuality; he and Gray converted to Roman Catholicism and led, or affected to lead, celibate lives. *The Blackmailers* is evidently designed as a hostile rewriting of some Wildean motifs.

The first act is a social evening at the Bond-Hintons, where complex relations are obscurely hinted at. In act II it becomes apparent that the charming Claud Price is a blackmailer: despite rumours that he is a bad lot, he is skilled at finding out scandalous things about people. Mrs Bond-Hinton is one of his primary resources, for he has been her lover (her husband has mistresses). These heterosexual and professional interests coexist with an apparent same-sex attraction when Price recruits a family friend, young Hal Dangar. Price calls Hal 'Hyacinth' because he first met him when he was a child and had golden curly hair. He puts his hand on his shoulder; Hal will be a pupil, a comrade, will get to be the man he should be, will be lonely no longer. Hal likes all this but is ashamed at the prospect of becoming a blackmailer. In act III the plot gets very complicated; there is potential at every turn for scandalous exposure. Resolution is promised when Hal transfers his affections to Mr Bond-Hinton: if only he had had such a father to set him up in a steady way. But Bond-Hinton is merely using Hal in a ruse to expose his wife. In act IV, consequently, we hear that a warrant for blackmail is being issued against Price. Hal is arraigned before his family elders, who give him two choices: go to New Zealand or remain in England as an outcast. In fact he has a third choice: he comes to the point of killing himself (he has a potion in his pocket). Then a fourth choice appears: a letter from Price, drawing him to Paris where he can continue as a blackmailer. He goes. Even as queerness may not separate itself out clearly from other disreputable practices, *The Blackmailers* shows, scandalous suspicions may run into all kinds of avenue, queerness among them.

People wonder why Wilde allowed himself to be taunted by Queensberry into suing for libel when the allegations against him could be substantiated. Fear of exclusion from Society led Wilde into this course: 'He goes from restaurant to restaurant looking for me, in order to insult me before the whole world, and in such a manner that if I retaliated I would be ruined, and if I did not retaliate I would be ruined also.'[34] Mrs Erlynne warns:

You don't know what it is to fall into the pit, to be despised, mocked, abandoned, sneered at — to be an outcast! to find the door shut against one, to have to creep in by hideous byways, afraid every moment lest the mask should be stripped from one's face, and all the while to hear the laughter, the horrible laugh of the world, a thing more tragic than all the tears the world has ever shed. (*Lady Windermere's Fan*, 57)

This is why Wilde stayed: if he were to flee, he would forfeit his place in Society for ever. Wilde's brother told Yeats that Wilde 'considered that his crime was not the vice itself, but that he should have brought misery upon his wife and children, and that he was bound to accept any chance, however slight, to re-establish his position'. This meant staying, either to be acquitted or to 'purge his offence', whereas 'if he runs away he will lose every friend that he has'.[35] This practical assessment of his chances of maintaining the social expectations of himself and his family is enough to explain Wilde's actions; we don't need to postulate a masochistic or 'feminine' drive towards self-sacrifice (arguments along those lines usually tend towards a stereotypical notion of what queers really want).

As Claude Summers observes, this does not make Wilde the subversive that we might wish him to be.[36] The odd-person-out was Queensberry. His first concern should have been to protect his family from scandal, but he was obsessed with Douglas and Wilde; he was the one who didn't play the game.

Deciding whether Wilde's writings are progressive or reactionary is in my view not a sensible project. As I have been arguing, it is a mistake to posit a unitary 'audience response'. His comedies have held the stage before basically conservative, boulevard audiences for a hundred years; they afford ample scope for indulgence in deference towards the upper classes. At the same time, successful plays are usually risky; they flirt, at least, with the danger that prevailing values might not be satisfactory, or might not prevail. In the face of such provocation, some audience members will retreat into conformity, while others will entertain more radical possibilities.

For Better and for Worse: Somerset Maugham

Somerset Maugham was twenty-one at the time of Wilde's trial and conviction in 1895, and, biographers agree, was profoundly affected — like other queer men of his class. Frank Harris explains:

The truth was that the cultured aesthetes . . . had been thunderstruck by the facts which the Queensberry trial had laid bare. For the first time they learned that such houses as Taylor's were under police supervision, and that wretched creatures like Wood and Parker were classified and watched. They had imagined that in 'the home of liberty' such practices passed unnoticed.[37]

Maugham's friend Ellingham Brooks thought it wise to go to Capri, and Maugham joined him there. Actually, it doesn't sound so bad, does it? − we may bear in mind the privilege of these men as well as their oppression. Despite these anxieties − or, indeed, because of them − Maugham is in many ways Wilde's most obvious follower. He cultivated members of Wilde's circle − Robert Ross, Laurence Housman, Robert Hichens, Reggie Turner, Mabel Beardsley, Ada Leverson − as if, Ted Morgan remarks, to 'establish a link with a writer whose life-style he admired but dared not emulate'.[38]

It seems right to claim Maugham for gay drama: he embodies so much that is brave and despicable about the pre-Stonewall queer man. Sean O'Connor says he shares with Wilde, Coward and Rattigan 'a particular way of looking at the world, a strategy of discussing relationships and a similar agenda'.[39] Queerness in Maugham's plays emerges mainly through a preoccupation with scandal.

In *The Circle* (1921) Elizabeth, who is married to Arnold, is in love with Teddie. Their older counterparts are Lady Kittie, Arnold's mother, and Lord Porteous, her lover. They ran away when Arnold was an infant, precipitating scandal, exile and ostracism:

because we couldn't get the society we'd been used to, we became used to the society we could get. Loose women and vicious men. Snobs who like to patronise people with a handle to their names. Vague Italian princes. . . . Things are more difficult when you are not married − Believe me, it's no joke when you have to rely only on yourself to keep a man.[40]

Because Lady Kitty and Hughie now appear stodgy and trivial, their love seems to have been a mistake, and young Arnold and Teddy risk repeating it: that is 'the circle'.

However, the moral of the play is not that one should respect established institutions. The other characters are not very exciting either, and Lady Kittie and Hughie did have something special once. She tells her husband, 'if I had

my time over again I should be unfaithful to you, but I should not leave you';
and he implies acquiescence by remarking how he has managed to entertain
himself discreetly with a sequence of young women (IIb, 54). Ideally, one
would accomplish the excitement of romance without the stigma of scandal.
However, Maugham doesn't attempt to devise a compromise conclusion; at the
end Arnold and Teddy run away after all.

Meanwhile, Arnold, Lady Kitty's abandoned son, shows distinct signs of
queerness. He is meticulous about the placing of the chairs in his drawing room
and he, not his wife as is supposed, made the room 'nice'; he 'should have been
an interior decorator', she remarks (IIb, 47). He says 'a man marries to have a
home, but also because he doesn't want to be bothered with sex and all that sort
of thing' (IIb, 57); they have no children. These hints of queerness were picked
up by Edith Oliver, reviewing a revival of *The Circle* in 1986.[41] Note that this
is not scandalous in itself − Arnold leads a frigidly exemplary life. But
scandalous matters are connected: because he fails to inspire his wife, she takes
up with another man.

Maugham's investment in this topic was specific. In 1914–15 he met Gerald
Haxton, an American who had grown up in England and was then aged twenty-
two (Maugham was forty). In 1919 Haxton was declared an undesirable alien,
either because of gross indecency charges from which he escaped on a techni-
cality, or because he had been involved in espionage. This meant that
Maugham had to live abroad if he wanted to be with his lover. Faced with a
choice between the self-repression of Arnold and the exile of Elizabeth,
Maugham opted for the latter.

Our Betters (1917, Broadway; West End, 1923) is about Americans making
it in London Society. It was written in 1915 but not produced because the
Foreign Office thought it might discourage the USA from coming into the war.
'If one wants to be a success in London one must either have looks, wit, or a
bank-balance', Pearl the hostess declares to Fleming, who is visiting England
(IIa, 12). Or, of course, be of high social rank, but we see no one like that. Pearl
is both secure and endangered, for she is the wife of Lord Grayston, whom we
never see, and mistress of the wealthy and elderly Arthur Fenwick, who likes
to call her 'girlie'.

Among these people, sexual adventures are taken for granted. The
Duchesse de Surennes, for instance: 'She was a Miss Hodgson. Chicago people.
Of course, they're nobody in America, but that doesn't matter over here. She
adores good-looking boys, and I daresay she's getting rather tired of Tony',
Pearl explains (IIa, 13). Tony Paxton is far from reliable − having nothing to

do all day, he spends his time running after Gaiety girls. His manipulation of the Duchesse is explored in detail, as he turns peccadilloes into profit. 'Of course I care for you', he tells her. 'If I didn't, d'you think I'd have let you do all you have for me?' (IIa, 65). She agrees to buy him a sports car. 'You seem to have a passion for rotters, and they always treat you badly', Pearl tells the Duchesse (IIa, 21).

As in *A Woman of No Importance*, there is an innocent young American visitor, though Maugham makes this figure male. Fleming blurts out:

> There's something in these surroundings that makes me feel terribly uncomfortable. Under the brilliant surface I suspect all kinds of ugly and shameful secrets that everyone knows and pretends not to. This is a strange house in which the husband is never seen and Arthur Fenwick, a vulgar sensualist, acts as host; and it's an attractive spectacle, this painted duchess, devouring with her eyes a boy young enough to be her son. (IIa, 53)

Fleming sees only the half of it. Tony is flirting with Pearl, who is attracted by the thought that he is somebody else's property. The climax of the action occurs when the Duchesse contrives that they shall be discovered making love in the garden tea-house, threatening her relationship with Tony, Pearl's with Arthur, and scandal for all concerned. 'The slut. The slut', Arthur exclaims, to gasps from the audience (IIa, 76, vii).

There is no direct mention of same-sex scandal, though the description of the Duchesse makes her seem very camp – 'a woman of opulent form, bold, self-assured and outrageously sensual. She suggests a drawing of a Roman Emperor by Aubrey Beardsley' (IIa, 16). Thornton Clay has an effusive manner, is somewhat overdressed, is unmarried, and has the style of a bitchy queen. He is the only one of her acquaintance with whom Pearl has not had an affair, the Duchesse alleges; 'Thornton never makes love to me except when other people are looking. He can be very passionate in the front seat of my box at the opera', she replies. 'This conversation is growing excessively personal', he says (IIa, 98). The queerest character in *Our Betters* is Ernest. He is a dancing master and Pearl's *coup de grâce*: by bringing down from London this socially desirable figure, she ensures that no one will cause an indelible scandal by leaving the house party. 'He is a little dark man, with large eyes, and long hair neatly plastered down. He is dressed like a tailor's dummy, in black coat, white gloves, silk hat, patent leather boots. He is a dancing master, and overwhelmingly gentlemanly. He speaks in mincing tones' (IIa, 115). In

Desmond MacCarthy's perception, Ernest's presence is the final condemnation of these people: 'their lack of all standards, even of superficial elegance, is deliciously suggested by the enthusiastic reception of "Ernest", on whose egregious vulgarity and capers the curtain descends'.[42] (I discuss provocative representations by Maugham of bachelors and independent women in chapters 6 and 7.)

The interest of *Our Betters* to sexual dissidents depends less upon such hints than on a substantial equivalence with events in Maugham's household. Ted Morgan is clear that Maugham 'modeled the gigolo', Tony Paxton, on Maugham's partner, Haxton.[43] He was charming and genuinely likeable, but he gambled, cheated at cards, and was prone to becoming drunk and offensive. He frequented disreputable bars and was indiscreetly promiscuous. Commentators generally write disapprovingly of all this, but Bryan Connon points out that Maugham's best work was produced while Haxton was with him.[44]

However, the point is not that Maugham was writing autobiographically, but that queer and illicit straight liaisons are subject, alike, to characteristic patterns of discretion and scandalous exposure. In 1966, shortly after Maugham's death, Beverley Nichols published *A Case of Human Bondage*, a bitter response to Maugham's 'libel' upon his wife, Syrie, in his autobiography *Looking Back*.[45] Nichols hints as broadly as he can that the relation between Maugham and Haxton involved love, on Maugham's part at least, and sex. Among other scandalous events, Nichols describes a weekend party at Syrie's villa in Le Touquet in 1925. On returning from the casino, hearing a ghastly noise from the next room, Nichols entered, he says, to find Haxton naked on the floor, covered with bank notes. As he stood staring, Maugham appeared behind Nichols, furious at finding him in Haxton's room. As in *Our Betters*, the kept boy is discovered (apparently) *in flagrante*. In this case it is not the guest's boy with the hostess, but the hostess' husband's boy with the guest.

Now, the house party with Syrie was in 1925, ten years after *Our Betters*. The presentation of such a closely equivalent situation was possible not because Maugham was skilled in psychic anticipation, but because it is in the nature of such liaisons to produce such scenes. We are observing a pattern of dissidence, exploitation and scandal that ran through a range of illicit relations and activities, queer and straight. Indeed, Bryan Connon says this was one of two occasions when Nichols appeared in such a compromised manner: he was discovered also by Coward with his lover, Jack Wilson.[46] The repetition, again, is not uncanny; indeed, Nichols says that virtually the same thing happened again, thirty years later, with Maugham's later companion Alan Searle.

We are looking at what I have called a *subcultural myth* — a collective, ongoing, lived scenario through which we create and recreate ourselves. The composition of such stories is shared by a number of people, partly in collaboration, taking particular forms in varying historical circumstances. As we tell our myth, it tells us.[47]

Coward treated similar situations in *Bitter Sweet* (1929), and in 'Nature Study', a story in the volume *To Step Aside* (1939). As Philip Hoare observes, 'Nature Study' seems drawn from Somerset and Syrie Maugham; also, it recalls aspects of Coward's deteriorating relationship with Jack Wilson, who married Natasha Paley in the wake of a scandalous affair with David Herbert.[48] Similar events recur repeatedly, in biographical and fictive representations, because they are in the structure of the kind of liaison these men were pursuing.

It might be supposed that scandalalous exposure is a malfunction — a point at which the system has failed to contain the passions of its subjects. However, it may not, always, entail the triumph of orthodoxy. It may mark what I have called a faultline in the prevailing arrangements, a pressure point at which change is stirring.[49] For while scandal was about policing Society, it was also about breaking the rules. In one aspect, this was a matter of individual distress, boldness, and often tragedy. In another aspect, it marked a structural faultline at which the system was struggling to maintain equilibrium. While in many cases scandal ruined the perpetrator, in others a change in the boundaries was forced. In the next chapter I consider bohemia as a place where the authority of Society might be refused and the spectre of scandal repudiated.

3

Society and its Others: Bohemia

A Place for Us?

World War I almost wiped out Society, but those who enjoyed its privileges laboured to restore as much of it as possible. While T.S. Eliot was lamenting over a heap of broken images in *The Waste Land*, Samuel Hynes points out, 'Society (with a capital S) was much the same: there were still top hats at Ascot, and young ladies were presented at Court, and Parliament still adjourned for the grouse and salmon season.'[1] Now, even more, entertainment and spectacle became the primary effect, with special emphasis on the débutante's 'coming out'. At the same time, Society helped to generate its (partial) others — social locations which supported alternative, even oppositional, attitudes. While scandal was a relatively *ad hoc* challenge to the authority of Society, bohemia constituted a fairly sustained alternative, affording principled justification for what would otherwise have been merely disreputable behaviour.

When we look at the wealth, authority and tentacular organisation of an institution such as Society, and think of the fate of transgressors such as Wilde, it is easy to suppose that the dominant ideology must have swept all before it. However, as Raymond Williams argues, classes throw off fractions partly at odds with core ideology: 'a social class is by no means always culturally monolithic. . . . groups within a class may have alternative (received or developed) cultural, often religious, affiliations which are not characteristic of the class as a whole'.[2] Williams particularly remarks on *middle-class dissidence*, which has tended since the time of the Romantics to organise itself around literature, art, theatre and so on. That is because of 'an increasing general-ization and development of the idea that the practice and values of art are neglected by, or have to be distinguished from, or are superior or hostile to the dominant values of "modern" society' (72). This insight is important because it enables us to theorise much of the oppositional impetus that we find across a great range of high-cultural work in modern times.

In the late nineteenth and early twentieth centuries more specifically, Williams points to the growth of cities as spaces where dissident groups might gather: 'within the new kind of open, complex and mobile society, small groups in any form of divergence or dissent could find some kind of foothold'.[3] He doesn't quite mention bohemia, though he writes of the Pre-Raphaelites as pursuing 'a certain set of alternative moral and social attitudes, much more open and relaxed ("bohemian") than the norms of their class'.[4] I think bohemia as a social category enables us to ground the dissident middle-class fraction that sponsored avant-garde theatre and partly accommodated sexually dissident practice.

Henry Murger gave imaginative substance to bohemia in his novel *Scènes de la vie de bohème* (1848; 'Bohemian' because like gipsies). By the time of Puccini's operetta of 1896, *La Bohème*, based on Murger's story, bohemia had passed through several phases. Colin Campbell calls it 'the social embodiment of Romanticism':

> We may define Bohemianism as an unconventional and irregular way of life, voluntarily chosen, and frequently involving artistic pursuits, of those Romantics who are self-consciously in revolt against what they see as a utilitarian and philistine society, and who find mutual support against its 'corrupting' influence in coterie behaviour. . . . They tend to form intellectual circles, often around a café or restaurant . . . where they meet to talk, gossip, recite, or hold verse competitions, get drunk, practise their wit, flirt, argue, or even brawl.[5]

By the turn of the century, bohemias were flourishing in London and New York, as well as Paris.

In the novel *Despised and Rejected* (1918) by A.T. Fitzroy, a pseudonym of Rose Allatini, Antoinette, who has lesbian inclinations, and Dennis, who is in love with Alan, find a supportive environment in a pacifist-socialist-artistic-bohemian tea-shop set, which includes Sinn Feiners (one of whom is killed in Easter 1916), flappers, actors, poets, Jews and people living in sin. 'The atmosphere became smokier and smokier, and bits of *risqué* stories became mingled with political arguments, theatrical jargon with the orders for meals;

and the mournful lilt of the Irish voices was a queer contrast to the high-pitched shrieks and giggles of the flappers'; to Antoinette 'it was all very delightful and unconventional'.[6] 'Isn't it too Bohemian for words?' her friend exclaims (203–4). There Barnaby, the wise pacifist writer and activist, finally expounds Edward Carpenter to Antoinette: gays are 'intermediate types' from whom 'a new humanity is being evolved' (348–9).

Despised and Rejected was prosecuted successfully as likely to prejudice recruiting for the war, but the reception had not been totally unfriendly.

> The author's sympathy is plainly with the pacifists; and her plea for a more tolerant recognition of the fact that some people are, not of choice but by nature, abnormal in their affections is open and bold enough to rob the book of unpleasant suggestion. As a frank and sympathetic study of certain types of mind and character, it is of interest; but it is not to be recommended for general reading.

So the *Times Literary Supplement*.[7]

In New York the emergence of Greenwich Village and Harlem as queer milieux occurred alongside their cultivation by bohemians. 'By the 1920s, young American intellectuals, bohemians, and generic nonconformists were determined to rout with a vengeance the last vestiges of Victorianism', Lillian Faderman says.[8] Queerness was most at home at the edges of society – waterfronts, boarding houses, red-light districts, bohemias, including 'theaters that hosted touring companies: all of these constituted places freed from the bonds of family and community', John D'Emilio and Estelle B. Freedman observe.[9] In *Rebels in Bohemia*, his study of Greenwich Village in 1911–17, Leslie Fishbein writes of 'the growing recognition and acceptance of homosexuality' as an aspect of a 'sexual revolution'. He refers to the influence of Walt Whitman, and to courageous pronouncements by Emma Goldman, Margaret Sanger and Mabel Dodge.[10]

Harlem, Kevin J. Mumford argues, instanced 'a kind of affinity between homosexuals, black/white sex districts, and African-American culture more generally'. Following Carl van Vechten, the queer novelist and critic who helped promote the Harlem Renaissance to white socialites, Mumford argues for a distinction between fashionable slumming and the bohemian, since the latter, 'in certain respects was more like the homosexual – a socially repressed cultural outsider – than like the mainstream white urbanite'.[11] Faderman also holds that Harlem was a legitimate refuge for homosexuals, while pointing out that black people were often as ambivalent about them as whites.[12]

Mark, the queer, white protagonist in Blair Niles' novel *Strange Brother* (1931), finds himself at ease in Harlem speakeasies: 'In Harlem I found courage and joy and tolerance. I can be myself there – just as I'm being myself with you. They know all about me, and I don't have to live a lie.' However, Mark brings his problems with him: 'It's as though I had the body of a man and the psychology of a woman! I'm what you might call a half-man.'[13] He finds some consolation in the writings of Carpenter and Whitman.

Up to a point, bohemia allowed women to live more independently, sheltering both upper- and lower-class lesbian subcultures. Elizabeth Wilson remarks this in Paris, Chicago and New York.[14] Faderman says bohemia placed a new value on the unconventional and daring and encouraged some women in bisexual experimentation; others were 'voyeuristically intrigued with lesbianism'.[15] At the same time, ideas of liberation and fulfilment put more pressure on women to be heterosexually active; companionate marriage was supposed to be the answer to Victorian repression. All too easily, in this context, lesbianism became the villain, as in *The Captive* and *Wise To-Morrow* (see chapter 7). Henry F. May, while noting Emma Goldman's championing of 'the intermediate sex', adds that neither socialists nor feminists necessarily approved of sexual dissidence: many looked for a purer form of marriage and sought to reject imputations of male effeminacy and female masculinity.[16]

To be sure, there was little chance of a specifically queer milieu: 'these communities exist in a fluid and contingent relation to other disenfranchised populations: the bohemian artist community, political extremists, sexual profligates, the entertainment demimonde, the criminal underground', Joseph Boone remarks.[17] And not all of those who experimented with same-sex affairs defined themselves as homosexual. Nonetheless, George Chauncey remarks, bohemians generally were believed to be queer. They 'were often regarded as unmanly as well as un-American, and in some contexts calling men "artistic" became code for calling them homosexual'; Oscar Wilde would be invoked.[18] It is hard to envisage the emergence of twentieth-century queer discourse without a social location in which it might be expressed and even affirmed. Bohemia afforded that.

Staging Contest

Social formations develop institutions through which to explore their concerns and assert their interests, and bohemians created, among other things, new kinds of theatre. Broadway and the West End were situated on extremely valuable real estate and their priorities were commercial. They tended towards monopoly organisation, whereby they owned not just metropolitan, but touring theatres, so they could control the entire commercial life of their product. The 1920s, before talking pictures fully got going, were the most splendid period on Broadway, but, Andrew B. Harris observes, this was not a period of artistic freedom:

> At the height of their power in the mid-1920s, the Shubert circuit consisted of eighty-six first-class theatres in New York, Chicago, Philadelphia, and Boston, and twenty-seven in other major cities. They could seat one hundred and thirty thousand ticket buyers a night with a weekly box office of $1,000,000. Besides their real estate holdings, the Shuberts booked seven hundred and fifty theatres or about 60 per cent of all legitimate theatres in the United States and Canada.[19]

Most straight (i.e. non-musical) plays were originated by independent producers, but they had to work the commercial system. They would raise financial backing from stage-struck 'angels', try out the production out of town, and 'bring it in' to Broadway if it was successful. 'By 1920 at the latest', Gerald M. Berkowitz says, 'New York City had achieved an absolute dominance and virtually absolute monopoly of the American theatre, with the rest of the country reduced to local amateur fare and touring companies of last year's New York hits.'[20]

Of course, conditions varied through the decades, and the London West End was not the same. The domination of commercial interests was similar, though, and persistent. In the 1950s particularly there were complaints that West End and provincial British theatre was controlled by 'The Group' — companies 'connected by the presence on all their Boards of . . . powerful and experienced magnates'. By the 1970s the web of theatre ownership involved commercial television as well.[21]

Financial pressures made Broadway and the West End innately conservative. Bohemians, in reaction, cultivated avant-garde modes of writing and informal performance spaces. By so much as conventional theatre was stuffy, trivial, cautious and middle-brow, their writing was surreal, earnest, outspoken, symbolist. Their spaces were salons, cafés, warehouses and colleges. And they foregrounded dissident sexualities.

Avant-garde writing and informal performance spaces are often ephemeral, and hence hard to plot. Sue-Ellen Case invokes the personal performances of Natalie Barney in her garden in Paris in the early decades of the twentieth century.[22] In the next few pages I retrieve dramatic texts by Alfred Jarry, Henry B. Fuller, Edna St Vincent Millay and Djuna Barnes, written in the heyday of bohemia between the 1890s and the 1930s. The contexts from which they derive are too various to support much of a theory (it is doubtful whether the Jarry and Fuller plays were performed), but they indicate the opening up of sexual topics that became possible when an author envisaged him- or herself as a bohemian dramatist.

Alfred Jarry was the author of *Ubu Roi* (1896), the founding text of Dada, surrealism and absurdism. His play *Haldernablou* (1894) is usually taken as alluding to his relations with Léon-Paul Fargue, a bisexual poet.[23] Duke Haldern tells Ablou, his page, that love exists only outside sex ('Hors du sexe'): he wants someone who would be neither man nor woman nor altogether a monster − a devoted slave ('esclave dévoué') whose speech would not disrupt the harmony of his sublime thoughts (216). At Ablou's instigation, the relationship becomes sexual, but Haldern is seized with religious fervour, declares that Ablou is 'impur et vénal' and, quoting the theological injunction that it is necessary to destroy the beast with which one has fornicated, strangles Ablou (227).

Henry B. Fuller, the Chicago novelist, experimented with plays in the expressionist mode of Richard Wagner and Maurice Maeterlinck. In *At Saint Judas's* (1896) the Bridegroom and his Best Man wait in the sacristy for the Bride; they have been very close: 'You have shared my thoughts, my ideas, my secrets, my ambitions. We have eaten together; we have slept together; we have fought side by side. We are of the same age, the same height − my eyes have always been able to look level into yours', says the Bridegroom (89). However, in the more psychological climate of 1896 the heroic friendship of Wagner's *Tristan and Isolde* (1865) does not yield so conveniently to heterosexual union. The Bridegroom rehearses the rumours that have threatened the marriage − they are reflected in tableaux of knights and damsels in the eight vaulted windows. The Best Man eventually admits that he has engineered these impediments: 'We have been friends always . . . I have loved you all my life. . . . The thought of *her* made me mad − made me desperate . . .' (98, Fuller's pauses). He is the Judas of the title − he must kill himself.

Edna St Vincent Millay wrote *The Lamp and the Bell* (1921) to be performed at the fiftieth anniversary of the Vassar College Alumnae Association; all the parts were taken by alumni — that is, of course, by women. Princess Beatrice and Bianca, her friend, are in love, the court ladies say: 'I vow I never knew a pair of lovers / More constant than those two' (278). They are like the young women in *As You Like It*. For the ladies, this has no sinister implication; they wonder who will marry first, and whether they will still be friends. However, Bianca's mother, the stepmother of Beatrice, is uneasy. What can they talk about but things they had better 'Leave undiscussed? — you know what I mean, — lovers, / And marriage, and all that — if that be all.' 'They grow too much attached. They grow to feel / They cannot breathe apart. It is unhealthy' (284–5). Bianca is sent away. Beatrice and the visiting King Mario become attached, though he is puzzled because she runs and whistles like a boy and jousts properly with her sword, not as if it were a needle. But when Bianca returns, she and Mario fall in love and marry; Beatrice steps aside, declines another proposal of marriage, and on the death of her father becomes queen. In a strange and rather unclear episode, some years later, Beatrice kills Mario — unwittingly in a mêlée during an attack by brigands. The two women do not meet again until Bianca is on her deathbed, when Beatrice comes to Bianca, who dies passionately in her arms — very much in the manner of Tristan and Isolde.

Millay's love affairs at Vassar, until she was twenty-five, had been with women, Faderman reports, but in the 'bohemian' atmosphere of Greenwich Village she came under pressure to sleep with men.[24] The story of *The Lamp and the Bell* enables her to review, and invite the alumni in the cast and in the audience to review, the importance of their relations with both women and men. In the 1920s M. Carey Thomas attended a college play along similar lines, and 'was grieved that this sort of thing . . . would make it difficult for women to develop the warm and close relationships some of them needed so very much'.[25]

The Dove (1926) by Djuna Barnes was performed at the Studio Theatre, Smith College, and also at the Bayes Theatre in New York. Its three characters all seem to be lesbians. Vera is small, thin and dark, the Dove is 'a slight girl barely out of her teens; she is as delicate as china with almost dangerously transparent skin' (149). As she and Vera wait for Amelia, the Dove is polishing the blade of an immense sword. Vera and Amelia, Vera says, have 'made it our business to know — everything', but they lack the courage of their convictions: 'we collect knives and pistols, but we only shoot our buttons off with the guns and cut our darning cotton with the knives, and we'll never, never be perverse though our entire education has been about knees and garters and pinches on hindquarters — elegantly bestowed.' She wishes that the Dove 'had lived all we pretend we have . . . someone like you should know — everything' (151).

The Dove remains there, she says, because she loves Amelia: 'Another reason for going away', Vera says. When the Dove first saw Amelia in the park she 'bowed to her in an almost military fashion, my heels close together' (152–3). She seems to challenge them to be more than 'two splendid dams erected about two little puddles'; she is 'dangerous', a bit like Hedda Gabler — for her pacific name is perversely given (157). Amelia appears, behaving histrionically; finding the Dove's hand by mistake 'she clutches it convulsively. Slowly THE DOVE bares Amelia's left shoulder and breast, and leaning down, sets her teeth in. Amelia gives a slight, short, stifled cry.' The Dove bows a deep military bow, goes out into the entry, fires a shot: she has put a bullet through a picture they have there, Carpaccio's *Two Venetian Courtesans*. '*This* is obscene', she says, 'slowly, but with emphasis' (161). Does she mean the picture or the bullet hole; has she done something authentically perverse, or just made another gesture?

Barnes came from a bohemian family (her father believed in polygamy) and had worked with the Provincetown Players in Greenwich Village. At least two other short plays by her are intriguing from this point of view. In *Two Ladies Take Tea* (1923) young Fanny means to capture the husband of the magnificent Countess (of uncertain years). Fanny has 'a beautiful foot', she says. 'It looks well in a stirrup, descending a staircase, on a neck.' Fanny agrees: 'My dear Countess, you are brilliant, adorable, fascinating! Were I a man I would choose you, of course. But men are fools, they adore safety' (129). The Countess wins by observing that the Count is not worth taking — he 'has one of those debauched skulls that come to a family only when the blood can feel no more terror, the heart no more anguish and the mind no further philosophy' (130: presumably this is syphilis). However, her son is available. In *To the Dogs* (1929) a woman mocks and repels a young man who thinks he is impressive enough to make love to her. He calls her 'a queer woman' — 'Yes, that does describe me' (140). This bohemian/avant-garde concept is still, after World War II, available for Genet's plays; I discuss *Deathwatch* in chapter 6 and *The Maids* in chapter 9.

A further new institutional break occurred around 1920, when enthusiasts for alternative drama began to establish regular performance spaces — little theatres. Much of the most vital and influential drama between the wars was presented here. In Britain little theatres were usually organised as clubs, and hence assessed as 'private' in relation to the censorship regulations; consequently (and it is a nice illustration of how repression produces culture as well as controlling it), they made a point of attempting plays which featured sexual dissidence.

Ackerley's *The Prisoners of War* (1925) was produced initially at the Three Hundred Club in London in 1925; the Cambridge Festival Theatre staged banned plays between 1926 and 1932, including Wilde's *Salomé*, which was produced also by the People's National Theatre. *Richard of Bordeaux* was initially a Sunday night production at the Arts Theatre Club; *Vile Bodies* (1931 – based on Evelyn Waugh's novel) was first performed there, and *The Captive* in 1934; the Arts was one of the places where Radclyffe Hall and Una Troubridge socialised with Gladys Calthrop and John Gielgud.[26] The Stage Society produced *Young Woodley* and Luigi Pirandello's *Six Characters in Search of an Author*, both of which had been banned; *Journey's End* was first performed by them because mainstream managements felt the public would not accept a war play. At the Westminster Theatre *Children in Uniform* and Eugene O'Neill's *Desire Under the Elms* were presented.

The Gate Theatre was founded in 1925; Norman Marshall, who ran it in the mid-1930s, says its 'policy was simply to present plays which would not normally be seen in any other theatre, either because they were too sophisticated to appeal to a large public, or because they dealt with subjects frowned upon by the Censor, or because they needed a smaller and more intimate auditorium than any West End theatre possessed'.[27] Banned plays produced at the Gate included *Desire Under the Elms*, *Salomé* and *The Children's Hour*. The Gate, and Robert Morley, had a big success with *Oscar Wilde* by Leslie and Sewell Stokes – a fairly straightforward account which leaves no doubt that Wilde was having indiscreet sexual relations with numbers of boys. I discuss most of these plays elsewhere in this book.

Katharine Cockin likens the theatre club to the social club – such as the Cave of Harmony, which Edith Craig and Radclyffe Hall frequented. She quotes Vera Brittain's evocation, in her book on *The Well of Loneliness*, of clubs where 'those believed to be specialists in the practices vaguely known as "vice" were welcome. . . . The locked-cupboard atmosphere of these places gave them their attraction.' Cockin believes that theatre societies, 'which functioned along comparable lines, may have attracted a similar public image. The "club" was a site of popular anxiety, with its alternative culture, unregulated practices and the connotations of recruitment, membership as well as informal associations.' Nor was it all image: these were 'oppositional spaces'.[28]

In the United States the little theatre movement deferred initially to Broadway and tours on the Shubert circuit. 'In spite of hometown chauvinism and a spirit of anti-commercial rebellion, local audiences did not trust themselves to know what was good', Harris says.[29] The Provincetown Players (1915–29), the Washington Square Players (1914–18) and the Theatre Guild (1918–40) changed this – though mainly from within the New York scene. Helen Deutsch and Stella Hanau observe:

> The little theaters were manned largely by the pre-war younger generation, who held memories of repressed Victorian childhood and had been the intelligent minority at college. They had been stirred by Isadora Duncan, had listened to Eugene Debs, had discovered Krafft-Ebing, and had wondered why professors of dramatic literature damned Strindberg as decadent and Schnitzler as immoral.[30]

Robert Károly Sarlósa characterises the Provincetown Players as a 'gathering of rebellious, bohemian artists and intellectuals'.[31] In their first play, *Suppressed Desires* (1915) by George Cram Cook and Susan Glaspell, the enthusiasm of a bohemian amateur Freudian is mocked in some detail. I discuss in chapter 7 Glaspell's play *The Verge* (1921), in which Claire is driven into weird ways by frustration with the roles of wife and mother. Provincetown performed Theodore Dreiser's psychoanalytically informed drama, *The Hand of the Potter* (1921). *Strange Interlude* (1927) by Eugene O'Neill, the great 'discovery' of Provincetown, was appreciated by progressive audiences, and, correspondingly, upset the mayor of Boston by its references to abortion and incest. I consider in chapter 6 whether the effeminacy of the character Charles Marsden requires us to read him as 'really queer'. The last play produced by this company, *Winter Bound* (1929) by Thomas H. Dickinson, is about two women, one 'masculine' and one 'feminine', who withdraw together to a Connecticut farmhouse, only to find a local male who makes the relationship into a triangular struggle. This sounds very like D.H. Lawrence's novella *The Fox*.

Women figured particularly in the little theatre movement. The professional stage was still a less-than-reputable place for a woman, and she could hardly expect to be taken seriously there; this did not discourage those of radical disposition, though it did make alternative theatre more rewarding. Performers such as Janet Achurch, Florence Farr, Elizabeth Robins, Marion Lea, Lena Ashwell, Olga Nethersole, Lillah McCarthy and Gertrude Kingston set up companies devoted to a more thoughtful and serious repertoire than professional theatre normally attempted.[32] I noted in chapter 1 the companies organised by Edith Craig to present plays on feminist and other progressive themes; the Pioneer Players performed *The Verge* in 1925.

The Mothers (1915), a one-act play by Edith Ellis set in Cornwall, was premiered at the Little Theatre in Chicago. Selina is having a sad and subdued row with Mark, her husband, over his attentions to a widowed neighbour, Hannah. He leaves and Hannah appears. Selina, indignantly, accuses Hannah of stealing, but Hannah says she had believed Selina to be an uncaring wife; lately, though, she has a different feeling: 'I grew to care for you in a strange, silent way because I understood.' The women embrace and kiss 'very tenderly' and draw away only 'slowly'. The men are like children and the women are mothers together, they say; no, sisters. 'I'm real refreshed', Selina says; 'I feel fortified all through my system' (45–6). They hold hands and suddenly kiss. As Jill Davis puts it, 'the play images likeness and/as desire. Hannah enters as the "other" woman but difference is erased through mutuality, through sharing, and is finally eclipsed in speaking which is almost choral.'[33] Mark returns, in full retreat: he has met Hannah and is suddenly convinced she is seeing another man – 'Her eyes had tales in 'em, and I guessed to oncet and she couldn't deny' (*sic*). He's right off her. 'It mayn't be no man at all', Selina hints. 'If it bean't no man, who the devil should it be? A woman?' he replies. Incredible as it seems to Mark, Hannah's sparkle does follow her embraces with another woman. 'Perhaps nobody don't never know another', Selina muses (46–7).

As Jerrold Siegel points out, bohemia was not altogether detached from Society and respectability. Rather, it was where the bourgeoisie experimented with the limits of its ideology of individual freedom and personal development. 'Bohemia grew up where the borders of bourgeois existence were murky and uncertain. It was a space within which newly liberated energies were continually thrown up against the barriers being erected to contain them, where social margins and frontiers were probed and tested.'[34] Leonora Davidoff quotes a Victorian commentator who describes bohemia as 'That section of Society which lives out of Society'.[35] Enter Noël Coward.

From Bohemia to Bright Young Things

Though he soon moved beyond them, bohemia and the avant-garde were springboards for Coward. He had been immersed in queer/bohemian/theatre circles since he had been targeted as a boy actor by 'stage-door johnnies', and taken up by the artist Philip Streatfeild at the age of fourteen (Streatfeild was thirty-five).[36] In 1964 Coward published a story, 'Me and the Girls', in which an elderly camp queen who believes himself to be terminally ill reminisces:

> Those were the days all right, days of glory for child actors. I think the boys had a better time than the girls on account of not being so well protected. I shall never forget those jovial wet-handed clergymen queuing up outside the stage-door to take us out to tea and stroke our knees under the table. Bobby Clews and I used to have bets as to how much we could get without going too far. I once got a box of Fuller's soft-centres and a gramophone record of *Casse Noisette* for no more than a quick grope in a taxi.[37]

By the age of eighteen, at the end of World War I, Philip Hoare says, Coward had found his way into 'an emerging Bohemian set which would dominate the avant-garde reaches of society in the post-war years'.[38]

After 1918 bohemianism was boosted by a wider revulsion against the 'Victorian' seriousness that was seen as having produced the war, and, even more, against the phoney attitudes that accompanied it: 'They refused to grow up into men of responsibility, fathers of families and of the state, soldiers', Martin Green says.[39] Samuel Hynes draws on writing by Evelyn Waugh, C.E. Montague and Beverley Nichols to delineate a post-war generation determined to overthrow parental values.[40] At this point it might be better to accept that 'bohemia' became attentuated to the point where the concept is no longer pertinent. However, I believe it remained effective as an inspiration and authorisation, even among those who were perhaps abusing it. Bohemia was the ground on which scandal might be redefined as principled innovation, fun, and the authentic way to live.

Coward's *The Vortex* (1923) both represents and is itself a product of bohemia. It was performed at a little theatre, the Everyman in Hampstead, after West End managers had refused it. Its manner may be termed avant-garde in the sense that it displays, uncompromisingly, aspects of contemporary life which mainstream audiences would find rebarbative. 'The picture of a frivolous and degenerate set of people gives a wholly false impression of Society life and to my mind the time has come to put a stop to the harmful influence of such pictures on the stage', declared the Lord Chamberlain. Coward insisted that his play had a strong moral, and got it through.[41] The youngsters, Nicky (played by Coward) and Bunty display casual attitudes and behaviour – they have been living independently in Paris and he has been working at music composition. Further, *The Vortex* places bohemian attitudes in the English country house: Florence, Nicky's mother, is an actress and has adulterous affairs – in the play, with Tom Veryan who is Nicky's age. This, a modern reader has to realise, is appalling enough, especially when Florence makes a hysterical scene in front of house-guests.

No one is said to be a homosexual, but queerness is certainly part of the ambience. Pawnie is described as 'an elderly maiden gentleman' who makes 'a "Fetish" of house decoration'. Helen is doubtful about his bathroom: 'Personally, it would make me self-conscious to sit in a bath surrounded by frisky gods and goddesses all with such better figures than mine' (167–8). Pawnie's taste for decadence is confirmed when he remarks that Florence is 'a couple of hundred years too late – she ought to have been a flaunting, intriguing King's mistress, with black page boys and jade baths and things too divine – '(170). He uses the same scent as Florence. There is nothing to code Helen specifically as lesbian, but she has no lover in evidence, is very attached to Florence, and holds her own in conversation.

Tom is the straight guy in all this gender disturbance. He is 'athletic and good looking', the stage direction says; 'one feels he is good at games and extremely bad at everything else'. Florence prefers his cigarettes to Pawnie's because they are 'a special rather hearty kind'. Tom contributes nothing to the conversation – though the camp Pawnie still contrives to flirt with him:

TOM (*shaking hands*): How are you?
PAWNIE: Very well, thank you – how sweet of you to ask me? (173–5)

Helen finds Tom's dancing 'too athletic'. 'Anyhow', Pawnie replies, 'I'm sure he's a success at the Bath Club' (201–2). Nicky is posed against Tom's hearty affect. When Florence tells him Tom is the very nicest type of Englishman he says he hates that type. Tom was at Sandhurst, the upper-class training college for officers: 'Such a pretty place', Nicky remarks. 'It seems so funny you being in love with that sort of chap,' Tom tells Bunty; 'you know – up in the air – effeminate' (196–8). Indeed, she breaks off the engagement: 'You're not in love with me, really – you couldn't be!' (217).

For those who were keeping up with psychoanalysis, Nicky's 'weak' father and infatuation with his mother would connote homosexuality. 'I've grown up all wrong', Nicky says: 'Of course it's your fault, mother – who else's fault *could* it be?' (237). Nicky's confrontation with his mother over her adultery is very like Hamlet's — George Street, the Lord Chamberlain's reader, thought Coward might plead Shakespeare as a precedent — and the buzz idea was that Hamlet had an unresolved 'Oedipus complex'.[42] Freud's remarks in *The Interpretation of Dreams* (translated in 1913) had been developed by Ernest Jones in a notorious essay of 1910 (reprinted in 1923). T.S. Eliot in his *Hamlet* essay of 1919 adduced also Shakespeare's sonnets: '*Hamlet*, like the sonnets, is full of some stuff that the writer could not drag to light, contemplate, or manipulate into art. And when we search for this feeling, we find it, as in the sonnets, very difficult to localize.'[43] We all know what that is.

The point, I believe, is not that Nicky's drug-taking is standing in for queerness; rather, as John Lucas suggests, queerness and drug abuse belong together among the disreputable practices to which you become vulnerable once you embark on scandalous/bohemian behaviour.[44] Queerness is part of a pattern when James Agate says Nicky is 'tarred with the degenerate brush. He dopes, his tongue takes the convenient path of the "too adorable", "too divine", and "too perfectly marvellous".'[45]

Coward again uses the figure of the actress-mother to infiltrate bohemia into the country house in *Hay Fever* (1925). 'I'm devastatingly, entirely lacking in restraint', Sorel says. 'So's Simon. It's Father's and Mother's fault, really; you see, they're so vague — they've spent their lives cultivating their Arts and not devoting any time to ordinary conventions and manners and things' (284). Queerness again lurks around. Simon is said to be broad-hipped and uninterested in boxing — 'so dreadfully un — that sort of thing' (270). 'Abnormal, Simon, — that's what we are. Abnormal. People stare in astonishment when we say what we consider perfectly ordinary things', says Sorel (254).

Coward carries these themes into the camp of the enemy in *Easy Virtue* (1926). Young Mr John has married Larita, and takes her to the family home, which is dominated by Mrs Whittaker and her daughter Marion. They disapprove strongly of Larita, who is not only divorced but, it is revealed, has been the subject of an article in a newspaper about her alleged lovers. They accuse her of marrying to restore her position in Society, but it is evident that she loves John and has no concern about such standing as might be conferred by the Whittakers. She is irritated by their self-righteousness and bored by their endless games of tennis; she is reading Proust's *Sodom and Gomorrah*.

John reverts to type and Larita leaves. As in *Lady Windermere's Fan* and *The Circle*, the *déclassée* but interesting, capable and good-hearted woman is driven out by scandal. However, in *Easy Virtue* conventional mores are confronted by a confident bohemian integrity, fortified by Freudian theory. Mrs

Whittaker is accused of 'the stern repression of any sex emotions'; Marion's clothes are 'slightly mannish' and her manner notably hearty (499–500) – she calls other women 'old girl' and 'old thing'. Larita tells her: 'All your life you've ground down perfectly natural sex impulses, until your mind has become a morass of inhibitions – your repression has run into the usual channel of religious hysteria. . . . You swear and smoke and assume an air of spurious heartiness because you're not sure of your own religion and are afraid of being thought a prude' (582–3). Mrs Whittaker responds by calling Larita a moral degenerate, but the bohemian version plainly has greater explanatory power. It affords a base from which to challenge the authority of Society.

Semi-Monde (1926) was considered impossible to perform in Coward's lifetime, mainly because of the explicit queer liaisons among its characters. However, this is a reason for taking it seriously as perhaps indicating how Coward would have preferred to depict Society. The play is set at a Paris hotel in 1924–26. Its forty-two characters appear mainly in couples – sometimes in love, sometimes squabbling, most often rather bored. As the months pass, they change partners, appearing in new combinations with varying compounds of deceit, romance, pique and anger. The main motif is repetition: their new liaisons promise to repeat the modes they have already displayed.

There are stereotypically queer characters in *Semi-Monde* – quarrelsome women and camp men. But the straight/gay distinction doesn't go without saying. There are also intense, collusive relations among women who are living heterosexually, and Cyril Hardacre transfers his allegiance from men (Beverley and before him Francis) to Norma, via a liaison with the lesbian Inez. Beverley takes Cyril's defection with only a mild complaint: 'You're becoming far too hearty these days, Cyril. . . . Even if you are reverting to the commonplace, surely there's no necessity to be so truculent about it.'[46] Coward is evoking a far more open-work sex/gender pattern than we have imagined for him and his generation or, indeed, created for ourselves. 'Demi-monde' was the term for people whose scandalous life had caused them to forfeit their place in Society. 'Semi-monde' is not the same: the large cast, some of them unnamed, gives an impression of an entire society. These people are not a subordinate group, they are half the world. There are no arbiters of taste and social standing – no Lady Windermere, no puritans, American or otherwise, no Lady Bracknell. Some people are best avoided because one has been or is being unfaithful to them, but no one suggests that someone is inappropriate to know.

As Philip Hoare reads *Semi-Monde*, 'Coward's attitude is defined by his tone – rejecting promiscuity and effeminacy, he assumed the stance of

Jerome, normal and straightforward.'[47] This may be right; perhaps Coward means to expose the shallowness of these people. But if that was his intention, he scarcely tried to envisage either the values or the social structures through which they might be corrected or displaced. And Jerome has been conniving in the seduction of his daughter, Tanis, in order to facilitate his own love-making with a much younger married woman, so it is doubtful whether he can represent a normative stance. 'We've got to behave decently — that's what's so damnable', Jerome says to Tanis (II-1-15). But they don't; 'I think my conscience must have died', she remarks (II-2-23).

The dominant value in the play seems to be the more bohemian one of being who you truly are and doing what you truly want to do. Norma tells Cyril, in respect of his sexuality, 'I realised in Cannes that you were in quite the wrong métier and not particularly happy in it. It's awfully difficult to find one[']s level these days — nothing matters really except being sure of what you want — and you weren't' (I-3-23, 24). This libertarian authenticity rarely authorises the normal and straightforward. And although these people are often unhappy, they also have quite a good time and don't hurt each other very much; it does not appear that they would find life more rewarding if their relationships were more firmly regulated.

Partly as a consequence of Coward's prominence, bohemianism became a fashion among leisure-class young people in the 1920s — 'Bright Young People', they were called, or 'Bright Young Things'. Robert Graves and Alan Hodge place this moment in the 'long weekend' between the world wars:

> In younger London Society . . . the correct thing to do, for intelligent young people with a fixed income and no particular vocation, was to call themselves 'artists' and live in Chelsea studios. There they gave 'amusing' parties and played at being Bohemian. Bohemianism was understood to mean a gay disorderliness of life, cheerful bad manners, and no fixed hours or sexual standards.[48]

Coward's plays both reflected and stimulated a stance of irresponsible wit, affectation and high spirits. They 'caught the sophisticated spirit of the age', Cecil Beaton says, and theatre was important in a 'whole new spirit of affectation and frivolity'.[49] Philip Hoare confirms:

> The theatre was the nexus of this culture of pleasure, and was also peculiarly open to outside influences; from the new syncopation from across

the Atlantic to the avant-garde from Europe, their influence was often felt first in the world of theatre. . . . It was also a liberating arena for women. The stage was one of the few places where they could pursue and succeed in independent careers. . . . The theatre's mixing of class and sexuality, and its susceptibility to the suspiciously new, combined to produce a threat to the moral status quo. The old social demarcations had gone.[50]

That is perhaps a bit too enthusiastic; it would be better to say that social demarcations were partly reformulated.

In the United States also, Coward's early work was produced with great success as, during the fervent social conflict of Prohibition, bohemia filtered out from Greenwich Village and become fashionable. 'In Philadelphia', Malcolm Cowley wrote, 'young married couples . . . would encourage their guests: "Don't stand on ceremony; you know we are thorough bohemians."'[51] This included sexual dissidence. Chauncey says:

> The pansies soon made their way onto the stages of Times Square as well [as the square itself]. The district's impresarios were constantly searching for new angles that might attract a crowd, and the growing competition among the theaters, cabaret revues, nightclubs, and speakeasies encouraged them to vie with one another in challenging the conventional limits placed on entertainment and satisfying the customers' appetite for new and ever more sensational thrills, a tendency that only accentuated at the end of the 1920s when the Depression devastated their industry.[52]

'By 1930, promiscuity was tame and homosexuality had become the expected thing', wrote Caroline Ware.[53] An essay in the journal *Current Psychology and Psychoanalysis* complained in 1936 that a New Yorker returning to the Village after an absence of twenty years had been startled to find that 'persons with abnormal sex habits flaunt their traits in the Village. One sees many of them — the boy assuming the usual feminine characteristics and obligations, the girl the Lesbian, who apes her brother.' Further, 'sight-seers from all parts of the city made pilgrimages to view these misfits on parade'.[54]

Max Ewing's novel *Going Somewhere* (1933) illustrates a merging of international Society, theatre, bohemian and queer circles in Paris, London and New York. Ewing was a young New York writer who moved in the gay and Society circles around Carl van Vechten. In Paris a male friend is 'frightfully sweet', the Princesse appears 'rather queer'; the Baronne bows only to those who were written about (under pseudonyms) in Proust.[55] In London there are parties where everyone comes as a sailor, and the protagonist writes a revue song, 'Matelot Mad'. They take the show to New York, where they go to the Cotton Club in Harlem and a Society party. Another novelist, Wyndham Lewis, protested ferociously in *Apes of God* (1930) that since the War 'everyone able to afford to do so has become a "bohemian". . . . The well-off find the studio-café society the only one in which they are free to live as they choose.'[56] This is disastrous because they are blocking the avenues of artistic innovation − driving up rents of studios − and, in their dabbling, trivialising Art.

Coward complained that 'with the present democratic destruction of all social barriers, "Society", like a reservoir suddenly released from its dam, has effusively swirled into the theatre', filling actors and actresses with social ambitions. Meanwhile 'the number of "Society" girls who are taking up acting at the present moment is positively frightening'. Hence his well-known song refrain, 'Don't put your daughter on the stage, Mrs Worthington'.[57]

Exploitation and Backlash

None of this is to say that anything went; part of my underlying thesis is that lesbian and gay subcultural modes emerge through cultural struggle. In New York performances of Mae West's plays sold out, but critics dismissed them as vulgar and exhibitionist, public decency lobbyists called for their closure, and Equity and other theatre organisations disowned them. *Sex* (1926) was raided by the police, and West and the entire cast were prosecuted successfully although the play had been running for a year; in the face of this, and the raiding and closure of Bourdet's play *The Captive* (see chapter 7), West abandoned *The Drag* (1927) before it reached Broadway. One outcome was that the state legislature prohibited plays 'depicting or dealing with, the subject of sex degeneracy, or sex perversion'. West's *The Pleasure Man* (1928) was prosecuted inconclusively in 1930.

Sex features a good-hearted prostitute and a Society woman who goes slumming in the red-light district; *The Drag*, which I discuss as a thriller in chapter 9, presents both anguished and exuberant queers. *The Pleasure Man* centres on a bohemian vaudeville troupe that includes a number of drag artistes and a drag party (see chapter 6). Despite, or because of, her status as a queer icon, West's plays haven't had a good press among gay commentators. Kaier Curtin highlights her homophobic remarks and concludes: 'Actually, her persistent, mercenary attempts to exploit gay transvestites in the 1920s stirred neither public tolerance nor compassion. It [sic] reinforced the stereotyping of gay men as vulgar, sex-obsessed effeminates who wear women's clothing at drag parties.'[58] However, drag features only in *The Pleasure Man* where, as Robertson and Schlissel say, the energy is in the drag queens.[59] The title figure is the heterosexually identified man who seduces and abandons women. 'If you're a man, thank God, I'm a female impersonator', he is told (187). Drag has the moral authority.

As we should expect, playwrights took diverse attitudes to the convergence of bohemian, queer and leisure-class formations. *Spring Cleaning* (1925, West End and Broadway), by the popular playwright Frederick Lonsdale, is designed to repudiate bohemian ideas that romance and fun might be more worthwhile than staying faithful to a husband when he has become inattentive and boring. After ten years of marriage Margaret has got in with a loose set – philandering men, including Ernest who is wooing her, and unfaithful wives. Her husband, Richard, disapproves in principle of such people – 'men of good families, content to live on the glory of their ancestors and the money they left them to live on. Born to be an example to the working classes', he exclaims (81–2). Margaret is manipulated into staying with Richard. 'I have always known it!' Ernest cries; 'You are middle class. You are in love with your husband' (138).

A secondary theme features Bobby. All the men – adulterous and faithful – unite in despising him. He is described as 'an effeminate boy of twenty-two. Very over-dressed.' Immediately upon entrance he seizes upon a cushion and declares it 'perfectly gorgeous'. Ernest says he's 'a dreadful fellow' and Archie blasphemes; the women refer to him as a powder-puff and a fairy. Richard calls him 'Miss' and 'that caricature of a human being', and threatens finally if he sees him again to 'put you on my knee and smack you' (27, 81, 90). Bobby does nothing to provoke all this, other than be there; indeed, he has no function in the action other than to be vilified. He is the culminating instance of what is going wrong with Society. James Agate wondered how the actor, Denys Blakelock, would survive playing such a '"fairy". Perhaps he should now play a plumber by way of antidote. In the meantime he gets shouts of laughter.'[60]

Vile Bodies is a stage version by H. Dennis Bradley of Evelyn Waugh's novel (published in 1930). It was performed at the Arts Theatre Club and in the West End the following year, but the bowdlerisation required by the Lord Chamberlain did it no good and it flopped. In the published text all the men are effete and all the women are independent-minded; 'Say what you like', a waiter says of Adam and Nina, 'you must agree they are a couple of Bright Young People' (88). Miles Malpractice's part is noticeably larger and gayer than in the novel. He is said to be looking 'terribly *tapette*' (catamite, fairy, nancy) and to be above suspicion . . . in his relations with women (11). A customs officer who opens Miles' suitcase supposes it to belong to his lady friend, but no — those are indeed his pyjamas with lace round the bottoms. His 'new boy friend' is a dirt-track racer, and we have a scene at the racetrack, with Miles suitably uncomfortable in such a masculine milieu.

Nor is queerness the aberrant experience of the lone individual in *Vile Bodies*. The waiter at Lottie Crump's hotel is referred to by her as 'my young Italian *queen*', 'Fairy Prince' and 'Pansy' (35, 139). And Chastity — one of Mrs Ape's chorus of beauties (or is it a front for prostitution? — the boundary is not very clear) — is teased by the other girls because she went out for a drive with Mrs Panrast in her Rolls-Royce. A man would have been understandable; well, Chastity says, she thought Mrs Panrast *was* a man! — she was sitting at a table so you couldn't see her skirt, and 'she looks like a man and — and — and she *goes on* like a man'. Chastity won't say what happened in the car. 'We're all liable to make mistakes, nowadays', Mrs Ape allows (95–6). Waugh's theme seems to be that all this is too trivial to be noticed though, of course, he is noticing it. It comes to no good: the play ends, abruptly, with a new outbreak of war. While some characters reportedly do well out of it, others grope their way through a desolate battlefield.

In Ivor Novello's comedy *Fresh Fields* (1933) the sisters Lady Mary (widowed) and Lady Lilian (single) slide towards a bohemian lifestyle because they have run out of money, but they display quite an aptitude for it. Lady Lilian takes a job as agony aunt, revealing a more-than-ladylike knowledge of life; Lady Mary invites a wealthy but 'common' family returning from Australia to stay as paying guests with the expectation that she will introduce them into Society. The reluctance of Tim, Lady Mary's son, to marry is just another embarrassment. They talk as if he were queer: 'Mr Tim hasn't seemed attracted to anyone'. 'Attracted? I believe he hates women' (6). 'I don't want to marry, and I'm not going to marry', he says. 'I hate the only girls I've ever met — silly, hard, empty wimps' (10–11). Una, the daughter in the Australian family, shows her interest in Tim by whistling Coward's 'Mad About the Boy' — an ambiguous signal; he rebuffs her. Lady Lilian also has not married, it is said because she 'got in with that artistic crowd — everything was too — too — Not a man amongst them, not what I'd call a man' (38). The problem is not Tim's sexuality but the loss of an opportunity to save the family from scandal by restoring its fortunes. Lady Mary doesn't care whether he's met a girl he likes: 'But you haven't got to! Marry someone — nominally! Grab your money — divorce, and we're all comfortable' (11). *Fresh Fields* is a comedy, so it is all magically resolved when the dreadful Australians turn out to be lovable after all. The relaxation of Society's controls has humanised everyone.

Rodney Ackland's *Birthday* (1934) stages a confrontation between the respectable household of Mary and a 'Bohemian' set that moves in across the street. It becomes evident that Mary's decency is designed selfishly, to keep her daughters at home — both the married Lallah and the unmarried Rosamund. The latter falls in love with the principal bohemian, Mark, and is persuaded to go off with him despite his being married. Queerness, again, is almost incidental: Tony Willow — played by Ackland — is a 'graceful young man'. He writes articles for women's magazines and his photograph has appeared: 'The most delicious picture of me. You *must* look' (56, 60).

The best play in this vein should have been Ackland's *The Pink Room* (1952). A censored version was shown at the Lyric, Hammersmith, but Ackland's purposes were not realised until the Orange Tree and BBC Television production, titled *Absolute Hell* (1988).[61] The customary disarray of people whose bohemian lifestyles cast them adrift in a Soho drinking club (*La vie en rose*) is placed in the context of appalling reports from the Nazi death camps (it is 1945). For the 1988 version Ackland made implied situations clear and frank: Maurice Hussey, the film producer, and his manservant, Cyril Clatworthy, are obviously queer, the part of R.B. Monody, the lesbian critic, is enlarged, and women and men demean themselves to gain the favours of US servicemen. Hugh Marriner, the alcoholic writer, is left by a boyfriend, Nigel, rather than a wife. Nigel means to marry Victoria, who will finance his work as a dress designer; however, he finds that he can't live with her after all. In an unusually positive gay love scene, he reinstates the relationship with Hugh — though (as in Shakespeare's *Love's Labour's Lost*) it must endure a separation of six months while Nigel makes himself useful by working with displaced persons in Germany.

The system was quite ready to obstruct work which might be difficult to assimilate. In fact, the price for public representation has always been compromise, and the political impetus of dissident fractions of the middle class has always been vulnerable to incorporation. The Pre-Raphaelites, Williams says, 'were in conscious opposition to the main cultural tendencies of their [commercial bourgeois] class' but 'they may finally be seen as articulating and expressing them'. And Bloomsbury, with hindsight, was 'expressing at once the highest values of the bourgeois tradition and the necessary next phase of a bourgeois social and cultural order'.[62] This is not to say that these formations had no radical potential (if we wait for an unadulterated movement it will be a long time). Campbell is severe when he says bohemians 'are nearly always the sons (and nowadays also the daughters) of fairly affluent, middle-class parents, who have eschewed a more conventional career − in preparation for which their parents would have supported them − for the more disreputable "dabbling" in art'.[63]

But the ambivalent allegiance of much of this work does indicate why it was so easy for bohemianism to become a fashion accessory. Fishbein summarises:

> Ideas that had been avant-garde in the prewar years - Freudian psychology, birth control, bohemianism − became the clichés of the postwar era. . . . During the 1920s the prosperous scorned respectability to pursue bohemianism on a large scale; the speakeasy captured the Village manners and mores for the middle class. Once radical writers and artists were recruited by enterprising businesses to spread the new taste in salable form throughout the land.[64]

The theatres, the plays and the audiences may have begun in a radical frame, but the outcome was a new, middle- to highbrow audience, for instance at a little theatre such as the New York Theatre Guild, Joel Pfister shows. 'Through its sophisticated, cosmopolitan, and tasteful productions, the Guild not only challenged the traditional commercial entertainment that had prevailed on Broadway, it helped *establish* what probably was a primarily university-trained, white-collar audience that sought "adult" art and culture, not merely amusement, at the theatre'.[65]

Of course, Bright Young Things did not engross all the cultural energies of the inter-war decades. Goldring distinguishes the 'continuous "wild party" thrown during "the Twenties" by the irresponsible youth of the monied classes, the "Socialites" and a section of Bohemia', on the one hand, and 'the rather feverish attempts to free themselves from pre-war restrictions and repressions, and to work out a new and better code of sexual morality, made by the essentially virtuous young of the educated and hardworking middle class'. By 1930, Goldring adds, the remnants of the Bright Young People 'ceased to impress a Bohemia already purged of wasters and beginning to take its work seriously'.[66]

As for Coward, he did take his queer bohemianism seriously at times. In *Design for Living* (1933) Gilda declares: 'we shall have to live and die our own way. No one else's way is any good, we don't fit.' Leo adds: 'We have our own decencies. We have our own ethics. Our lives are a different shape' (462–3). I explore in chapter 5 how Coward managed to insinuate queer connotations into West End plays, and how far that contributed to a breakthrough in sexual dissidence. But, from the start, he was more interested in taking bohemian values back into Society than in preserving the purity of an oppositional vision; and, reasonably enough, he wanted to work in financially solvent theatres. So while bohemia was a springboard from which to infiltrate the mainstream, his poor-boy craving for success allowed the mainstream to co-opt him. One of the subsidiary motifs in *Design for Living* is a fear that the characters may be losing their integrity as they become successful.

4

Emergings

A Preoccupation

The theatre critic St John Ervine wrote in 1933:

> I do not think I am exaggerating when I say that if either *La Prisonnière*
> [*TheCaptive*] or *The Green Bay Tree* had been performed in England
> before 1914, the vast majority of people would not have known that each of
> them treats of sexual perversion or that there was such a subject to treat. I
> doubt if there was one person in a thousand who, before 1914, knew the
> meaning of the word *Lesbian*.[1]

In that twenty-year period, homosexuality became a preoccupation of the
intelligentsia in Britain and North America.

It has never been doubted that many men had same-sex liaisons in the first
half of the twentieth century. Court cases were the tip of an iceberg. Lesbian
practice has been harder to see, but once you ask people, as Elizabeth Lapovsky
Kennedy and Madeline D. Davis did in Buffalo, New York, you find there was
plenty going on.[2] In Britain the Lesbian Oral History Group and Emily Hamer
have found significant records of lesbian life.[3] George Chauncey's definitive
study, *Gay New York*, finds that, especially during Prohibition (1920–33),
lesbian and gay life flourished in Greenwich Village and Harlem, and people
came from outside to look.[4] I am interested here in something further: the
emergence of homosexuality *as a topic in intellectual life*.

T.W. Heyck writes of the mid-Victorian man of letters as sharing with a
mainstream readership fundamental middle-class values and concerns about

social relations and public order. But towards the end of the century an increasing specialisation and self-consciousness among writers, scientists, artists and thinkers produced a change, which Heyck identifies as a development from men of letters to intellectuals. The latter were more ready to think of themselves as critical, marginal, alienated.[5] Like many bohemians, many intellectuals were of 'good' family (Edward Carpenter, for instance; most of Bloomsbury); Noel Annan demonstrated in 1955 the upper-middle-class family network within the 'intellectual aristocracy'.[6] Where they could afford it, they generally did enough to maintain their status in Society. But their attention and their allegiances were elsewhere. If they had little or no independent income, they got by, in bohemian manner, on temporary and part-time jobs as schoolteachers, proof-readers, translators, and by scrounging. They involved themselves with little theatre and little magazine ventures. Leading feminists thrived in these circles.

It is in this social formation that homosexuality became a topic. For the radically minded, it afforded an exciting new framework for apprehending the world; writers and artists seized the potential for newly focused emotional, social and physical experience. For more conservative-minded people, the topic fed anxieties about manhood, womanliness and degeneracy, especially in schools. Sexuality was a site of contest: while radical elements sought to recognise and explore it, conservative elements strove to suppress or contain it. Radclyffe Hall's *The Well of Loneliness* was prosecuted successfully in England in 1928. But forty writers signed a protest in *The Times* newspaper, including Arnold Bennett, Laurence Binyon, John Buchan, E.M. Forster, Storm Jameson, Rose Macaulay, Desmond MacCarthy, Vita Sackville-West, George Bernard Shaw, Lytton Strachey, Leonard and Virginia Woolf; Vera Brittain and Bertrand Russell also defended *The Well*. It was available in Paris, and prosecution was unsuccessful in the USA, where it sold well.[7] James Douglas believed that his violently hostile review in the *Sunday Express* was appropriate precisely because sexual dissidents were asserting themselves: 'I am well aware that sexual inversion and perversion are horrors which exist among us today. They flaunt themselves in public places with increasing effrontery and more insolently provocative bravado.'[8] (I discuss the impact of *The Well* on lesbian identities in chapter 7.)

This point is important because the story we have told ourselves emphasises restraint and inhibition. For many lesbians and gay men, that was indeed their experience. However, I have argued, censorship indicates an area of pressure, not an absence. The social order promoted same-sex awareness, as well as penalising it, through a continuous flirtation with the impermissible. To be sure, individuals were subjected to vicious penalties, but these too made homosexuality present, even while forbidding it. We are looking at what I have called a faultline in the system: a point where the dominant ideology is under strain, where powerful competing concerns produce urgent ideological work.

World War I confirmed the radicalisation of intellectuals. While extreme right-wing ideas and attitudes circulated, resistance to them developed as well. Samuel Hynes says that events such as the Allan/Billing trial and the Allatini trial (see chapters 2, 3)

> intensified and solidified what was worst and most repressive in wartime English society, and by so doing helped to create a post-war sub-culture of outsiders, composed of an odd mixture of persons − opponents of the war, artists, homosexuals − whom the war spirit had identified as subversive. . . . Oscar Wilde had seemed dead in 1914, and pacifism had scarcely been born. But in 1918 both were alive and vocal.[9]

For young people in particular, Christopher Hollis recalls, to take an interest in homosexuality was a way of separating themselves from their parents' generation.[10] That meant Wilde: a split between athletes and aesthetes dates from this point. Louis MacNeice found that at 'Oxford homosexuality and "intelligence", heterosexuality and brawn, were almost inexorably paired. This left me out in the cold and I took to drink.'[11] The Oxbridge pattern fed back into public schools. At Harrow, where Terence Rattigan was a pupil, it became fashionable for boys in rebellion against school values to proclaim their genuine or affected homosexuality.[12] The sissy − that despised other of the Victorian boys' story − returned to challenge the system. There was a contest about the kind of place Britain should be, and it was focused partly on ideas of sexuality. What some people thought of as thrilling, and others as the harmless outlet of an unfortunate minority, others again thought of as the end of Christian decency.

Psychology was the key because it had a big investment in sexuality and seemed intellectually, indeed scientifically, authoritative. Havelock Ellis' *Sexual Inversion* was withdrawn before publication in 1897 (there was a German edition in 1896), largely because the Wilde trials suddenly altered the climate. But while this made Ellis' text hard to get in Britain (it was published in the USA in 1901, 1915 and 1936), it became 'a "dirty book" with a secure black market'; hundreds of men and women wrote to Ellis about it.[13] Central texts on homosexuality by Freud appeared in English translation – *Three Contributions to the Theory of Sex* in 1910, 1916, 1918, 1930 and 1938; *Leonardo da Vinci and a Memory of his Childhood* in 1916 (New York) and 1922 (London); the 'Wolf Man' and Schreber casenotes in 1925. Supporting the criminalisation of lesbianism in the House of Commons in 1921, Ernest Wild acknowledged that many members might doubt that such practices occur. But 'if they were to consult any neurologist, any great doctor who deals with nerve diseases, they would soon be told that this is a very prevalent practice'.[14]

Much of Freud's influence was felt through the generally cruder extrapolations of his followers. They fixed homosexuality as a clinical entity, presented it as a problem of gender identity (and thus a version of the feminine soul in the masculine body), related it to narcissism, and attributed it to an arrested resolution of the 'Oedipus complex', Kenneth Lewes shows.[15] Popularisations flourished. A.G. Tansley in *The New Psychology and its Relation to Life* (1920), which ran through many editions, summarised:

> In childhood the sexual instinct, having as yet no means of normal biological expression, finds all sorts of objects on which it tries, so to speak, to expend its energy, and this process, under suitable conditions, may very easily result in the establishment of various forms of sexual perversity. If the proper sequence of stimuli is forthcoming development proceeds in the proper biological channel, the typical heterosexual reaction takes place, and these early experiments are discontinued, since nearly the whole energy of sex is absorbed in the heterosexual channel.[16]

Despite such notions as 'the proper sequence of stimuli' and 'the proper biological channel', Tansley does allow that same-sex feelings are normal and that they may persist in everyone. Joel Pfister demonstrates US interest in popularisations – much of which went into self-help channels, where the idea was to normalise yourself so as to be ready for whatever tasks capital and Uncle Sam might require of you.[17] Abraham A. Brill remarked that patients often 'do not know that they are homosexual'; he and other psychoanalysts were keen to tell them.[18]

If queer intellectuals today regard much of the Freudian project with suspicion, for many, initially, it was a powerful solvent of traditional decencies. 'Idealistic young intellectuals' discovered in Freud what Nathan G. Hale, Jr. terms 'a sweeping criticism of traditional sexual mores and virtues':

Young writers first proclaimed their vision of psychoanalysis in the bohemias of Chicago and New York. . . . Both psychoanalysts and intellectuals stood for greater frankness in life and literature and opposed 'rigid' moral judgments. Just as the patient should squarely face his repressed impulses, so writers should deal realistically with the whole range of human passion. Honesty would purge the soul of failure, longing, and conflict.[19]

As Jonathan Dollimore has said, rather than use psychoanalysis to 'explain' sexuality, we should regard that preoccupation as one aspect of a larger historical development whereby homosexuality is made the focus of fundamental social, psychic and aesthetic conflicts.[20]

Theatre was one of the places where psychological ideas about sex circulated. Theodore Dreiser in *The Hand of the Potter* (1921) has a journalist appeal to Ellis, 'Kraft-Ebbing' and Freud to explain the behaviour of a psychopathic killer of small girls: 'I've been readin' up on these cases for some time, an' from what I can make out they're no more guilty than any other person with a disease' (377–8). Already I have shown Coward's plays to be dotted with Freudian concepts, including the deployment in *The Vortex* of the notion that Hamlet might have an 'Oedipus complex'. Also in that play, the effeminate Pawnie is said to make 'a "Fetish" of house decoration' (the quote marks and capitalisation indicate novelty; later editions remove them), and Nicky is said to be 'suffering from a slight inferiority complex' (167, 211) — Alfred Adler's *Study of Organ Inferiority and its Psychical Compensation* had been translated in 1917.

Self-conscious Freudian innovation also occurs in *The Prisoners of War* (1925) by J.R. Ackerley, set at the end of the war. Young Conrad doesn't have a framework for understanding Adelby's suggestion that his problem might be related to 'what clever people call your ego'; Conrad thinks this means he's selfish; nor does he see the relevance of Adelby's suggestion that pacing the pattern in the carpet might be significant (105–6). However, the audience is expected to get the point. Mae West in *The Drag* (1927) sets up its theme by having a doctor read Karl Heinrich Ulrichs, who had introduced the term 'invert'. The Freudian Karl Menninger, mainly with *Strange Interlude* (1927) in mind, said that Eugene O'Neill had introduced more people to psychoanalysis than all the scientific books put together.[21]

Maugham deploys an amusingly simplified Freudian explication in his last play, *Sheppey* (1933). Sheppey, a barber, wins the Irish Sweepstake and decides to give it all away to thieves and prostitutes and live like Jesus. Members of his family are upset, and have Sheppey analysed by a mental specialist, who wants to certify him. 'A sane man takes money from the poor. He runs chain stores, founds building societies, or engages in municipal work', Dr Jervis explains;

> The normal man is selfish, grasping, destructive, vain and sensual. What is generally termed morality is forced upon him by the herd, and the obligation he is under to repress his natural instincts is undoubtedly the cause of many disorders of the mind. Dr Ennismore said to me just now that he had little doubt that philanthropy in general could always be ascribed to repressed homosexuality.

By way of elaboration Jervis specifies 'a distinct father-complex', 'Oedipus and all that', and 'religious paranoia'.[22]

The British literary intelligentsia strove to address sexuality, despite the possibility of prosecution. Many fictional treatments got into print. *David Blaize* (1916), E.F. Benson's novel about an intensely romantic love affair between schoolboys, attracted letters of gratitude from mothers and from soldiers in the trenches, and of complicity from boy-lovers.[23] Alec Waugh was more straightforward about sex in public schools and caused a furore with *The Loom of Youth* (1917). Ernest Raymond in *Tell England* (1922) dwelt upon intense friendships as a way of establishing the *esprit de corps* that would be needed in the trenches. Robert Graves in *Goodbye to All That* (1929) discussed and partly defended homoerotic relations in schools. Lawrence's *Women in Love* was published in 1922, with the mysterious Brüderschaft between Birkin and Gerald, and with the degenerate Loerke, though without the cancelled opening chapter; in *Studies in Classic American Literature* (1923) Lawrence attended to male comradeship in American poetry. T.E. Lawrence in *Seven Pillars of Wisdom* (1922, 1926) wrote candidly of the customs of Bedouin youth; E.M. Forster, reviewing the edition of 1935, remarked 'a sexual frankness which would cause most authors to be run in by the police'.[24] Naomi Mitchison, anticipating Mary Renault, explored same-sex passions in classical Greek and Roman settings in stories published in 1928 and 1929 ('O Lucky Thessaly!', 'A Matter of No Importance'). Ronald Firbank paid for his novels to be published between 1915 and 1923; in 1929, after his death, Duckworth published a collected edition; 'Queer modernism', Joseph Bristow calls them.[25] In *The Apes of God* (1930) Wyndham Lewis satirised the cultural scene as corrupted by homosexuality. Neville is in love with Percival in *The Waves* by Virginia Woolf (1931).

André Gide's *L'Immoraliste* (1902) was published in translation by Cassell in 1930; *Der Tod in Venedig* by Thomas Mann (1912) was translated in 1928 for Secker and Warburg; translations of Marcel Proust's *À la recherche du temps perdu* (1913–27) appeared under the imprints of Chatto and Windus and Random House in 1922–32. Walt Whitman was available. Blair Niles' *Strange Brother*, suggesting that these matters might be managed better in Harlem, was published in the USA in 1931 and in Britain a year later.

Radclyffe Hall had been broaching lesbian themes in her writing for some time before *The Well of Loneliness*. *Regiment of Women*, published in 1917 by Clemence Dane, suggested that women might be subject to excessive passions and that single-sex schools might be unhealthy places. *The Rainbow* by D.H. Lawrence was seized by the police in 1915, J.C. Squire was told, because it 'mentioned sapphism' (Ursula has a substantial lesbian relationship with a teacher); however, a slightly expurgated version was published in the USA in the early 1920s and in England in 1926.[26] In Lawrence's novella *The Fox* (1922) the boy has to kill to get his woman away from her female lover, but still he can't possess her. Judith in Rosamond Lehmann's *Dusty Answer* (1927) is bewildered by her love for Jennifer, Jennifer's for Geraldine, and Roddy's for Tony. Compton Mackenzie's *Extraordinary Women* (1928) presents expatriate lesbians on Capri as merely trivial — they drop into French or Italian for the more intimate parts of their dialogue. With faintly oppressive geniality, Woolf's *Orlando* (1928) invites the reader to consider how one person (Vita Sackville-West, as it might be) can be both man and woman, and marries him/her to the woman/man Shelmerdine. Elizabeth Bowen in *The Hotel* (1927) and *The Last September* (1929) accords delicate intensity to lesbian affairs, even while presenting them as neurotic and to be set aside as the condition for entry into adult femininity. The blues singer in Niles' *Strange Brother* refers casually to her female lover. 'Michael Field' in *Works and Days* (1933) and Gertrude Stein in *The Autobiography of Alice B. Toklas* (1933) allow readers to see portraits of marriages that are not heterosexual. Colette represents lesbian experience in several novels, most diversely in *The Pure and the Impure* (1933). In *More Women Than Men* (1933) by Ivy Compton-Burnett, Josephine swears a partnership in their lives as well as her school with the 'masculine' Miss Rossetti and falls into her arms, while the 'womanly' Felix quits his elderly partner of twenty-two years (on whose knee he is wont to sit) to assume family responsibilities. In her comic novel *Devoted Ladies* (1934) M.J. Farrell (Molly Keane) makes almost all the characters lesbian or gay — and variously treacherous, predatory, pathetic and doomed; 'Before then no-one thought anything of two elderly ladies setting up house together', she recalled when her book was republished in the 1980s. 'I was excited by finding out about lesbians and homosexuals. It was new. It made a subject.'[27] Sylvia Townsend Warner in *Summer Will Show* (1936) elaborates a triangle in which the women constitute the two points that count. Djuna Barnes evokes a distinctly queer range of people under the prestigious Faber imprint in *Nightwood* (1937).

I have written the foregoing paragraphs from a mainly British point of view, but most of these texts, and others additionally, figured in the United States (I discuss Greenwich Village and Harlem as bohemian contexts for the development of dissident sexuality in chapter 3). Henry F. May characterises *The End of American Innocence* like this:

> To the intellectuals, censors were nasty and cruel old men, inflicting on others their own frustration, denying to America the possibility of free and joyous self-expression. To some of the conservatives in the prewar years, a strange flood of filth was welling up from mysterious sources. Erotic plays and books, divorce, free love, lascivious dances, birth control were menacing not only American culture but the possibility of moral restraint, the sheet-anchor of any and all civilization.[28]

These quarrels filtered into the popular press. Laurence Senelick shows how the fairy and the maidenly male were introduced to the American public in the 1920s through gossipy periodicals such as *Broadway Brevities* and men's magazines such as *Hot Dog*.[29] Harry M. Benshoff, combing through *Esquire* of the 1930s, finds a surprising openness to more or less gay topics. 'In its first few years [from 1933], the magazine ran cartoons and joked about pansies and eunuchs, as well as occasional essays on homosexual men such as Cole Porter, tennis ace "Big Bill" Tilden, or painter Paul Cadmus; in most of these stories it is possible to discern homosexual innuendo (or just as easily ignore it).'[30]

Looking back from 1961, Julian Symons declared that 'The Thirties' were marked by 'the demand for unlimited personal freedom', and that this 'might also be called the homosexual decade, in the sense that in these years homosexuality became accepted as a personal idiosyncrasy'. As written, that is a ridiculous statement: innumerable lesbians and gay men suffered bitterly for their little peculiarity.[31] However, in respect of the literary and artistic intelligentsia, Symons has a point.

Boys Will Be Boys

'If all persons guilty of Oscar Wilde's offences were to be clapped in gaol, there would be a very surprising exodus from Eton and Harrow, Rugby and Winchester, to Pentonville and Holloway', W.F. Stead remarked in 1895, in response to the Wilde trials. 'But meanwhile public school boys are allowed to indulge with impunity in practices which, when they leave school, would consign them to hard labour.'[32] In many places, boys messing around together had been only vaguely stigmatised, and hero-worship had been thought acceptable within an ideology of respect for seniority and manliness. Romantic friendship was not much discouraged − it is justified in Horace Annelsey Vachell's novel *The Hill* (1905), though eroticism between the boys is kept precariously at bay, as Bristow shows.[33] In the 1920s, same-sex activity was still often regarded as the kind of messing about any boarding-school boy might do; no distinct ethos accompanied it (for instance it was not thought incompatible with expertise at games). Few of these sexually-active boys seem to have regarded themselves as homosexual or potentially homosexual.

All these attitudes persisted, in varying combinations, up to the 1960s. But the emergence of homosexuality *as a condition* imposed an intense anxiety. Once more, we need Foucault's argument: it is during this period that people in the West came to demand of sex 'that it tell us our truth, or rather, the deeply buried truth of that truth about ourselves which we think we possess in our immediate consciousness'.[34] This post-Freudian tendency to posit sexuality as the inner and underlying reality of the individual exerted pressure upon the casual same-sex incident and the romantic friendship, demanding that they either proclaim their innocence explicitly or, better still, acknowledge their underlying sexual motivation.

For young people especially, homosexuality emerged around them as a concept while they continued in customary ways. As an informed teacher, parent or fellow-student introduced new ideas, they found themselves under sudden suspicion of they-knew-not-what. Significant others divided over whether they were exhibiting harmless calf-love or monstrous perversion. Sometimes the thought that they might be radically different from other people dawned upon them, obscurely and gradually, as they moved out into the world. Plays of this period show a double emergence: the individual comes to consciousness of his or her dissident sexuality even while the concepts through which such realisation can occur are being established.

People who wanted to get homosexuality onto the agenda often concerned themselves with schools. 'What we need first of all is a much greater degree of sincerity concerning the actual facts', Ellis wrote in *Sexual Inversion*. 'The school is undoubtedly the great breeding-place of artificial [i.e. non-congenital] homosexuality among the general population – at all events in England. . . . It is very unfortunate that school authorities do their best to ignore and conceal the facts.'[35] The irony was that public (i.e. private) schools had been designed, in a pre-Freudian era, to keep young men away from the softening influence of women so that they would be able to take their place as controllers of men on landed estates, in industry and in the empire. Now the very institutions that were supposed to protect men from effeminacy were being exposed as the ones where inverted practices flourished. By 1935, Douglas Goldring considered, the topic had been transformed. He could scarcely recall boys with 'ingrained homo-sexual tendencies' at his school at the turn of the century, while 'of the young public school and university men I have come across in recent years, fully seventy-five per cent. are quite openly and even conceitedly homo-sexual'.[36] Of course, that can't have been the case, but it is significant that it appeared thus. Perhaps the change is due to the War, Goldring muses, or to the openness with which scientific theories of sexuality are discussed.

Writers struggled to sort this out, often with an awkward and embarrassed sense that they might have to revise some of their own emotional commitments. Richard Aldington in *Death of a Hero* (1929), Martin Taylor says,

> was attempting a retrospective defence of a type of relationship that had since come under close scrutiny. . . . The work of the post-war psychologists had made it difficult to distinguish the threshold between friendship and homosexuality, maintaining that when the erotic forces of physical attraction motivated a relationship between men, it could then be termed homosexual rather than platonic.[37]

Robert Graves was distressed when the erstwhile object of his romantic schoolboy attentions, the innocence of which he had strenuously maintained, took up a queer lifestyle. Invited to write a play, Graves produced *But It Still Goes On* (1930). Dick and Dorothy are brother and sister; David is in love with Dick and Charlotte is in love with Dorothy. Charlotte speaks of 'men of David's – what *is* the word? – of David's persuasion', but Dorothy distrusts 'your fantastic Freudian stuff about maternal fixations' (231–2). Despite qualms of various kinds, David marries Dorothy and Charlotte tries to marry Dick; he rejects her because of her lack of sexual passion so she marries his father. David – who has been shown in an oyster-bar in the West End with a lower-class youth 'dressed somewhat effeminately' – is found doing 'disgusting and horrible' things on Hampstead Heath (250, 303). Both marriages end violently, not to say melodramatically. Such an explicit play could not be produced, but Graves published it.

So was there no place for a noble love between men? Were all the historical instances, from the Theban Band through David and Jonathan to Tennyson and Hallam, really perverted? Theatres in Britain and the USA were places where the question was contested.

John van Druten's case in *Young Woodley* (1925) is that the sensitive youngster will be all right if you don't harass him with exaggerated suspicions. Woodley, the boy whom we may have to worry about, writes poetry on the subject of 'dark-eyed maidens, supple limbed' (148), and says he has trouble relating his ideal feelings about women to the sexual opportunities that present themselves. However, he plays sports, and is in love with Laura Simmons, the housemaster's wife. Meanwhile Mr Simmons has taken against Woodley and his poetry, and is ready to imagine the worst:

There is a surliness and cynicism about that boy, a sort of superiority. It is all this intellectual flapdoodle. He imagines himself too good for everyone. This rubbish about writing poetry. It is not healthy or normal in a boy. It all comes down to the same thing in the end. Sex. It is at the bottom of all the trouble. The school is going through a bad period; these things come in waves. A few of the wrong men at the top and the harm is done. (179)

He says Woodley behaves 'like a hysterical school girl' (220).

It transpires that Mrs Simmons is disillusioned with her husband and the narrowness of his attitude towards the boys; she is strongly drawn to Woodley; they read poetry to each other and embrace rapturously in a long kiss. So there is nothing queer about sensitivity, and Woodley has a promising heterosexual future. Notwithstanding, the Lord Chamberlain regarded the play as 'an attack upon the public school system, liable to cause offence to scholastic bodies and pain to parents and guardians'; it was produced successfully on Broadway.[38]

Yet the topic was awkward. A boy needs a father-figure as a role model – Woodley's father stands by him at the end; he will try to be more 'intimate';

they will play golf together. In an autobiography, *The Way to the Present* (1938), van Druten tells how close *Young Woodley* was to his own experience. However, the first two pages announce a bad relationship with his father as the leading motif: 'The antagonism which existed between us, the almost violent lack of sympathy I had for him, could only be explained, I think, by a process of psycho-analysis' (11–12). Again: 'I had thrilled to *Dorian Gray* and met trouble with Father over it' (127). In this text van Druten allows the fate of the sensitive boy to seem more problematic. Also, he is uneasy about romantic friendship and Vachell's novel *The Hill*. 'There is nothing in the story that is in the least perverted or abnormal', he avers. 'But I do not think it a good book for boys. It encourages the longing for romantic friendship, so that the juvenile reader takes it for something fine and ultimate, instead of for what it is – a temporary canalization or sublimation of the normal sex instinct' (104–5). Van Druten wants to reaffirm the innocence of boyish love, but anxiety about the queerness he is trying to repudiate breaks up the picture.

Other dramatists reworked these images in other ways. No misgivings are admitted into *Ah, Wilderness!* (1933) by Eugene O'Neill. There is 'something of extreme sensitiveness' about young Richard: 'a restless, apprehensive, defiant, shy, dreamy selfconscious intelligence' (23). He reads a lot – not just Ibsen and Shaw, who are dangerously socialistic, but Wilde and Swinburne. However, he applies their romantic intensities to Muriel. When she is forced by her father to dismiss him, he is drawn into a house of ill-repute but shrinks from sexual involvement there. This is because he is saving himself for a true and decent love with Muriel, not because of the taint of queerness. His father is supportive but firm, his mother loving but not to be taken too seriously in early manhood. His mother's brother is unmarried, because he is locked into an unfulfilled romance with his father's sister.

Whiteoaks (1936) by Mazo de la Roche (from her novel) is more adventurous in its treatment of boyish proclivities. Eighteen-year-old Finch is 'very sensitive and nervy' and lives for his music; under pressure he becomes hysterical. His family is dominated by a portrait of the grandfather in military uniform. 'Farming and horses, yes, but music . . .' (2, 30, de la Roche's pause). Finch is forbidden to play the piano until he has passed his exams, but he goes to town on the pretext of studying with a friend and plays with a band in a café. He drops a letter from one of his fellows and his brother reads it out: 'A letter of yours, eh? Listen to this, Renny! "Darling Finch". My God! That this sort of muck should be written to a brother of mine!' Renny, a stepbrother, says he's disgusted: 'I'd rather you had spent last night in a brothel than to find you carrying that sloppy letter about!' (66–7). They resort to talk of how manly the grandfather was, and all the men of the family.

At first Finch can't see what's so wrong about the letter; this suggests that nothing very sexual has occurred. When left alone, he realises: 'A pause – then his face is illuminated by understanding. He wildly tears the letter into several pieces and throws them into the fire' (69). There is no further elucidation in the text; in this mime we have to read the dawning of Finch's awareness that his sexuality is in question. He makes as if to throttle himself by twisting a towel around his neck, but revolts from that. 'He sinks with a gasp of relief to the piano seat. There is a pause, then he brings his hands down in a wild tumult of sound, challenging and triumphant.' He is choosing a life of defiance, but it is unclear whether that means a life of queerness or a life in which misinterpretations will be shrugged off. 'That boy's a bundle of nerves lately', his uncle remarks (69).

The main action in *Whiteoaks* is the competing of the men and boys for the favour of Adeline, the grandmother, who is 101 and declares that she will not divide her wealth. 'You're a queer boy', she says to Finch, 'but I like you' (42). So she leaves him the money, and the clumsy and materialistic people are disappointed; despite the Ivy Compton-Burnett dialogue, the theme anticipates *Cat on a Hot Tin Roof* (1955). *Whiteoaks* was presented successfully in Canada (where it is set), London and New York. The censors found nothing sufficiently explicit to justify an objection, but critics picked up a queer message, discerning that Finch had fallen among 'evil companions, such young men as write love letters to each other'.[39] According to Kaier Curtin and Nicholas de Jongh, *The Good* (1938) by Chester Erskin, which received nine performances on Broadway, presents in similarly sympathetic terms a sensitive and emotional boy who is in love with his choirmaster.[40]

George and Margaret (1937) by Gerald Savory depicts another family under a scarcely articulated threat of queerness. Young Dudley invites Roger to stay – they are both musicians. Frankie, Dudley's sister, falls in love with Roger, but her mother doubts 'if he's the marrying sort, you know. These artistic types very often aren't' (38). But then, Frankie's current beau is a bit suspect too; 'I think men should prefer the company of women', her father remarks, 'but they shouldn't dress as if they do' (23). Frankie, frustrated by Roger's reserve, tells him he is 'rather a weak character' and 'probably effeminate' (47–8). But eventually they get it together. Meanwhile the older brother, Claude, is challenged on his role as a scoutmaster: 'Seen any Girl Guides lately?' Dudley asks. 'Segregation of the sexes is necessary to scoutcraft',

Claude replies; 'How can we teach them to be men if they're mixing with girls all the time?' 'I should have thought it would have been the best way', Frankie chips in (21). Claude turns out straight, though at the expense (as his mother sees it) of marrying the parlourmaid. Dudley, however, remains a loose end. He needs a woman behind him to help him believe in his genius as a musician, Frankie muses. Perhaps there is one, their father says; 'No, there's not. I should know at once' (22). *George and Margaret* ends without resolving this misgiving.

'The Army with its male relationships was simply an extension of my public school', said J.R. Ackerley.[41] In fact, World War I made sexuality more problematic. On the one hand, it intensified and relegitimised emotions between men. Maugham felt able to present in *The Unknown* (1920) an ex-soldier who speaks lovingly of a dead friend: 'It's difficult to explain what it was like. It seemed to shine about him like a mellow light. It was like the jolly feeling of the country in May. And do you know what it was? Goodness. Just goodness. He was the sort of man that I should like to be' (IIIb, 58). In Graves' *But It Still Goes On* David remarks: 'Do you know how a platoon of men will absolutely worship a good-looking gallant young officer? . . . they don't realize exactly what's happening, neither does he' (245). At the same time, the War encouraged attention to mental illness. As Jeffrey Weeks explains, 'The shell-shock and other psychological disorders, and the disturbance of traditional liberal views of human nature that the war produced, opened the way to new forms of treatment.'[42]

Ackerley's play *The Prisoners of War*, set in an internment camp in Switzerland, centres upon Conrad's perplexity at emotions which, the audience is meant to deduce, are homosexual. He doesn't like women − when Madame Louis refers to 'the fair sex' he snaps back, 'Which sex is that?' − and is a virgin at twenty-four (119, 95). However, he draws no particular conclusion from all this. He quarrels incessantly with young Grayle, the unresponsive object of his enigmatic attentions, and suffers what would come to be regarded as psychosomatic symptoms − neuralgia and eventually a fit and delirium. As well as being a prisoner of war he is a prisoner in his own head. At one point Conrad risks a relatively direct appeal to Grayle − 'You could help me no end, you know, if you were decent to me' − and strokes his head. 'Look out!' Grayle exclaims: 'Someone might come in!' Grayle, the stage direction remarks, 'has been educated at a good public school' (102). For it is not that these young men have not come across same-sex passion, but that they have no framework for conceptualising it. Ackerley records how at the time of the action of the play he was mystified by the question 'Are you homo or hetero?' 'So far as I recall I

never met a recognisable or self-confessed adult homosexual (except an
ancient master at school, called "the Nag", who was mysteriously sacked) until
after the war.'[43]

Of course, the play is written with hindsight: Ackerley is exposing the
confusions of his slightly-younger self. During his internment he read
Plutarch, Otto Weininger and Edward Carpenter, and by the time the play was
produced he was considerably more experienced, both sexually and intellectually (particular friends included E.M. Forster and Goldsworthy Lowes
Dickinson). He allows an informed audience to see what is troubling Conrad.
James Agate said in his review that the play concerns 'the least understood of
abnormalities' — 'It jumps to the eyes that the problem is not one of
depression but of repression.'[44] Notice the tone, there, of telling us something
that we might not quite have worked out for ourselves; Agate is assuming an
uneven development of such ideas. Phyllis Whitworth, who ran the Three
Hundred Club where *Prisoners* was being produced, was disconcerted to hear
that it was being spoken of in anticipation as a homosexual play. She wanted
to cut the bit where Conrad strokes Grayle's head, but Ackerley 'insisted that
since Mrs Whitworth had read the play several times without recognizing its
homosexual element until someone pointed it out to her, then it was safe to
assume that her lady subscribers would be similarly insulated by their
innocence'.[45] The censor worried about the play, but found little to object to:
'The sentimental friendships and jealousies between the officers have no
sinister suggestion in any coarse sense.'[46]

This indeterminacy perhaps explains why, despite excellent reviews, *The
Prisoners of War* ran for only twenty-four performances after transferring to
the West End. It stirred people interested in this risky new subject, but didn't
communicate far beyond that constituency. By 1935, when it was produced in
New York, following the success of *The Green Bay Tree* and *The Children's
Hour*, it seemed implausibly naive.[47] Ackerley too found this when he was
older. He longed to eradicate the line where Conrad says he is fond of Grayle
because 'He's clean. Fills gaps': 'I saw that Freud had got away with more than
I intended.'[48]

Discussion about *Prisoners* often focuses on two other young officers,
Rickman and Tetford, and whether Freud got away with something there as
well. Already in 1935, Curtin notes, critics of the New York production found
the sexuality of these characters suspect.[49] Rickman and Tetford are buddies:
they go to town together to hunt for women. But Tetford seems specially
aware. He suggests that Conrad is in love with Grayle and condemns the

latter's lack of consideration; when Rickman pays too much attention to Grayle he sets out, explicitly, to reassert his claim on Rickman. They resolve to become partners after the War in the tough Canadian lumber camps (Rickman is Canadian). In this scene Tetford touches Rickman's head such that, the stage direction says, 'one is reminded' of Conrad's gesture towards Grayle. He puts his hand on Rickman's shoulder, and Rickman links a finger in Tetford's other hand; when Conrad enters they release hands 'without embarrassment'. As he thinks of flying away to this new life, Tetford rests a tennis racket 'on the floor between his legs, and is dreamily working the handle to and fro as though it were the joy-stick of his aeroplane'; he gets Rickman to sit behind him (128–30). This phallic moment is also the point at which the internment of this potentially dynamic group of young men seems specially sad; Conrad's fit follows immediately.

De Jongh complains that Ackerley contrives sad endings for effeminate homosexuals, whereas 'the archetypically masculine Tetford and Rickman are allowed to look forward to homosexual happiness together'.[50] To Peter Burton, this 'friendship' is surely 'emotionally homosexual', 'subliminally homosexual?' Surely it '*has* turned into love?' However this, Burton says, is 'to our eyes today'.[51] Ackerley insisted that he did not intend Tetford or Rickman to be perceived as queer. He wrote to Stephen Spender in 1955, when the play was revived in London:

> As for homosexuality. I'm sorry you thought that there were 'one or two' homosexual characters. If that were so it would certainly be a fault, but it was not intended. . . . There is only one homosexual character, Conrad himself. The rest are entirely normal. And although Tetford regards Rickman as *his* pal, the notion of their going to bed together ought to be as unthinkable to the audience as I meant it to be to them.[52]

The idea, evidently, was to indicate that 'innocent', loving, man-to-man relationships were still possible. Conrad is different: he speaks of people such as himself as 'a race apart. Temperamentally unsound' (*Prisoners*, 126). 'He was so nervy and highly strung', says the motherly Mrs Prendergast of Conrad – 'He was like a woman in some ways' (132). But Freudian assumptions were making it increasingly difficult to bracket sexuality.

The topic was further inflected for Ackerley, as for so many other gay men, by his distress at any prospect of effeminacy. He has Adelby say that as a boy he was stirred by 'tales of the heroes' in Plutarch's *Lives* – the Theban Band.

'It's a pity we've lost all that, that great hero-worship. Each man used to take his intimate friend to war with him, didn't he? And they'd protect each other. It gave a man something *real* to fight for' (105). In those times same-sex passion was compatible with soldiering. But this remains an aspiration. Ackerley, like Carpenter, Forster, Lowes Dickinson and others who proclaimed the manliness of same-sex passion, never quite expels a residuum of effeminacy from his concept of queerness. I pursue these themes in chapter 6.

The straight alternative to *Prisoners*, by general agreement, is *Journey's End* (1928) by R.C. Sherriff. It was produced initially at a club theatre because it was doubted that people were ready for a play about the War. Stanhope, the company commander, is a good officer but because of nerves he is drunk much of the time (he's only twenty-one or so; everyone else who came out with him is dead or wounded). Fortunately he has a committed friend and invaluable support in Osborne, an older officer generally called 'Uncle'. The arrival of an inexperienced younger officer, Raleigh, is troubling for Stanhope because they went to the same school: Raleigh has hero-worshipped Stanhope, and Stanhope is engaged to Raleigh's sister.

Journey's End is not just a different version of the War from *Prisoners of War*: it stages an explicit counter-argument about homoeroticism. In both plays we have a nerve-shattered captain, but in Sherriff's account he is distressed by his duties as an officer, not by passion for a young colleague. Failure of manliness in *Journey's End* is not to do with sexuality, but with loss of nerve in battle. Hibbert, who is cracking up, is told to 'try and be a man' (80). Osborne, the wise, older officer, corresponds to Adelby in *Prisoners*, but Osborne has been a champion rugby player and when at home plays tin soldiers with his two sons, whereas Adelby's heterosexual relations are somewhat insecure. Stanhope speaks of Osborne as 'The one man I could trust – my best friend – the one man I could talk to as man to man' (121).

Fortified by all this uncomplicated manliness, Osborne is able to give frank but decently reticent expression to homosocial feeling. He says a couple of times what a good-looking youngster Raleigh is, and enthuses about Stanhope: 'You don't know him as I do; I love that fellow. I'd go to hell with him.' 'Oh, you sweet, sentimental old darling!' exclaims another officer (22). Osborne counsels Stanhope about Raleigh and about taking a rest. 'Dear old Uncle!' Stanhope responds, 'Make you a little apron – with lace on it.' Osborne persuades him to go to bed: 'Kiss me, Uncle', Stanhope says. 'Kiss you be blowed!' Osborne replies (50). Such affections are allowed to men whose manliness is beyond question. While *Prisoners of War* focuses on what was generally regarded as unhealthy feeling and has difficulty keeping Rickman and Tetford clear of it, *Journey's End* reasserts the simple decency of man-to-man emotions. Adelby associated hero-worship with the Theban Band; Osborne reassures Stanhope that it is is 'quite natural' for Raleigh to make him a hero. 'As long as the hero's a hero', Stanhope says (44): his fear is not that there is something improper about Raleigh's feeling, but that his sister will hear that Stanhope drinks all the time. In fact Raleigh writes home a letter of newly intense admiration for Stanhope, so there is not a problem. He dies with Stanhope by the bed holding his hand.

In *Post-Mortem* (written in 1930) Coward responded, in turn, to *Journey's End*. His play starts in the trenches, where a nice, clean-looking young officer, Babe Robins, is distressed at the death of a confrère, Armitage. Then another officer, the idealistic John, is killed. The main action of the play is the return of the ghost of John after thirteen years to the England of 1930. He discovers various inadequacies and betrayals among his former family and friends. Babe now has the look of any average, prosperous young man in the motor business, and is upset when John says he loved Armitage: 'Look here, don't you talk such bloody rot.' But there was nothing to be ashamed of, John avers: 'There is no slur in that. It was one of the nicest things about you, wholehearted, and tremendously decent. It must be a weak moral code that wishes to repudiate it. Love among men in war is gallant and worth remembering. Don't let the safe years stifle that remembrance' (631). However, an older and now-aggressively-cynical ex-officer says the exchange displays Babe's repressed homosexuality: 'Excellent psychology. You got him on the raw. Hero-worship. "Greater love hath no man, etc., etc." Heart interest. Sex confusion. He'll be like that until he dies' (635). Gallant or queer — there is the debate. Coward didn't try to get *Post-Mortem* produced, but he published it in *Play Parade* (1934) with his major plays to date.

World War I is a key myth in Britain. It represents both ultimate heroism in the service of nation and (for those of a critical cast) an extreme instance of the cruelty and wastefulness of capitalism. In both these versions, bonding between soldiers is a crucial index of human feeling, either revalidating the system or exposing its inhumanity. Yet the emergence of sexuality as a topic has made it rapidly apparent that the entire scenario of heroic devotion is available to queer reinterpretation. These plays are trying to handle that instability; even in recent years we have seen only reluctant recognition that the admired 'war poetry' of Wilfred Owen and Siegfried Sassoon is founded in same-sex passion.

The circulation of this discourse was uneven, then. As a young schoolmaster in the 1930s, T.C. Worsley says, he knew 'no word for those who nowadays would be summarily described as "Queer" or "Bent". . . . The vice, if it is one, was hinted at in the wary disapproval with which any close association between boys and masters, or elder and younger boys was regarded. But without any nomenclature to describe it, it remained unspecified in everyday conversation.'[53] He had never felt any inclinations towards women − a boy one year older had 'engaged my affections to an absurd and exclusive degree. I thought of no one else. I didn't think of him, let me say, in any sexual connection. I didn't at the time even know I could' (23). Worsley did not understand his own emotions as queer, but a woman to whom he had been trying to make love took him to see Mordaunt Shairp's play *The Green Bay Tree* and told him. '"You're a homosexual", she said quite kindly' (26).

Stevan in *The Rats of Norway* (1933) comes close to Worsley's experience. The play, by Keith Winter (who was having an affair with Coward), ran for several months in the West End and was produced unsuccessfully in New York in 1948. It is concerned with the steamy liaisons of teachers in a Northumbrian prep school − a cut-off, unreal place, it is suggested (the boys don't figure). There is a manifestly queer master among them, Chetwood: 'a slim, effeminate youth with a sulky and rather silly sort of beauty which only just fails to impress' (10). However, he is not taken seriously and the play is not much about him. Stevan, a new teacher, takes against Chetwood and is rude to him at every opportunity, and seems to fall in love with a woman colleague, Tilly. Meanwhile the drunken and tortured Sebastian has a torrid affair with Jane, the headmaster's impressive wife. Nonetheless, 'A current of deep sympathy seems to flash between the two men', Stevan and Sebastian (79), though it is virtually unexpressed and hence hardly apparent until Tilly works out that she is in the way. Sebastian has a heart attack and dies in Jane's bed, so her husband becomes aware of her infidelity, but her final words are for Stevan: 'You loved him too, didn't you? . . . More than Tilly?' 'Yes' (104).

What is striking here is the conjuncture of Chetwood and Stevan. By 1933 we know what a queer looks like, but still he is *someone else*. The feelings of the presumptively straight Stevan and Sebastian can still take them by surprise.

Girls in Trouble

Lillian Faderman points out that while only 10 per cent of American women generally remained single, between 1880 and 1900 about half the women who had attended college did so.[54] Women who had opportunity, in other words, were opting away from household arrangements that would subordinate them to men. They preferred a career and the company and affection of other women. However, the suggestion that there was something 'abnormal' about this was not often heard. Carroll Smith-Rosenberg concurs: there had been occasional notorious discoveries of lesbian passion, but these did not influence the self-perceptions of bourgeois and educated feminist women. Such women 'praised the feminine qualities of the women they loved; they certainly did not practice cross-dressing. None of them reported feeling that a male soul inhabited her female body.'[55] These women rested on the tradition of romantic friendship; they didn't have to wonder whether they were manifesting a perverse sexual orientation, or a lesbian sensibility.

Sheila Jeffreys is suspicious of the energy expended by Faderman on proving that such women did not have genital sex: even if the topic was not much talked of, they might have discovered it through affectionate embraces.[56] That seems likely enough; the further question, still, is whether what they were doing was likely to be recognised as sexual and as signifying a lesbian personality-type. At the trial of Marianne Woods and Jane Pirie, two schoolteachers accused by one of their pupils of indecent practices in 1810, their advocate argued that 'their private parts were not so formed as to penetrate each other, and without penetration the venereal orgasm could not possibly follow'.[57] I think this is important: people had difficulty envisaging *as sexual practices* those other than, or other than leading to, heterosexual penetration. That is why, famously, Queen Victoria was unable to imagine lesbianism (or was she, perhaps, protecting her sisters?).

Nonetheless, there certainly were women who regarded themselves as Sapphists (the more usual term) before the 1920s; Emma Donoghue quotes instances in *Passions between Women*, and Dell Richards enumerates others in *Lesbian Lists*.[58] Frank Wedekind presents a lesbian in one of his *Lulu* plays (1895) − another evocation of sexual dissidence in bohemia. Among the admirers of Lulu is the Countess Martha Geschwitz, who appears wearing 'a pale-blue Hussar jacket edged with white fur, with silver-braid facings, white bow-tie, close fitting stand-up collar and stiff cuffs with enormous ivory cuff-links'. She expresses abhorrence at the idea of sleeping with a man: 'I can't − I can't − not a man' (154, 174). Like the men in Lulu's life, Geschwitz grovels at her feet (literally); Lulu calls her a monster and tells her 'Go to the Moulin Rouge! Go to a circus' (162). She suffers mental torment and a slow, painful death. Wedekind said he meant to show Geschwitz as a fatally flawed, tragic figure, but in Nina Rapi's reading she is degraded.[59] She could be both. *Lulu* was not produced until 1987 in German, 1992 in English. G.W. Pabst's film *Pandora's Box* (1928) presents the Countess only briefly; Alban Berg's opera, *Lulu* (1937) seeks to make her devotion appealing.

Faderman notes *March Hares* (1921) by Harry Wagstaff Gribble as one of a number of plays and novels that 'brought fascinated views of lesbians to literature and the American stage'; Donald L. Loeffler believes the play exhibits 'latent homosexuality'.[60] I find this text hard to interpret — it is subtitled 'a fantastic satire'. Geoffrey and Janet both live in the house of Janet's mother, Mrs Rodney; they have been engaged for three years and run a drama school together. Because she is annoyed by Geoffrey's lack of amorous attention, Janet brings a woman-friend, Claudia, into the house — she calls her 'an affinity'. Janet speaks of Claudia in exalted tones; she depends on her in her elocution teaching: 'I can think more clearly when she is in the room. When one of my pupils has difficulty with a gesture or intonation, and I cannot give quite the right correction, I look at Claudia for a moment or two, and — I get the exact shade or tone I want' (14).

Geoffrey, to get even, invites into the house a male friend, Fuller: 'So I said to myself — "Well, if I can sacrifice three of the best years of my life to a steady concentration upon Janet merely to be told at the end of that period that she has found an affinity in someone else — why shouldn't I look for an affinity, why shouldn't I bring back a companion?"' (12). Fuller arrives carrying a handbag. 'A handbag?' Mrs Rodney exclaims — with a Lady Bracknell intonation? However, the stage directions describe Fuller as 'a very normal young man' (6); he agreed to come for the adventure, he says. All the characters say both admiring and rude things about each other in various combinations, apparently competing for attention. The two women become rivals over the men, while complaining that neither Geoffrey nor Fuller is red-blooded. After slapping each other, Janet and Geoffrey are inspired to renew their engagement; it turns out that Claudia is married already; Fuller is left standing. I can't see any signal that tips these homosocial relations into same-sex passion; but then, what signal should we expect? *March Hares* is either flirting outrageously with the prospect of homosexuality, or is entirely oblivious to it. Perhaps Gribble didn't quite know which; perhaps audiences divided in their responses. Once more, we are looking at a confused and uneven development.

Children in Uniform (1932, called *Girls in Uniform* on Broadway) by Christa Winsloe arrived in the West End and on Broadway after success in

Europe and as a film. Manuela is fourteen and her mother is dead. She is placed in a harshly disciplined boarding school which aspires to inculcate Prussian values: 'Our girls need more discipline, more self-control. . . . If we pamper our children, Kesten, how can Prussia rise again?' the headmistress demands (43–4). The other girls are already entranced by one of the teachers, Fräulein von Bernburg, who kisses the girls in Manuela's dormitory goodnight. Von Bernburg is 'Tall, straight, dark, aristocratic, strong, with beautiful brown eyes, and a direct look, a strong but sensitive mouth' (34). In a context where the girls are passing each other love-letters, Manuela's crush on her teacher begins immediately. 'I can't in the least imagine how she would kiss. And yet it must be just like a mother. . . . I never wanted it to be the same as much as I do now, but I don't know how I can wait. I feel as if I might choke − or scream − or become dumb − '(46).

A French (and hence flighty) teacher, Mademoiselle Alaret, asks von Bernburg, 'teasingly', whether she doesn't specially like Manuela. But von Bernburg interprets the topic solemnly and responsibly, expressing sympathy for the confusion of all the children. 'If once we were weak, if once we were to give way to our feelings, we should be lost' (41). This could mean: We would all plunge into lesbian affairs, but von Bernburg's demeanour indicates that it means: We would be unable to maintain the disciplined ethos of the school.

Manuela gains considerably in confidence, and is to perform in Voltaire's tragedy, *Zaïre*. She is to act a knight who protects his erring sister, played by the gentle Edelgard, who is in fact devoted to her and whom she in fact protects. Manuela is exhilarated at the prospect of impressing von Bernburg: 'When I'm dressed in my silver armour, with my hair quite free, then, she will see me properly for the very first time! . . . Let me dream I am a knight, a knight who has come to free her' (55–6). Manuela laughs boyishly, is said to look just like a boy. She receives a proposal of marriage from the fencing master, but the prospect of seeing him makes her feel sick. Meanwhile, von Bernburg is beginning to compromise the stern principles of the school: sympathetically, she gives Manuela one of her chemises.

Manuela is a triumph in *Zaïre* − all the girls court her. There are dangers, however. 'If once you become an actress, you will be no longer fit for society', Oda warns. 'And, of course, you couldn't marry, either.' 'That wouldn't worry me. I shan't marry, anyway', Manuela replies (73–4). She drinks all their glasses of punch and blissfully proclaims her love for von Bernburg, and that it is reciprocated. Unfortunately the headmistress has entered: 'Revolting! A scandal! A scandal!' (78). Another teacher says Manuela is 'a lost girl' and 'morbid' (94).

The allegation that von Bernburg has reciprocated Manuela's passion is not credited (it would be a different matter today), and her concern remains humanitarian and maternal: 'I cannot bear to see her treated unjustly. Because I love her as if she were my own child'. She remains sympathetic and firm, telling Manuela that they must never meet again: '(*painfully*): You must not love me so much. It is wrong, it is harmful — it is a sin' (87, 99). Von Bernburg confronts the headmistress: 'I am much nearer to the girls than you are. I love them.' Anyway, this is not the way to train leaders: 'Here — you train women for sergeants, not mothers of generals! Here no leader could rise, no Joan of Arc in her shining armour.' Manuela 'cried out her sin and perversity', the headmistress says, but von Bernburg replies: 'She cried out her longing! Her longing for warmth and affection! She has not yet become crushed and stupid. Sin! Why, she doesn't know its meaning!' (101–3). Manuela throws herself out of a window and dies; the headmistress says they must call it an accident (in the film Manuela is saved by the other girls).

Curtin summarises US responses: 'The critics in 1932 viewed *Girls in Uniform* as an examination of the brutal, prudish reaction of an individual personifying the Prussian educational system to a harmless, passing schoolgirl's crush.'[61] That is not quite right: some of the critics he quotes explicitly asserted a 'harmless' reading over the lesbian reading which they admitted was possible, at least for those who were minded to make it. So Richard Lockridge in the *New York Sun*:

As was probably inevitable, the play has been interpreted by some who have seen it, on the stages of London and Berlin and on the screen here, as a study of those tendencies described by one of the mistresses as 'unhealthy'. And, of course, if a schoolgirl 'crush' is unhealthy, then Manuela's feeling for her teacher was something to be hushed. But if we are not too regimented by prevailing misinterpretations of 'modern psychology' — if we are not unperceptive as Manuela's persecutors — we can see it only as a story of an innocent child cruelly and needlessly murdered.[62]

The play is certainly open to the thought that it is von Bernburg who is mistaken — failing to recognise the lesbian basis not only of Manuela's passion but of her own sympathy. For Lockridge such a reading would accord with 'prevailing misinterpretations of "modern psychology"'. Perversely, for the modern reader, the 'liberal' view when these plays were initially presented was that there is nothing to worry about: it is nasty, suspicious people with sex on the brain who think otherwise. Today, we would prefer to see the possibility of lesbianism among young women taken seriously.

The Children's Hour (1934) by Lillian Hellman was banned from other than club production in England, despite a successful Broadway run. The historical events on which Hellman based the play have already been mentioned: in Scotland in 1810 a set of judges was divided and baffled by accusations of sexual indecency against two teachers. They did not think the offences impossible, but they did make comments such as: 'I cannot think or admit that it furnishes any presumption against the plaintiffs because they formed a friendship of great warmth and they sometimes slept in the same bed together. These are the natural presumptions of innocence in my mind.' The fact that the pupil making the accusation was half Indian was taken as an explanation of her knowingness: 'she was no stranger to those impure ideas which she had imbibed partly from her Eastern education, and partly perhaps from that precocity of temperament which she owed to an Eastern constitution'.[63] Characters in *The Children's Hour*, set in the present-day of 1934, register surprise and dismay at the allegations against Karen and Martha, but not incomprehension or disbelief. The grounds of suspicion have changed.

Martha is certainly attached to Karen. She is disappointed that their vacation will not be 'just you and me — the way we used to at college' (18). She doesn't want Joe, Karen's fiancé (a doctor), along with them; she has been hoping they won't marry after all. She says she is concerned for the school they have built up, but evidently she sees Joe as a rival. Martha's aunt, Mrs Mortar, has been on the stage and has no doubt about what is going on: 'it's unnatural, just as unnatural as it can be. You don't like their being together. You were always like that even as a child. If you had a little girl friend, you always got mad when she liked anybody else. Well, you'd better get a beau of your own now — a woman of your age' (25). Joe, meanwhile, puts the best construction on things: 'I know how fond you are of Karen, but our marriage oughtn't to make a great deal of difference' (28).

Mary, who accuses the two teachers, is a disturbed youngster — dishonest, bullying, blackmailing, unresponsive to the caring concern of Karen. She and the other girls have been reading *Mademoiselle de Maupin* (1835) by Théophile Gautier, which includes lesbian episodes, and they have overheard the talk about Martha's 'unnatural' attachment to Karen. We see Mary piecing together an accusation, pragmatically, and only partly aware of its import, as she manipulates her grandmother, Mrs Tilford. The latter is a kind and reasonable woman, who means to be firm with Mary and is reluctant to believe ill of Karen and Martha. But Mary's accusation is definite and circumstantiated; to a woman such as Mrs Tilford, *The Children's Hour* says, lesbianism is far from her thoughts but eventually credible. 'There's something wrong with Karen', she tells Joe, 'something horrible' (65). Mary must have got such an idea from somewhere, and observation is the most likely source.

Criticism has tended to focus on the question of whether Martha — the more promising candidate — is really lesbian or not. The children's evidence was false, Mrs Tilford learns at the end of the play: 'I know it wasn't true, Karen', she says (110). However, this is shortly after Martha has confessed to Karen: '*I have loved you the way they said*' (104). Commentators have complained that this confounds the issue. Just when we were warming to a civil liberties theme — passionate friends are entitled to freedom from arbitrary slander, specially when they are women trying to make an independent way in the world — our commitment is confounded; Martha says she is 'guilty' after all, and indeed 'dirty', and kills herself. As Eric Bentley puts it, there are two plays in *The Children's Hour*: one in which society punishes the innocent and a second, which takes over suddenly at the end, in which society punishes someone guilty of lesbianism.[64] The audience is engrossed in the first story, and there is little time for giving a moral context to the second. What becomes difficult to frame is the homophile question: Why should these women *not* have had lesbian relations?

These arguments do not reach what is, I think, most interesting about *The Children's Hour*. Actually it is plain all the way through that Martha is in love with Karen, and almost equally plain that the women have not been enjoying sexual relations in the manner alleged. Neither their feelings nor their behaviour are uncertain. What is at issue is whether their passionate friendship now has to be 'recognised' as 'actually' lesbian. Or, to put it another way, it is the misfortune of Martha and Karen to be situated at the point where our cultures decide to review the concept of romantic friendship, sorting out which relationships should be redefined as 'really' lesbian.

For in 1934, unlike the historical trial date of 1810, lesbianism is not hard to envisage. Karen protests: 'But this isn't a new sin they tell us we've done. Other people aren't destroyed by it.' Martha replies: 'They are the people who believe in it, who want it, who've chosen it.' So there are purposeful lesbians, and they manage to live their lives. But 'We aren't like that. We don't love each other', Martha avers (103). It is this disclaimer that prompts her reversal: she has indeed, after all, loved Karen '*the way they said*': 'maybe I wanted you all along; maybe I couldn't call it by a name; maybe it's been there ever since I first knew you'. There is no new evidence for this; rather, the old feeling is being given 'a name'. 'There's something in you, and you don't know it and you don't do anything about it. . . . I didn't even *know*' (103–5).

I discussed in chapter 2 *Mademoiselle de Maupin*, which Mary and the other girls have been reading. D'Albert can engage in passionate involvements with women and men without having to define himself as homosexual or heterosexual. Similarly, the woman who calls herself 'Théodore' is not cross-dressing in order to facilitate lesbian affairs; she wants to conduct a thorough analysis of men. To be sure, she is fond of Rosette, who, believing her to be a man, loves her passionately. And Rosette eventually places herself on the lap of 'Théodore', who finds herself responding sexually: 'I felt her half-naked and insurgent breasts leap against my breast, and her fingers tighten about my hair. A thrill ran through my body and the nipples of my breast grew hard.'[65] However, this does not much disconcert 'Théodore', or oblige her to come to terms with what we might call 'her lesbianism'. She muses: 'As I have not yet loved a man, the excess of my affection has overflowed in some sort into friendships with girls and young women; I have brought to these the same abandon and exaltation that I put into everything I do, for moderation in anything is impossible to me, especially in any matter affecting the heart' (215).

The more daring move is still to follow. 'Théodore''s close encounters with men lead her to decide that she doesn't much like them:

> The fact is that I really belong to neither of the two sexes: I have not the imbecile submissiveness, the timidity, or the littleness of women; neither have I the vices of men, their disgusting crapulence and bestial propensities. I belong to a third sex which has as yet no name, either higher or lower than the other two, either more defective than they or superior to them. I have the body and soul of a woman, and the intellect and strength of a man. . . . My ideal would be to have each sex in turn so as to satisfy my dual nature. (266)

She carries through this analysis by going to bed with both d'Albert and Rosette in the same night, and then rides off with her cross-dressed, female page, in quest of further adventures.

In a girls' school of the 1930s, this book from the 1830s would indeed seem pornographic — and perhaps it is, though I find a saving specificity at moments like that when 'Théodore', finally unclothed for d'Albert's gaze, complains that she is cold (278). What is sad, surely, is that such expansive writing should incite the closed-down thoughts of Hellman's characters. *Mademoiselle de Maupin* was a fantasy even in the 1830s, but it does point towards a sex/gender system that was slower to compartmentalise intimate experience, including friendship and sexual passion. That is the change registered by *The Children's Hour*. Women were caught between residual and emergent views of their behaviour; much of the cultural work in fiction and theatre is engaged with this faultline.

5

Noël Coward's Audiences

Gay Coward?

Noël Coward occupies an uncertain place in British and US queer theatre history. For Nicholas de Jongh only *The Vortex* claims a mention; John Clum discusses only *Design for Living*; in a list of homosexual plays on Broadway before 1950 Donald Loeffler includes only *Design for Living*. Kaier Curtin discusses *The Vortex* and *Design for Living*, but as lamentable instances of closeting. Other commentators regard everything Coward wrote as ineluctably queer. Sean O'Connor says his work is 'littered with subtextual resonances for those who found the prevailing moral code difficult to live within or just plain wrong', but he takes no interest in *The Vortex*.[1] According to John Lahr, in *Hay Fever* 'the homosexual sense of the capriciousness of life is matched by a capricious style'; *Private Lives* displays 'the aesthetics of high camp' and hence 'an essentially homosexual comic vision of the world that justifies detachment'; in *Design for Living* 'the homosexual daydream of sexual abundance comes true'; and in *Blithe Spirit* Charles' discovery that he is living with his dead wife as well as his live one suggests both 'the schizophrenic quality of homosexual life' and 'the homosexual nightmare of female suffocation'.[2] It's a good job Coward didn't write thrillers, for they would presumably witness to the homosexual desire to kill people or be killed.

It is not easy to get a fix on Coward. We have made much of 'Mad About the Boy' – it includes the lines: 'Housman really / Wrote *The Shropshire Lad* about the boy'. But in its initial context, in *Words and Music* (1932, 133–40), the well-known refrain is interspersed with verses in which a Society woman, a schoolgirl, a cockney woman and a prostitute present their particular perspectives on a young male movie star. And Coward insisted that he never sang the song himself. On the other hand, he did want to add, for a New York revue in 1938, a stanza to be sung by a businessman in his office:

Mad about the boy,
I know it's silly,
But I'm mad about the boy,
And even Doctor Freud cannot explain
Those vexing dreams
I've had about the boy.[3]

Coward was ready to extend the scope of same-sex allusion, but didn't want it too close to his backyard. Again, 'Matelot' (from the revue *Sigh No More*, 1945) strikes Adrian Wright as 'blatantly a homosexual love song', and Hoare says Coward wrote it for his lover and protegé Graham Payne, but the song is actually about the spirit of the father calling his son to follow him as a fisherman.[4]

For me, a principal revelation in Philip Hoare's splendid biography was Coward's dislike of effeminate homosexuals. In 1929 he warned Cecil Beaton against looking or sounding queer:

Your sleeves are too tight, your voice is too high and too precise. You mustn't do it. It closes so many doors. . . . It's hard, I know. One would like to indulge one's own taste. I myself dearly love a good match, yet I know it is overdoing it to wear tie, socks and handkerchief of the same colour. I take ruthless stock of myself in the mirror before going out. A polo jumper or unfortunate tie exposes one to danger.[5]

Again, rehearsing with Marlene Dietrich in 1935, Coward exhorted her: 'Marlenah! I must not appear effeminate in any way. Do be a dear – watch out for anything that could be considered less than "butch", if you see me being at all "queer", tell me immediately.'[6]

I had been inclined to welcome the song 'We All Wore a Green Carnation', from Coward's musical *Bitter Sweet* (1929), as an exuberant triumph of sanctions-busting, in which Coward's genius overwhelms the censor and gains an expression of queerness rampant. (The green carnation, of course, was the emblem of Wilde and his circle.) But the song makes better sense if regarded in the way Hoare proposes: as 'Noël's comment on the Uranian decadents, purveyors of a camp sensibility he eschewed', signalling 'disdain for the more obvious members of the homosexual fraternity'.[7]

> Haughty boys, naughty boys, dear, dear dear!
>   Swooning with affectation.
>   Our figures sleek and willowy,
>   Our lips incarnadine,
>   May worry the majority a bit. (*Bitter Sweet*, 156–7)

The Lord Chamberlain could hardly miss the point; evidently he thought the song so hostile to gays as to be harmless to the body politic. *Bitter Sweet* contains another song in similar mode, 'Tarara boom-de-ay', sung by the same four 'exquisites': 'Now that we find the dreary nineteenth century is closing, / We mean to start the twentieth in ecstasies of posing' (149–50).

An episode in *This Year of Grace!* (1927) is similarly dismissive of effeminacy. A newspaper vendor and an Underground booking-clerk, Fred and Harry, speak rudely to a couple of smart young ladies who think it a marvellous adventure to put money in the ticket machine. 'Wot do they want to come nosing round 'ere for – bloated aristocrats?' Fred demands. Harry thinks the answer is birth control – eliminating such people – but Fred disputes it. Then Charles, 'a very exquisite young man', enters and Fred calls off the argument. 'It's all right – you've won. I'm all for birth control.' Charles tries to buy a ticket, but can't make the machine work; 'I said shake it – not stroke it!' Fred exclaims. Where's he going, anyway? – Queen's Gate. ''Arry, that's wot the Russian Ballet's done for England' (8–9). Coward was still mining this vein in 1945. *Sigh No More* includes a skit on the theme 'I Wonder What Happened to Him?' For instance young Phipps 'Who had *very* large hips / And whose waist was excessively slim?'

> Well, it seems that some doctor in Grosvenor Square
> Gave him hormone injections for growing his hair
> And he grew something here, and he grew something there.
> I wonder what happened to her – him?[8]

The reason I had not anticipated Coward's hostility towards effeminacy is that, to my lower-middle-class, scholarship-boy, Royal-Court, 1960s, Gay-Lib sensibility, Coward's persona *in its entirety*, and all his characters and everything to do with his kind of theatre, appeared tinged with effeminacy. It hardly occurred to me that, within the mid-century spectrum of queerness, Coward would regard himself as 'straight-acting' (as contact ads today sometimes promise and demand). I now attempt a more careful analysis of Coward's interventions in the sex/gender system in *Private Lives*, *Design for Living* and *Present Laughter* (*The Vortex*, *Hay Fever*, *Easy Virtue* and *Semi-Monde* are considered in chapter 3).

Private Lives (1930) places in adjacent suites of a Riviera hotel two honeymooning couples, and it quickly emerges that Elyot and Amanda, who are now married to Sybil and Victor, were previously married to each other. Elyot and Amanda rediscover their mutual fascination and run off together; they quarrel violently and return and are forgiven by their new spouses; at the end they leave together after all. In this instance, Coward does risk some confusion around gender identities. While Sybil and Victor have strongly conventional ideas of masculine and feminine roles, as of other things, Elyot and Amanda don't take them seriously. Sybil hates 'these half masculine women who go banging about'; she likes 'a man to be a man'. 'If you feel you'd like me to smoke a pipe, I'll try and master it', Elyot responds (471–2). Amanda claims notable scope for the independent-minded woman. Elyot thinks it's all right for him to have affairs because he's a man – 'It doesn't suit women to be promiscuous.' 'Excuse me a moment while I get a caraway biscuit and change my crinoline', Amanda quips – 'It doesn't suit men for women to be promiscuous' (509). As in Wilde's plays, these anti-sexist implications are obscured if one re-genders the couples, as Lahr suggests, and imagines them all to be gay men. We may, in fact, discern a pattern, whereby gay writers who utter effective critiques of the sex/gender system generally, and of the situation of women in particular, are set aside as revealing merely the triviality and tragedy of the supposed homosexual condition (I discuss Tennessee Williams in chapter 10).

Design for Living (1933) was performed on Broadway but banned in London until 1939, apparently because of its heterosexual explicitness; it is surely the queerest of Coward's plays. The main characters are again artistic, bohemian, and defiant of sexual conventions.

OTTO: We are different. Our lives are diametrically opposed to ordinary social conventions; and it's no use grabbing at those conventions to hold us up when we find we're in deep water. We've jilted them and eliminated them, and we've got to find our own solutions for our own peculiar moral problems. . . . We're not doing any harm to anyone else. We're not peppering the world with illegitimate children. (404–5)

At the opening Gilda is supposed to be living with Otto, but there is some embarrassment when their friend Ernest calls. The reason, it emerges, is that Leo has spent the night with Gilda. At the start of the second act Leo is in Otto's place (anticipating John Osborne's *Look Back in Anger*); they are restless, and still talk of loving Otto. When Otto returns, he and Gilda sleep together; as a consequence, Gilda feels free of both of them and leaves. 'She's escaped!' Otto cries (421).

Leo and Otto, each with the same farewell note from Gilda, remain to comfort each other. They get drunk together, touch and hold each other, thank God for each other and agree that they will be better off without her:

OTTO: . . . We were both damn fools in the first place, ever to have anything to do with her.
LEO (*admiringly*): You're awfully strong, Otto! Much, much stronger than you used to be. (428)

There are sexual innuendoes ('Armadildo' sherry, 430). However, it is suggested finally that much of this is bravado: 'we're going to be awfully — awfully — lonely — [*They both sob hopelessly on each other's shoulders as the curtain slowly falls*]' (432).

How might audiences interpret this moment? The classic homosocial relationship effects male bonding via (purported) desire for a woman, but disavowal of homosexuality is usually a condition of such bonding.[9] People accustomed to that pattern might take it for granted that sexual passion between the two men is out of the question. In London in 1939 Herbert Farjeon complained that the amiability of Otto and Leo towards each other in the ensuing act was inconsistent with their earlier hostile behaviour; so he, for one, did not confess to discerning any underlying vein of passion between the men.[10] To a Freudian, however, it was obvious: 'I do not know whether the author of the play knew our psychological concept of homosexuality', Abraham A. Brill remarked, rather patronisingly, 'but all the essential factors of it were cleverly depicted. The narcism [*sic*] was expressed by making the two men look and dress almost exactly like; they even kiss each other.'[11] This is in Brill's chapter on 'Polymorphous Perversities'.

The third act of *Design for Living* discovers Gilda married to Ernest; Leo and Otto reappear, having travelled the world together; she flees, leaving them in the apartment. Ernest returns home to find Leo and Otto emerging from the bedrooms (or bedroom) in Ernest's pyjamas. They are the third couple discovered by Ernest getting out of bed — the triangle is complete.

Once more, it is not necessary for an audience to imagine that queerness is the unique key to the text − but nor, in such a bohemian milieu, can it be ruled out. After all, Otto and Leo knew each other first, Ernest points out. 'Yes, yes, yes, yes', exclaims Gilda, 'I came along and spoilt everything!' (352). But that says more about Ernest. Attempting to explain the play as a mask for the 'real' feeling between the two men would be a mistake; the queer interest is in the threesome. As Leo sees it, 'It doesn't matter who loves who the most; you can't line up things like that mathematically. We all love each other a lot, far too much. . . . I love you. You love me. You love Otto. I love Otto. Otto loves you. Otto loves me. There now! Start to unravel from there' (360−1). At the end, Leo and Otto demand that Gilda go with them − both of them. She agrees: 'we're all of a piece, the three of us' (462). Ernest swears that he will never understand 'this disgusting three-sided erotic hotch-potch' (463); they abandon him.

Ernest's position is significant. The stage directions introduce him as rather precise in manner. He is said to be distrustful of women and a permanent spectator; he goes 'on a world cruise with a lot of old ladies in straw hats' and this instances how his life is 'sterile' (400−1). He loves the three principals a lot − though Gilda 'a little less than Otto and Leo', she notes, 'because I'm a woman and, therefore, unreliable'. But then, his way of loving is limited anyhow: 'Your affection is a scared thing, though. Too frightened; too apprehensive of consequences' (352-3). Ernest is flustered by the principals' switches of partner:

LEO: Ernest's often in a fluster. It's part of his personality, I think.
OTTO: Ernest hasn't got a personality.
GILDA: Yes, he has; but it's only a very little one, gentle and prim. (366)

He is the fourth character in a scenario where three is company. They are artists whereas he is a dealer − an unimaginative and mercenary parasite. He urges them to live more conventionally, to abandon their bohemian frivolity. His marriage to Gilda is mocked: 'You're a dear old pet, Ernest, and we're very, very fond of you and we know perfectly well that Gilda could be married to you fifty times and still not be your wife' (453). At the end he is made to parrot conventional decencies: 'There isn't a decent instinct among the lot of you. You're shifty and irresponsible and abominable, and I don't wish to set eyes on you again − as long as I live' (463). He storms out, falling over a stack of paintings − a final sign of his difficulty with creativity. As with Malvolio in

Twelfth Night, the character who cannot handle the demand to be heterosexually festive is excluded. In Lahr's view, 'Coward's comic revenge at the
finale is the victory of the disguised gay world over the straight one.'[12] But the
victory of Leo, Otto and Gilda is over the sterile, conventional, effeminate
queer, represented by Ernest.

In fact, a pattern takes shape in these plays, whereby the principals may be
somewhat effeminate, but the really despicable queer is someone else. If Nicky
in *The Vortex* (played by Coward) strikes one as rather queer when compared
with Tom, his character is sheltered from inferences of excessive femininity
through juxtaposition with Pawnie. Harry Benshoff in his study of homosexuality and the horror film calls this 'inoculation': the manifest queer
exonerates the others.[13] So with *Third Person* by Andrew Rosenthal (discussed in
chapter 1): Kip's background is exposed by Felix, who understands and is hostile
to Kip because of his own ancient and unrequited attachment to Hank (Felix's
wife says their marriage is a mockery). Behind the never-quite-audible homosexuals there is a real one – typically covert, treacherous and malicious. So
homosexuality may be redeemed, as Stephen Rooney puts it, by getting
defined against a more unattractive version of itself.[14]

The queerest moment in *Design for Living*, on the other hand, is surprisingly
straightforward. Leo is visited by a reporter, whom he attracts and teases with
charming-infuriating replies to his questions. Suddenly Leo switches mood:
'don't write down any of this interview; come and see me again', and they
arrange to talk on the telephone the next day (387–8). There is no 'good' reason
for any of this: what we are seeing is Leo making an assignation.

In *Present Laughter* (1942) Garry Essendine is a famous and attractive
actor, pestered by admirers whom he tries to shake off. As the play opens
Daphne Stillington, a new acquaintance, emerges from the spare room. Other
casual liaisons are mentioned, and there is talk of men as well. A young man
went to the Slade School because Garry allowed him to think he 'minded so
passionately about his career'; an Indian whom he met in a bar in Marseilles
'was wonderful' (151, 222). There is an admiral's son: Garry 'swore to him that
if he left the Navy [he]'d give him a job on the stage' – 'Absolutely
marvellous, if it's the one I think it is [which other ones were there?], vast
strapping shoulders and tiny, tiny hips like a wasp – .' Old gentlemen in the
city will back Garry in plays, especially if they are not married (224, 244).

The male counterpart of Daphne Stillington is Roland Maule. This 'a bit
wet' young man from Uckfield refuses to be put off; he has been studying

psychology, he tells Garry, 'because I felt somehow that I wasn't at peace with myself and gradually, bit by bit, I began to realise that you signified something to me. . . . I feel much better now because I think I shall be able to sublimate you all right' (206, 174–5). He feels better still on his next visit; 'Couldn't I stay a little longer, you see every moment I'm near him I get smoother and smoother and smoother, and my whole rhythm improves tremendously' (213). Like Garry's other admirers, Roland declares that he is going to accompany him on a tour in Africa, 'To be with you.' Daphne promised not to make demands − 'I don't want you to marry me or anything like that.' Roland also promises no demands − 'You mean you don't expect me to marry you!' Garry quips (231–4). At the close of the play Garry and his entourage take off, leaving Daphne in the office and Roland in the spare room.

Arguably, Roland effects another inoculation, like Pawnie in *The Vortex* and Ernest in *Design for Living*: if Roland seems queer and Garry tries to avoid him, Garry can't be all that queer. There are two ways (at least) of reading such deployments of stereotypical gender-inverted men alongside relatively straight-acting types. In one, they may suggest that however bohemian the main characters might be, the real queers are someone else − trivial people − foolish, effeminate and marginal. In the other, they may suggest that homosexuals don't have to be effeminate. Queer impulses may occur among a range of people, not just the 'obvious' ones. It is hard to regard either of these inferences as progressive. Both imply that the effeminate homosexual is despicable and that the better type of queer might evade stigma by disavowing him.

A Knowing Subculture

So who was picking up all these queer nuances, and what were they making of them? If Coward was a pioneer of gay awareness, how did he get away with it? How far was he really compliant with conventional attitudes?

I have argued that it is a mistake to suppose a unitary audience response. Indeed, the development of little theatres institutionalised a split in audiences. In the wake of the censoring of his play *Young Woodley* in London in 1925, John van Druten proposed an extension of this principle − dividing theatre into two: one 'subject to censorship, where the audience would be thereby insured against having either their sensibilities shocked or their intellects assailed, and another where, free from censorship, they entered at their peril'.[15] Maugham opposed this idea. In an essay published with the second volume of his collected plays in 1931, he insists that drama 'must address itself equally to the working man in the gallery and to the gilded youth in the stalls. It must interest the stock-jobber who reads nothing but the *Financial Times* and the elderly spinster whose soul is sweet with memories of Italy and Greece.'[16]

James Agate complained in the *Sunday Times* that Coward was writing only for sophisticated people. *The Vortex*, he said, 'has a certain quality of heroic excitement which may make the galled Society jade wince, but will not wring the withers of the man in the street'.[17] Yet the play was successful. Reviewing *Hay Fever* in 1925, Agate again tried to specify an audience for Coward, while admitting his popularity: such plays 'appeal to an infinitesimally small and, I believe, purely Metropolitan audience. Their success is one almost entirely of curiosity, even of a more or less prurient itch from which the country as a whole is free.' The resistant audience seems to have retreated to the provinces; Agate adds: 'All the provincial managers are crying out against the "sex-play"' (242).

In fact, Coward had found another way. His project was to comprise both audiences in the one text, on the one theatrical occasion. Even while attracting the respectable, middlebrow playgoer, he managed to construct a *knowing subculture* of privileged insiders. He addresses two simultaneous audiences — the uninitiated and those in the know.

In a preface to *Private Lives* Coward attributes the play's success to naive enthusiasm:

> It was described in the papers variously, as being, 'tenuous', 'thin', 'brittle', 'gossamer', 'iridescent', and 'delightfully daring'. All of which connoted, to the public mind, 'cocktails', 'evening dress', 'repartee', and irreverent allusions to copulation, thereby causing a gratifying number of respectable people to queue up at the box office. (*Private Lives*, xiii)

Coward relishes the naivety of such 'respectable people'. In their curiosity they pay for the production, but they don't fully understand what is going on. And their exclusion — which was both a necessary defensive manoeuvre and part of the joke — effects an inclusion of the knowing.

In New York, Chauncey reports, Coward's audiences were composed partly of gay men; whether others knew it or not, '*they* were aware of their numbers in the audience and often shared in the collective excitement of transforming such a public gathering into a "gay space", no matter how covertly'. Oral history respondents specify Coward as 'the Mount Everest of double entendre'.[18] That audience was there for other plays too. A reviewer of a performance of Mae West's *The Drag* in New Jersey in 1928 remarked that 'the audience seemed to have been divided into two groups – those who fully understood the subject under discussion and those to whom the whole theme was a puzzle'. And *The Captive* by Édouard Bourdet (see chapter 7) was reported in 1926 as attracting a large proportion of gay men and women. But those plays were too explicit and got closed down.[19]

Coward's knowing plays helped to establish a milieu in which many lesbian and gay people could live with some protection and yet also with the validation of a certain public presence. For those who wanted to hear it, he contributed specifically to gay subcultural formation. As Andy Medhurst puts it, Coward's work 'can be productively mined for half-hidden endorsements of sexual options that strayed beyond the expected confines of domesticated hetero-sexual monogamy'. He 'shared and contributed to making the male homosexual structure of feeling'.[20] Although discretion and censorship were plainly techniques of control tending to produce subjectivities agreeable to the dominant order, they could not but facilitate the formation of a coherent subculture – one actually fortified, in some respects, by exclusion.

The key to Coward's triumph, and to his limitations, is his negotiation with effeminacy. The ambiguity, whereby both dandified leisure-class manners and the post-Wildean idea of the queer man were perceived as effeminate, facilitated both boldness and evasion, enabling Coward to express queerness while hardly exceeding the bounds of gentlemanly decorum. He could flirt with sexual dissidence while trying not to let it take decisive hold of public perceptions. This strategy was not without risk. Hoare summarises: 'In affecting anything other than the normal mode of masculine dress, Noël was opening himself to criticism. Those who knew about such matters whispered about his sexuality; those who did not, excused it as the garb of theatrical folk, who were "different". To the homosexual enclave within the theatre (and without), Noël became an icon.'[21] More exactly, he represented a certain kind of leisured discretion – which had the privilege of exuberance but, for most gays, could only be a metaphor for the kind of life they might aspire to live.

Ironically, Coward persistently overestimated the extent to which he was passing for straight. As he toured war-torn Britain with *This Happy Breed* (1942) he went on stage reeking of Chanel No.5 and 'kept up the appearance of a sybarite', and then expected Winston Churchill to place him in a high-powered intelligence and public relations role in the USA. Joyce Grenfell for one thought it was all very well for a playwright, but regrettable 'that the man who represents his country at a time like this should be famous as a "queer"'.[22]

Effeminacy worked less well for Coward in the United States. There too, it might mean class – the (perceived) effete, East-Coast, European-identified gentry – but that formation retained considerably less respect than the English leisure class at that time; it was seen as barely compatible with central 'American' values to do with pioneer masculinity. *Esquire* in 1945 thought it was a time for their reinforcement. An article entitled 'Farewell, Noël Coward' declared: 'we haven't time to toy with the less healthy facets of our emotions . . . . Where is the man? Your brilliance strikes us as a little tawdry. Like sequins in the morning sunlight. . . . There are crises that cannot be met in a silk dressing gown'.[23]

Coward's theatre emerges as more various, negotiable and appropriable than might have been supposed, but still it is doubtful how far it challenged wider audiences. Same-sex passion might emerge through the veil of discretion into misty visibility as the alternative that must, for a conventional West End audience, be held at the boundary of thought. But the trouble is, people generally are titillated, up to a point, by ideas and attitudes that they find improper; beyond that point, they repudiate them. Indeed, one of the most exciting quests in cultural analysis is for the instance of strategic textual deployment that might plausibly disconcert those actually likely to encounter it. In my view Coward hardly tried to catch the unwary. There are moments when the innocent reader may be enticed by the logic of character, action and dialogue into collusion with an unaccustomed awareness and even endorsement of sexual dissidence, but they are not sustained.

The price of infiltrating the system at one point may have been retrenchment at another. But finally it suited Coward to hold homosexuality poised at the brink of public visibility. Men like him benefited from the deferential inter-war social climate, in which leisure-class homosexuals were generally allowed to strain conventional taboos so long as they maintained a degree of discretion. While the hearties controlled the economic, political and coercive institutions, upper-class bohemians and aesthetes might play fairly safely at being bright young people. They might even criticise patriarchy, heterosexuality and the family – from within a theatrical institution that was hardly likely to offer a base for mass disaffection. After 1945 these conditions no longer pertained, and Coward appeared out of step and conservative.

Leisure-class male homosexuals contributed little to the movement towards law reform and gay liberation.[24]

Coward, meanwhile, saw no contradiction between his queerness and his patriotism; indeed, the two gelled perfectly in his esteem for service personnel. Walking through Leicester Square in 1952 he saw a banner for a heroic film starring Dirk Bogarde and Michael Redgrave: *The Sea Shall Not Have Them*. 'I don't see why not', cried Coward; 'everyone else has'.[25]

Gay's the Word

Commentators wishing to assert the effectiveness of our presence through history often claim that 'gay' has really always meant us. However, the fact that the word was used to mean a female prostitute in Victorian times (in London at least) is in my view not relevant. I think it is now clear that 'gay' acquired a gay meaning between World War I and World War II in the United States and was largely imported to Britain from there. Further, since we are talking about language change, and specially since we are talking about an out-group, it is imperative to consider who knows the new word or the new meaning. We are looking at a gradual infiltration, in which gay starts as the in-word of a leisured and artistic group (Coward specifically); is gradually extended through that subculture; and then on into queers generally; and eventually − in the face of some protest − into the straight world.

George Chauncey in *Gay New York*, focusing on the period of Prohibition (1920–33), argues that the main distinction initially was between being 'manly' and being 'a fairy' − more to do with gendering than sexual orientation. That arrangement is very often found, historically and geograph-ically. Then men who began to identify *as homosexuals* started to call themselves 'queer', while 'fairy' was used for the men who identified by gender attributes; many queers asserted their dislike for fairies. The queers then instated 'gay', which began to catch on in the 1930s, often as a code word. However, it was taken up by the flamboyant fairies, and came to refer to all kinds of people involved in same-sex practices. Thus the mode of categori-sation had shifted from one based on gender (fairies versus men) to one based on sexuality (gays versus straights). The primacy of 'gay' was consolidated during the war.[26] I return to some of these arguments in chapter 6.

Evidence from other commentators broadly confirms this account. Ronald A. Butters doubts that 'gay' appeared in North America before 1935, since it is absent from a collection of graffiti published in that year.[27] However, I think it was already current in leisured and artistic circles, though it may not have reached people whose opportunity for literary expression was confined to graffiti. John Boswell notes that the first public use of 'gay' in the United States 'outside of pornographic fiction appears to have been in the 1939 movie *Bringing up Baby*, when Cary Grant, wearing a dress, exclaimed that he had "gone gay"'.[28]

Donald Webster Cory attested to this gradual and uneven process in his groundbreaking book, *The Homosexual in America*, back in 1951. He says psychoanalysts have told him that patients were calling themselves 'gay' in the 1920s; note the class indicator there – only upper-class people had analysts.

> By the nineteen-thirties it was the most common word in use among homosexuals themselves. It was not until after Pearl Harbor that it became a magic by-word in practically every corner of the United States where homosexuals might gather, and in the decade following America's entry into the Second World War I find that it was used with increasing frequency not only by novelists, magazine writers, and gossip columnists, but even by radio announcers. And yet, even to this day, despite its decades (if not centuries) of use, it is practically unknown outside of homosexual circles, except for police officers, theatrical groups, and a few others.[29]

Cory adds that lesbians are beginning to use 'gay', and that the antonym is 'straight'.

Coward was at home in leisure-class/theatrical circles in New York; Hoare says he moved straight into a queer-bohemian set there in 1921.[30] I believe he picked up the US code word and brought it back to Britain, where its initial use in the 1930s was among leisured, artistic and theatre people. 'Gay' appears in the journal of the honourable Stephen Tennant in 1936.[31] Curtin writes, of New York:

> The adjective 'gay', ironically enough, was used in almost every review to describe Noël Coward's *Design for Living*. In 1933 the word still meant, to most people, an open lightness of heart and mood. In that sense, the play was unmistakenly gay; yet it seemed to a number of theatregoers to be 'gay' in the sense the word was being used in that decade by some American lesbians and gay men, especially in theatrical circles.[32]

Such half-knowledge was marvellously suited to Coward's purposes. 'Gay' was already collocated with Bright Young People and they were already effeminate.

By tilting it just a little he was able to foreground the trace of irregular sexuality. The Bright Young People who give their name to a Coward song in *Cochran's 1931 Revue* proclaim a stereotypical swathe of trivial and effeminate traits, and declare themselves 'Gay to the utmost degree'.[33] As I have said, 'Mad About the Boy' (1932) features ostensibly heterosexual adulation, but the final refrain evokes something more:

> He has a gay appeal
> That makes me feel
> There's maybe something sad about the boy.

The song appeared in Coward's *Words and Music* (139); elsewhere in this revue 'gay' appears ten times with a less specialised significance. We have both queer and gay in Coward's song, 'I've Been to a Marvellous Party' (from *Set to Music*, 1938):

> Everyone's here and frightfully gay,
> Nobody cares what people say,
> Though the Riviera
> Seems really much queerer
> Than Rome at its height.[34]

In *Design for Living* 'gay' is readable in more or less the general sense, but even there Coward seems to be stretching its connotations — almost playing on the fact that there is *not*, at that point, an entirely reliable homosexual implication:

LEO: A strange evening. Very gay, if I remember rightly.
GILDA: Oh, it was gay, deliriously gay. (365)

On that evening, it is explained, Gilda chose Otto in preference to Leo, the men fought, Otto fell in the bath and Leo turned the water on him. Again:

OTTO: A gay, ironic chance threw the three of us together and tied our lives into a tight knot at the outset. (405)

This is apropos of how Gilda has preferred Otto and Leo alternately. Once more in this play:

ERNEST: You seem very gay this morning.

GILDA: I'm always gay on Sundays. There's something intoxicating about Sunday in London. (409)

Actually Gilda is exhilarated because she has decided to free herself emotionally from Leo and Otto. These instances perhaps flirt with, without confirming, a queer meaning for 'gay'. They point towards where its boundary might be.

The complex hesitation around the word 'gay' in Coward's work is of a piece with other factors we have observed. It enabled him to promote gayness into public discourse under the cover of a more general context; at the same time, it enabled him to disavow gayness by submerging it in Bright Young People. But his main contribution was quite specific. He found homosexuality embedded in, perhaps trying to emerge from, a more general concept of bohemian-leisured exuberance, and elaborated that formation and its language in a way that strengthened the potential for a discreet queer identification.

If Coward anticipated the arrival of 'gay' in Britain and contributed certain inflections, it is pretty clear that its wider dissemination occurred through GIs during World War II. In January 1947 Kenneth Williams, performing for the armed forces in Singapore, juxtaposes two meanings in his diary: 'Went round to the gay bar which wasn't in the least gay and saw K. and Co.'[35] But his usage is unclear on New Year's Eve at the end of that year: 'we all joined Mum and Dad at Henekey's, very gay party. Continued afterwards here at 57 doing the hokey-cokey and all that' (18). And how are 'queer' and 'gay' demarcated in this entry of 1950? 'Saw queer drag show at the Royal. It was gay. Laugh. Met them all after, at our digs. They're charming' (51–2)?

In his unprecedentedly candid book *Against the Law*, published in 1955, Peter Wildeblood wrote, of Oxford after the war: 'I met a man with whom I had been at school. He had been a naval officer, with some staff appointment in Ceylon. He said that most of the officers at the station had been "gay", and looked at me as though this was some password to which he expected me to reply. I had not heard the word before, but apparently it was an American euphemism for homosexual.'[36] However *The Heart in Exile*, a novel by Rodney Garland published in 1953, which attempts, among other things, to display the scope of queer subculture in the 1950s, never uses 'gay' to mean homosexual. Colin Spencer in *Which of Us Two?*, commenting on a letter written in 1957, remarks that he used the phrase 'gay bar'.[37]

D.J. West in his study *Homosexuality* (1955) observed: 'A newcomer puts on just the shadow of a meaning look, remarks with just a tinge of the accepted inflexion, "Isn't it gay in here?" and, if he is a presentable young man, he is lonely no more [would it were so easy!]. An uninformed bystander would notice nothing untoward.' In 1960 Gordon Westwood reported 'gay' as American but known in Britain.[38] By 1964 it was being publicised in the Evening Standard: '"Gay" is what they prefer to call themselves. . . . the present use is largely American, but has caught on here.'[39] Several of the elderly informants in *Between the Acts*, oral histories from the late 1970s, express discomfort with 'gay' as a newish term, and two of them register it as 'American'.[40] In the collection *Walking After Midnight* John Alcock recalls a friend returning from the USA during the War and telling him that Americans said 'gay', not 'queer'. However, Bernard Dobson believes he didn't become acquainted with 'gay' until he joined the Gay Liberation Front in 1970.[41] And Andy Warhol says that when he met the Duchess of Windsor, presumably in the 1960s, and other socialites they 'said "gay" every other adjective and never once meant homosexual'.[42]

After all these indeterminacies, the word we selected to collocate with 'liberation' was 'gay', and its use still annoys reactionaries. Coward's strategic deployment of 'gay' protected his privacy but, in that very process, helped to edge the word towards public recognition. Like camp style generally, it came to signify not secrecy, but acknowledgement of the demand for secrecy and ironic refusal of it; and so became available for a new, more defiant phase of gay culture.

6

Gay Men and Gender

Bachelors

The exposure and conviction of Wilde contributed crucially to the establish-ment of the dominant twentieth-century metropolitan idea of the queer man, I argued in Chapter 2. Even so, effeminacy, aestheticism and a dandified manner did not correlate inevitably with queerness, and the bachelor remained a broadly plausible figure. In plays he is marginal, spending time with women, involved in gossip, useful as a commentator and facilitator because he isn't involved in the heterosexual pairing-off which is usually the central theme. People did not think, until quite recently, that anyone who wasn't manifesting some kind of heterosexual enthusiasm must be queer. An element of stigma did attach to fussy bachelors, mannish spinsters, sissy-boys and tomboys − violators of gender hierarchy. But it was not, necessarily, a cloak for awareness of same-sex practice.

Yet, even for the innocent or the resistant, the dim anxiety that there might be more to all this than meets the eye was sometimes inescapable. The author Beverley Nichols, as a boy in his teens during World War I, was taken up by an effeminate aesthete who lived nearby. Edwards and Beverley had sexual relations, but Mr Nichols (a businessman) managed to regard Edwards as a hell of a fellow with the ladies. However, Edwards gave young Beverley a copy of *The Picture of Dorian Gray*, and his father found him reading it. Instantly, Mr Nichols went frantic: he called Beverley a '"pretty little boy", enunciating the word "pretty" in a shrill parody of a homosexual voice as he hit him across the face. Then he spat on the book and tore the pages with his teeth. "Oscar Wilde! To think that my son. . . ."'[1] The real-life Edwards could still be perceived as a leisure-class philanderer, but he was transformed into a homosexual when the name of Wilde was uttered.

This indeterminacy led to a cat-and-mouse game in representations of the bachelor: he might or might not be queer — an audience is challenged, as it were, to acknowledge the possibility of sexual dissidence. Somerset Maugham flirts with this faultline more boldly than we might expect. Blenkinsop in _Mrs Dot_ (1908) has a silly name and is a bachelor of forty-five years. Lady Sellinger says she disapproves: 'you're a cynic, a millionaire, and a bachelor. And no man has the right to be all three.'[2] When Mrs Dot wonders why Blenkinsop never married, he says he has cultivated small talk, such that whenever the topic arises he is able to head it off (Ia, 128—9). Such epigrammatic evasions are of course Wildean, and grounds for suspicion in themselves. Blenkinsop has an unusually long speech attacking women for being tough and determined rather than 'the gentle sex' they are supposed to be (Ia, 145—6). So he doesn't like them because they aren't feminine enough for him!

Blenkinsop even has a sidekick — young Freddie — though there is no apparent emotional commitment between them. In the course of reviewing Freddie's qualities, Mrs Dot asks Blenkinsop whether anyone could fall in love with such a person: 'If you were a young and lovely maiden would you fall in love with Freddie?' His reply is bland but ambivalent: 'Well, if you ask me point blank I don't think I should' — if he were a maiden, that is (Ia, 130). The plot requires Blenkinsop to pretend to make love to Mrs Dot — which he does with alternate reluctance and enthusiasm, such that neither she nor the audience can be sure whether he means it. 'You're not a marrying man', she deduces (Ia, 163).

Jack Straw (1908) also has a bachelor figure, Ambrose Holland. He is 'a well-dressed, elegant man of five-and-thirty', and he opens the play on a distinctly queer note. He wants to choose a retired corner of the restaurant so he and Lady Wanley 'can gossip in peace'. She prefers a table where she will be seen; but the other side will be better, Holland says — 'The waiter's rather a pal of mine.' 'What queer friends you have', Lady Wanley opines (Ia, 189). Together, they organise the main action: in order to punish some snooty parvenus, they persuade a waiter to impersonate a Pomeranian arch-duke. Holland's relations with women and marital status are not discussed at all, and he has no particular same-sex commitments either. Compare the rake, Lord Serlo, who has been 'mixed up in one or two scandals' (Ia, 223); he 'spends all his time with stable boys and barmaids' (Ia, 240). If he's manly enough, he can do as he wants.

Charles Marsden, a novelist and a bachelor in Eugene O'Neill's *Strange Interlude* (1927), is another uncertain figure:

> His appearance is that of an Anglicized New England gentleman. . . . There is an indefinable feminine quality about him, but it is nothing apparent in either appearance or act. His manner is cool and poised. He speaks with a careful ease as one who listens to his own conversation. He has long fragile hands, and the stooping shoulders of a man weak muscularly, who has never liked athletics and has always been regarded as of a delicate constitution. (12)

Marsden is excessively attached to his mother, and regards sex with extreme distaste: 'to the devil with sex! . . . our impotent pose of to-day to beat the loud drum on fornication! . . . boasters . . . eunuchs parading with the phallus!' (14, O'Neill's pauses). Nina calls him a 'fussy old woman' and 'you slacker bachelor' (88, 91). In the view of Ned Darrell, a doctor, Marsden's novels have talent but lack depth: 'afraid he'll meet himself somewhere . . . one of those poor devils who spend their lives trying not to discover which sex they belong to!' (62, O'Neill's pauses).

Commentators complain, first, that Marsden is stereotyped as a homosexual and, second, that he is not even credited with sexual feelings for men. And that is despite seeming to be named after two of O'Neill's friends, the Greenwich Village painters Charles Demuth and Marsden Hartley, whom we now think of as queer. So disappointing is Marsden as a putative gay man that Jonathan Weinberg, quoting also work by Robert McAlmon and F. Scott Fitzgerald, says we must 'question the clichéd view of the avant-garde as a free space in which sexual experimentation and difference were accepted and even encouraged'.[3] Curtin complains that Marsden's timidity absolved critics, in 1963 and 1985 as well as initially, from having to notice gayness.[4] However, it is not necessarily appropriate to regard Marsden as 'really' queer. The question falls distinctively in *Strange Interlude* because, throughout, O'Neill has the characters speak their inner thoughts in broken soliloquy in alternation with the dialogue. Marsden, in his thoughts, displays absolutely no sexual interest in any of the men in the play; to the contrary, he tends to see them as rivals for the love of Nina — a love which he repeatedly states to himself, but which appears futile because of his unease with sex and his unattractiveness. Perhaps Marsden should be regarded not as a closeted gay, but as a heterosexual who lacks confidence with women. Not every disturbed person has to be claimed as one of us.

The main concern of *Strange Interlude* is Nina's attempts to reach satisfaction as a woman. In this scheme, Marsden's 'femininity' has a place, as part of her coming to terms with a principle of maleness which she refers to often as 'God the Father'. Initially Nina cannot contemplate Marsden as a lover: 'Pah! . . . how limp his hands are! . . . his eyes are so shrinking! . . . is it possible he loves me? . . . like that? . . . what a sickening idea! . . . it seems incestuous somehow! . . . no, it's too absurd! . . .' (204, O'Neill's pauses). But she relies on him as father-figure all the way through and at the end, exhausted by emotional complications and beyond a point where she feels it important to be sexually attractive, she and Marsden come together. It is possible to regard this final convergence either as a proper phase of rest and quiet in life, or as a defeat and a regression. Either way, homosexuality isn't the point.

Of course, this is an entirely legitimate angle for O'Neill to take. Yet, together with the relaxed attitude towards the sensitive boy in *Ah, Wilderness!* (1933; see chapter 4), it does stamp him as markedly disinclined to notice queer possibilities. By the time of *The Iceman Cometh* (1946), I argue below, sexual dissidence was more readily signalled and apprehended. So something is perhaps to be gleaned there in Jimmy Tomorrow, who has the manners of a gentleman and 'a quality about him of a prim, Victorian maid, and at the same time of a likable, affectionate boy who has never grown up' (6). Jimmy eventually discloses that his wife left him because he took no interest in her. He preferred drinking all night with his pals to being in bed with her. He can't recall why he married – can't remember whether she was pretty; perhaps he wanted a home. This sketch is not developed. The more significant male-to-male engagement, between Parritt and Larry, is organised homosocially, around their conjuncture as son and ex-lover of the same woman.

A prime reason for an enhanced awareness of queerness in theatre was Mordaunt Shairp's *The Green Bay Tree* (1933), a success in the West End and on Broadway. The play is about a leisured and exquisitely cultivated man, Dulcimer, and his adoptive son Julian: the latter is tempted away from marriage with the earnest Leonora (Leo for short) by luxury and idleness. Finally the biological lower-class father shoots dead the sterile father-figure; but Julian remains trapped and ends up replicating the initial behaviour of his patron. Dulcimer is called 'Dulcie', and has the affectation, amoral wit and concern with style and décor that mark the Wildean stereotype. When the play opens he is talking to his manservant and decides to arrange the flowers – echoing the discussion about Lord Goring's buttonhole in *The Ideal Husband*.

However, there is a problem: 'I'm terribly overdressed for doing flowers'; so he considers allowing the servant to arrange them. But there are tulips — 'I don't think I could trust you with a tulip.' Dulcimer puts on gloves and an apron, and does the flowers himself. When he has finished he demands: 'When on earth are you going to take all this [table of flowers] away? I look like a wayside shrine!' He wants to leave London because the road outside is going to be dug up: 'I refuse to stay here with the Square full of men frying bacon in tarpaulin huts' (56–9). If this camp insouciance seems charming, and I don't see why it should not, Dulcimer is soon revealed as cynically manipulative. He is determined to manoeuvre Julian out of the affair with Leo; 'he is to me youth and charm and companionship', he declares, in Wildean vein (93).

Yet *The Green Bay Tree* says almost nothing about genital sexuality. In Richard Findlater's view, it is so discreet that 'the audience might imagine that the moral corruption exercised by the central figure over the younger man was one only of cynical materialism and not sexual love'.[5] George Street, the Lord Chamberlain's examiner, supported a licence because he believed there is 'no suggestion of physical homosexuality'; to him, critics who thought otherwise were 'influenced by a desire to appear knowing or by the unfortunate fact that homosexuality is in the air very much at present or at least in the theatrical air'.[6] However, that way of putting it does indicate the likelihood of a 'knowing' audience. In just the manner I argued in respect of some of Coward's plays, Street recognises two groups: those already in the know cannot be helped; others may be safe so long as the play is sufficiently oblique.

Actually, as Jed Harris, New York producer of *The Green Bay Tree* observed, 'the suspicion had to be there. That's the only way you can explain what was going on.'[7] That seems right when Julian says he has had a marvellous afternoon and Dulcimer supposes that he has been enjoying the 'sweaty transports' of the Westminster Baths (57). Or when Leonora exclaims: 'I wonder how much you really care about him? I hope I shan't meet you one day in Piccadilly with a painted face, just because you must have linen sheets!' 'Haven't you any conscience at all about keeping him from what is normal and healthy?' she demands of Dulcimer (92–3). The negative alternatives behind this sentence — immoral, abnormal, unhealthy — add up, virtually, to queerness. Only this might seem to justify an imputation of evil: 'You fascinate me', she says, 'like a snake fascinates' (82). The title is a biblical quotation, offered by Julian's Bible-bashing father: 'I myself have seen the wicked in great power and spreading himself like a green bay tree' (76). Lady Violet

Bonham Carter remarked that 'many of those who saw "The Green Bay Tree" . . . regarded the situation it depicted as frankly homosexual'.[8]

The Green Bay Tree is the point at which the queer gent breaks his cover as an eccentric bachelor, as many reviewers recognised. 'Centuries back the Greeks had a word for it', one wrote; 'it is somewhat difficult at times to discover what *is* at the bottom of Mr Mordaunt Shairp's garden', said another, wishing he 'had not hesitated to call a spade a spade'. But they were generally appeased by the play's urgent hostility towards Dulcimer — the *New English Weekly* complained of his 'exaggeratedly mincing deportment and his ugly caressing of chairs'.[9] 'For American audiences', John Clum says, *The Green Bay Tree* 'established the stereotypical picture of the homosexual as wealthy, effete — and British'.[10]

Worrying About Effeminacy

As US commentators have shown, even drag queens might pass if they were positioned as skilled professional performers. In Mae West's play *The Pleasure Man* (1928) it seems plain that we are in queer company. The camp chat among the drag artistes is perfectly recognisable today:

FIRST BOY: I hear you're studying to be an opera singer.
THIRD BOY: Oh, Yes, and I knows so many songs.
FIRST BOY: You must have a large repertoire.
THIRD BOY: Must I have that too?
FOURTH BOY: Oh, look, I can almost do the split.
SECOND BOY: Be careful, dearie, you'll wear out your welcome. (191)

Nonetheless, there is an interesting exchange during the trial over the banning of the play in New York. The defence lawyer avers that 'there is nothing indecent in female impersonations on the stage'. No, not necessarily, the prosecutor agrees, 'but it is possible to have an obscene, lascivious performance under cover of a female impersonation'.[11] And the evidence in this case is that the artistes in the play wore the clothes and used 'the mannerisms of women' even when they were not performing on stage: 'They were not portraying female impersonators, but depicting degenerates or fairies at a fairies' party, given by a man who depicts a fairy type.'[12]

Marybeth Hamilton, taking up this point, finds that there was a 'legitimate' tradition of non-queer female impersonation in the USA, in which the magic of the transformation was regarded as supplying fairly wholesome amusement for a general public. The artistes might still be regarded with suspicion, but only sometimes with homophobic hostility. Several describe their families as supportive; sexuality just wasn't talked about. That legitimate tradition functioned *alongside* an underground, queer tradition which catered to emerging gay communities in the cities.[13] *The Pleasure Man* was defended as showing the one, but actually, the prosecutor said, revealed the other. Laurence Senelick and Sharon R. Ullman disclose a compatible story in the careers of female impersonators, specially Julian Eltinge, from the turn of the century through the 1920s. Eltinge's celebrity was at the price of tireless promotion of an image of him, off-stage, as virile to the point of pugilism.[14]

During World War II, Allan Bérubé says, the legitimate tradition of female impersonation was just about surviving a popular realisation that it might be seriously queer. Most soldiers watched the illusionists with awe — if they were sexy, ostensibly at least, it was because they looked like women. And there were humorous acts — husky men looking silly in women's clothes. At the same time, a gay spectator might turn on to the scenarios where men sing love songs to each other, and to the potential for *double entendre*, intended or not. 'The joke was on the unaware members of the audience — a subplot about homosexuality was being created right before their eyes and they didn't even know it.'[15] The tension between the two readings, the two audiences, was handled through camp, Bérubé adds, brilliantly. But a careful balance was necessary:

> whenever drag performances became explicitly homosexual and undermined the audience's heterosexual assumptions — when performers impersonated queers or seemed queer themselves — then spectators sometimes became offended and hostile, reviewers attacked the show directly as obscene, authorities closed the show and arrested the actors, and, in the military, discharged the soldier-performers as homosexuals.

As in plays by Coward, it was possible to insinuate gay interests alongside the mainstream, though at a risk and at a cost in secrecy and hence shame.

Drag flourished in British entertainments units as well; after all, women were not available. Peter Nichols evokes that scene in his play *Privates on Parade* (1977, Royal Shakespeare Company), set in Singapore in 1948. Despite official incomprehension and homophobia, gay men exploit the opportunity for flagrant camping and steady liaisons.

The Cold War climate of the 1950s did not immediately freeze out drag. In *An Evening at the Garden of Allah* Don Paulson publishes pictures and oral histories of a cabaret bar, which flourished in Seattle between 1946 and 1956. The clientele were both lesbians and gay men, almost all from lower classes; most of the performances were by local artistes, men dressed as women; they were virtually all white. Alongside this subcultural project, in which effeminacy equated with queerness, the Garden of Allah also featured the Jewel Box Revue, a professional touring company formed in 1939 to revive female impersonation. As Paulson suggests, this 'could be viewed as an early gay organization – gays, lesbians, bisexuals, and transgenders in financial, artistic, and social partnership'. However, 'while gays came to see the show, it was not geared for them. It was the straight audiences that supported the *Revue*.'[16] In the 1950s, still, drag allowed alternative interpretations.[17]

In *Gay New York* George Chauncey illuminates changes in queer self-perceptions in the first half of the twentieth century. He finds that until the 1930s men were not divided into 'homosexuals' and 'heterosexuals': this was not the primary axis of identification. A man displaying a committed feminine manner got called a fairy, but 'the "man" who responded to his solicitations – no matter how often – was not considered abnormal, a "homosexual", so long as he abided by the masculine gender conventions'.[18] In the middle class, initially, men who identified by sexuality started to call themselves 'queer', as opposed to the fairies who identified by gender attributes; the idea was to assert that you could be queer without being a fairy. However, especially through the ensuing adoption of 'gay', it came to be assumed that everyone involved in same-sex practices belongs ultimately together: they are all gay. And this has remained the dominant assumption. Yet a hierarchy persists, embarrassingly for many men, between 'masculine' = 'active' and 'feminine' = 'passive' gay men – corresponding, of course, to the hierarchy of men and women in our societies.

Chauncey's account is perhaps too schematic. Even the 'masculine' queers, he himself observes, 'were profoundly shaped by the cultural presumption that sexual desire for men was inherently a feminine desire'.[19] And the older pattern persisted, perhaps residually, way beyond the 1930s. During World War II in the USA, Donald Webster Cory reports, a sailor was able to assume that 'the stranger who performed fellatio' was 'homosexual', but not 'the man on whom it was performed'. 'The performer was a "fairy". The compliant sailor, not.'[20] In the revised edition of Gore Vidal's novel *The City and the Pillar* (1965), Jim Willard still worries about the relation between himself and mincing queens; he would sometimes 'study himself in a mirror to see if there was any trace of the woman in his face or manner; he was pleased always that there was not'.[21] Todd Butler makes an interesting distinction in a oral history of New York in 1960: 'It was unusual for somebody to be fully "out" and leading a gay lifestyle to be that butch. Usually, if you met somebody who was gay and butch, they were very uptight, closety types and very, very neurotic.'[22]

In England, certainly, the situation was confused. But there was a change: the spread of the idea of *the homosexual* led men who did not see themselves as fairies or pansies to recognise that they might be queer nonetheless. T.C. Worsley asks: 'How was I to tell? Homo, I certainly did seem to be. Sexual I certainly wasn't. The word, in any case, was not in general use, as it is now. Then it was still a technical term, the implications of which I was not entirely aware of; it implied, if anything, "cissiness". Cissy I certainly wasn't. Wasn't I on the contrary if not a tough, at least a masculine athlete?'[23] I noted in chapter 4 how men such as J.R. Ackerley would have liked to repudiate the fairies but, because gender inversion was intrinsic to 'homosexuality' as it had been constructed, this proved difficult. Mostly they ended up simultaneously adopting some effeminate manners while insisting that they were not really like that. Robin Maugham, according to Bryan Connon,

> could never relax in the company of effeminate men in public unless he was too drunk to care. Like Willie [Somerset Maugham] he did not understand why some homosexual men felt compelled to behave flamboyantly to challenge total strangers with their brand of sexuality. Camping about with friends in private was a different matter, though he never felt entirely at ease with this, but to be anything other than masculine in public was a betrayal of the male ethos.[24]

There was a countervailing discourse, drawing upon Walt Whitman, Edward Carpenter and 'uranian' writers, which asserted male same-sex practice as quintessentially manly.[25] However, this seems not to have had much purchase, and was unlikely to get onto the public stage.

Instability in the queer repudiation of effeminacy is exposed in Michael Hill's banned play *Tragedy in Jermyn Street* (1934). Terry has just become engaged to Janet, but runs into Marlowe — who ten years ago was expelled from school because of his affair with Terry. Marlowe is of a domineering and brooding temperament, and persuades the highly strung and hysterical Terry that he can never be happily married; indeed that they must go away together,

though they bicker continually. Terry has difficulty explaining his condition
to his fiancée: 'You know, Janet, some men and women are not quite normal.
They never have been normal, even when they were children.' They don't like
women. 'I know', Janet puts in, 'great big hearty creatures, who love to be
called a man's man. They drink beer and swear a lot, don't they?'

TERRY: I don't mean that. On the contrary, I'm talking about those men who
    have definite feminine traits in their psychological make-up.
JANET: Do you mean Nancy boys?
TERRY: No, I don't, and please don't use that revolting expression.
JANET: I'm sorry, but most people use it nowadays.
TERRY: Most people are very stupid. (*With a supreme effort.*) I'm like that.
JANET: Like what?
TERRY: Queer. (68)

Once Terry has accepted the 'feminine traits' theory, it is not easy for him to
separate himself from 'Nancy boys'. When he says, 'I'm like that', it sounds as
if he means he is like them; 'Like what?' Janet asks. 'Queer' doesn't resolve it.
And what about Marlowe? He seems over-emphatic in his 'masculine' manner:
'The time will come when people will be forced to realize that to be "queer",
is not of necessity to be vicious and that every "queer" person does not
necessarily dye his hair and decorate his face with filthy cosmetics.' After all,
'you and I know, that some of the greatest artists both contemporary and for
hundreds of years past have been "queer"'. But is art so masculine and healthy?
Even these creative people, according to Marlowe, have been 'mental
hunchbacks' (60–1).

It might be thought that Alexander the Great, at least, was a real man —
even if he was queer. In Terence Rattigan's *Adventure Story* (1949) Alexander
neither seeks nor gains heterosexual love. His most positive relationship is with
Hephaestion; perhaps the theatregoer recalls Christopher Marlowe's *Edward II*,
where the King's love for Gaveston is explained thus: 'The mightiest kings have
had their minions: / Great Alexander lov'd Hephaestion' (I.iv.390–1). Before
a big battle Alexander calls for his company during the night, asking 'I wonder
how many hours of sleep I must have robbed you of in your life, Hephaestion?'
The reply is, 'If you're awake, why should I want to sleep?' (47).

It becomes apparent that Alexander is conquering the world in order to repel
the accusations of his father, Philip of Macedon: 'Look down at me now and
sneer. Say — "See what a weak effeminate coward I have for a son"' (149). For

a proposed New York production, Rattigan strengthened this motif by inscrting a scene with Philip at the start, in which he attacks Alexander as 'an effeminate weakling, a mother's darling of doubtful paternity, so little fitted to be king that at twenty he hasn't even shown that he possesses the instinct of a man'.[26] However, Alexander's efforts lead him not into secure manliness but into despotism and 'barbaric' Persian customs. His most erratic violence occurs at the end of the play, in response to the accusation that 'Philip, at least, was a man' (190).

Men Together

Same-sex communities are often thought to promote homosexuality; we saw instances in schools and the army in chapter 4. Jeffrey Weeks terms this 'situational', remarking that it may hardly conflict with a straight self-identification.[27] Nonetheless, such is the dominance of gendering in our cultures, that within an all-male context some men are labelled masculine and others feminine, and the latter are perceived as the real queers. *Little Ol' Boy* (1933) by Albert Bein is set in a reform school. Lockett is anxious and bullied; the warden's wife tries to protect him. His life becomes more dangerous when he hero-worships the tough and experienced Barry, though Barry attempts to train him in masculine ways of looking after himself. The relationship becomes more intense as it becomes more threatened; Lockett dies in Barry's arms. The feminine is destroyed and the brutal regime is reasserted.

'Now Barabbas . . .' (1947) by William Douglas Home started at the Boltons Club, and transferred to the West End with glowing reviews. Richards is stereotypically queer: he 'speaks with a precious accent', has 'very long hair elaborately arranged' and 'theatrical gestures' (5); he has worked as a chorus boy and done a bit of ballet too. Paddy is a hard man, an Irish nationalist convicted of trying to blow up a railway line. 'They ought to hang the likes of you' (7), he says to Richards. He is even more contemptuous towards another prisoner, Medworth, whose crimes, we gather, involve under-age boys; when Medworth starts talking about David and Jonathan to young Roberts, Paddy warns him off. 'You're soft as butter', he says, whereas 'I'm just a tough, bone-headed Irishman' (54). However, a political saboteur may be queer, at least while he is serving a long sentence. Paddy and Richards become attached, and when Richards is moved to another prison Paddy turns his attention to Roberts, whose girlfriend has abandoned him. I believe the play means us to interpret the effeminate types as really homosexual and the others as victims of the prison system – for prison, as the Governor warns Paddy, 'is not a normal place to be' (64). The *Spectator's* critic noted 'the full weight of sadness and frustration that is the natural corollary to this unnatural life' (quoted on the dust jacket).

Jean Genet was not interested in reforming prisons, but in elaborating their fantasy potential. What is so distinctive and disconcerting about his writing, from a post-Stonewall point of view, is his total lack of interest in repudiating, explaining or justifying effeminacy. This is partly because he delights in the opportunity for resistance that it offers; partly because he is so sunk in a mid-century construction of homosexuality that he cannot begin to imagine 'liberated' notions, wherein gay men might be 'proud' and not inferior (= effeminate). In *Deathwatch* (1949, Paris; Off-Broadway, 1958), as in Genet's novels, there are masculine men: some of them are top dogs and others identify with the top dogs and compete for that status. But this masculinity is insecure, always needing to prove itself. 'A man doesn't have to strut. He knows he's a man and that's all that matters', Green Eyes asserts (29). However, he is fearful that his girl is betraying him. Only Snowball seems unchallengeable, but he is perhaps just an idea: 'He's got what it takes. Don't play around with him. He's a Negro, a savage' (8).

The true queers, the feminine-identified boys who make themselves available to the phallic types they worship, have the advantage of complete existence. Kate Millett writes: 'Genet's femininity is, as Sartre phrases it, a "hostile eroticism", delighted to ridicule and betray the very myth of virility it pretends to serve.'[28] In *Deathwatch* Maurice lives through the tattoo of Green Eyes' girl on his chest. He knows he is pretty, and cultivates camp mannerisms: 'Maurice. I'm telling you to stop. And stop tossing your head like a whore', Lefranc demands (38). Lefranc wants to inherit Green Eyes' authority, but Maurice, whose submissive femininity is a necessary condition for the manliness of others, taunts him with his inadequacies. The outcome is a murder.

Such themes were still running in John Herbert's *Fortune and Men's Eyes* (1967). When Smitty arrives in the reformatory he is young, inexperienced and not queer, he says – not like the impressive Queenie and the vulnerable Mona. Smitty is exploited by Rocky, but Queenie, who can recognise real macho when she sees it, puts Smitty up to quell Rocky and become the operator and bully of the block. The only way to avoid being a victim is to be meaner than the others; the effeminate boys are the only real queers, and their attempts to achieve self-respect are even more precarious.

Mince Tall

While a higher visibility for effeminate queerness made bachelors more vulnerable, female impersonation less viable, and a virile affect more necessary, casual representations in stage plays became more common. In 1929, in the wake of the banning of *Young Woodley*, John van Druten complained: 'One of the most surprising phenomena which I have recently noticed in the theatre is the portrayal, especially in farce, revue or musical comedy, of effeminate men, mincing and wilting in what the public regards as "Nancy" attitudes, to the shrieking delight of an audience — and this while any attempted mention, even, of homosexuality is utterly taboo in the serious theatre.'[29] Reviewing *The Green Bay Tree* in the *Observer*, Ivor Brown announced himself 'wearied beyond words with the easy laughter raised by parading effeminate men with all the mincing movement of their kind'.[30] In the introduction to *Tragedy in Jermyn Street* Hill objects, similarly, to the banning of his serious play 'in an age when sexual inversion is the subject of fifth-rate Music-Hall jokes made by sixth-rate comedians' and 'material for sniggers from gallery audiences' (8). The pattern was similar in New York. The protagonist in Blair Niles' novel *Strange Brother* (1931) observes: 'It used to be unmentionable. It was kept so hushed up that you might go through life to the grave and never hear it mentioned. Now it has evolved to the point where it's material for jokes.'[31] New York critic George Jean Nathan complained in 1945 that a caricature in a musical revue, *Laffing Room Only* (1944), had passed the 'moralists' while they tried to prevent serious gay character studies.[32]

It is not easy to track down these effeminate performances. The scripts may not be published, queerness is mostly in the business anyway, and reviewers consider such matters beneath their notice. Neil Bartlett has drawn attention to Arthur Law's play, *The New Boy* (1894).[33] The situation is that Dr Candy will leave his money to Mrs Rennick only if she has not married again, but she has a young husband, Archibald. So he pretends to be her son, and is drawn into the school as a pupil: he is humiliated by discipline, rugby football, and customary bullying; even approaches from a girl are embarrassing, since his wife is nearby. Now, the plot depends entirely on the heterosexual credentials of all the characters: the play is funny because the 'boy' is in fact the husband of the woman who is being wooed. Nevertheless, Archibald is repeatedly discovered in 'sissy' situations. Bartlett is surely right to hear queer resonances in the scene where the 'boy' is dandled on the knee of a suitor who is attempting to ingratiate himself with Archibald's wife (believing her to be his mother), specially when the suitor 'moves his knee up and down'; 'Don't joggle: don't joggle', cries the discomforted Archibald (32).

Another instance might be *The Torchbearers* (1922, Broadway; West End, 1925) by George Kelly, a gentle satire on the little theatre movement. 'I acted the part of the effeminate stage manager', Eddie Fuller says, in a Works Progress Administration (WPA) Federal Theatre tour of the play in 1936.[34] The language and posture of the stage manager in the printed text give no particular support for this interpretation of the character, but it is the obvious way to make the part interesting (Fuller recalls it because his trousers split and the leading lady's whisper was heard through the loudspeakers: 'Edward, your balls are hanging out'). Tucked into the Sussex University Library copy of *The Torchbearers* is a playbill for a performance by the St Peter's Players in St Peter's Hall, Cricklewood; the play may have furnished opportunity for innumerable amateur, queer events. Yet, even in such instances, it is not clear which audiences drew which inferences. A dancing instructor living in Cambridge says, of the period before 1945, 'They might call you queer, but probably only because of the way you talked, but they wouldn't think anything about sexually. They'd call you queer because they thought you was a bit girlish. But not because of the sexual act.'[35]

Even quite prominent plays need reviewing. In Sophie Treadwell's *Machinal* (1928) the range of doubtful sexual practice in a pick-up bar is rounded out by a 'middle-aged fairy' and the 'young, untouched' boy he is chatting up: 'Real amontillado is sunshine and orange groves – it's the Mediterranean and blue moonlight and – love? Have you ever been in love?' (32–3). Curtin draws attention to Moss Hart's musical *Lady in the Dark* (1941), which features a magazine office in which Russell Paxton is resident photographer. He bursts in: 'Liza, I've taken pictures of beautiful males, but this one is the end, the absolute end!' It is Randy Curtis, a movie star – 'Oh, I tell you he's godlike Liza, he's a beautiful hunk of man. . . . Now, Mr Curtis, I must have one more pose. I want to take you while you still have that gorgeous tan.' Curtin attests that Danny Kaye played Russell as a 'swish-stereotypical "fag" role'; in the recording I have heard Gene Crockett plays him thus, provoking tittering among the audience.[36] In Wolcott Gibbs' episodic *Season in the Sun* (1950) a limp-wristed male couple are refused accommodation, producing amusement among the principals ('They would have no trouble at all flying in and out of windows', the character note says – i.e. they are fairies). And is it irreverent to raise a question about Alexander MacColgie Gibbs in *The Cocktail Party* (1949) by T.S. Eliot? Alex is full of

Society gossip, apparently without a female partner or aspirations to have one, and has studied the native mind while travelling widely outside Europe. He insists on cooking a meal for Edward when his wife deserts him but cannot find sufficiently elaborate ingredients in the kitchen; recklessly, he uses all the eggs (they were rationed in 1949).

Coward was by no means the last person to insinuate queer effeminacy into revue. Hermione Gingold, Walter Crisham and Michael Wilding performed a song in the *Gate Revue* of 1939: 'All Smart Women Must'. It is about how fashion designers contrive to make women unattractive to men; the last lines warn: 'Dame fashion is a fairy / And fairies get you if you don't watch out.' The Lord Chamberlain's notes say 'this was sung by two effeminate men and a lesbian'.[37] *At the Drop of a Hat* (1957) was in more restrained mode; this elegant, sophisticated, and very witty sequence of songs by Michael Flanders and Donald Swan was not noted for camp humour. However, in 'Design for Living' (Coward's title, of course) the two men sing together of the decor in their home:'We live in a most amusing mews, / Ever so very contemporary.' They conclude:

> But though 7B is madly gay,
> It wouldn't do for every day.
> We actually *live* in 7A,
> In the house next door.[38]

This vein persists in the satirical 1960s: in *Beyond the Fringe* (1961, West End; Off-Broadway, 1962) three young men camp around in sou'-westers as they get ready to film a commercial. 'So I said to him, I said, do you do vests in mauve?' They are advertising Bollard, 'a *man's* cigarette'.[39]

Then consider Maitland, the manservant in *The Chalk Garden* (1955) by Enid Bagnold (a friend of Worsley). He was brought up in an orphanage where they played rounders rather than cricket, was imprisoned as a conscientious objector, blossoms when there is opportunity to be creative in the serving of lunch. He acts up and becomes hysterical when criticised: 'I have soft ground and hard ground to my feelings. You should mind where you step!' (21). He has no personal attachment other than to the child of the house; she checks when he calls her 'dearest'; he replies: 'Only in a sad sort of way, I have no dearest' (34). Is this not a camp part? And what about Willie Maltravers in *The Amorous Prawn* (1959) by Anthony Kimmins? He is 'a tall and rather precious chef', and very enthusiastic: 'Madam, my mind is reeling with menus' (319,

330). However, he is disappointed when American visitors only want steaks: 'I'm not one to give trouble, and I'm not easily upset, but I can't stand the monotony another minute. I'm giving notice' (343). In the film, directed by Kimmins (1962), Derek Nimmo plays Maltravers very campily.

7

Lesbians and Gender

Compton Mackenzie, setting his novel *Extraordinary Women* (1928) at the end of World War I, makes some of his lesbians purposefully manly; apparently this is a novelty on the Isle of Sirene (Capri). However, 'accustomed for years to the spectacle of ladylike men', the locals 'were not capable of being shocked by a gentlemanly woman'.[1] I showed in chapter 4 how the idea of lesbian relations emerged into the consciousnessess of many people. Here I explore through stage representation in Britain and the USA the pressures upon the independent woman, the sudden invocation of the predatory lesbian, and the decisive arrival of the mannish lesbian.

Compulsory Heterosexuality

The thought that marriage might be a trap for the woman had been announced, notoriously, in Ibsen's *A Doll's House* (1879) and reinforced in *Hedda Gabler* (1890). In Wilde's writings the nearest to successful marriages are in *Lady Windermere's Fan* and *An Ideal Husband*, but each of these has to be rescued by a more independent spirit, and depends upon significant deception between the principals. In *A Woman of No Importance* (1893) Mrs Allonby leads the women in an assault on the very idea of marriage. 'Happy marriages', says Lady Caroline, are getting 'remarkably rare'. 'Except amongst the middle classes, I have been told', Lady Stutfield reports (disavowing first-hand knowledge). 'I have noticed a very, very sad expression in the eyes of so many married men.' Mrs Allonby dismisses the very notion of an ideal husband: 'There couldn't be such a thing. The institution is wrong' (46–7). The

130

virtuous Miss Worsley is appalled. On her definition of natural womanly behaviour, the entire conversation should have been impossible: 'I couldn't believe that any women could really hold such views' (50). She wants fallen women punished along with men, and the children as well.

Wilde is foregrounding a dispute *within* the demand for female dignity and assertion. Women such as Miss Worsley deploy a rhetoric of purity within a reformist agenda, as a way of campaigning against male exploitation, especially by upper-class men and in prostitution. In his plays Wilde sets that aside, according significant power and wisdom to a feminine equivalent of the male dandy − leisured, flippant, knowing, and very clever. Mrs Allonby is unimpressed by such an accomplishment of the reformers as the recent Married Woman's Property Act, which allowed married women, for the first time, to retain and control property: 'All men are married women's property. That is the only true definition of what married women's property really is. But we don't belong to any one' (42). The strategy of the feminine dandy is to ignore marriage − some of these women have husbands but behave as if they had not, others manage without.

In mocking Miss Worsley's earnestness, Wilde had a point. As Frank Mort observes, the rhetoric of purity 'offered a set of concepts, a rhetoric of resistance and a strength of moral certainty powerful enough to take on the weight of the medical and political establishment'.[2] But demands for State regulation produced new laws, whose weight came to bear upon the victims rather than the powerful. The purity lobby scarcely touched the upper-class men with whom it had begun; it produced instead the Criminal Law Amendment Act of 1885, which, among other things, criminalised male homosexual acts in private.

By claiming femininity, Wilde's female dandies unsettle the idea of true womanhood. Take Mrs Arbuthnot's handwriting in *A Woman of No Importance*. 'She is one of the sweetest of women. Writes a beautiful hand, too, so large, so firm' (Lady Hunstanton). 'A little lacking in femininity, Jane. Femininity is the quality I admire most in women' (Lady Caroline). 'Oh! she is very feminine, Caroline, and so good too' (Lady Hunstanton; 32). If femininity is womanly and hence naturally good, Mrs Arbuthnot is 'very feminine'. But she asserts herself and her goodness in a middle-class way, and thereby becomes, like her writing, almost manly. 'You should hear what the Archdeacon says of her. He regards her as his right hand in the parish', Lady Hunstanton adds. The common phrase, which we almost hear, is 'right hand man'.

Entrusting women's independence to the feminine dandy incurs two costs. First, we may discern an underlying frustration. It is a joke in *A Woman of No*

Importance when Lady Hunstanton remarks: 'Dear Mr Cardew [presumably the Prime Minister], is ruining the country. I wonder Mrs Cardew lets him' (26). Actually, the leisure-class woman, we see in the plays, may not even go down to supper at a party without getting a man to escort her. Repartee and flirting are not going to achieve very much. Second, the feminine dandy can too easily be set aside as an unsatisfactory woman. According to Alan Bird, Wilde's women are 'domineering, powerful, ruthless, self-possessed and absolutely determined in their obsessive desires and loves, whether of money, marriage, social standing, or a son'.[3] In the view of Patricia Behrendt, the representation of Mrs Allonby and the others is misogynist: these women are 'tyrannizing, materialistic, and petty by nature'.[4] Such demands that women be like what they have always been said to be like are, of course, profoundly conservative.

Wilde's validating of dandy femininity was hardly pursued beyond his life and work, though something of it appears in George Bernard Shaw (I discuss *Mrs Warren's Profession* and *Getting Married* later in this chapter). Feminists generally explored marriage among less exalted classes and in a more earnest manner designed for little theatres rather than the glitter of the West End. Elizabeth Baker's *Chains* (1909) shows young people, inspired by one of them who is going to emigrate to make a new life, realising that the conventional wisdom about making a sensible marriage in good time is a snare. For the woman, it may mean release from shop or office work, but she has to hold her husband's attention. For the man, it means he must hold a job, however hard and humiliating the conditions. At least farming in Australia affords him somewhere else to go, and a prospect of male camaraderie. Maggie turns down an advantageous marriage and exuberantly maintains her independence, but no alternative future for her is indicated. However, there is no suggestion that she might not care for men as such; if anything, she seems keen on Charley.

In fact, the more prominent notion, which seemed particularly plausible in the wake of World War I, when so many young men were killed, was that the woman without a man to depend on must be disappointed, frustrated and probably bitter. While Victorian gender ideology had been reluctant to entertain the idea of female sexual passion at all, more advanced spirits were eager to co-opt women into companionate marriage and a heterosexual relation that would satisfy both partners. Victorian repression, it was held, from Freud to D.H. Lawrence and Marie Stopes, had prevented women especially from fulfilling themselves sexually. As George Chauncey, Jr., puts it, 'the resexualization of women — in one sense a progressive development —

was used to tie them to men, as the culture increasingly postulated the importance of women's sexual desire as a basis for their involvement in heterosexual institutions such as marriage'.[5]

Hence, in Sheila Jeffreys' chapter title, 'The Invention of the Frigid Woman': 'Spinsterhood, lesbianism, celibacy and heterosexual practices apart from sexual intercourse were condemned. The concept of the "frigid woman" was invented to explain why women were resisting this change in men's sexual expectations, and was used as a weapon to worry women into compliance.'[6] In Agatha Christie's play *Ten Little Indians* (1944) one of the characters is 'a tall, thin spinster, with a disagreeable, suspicious face'. She inveighs against 'low-backed evening dresses. Lying half-naked on beaches. All this so-called sunbathing. An excuse for immodest conduct, nothing more. Familiarity! Christian names − drinking cocktails.' She is sex-starved as well as bitter, an audience is likely to conclude (9, 16).[7] (The novel had been called *Ten Little Niggers* when it was published in England in 1939; subsequently it was called *And Then There Were None*.) The spinster is not inevitably frustrated for Christie; there are two unmarried ladies in *Appointment with Death* (1945), one feminine and one masculine (capable, bossy); neither of them is particularly eccentric, inadequate or perverse and both are treated with respect.

The thought that women and men might be happier without each other is entertained by Maugham in a comedy, *The Unattainable* (1916; produced as *Caroline*). 'It's really very pleasant to be one's own mistress', Caroline remarks to her maid. 'Ah, well, ma'am, you're one of the lucky ones; you can please yourself.'[8] The prospect of independent women is treated more severely in Maugham's *The Land of Promise* (1913). The play opens with conversation among women who are companions to old ladies. They dislike their subservience, though it enables them to cling to gentility. But a marriage might not be preferable. 'I shouldn't like to live with a man at all', Miss Pringle says; 'I think they're horrid, but, of course, it would be impossible if he weren't a gentleman.' Norah Marsh has some expectations of a small legacy from her deceased employer, so she says she'll marry − 'Never' (Ib, 221–2). However, Norah finds herself penniless, goes to her brother who is farming in Canada, has difficulty with her sister-in-law, and marries a poor − non-gentleman − farmer, Frank Taylor. It is very evident that she is repelled by the idea of sexual intercourse with him; she shudders at the thought (Ib, 267 − though the actor, Godfrey Tearle, was very handsome).[9] Norah demands: 'D'you want me to tell you in so many words that you're physically repellent to me? The thought of letting you kiss me horrifies and disgusts me' (Ib, 283). She actually tries to shoot Taylor, but the gun is not loaded. He will not tolerate refusal: 'Listen. There ain't a sound. It might be the garden of Eden. What's that about male and female created He them? I guess you're my wife, my girl, and I want you.' She is forced to submit: 'A look of shame, fear, anguish, passes over her face, and then, violently, a convulsive shudder runs through her whole body. She puts her hands to her eyes and walks slowly to the [bedroom] door' (Ib, 286).

After a while Norah gets a chance to return to her old life on advantageous terms, but finds she has come to love Taylor. Women 'have our part in opening up the country. We are its mothers and the future is in us. We are building up the greatness of the nation. . . . I can't go back to that petty, narrow life' (Ib, 308). The problem, in Maugham's presentation, is effete England, dominated by old ladies; the prairie offers a full life to real men and women. The name Norah is of course significant: *The Land of Promise* rewrites the conclusion of Ibsen's *Doll's House*.

Maugham's condoning of rape is extreme, even in the context of his time; the fact that the Lord Chamberlain licensed the play says a good deal about the gender politics of that (all-male) office. Some reviewers objected. To be sure, there was a precedent in Shakespeare's *Taming of the Shrew*. 'But that was jest: this was grim earnest; as minute, as realistic, as brutal as Zola unrestrained,' J.T. Grein complained in the *Sunday Times* (Grein was to be the producer of the Maud Allan *Salomé*). He continues: 'We admired the dramatist, but we found fault with his discretion. Physical subjugation of a woman is the most painful of all domination. And in this case there was not even the excuse of latent attraction on her part.'[10]

At the end of *The Sacred Flame* (1928), Maugham leaves 'two lonely women' who must 'cleave to one another' (IIIa, 319). They are the mother who has poisoned her invalid son, Maurice, and the Nurse who harboured a secret passion for him. The Nurse's love, Maurice's wife thinks at first, was 'rather horrible and disgusting', because of its perverse intensity and its focus upon a man incapable of having sex. An audience may infer that there is, in contrast, proper, healthy heterosexual love, and that it is understandable, if not right, that Maurice's wife should take up with her brother-in-law when her husband is incapacitated − compare *Lady Chatterley's Lover*. (It is to save Maurice from knowledge of this that his mother poisons him.) So two women are left together, in the wreckage of other, better kinds of love. The Nurse is on her knees clasping her arms around the mother − conveniently redirecting the passion that had been focused on Maurice. Those are the terms upon which two women may plausibly acknowledge a destiny other than marriage.

What is surprising, looking back at these plays by Somerset Maugham, is his reputation as a key figure in a theatre which, because of censorship and complacency, sustained a merely frivolous attitude towards difficult aspects of contemporary life. It is hard to envisage more aggressively unpleasant plays than *The Land of Promise* and *The Sacred Flame*.

With increasing urgency, feminist playwrights and their sympathisers struggled with the proposition that marriage was the only positive choice. Susan Glaspell in *The Verge* (1921), produced by the Provincetown Players in New York, shows Claire being driven into strange ways (she is obsessed with breeding a new plant in her greenhouse) by furious frustration with the role ascribed to her as wife and mother. 'We need not be held in forms moulded for us', she says — plants and people. 'Be the woman you were meant to be!' the others demand (64, 79). But even a passionate love affair is a trap — to be even more violently resisted. As David Sievers sees it, Claire is 'strangely troubled with the compulsion to break out of molds', and psychosis is the natural outcome. Her 'oversensitivity — and possibly her unconsciously homosexual wish to be "other" than woman — drove her past the verge of insanity'. I agree, rather, with Joel Pfister: the moulds, *The Verge* shows, are the problem.[11]

'I suppose I got to marry somebody — all girls do — ', Helen says in Sophie Treadwell's play *Machinal* (1928, Broadway; produced as *The Life Machine* in the West End in 1931). However, she doesn't want to remain unattached either: 'it's like I'm all tight inside — sometimes I feel like I'm stifling' (19). Her employer propositions her so she marries him; she finds him repulsive but forces herself to sleep with him. She is taken to a pick-up bar where she meets a man with whom she falls in love and has secret sexual relations for a year. She does need a man, then, but it has to be the right one. In Sievers' view, 'Miss Treadwell's portrait of an emotionally starved woman driven to murder by her fixated loathing of sex is a full-blown psychological study.'[12] But, this is, again, to overlook the slanted range of choices which Sophie is able to discern.

In *The Verge* and *Machinal* the women's frustration with marriage leads to a nervous breakdown. However, while it may strike us that such protagonists might be happier with another woman, the more legitimate inference from the playtext is that they need a fairer and more sensitive adjustment of the terms of heterosexuality.

Lesbian Predators

Children in Uniform and *The Children's Hour*, I argued in chapter 4, illustrate how the thought that some women might prefer lesbian relations was not easy to conceive or to announce before the 1920s. However, *The Mothers* by Edith Ellis, *The Lamp and the Bell* by Edna St Vincent Millay, and *The Dove, Two Ladies Take Tea* and *To the Dogs* by Djuna Barnes are more adventorous (see chapter 3). Also, there is *Criss Cross* (1899), a short, early play by Rachel Crothers, who was to become one of the most fruitful Broadway dramatists of her generation. Ann is a successful writer, and regarded with awe by others; Cecil, a younger woman and her cousin, is enthusiastic about Jack, a painter. But Ann wants to change the subject; she isn't going to dress up for his visit. Cecil's anxiety is that Jack doesn't care for her as he used to, whereas Ann is 'so strong, and sure of things' and has 'never loved anyone' (27). When Jack comes, Ann gets him to propose to Cecil, despite his evident interest in Ann herself. So she is left alone for the curtain speech: 'If I could only tell it to somebody – only say it aloud to myself – just once – it would not be quite so hard!' (29). Evidently Ann has sacrificed her own love, but is it for Jack or Cecil? She is certainly interested in Jack as a fellow-artist, but she speaks urgently of her relationship with Cecil: 'If I were a man, now, it would be so easy. So easy to take her up in my arms and shield her against the whole world. There's such an honest, trusting light in the girlish eyes she raises to me' (28). Ann would like to be in Jack's place, but there seems to be no prospect of this. It doesn't get said aloud, but an audience may infer it.

While many commentators were unwilling to acknowledge the existence of lesbians, some were keen to warn against their corrupting influence. A.G. Tansley in *The New Psychology* (1920) says that among women 'superficial manifestations' of feeling

> grade imperceptibly into the extreme forms of homosexuality on both the physical and the psychical sides. Even without expression in the most extreme forms they may absorb so much of the sex energy of a woman that not enough is left for the development of the normal channels, with a resulting disinclination for marriage, or at any rate for normal sexual relations with a man.[13]

So a woman may be drawn away from heterosexuality by even a slight lesbian inclination.

These perils are broached in Clemence Dane's novel *Regiment of Women* (1917; Dane was the pseudonym of Winifred Ashton). Clare, a schoolteacher, habitually attracts younger women to her but then, being unable herself to love, plays cruel games with them. 'It's vampirism', she is eventually told.[14] She drives a girl in the school to suicide, though it is reckoned generally to be an accident. Her other relationship is with Alwynne, a nineteen-year-old teacher. Alwynne's aunt tells Roger, who wants to marry Alwynne, that Clare is 'abnormal, spiritually perverse and she's fastened on the child. They adore each other. It's terribly bad for Alwynne. As it is, it will take her months to shake off Clare's influence, even with you to help her' (288). And there are sexy moments: Clare 'put her arms round Alwynne and kissed her passionately and repeatedly' (73). Yet Alwynne is able to regard such intense friendship not as a perversion, but as a reasonable alternative to marriage: 'if you've got a — a really real woman friend, it's just as good as falling in love and getting married and all that — and far less commonplace. Besides the trouble — smoking, you know — and children' (296). Her aunt disagrees:

> How can you weigh the most intimate, the most ideal friendship against the chance of getting married? . . . The brilliant woman — the rich woman — I don't count them, and there are other exceptions, of course; but when her youth is over, what is the average single woman? . . . We're not children. We both know that an unmated woman — she's a failure — she's unfulfilled. (335)

Yet that aside about the rich woman is perhaps important: is it, as some feminists were saying, that marriage was an unfortunately necessary meal ticket for the 'average' woman? Eventually Alwynne decides to marry Roger, though this is because Clare is so unpleasant, rather than because Alwynne accepts, explicitly, the priority of marriage.

The most notorious lesbian play of the 1920s was *The Captive* (1926) by Edouard Bourdet. Irene, who is twenty-five, is annoying her rather bullying father by going out by herself and refusing to accompany him on a diplomatic posting to Rome (her mother is dead). But where is she going out to and why does she want so much to remain in Paris? She is forced into a lie — that she has hopes of a marriage proposal from Jacques. She persuades Jacques to collude with this, though he doesn't like it because he actually *is* in love with Irene and *has* proposed marriage; she turned him down. 'If I had told the truth, no one would have understood it', Irene says (62). Jacques decides to find out what is going on, and gets to talk to d'Aiguines, the man of the house where Irene is spending her time. But he is not the lover, as Jacques has supposed: 'Hers is quite another kind of bondage.' For 'it is not only a *man* who may be dangerous to a woman. . . . In some cases it can be another woman' (145). Nothing can be done about it, d'Aiguines insists. He speaks with authority: it is his wife who is the lover of Irene, and it has made him old before his time. Madame d'Aiguines does not appear in the play; perhaps that would be too much to ask of a mainstream audience.

Irene pleads with Jacques to help save her: 'You've got to treat me like a crazy person — a sick person — and take care of me'. If she falls entirely into the clutches of her lover, there will be no return; 'It's like — a prison to which I must return captive, despite myself' (169, 171). She wants Jacques to cure her by marrying her, and eventually, despite a moment where her physical aversion to love-making with him is revealed, he agrees. In the third act, it is apparent that their marriage lacks passion. Jacques gets in touch with his former mistress, and Irene is approached again by Madame d'Aiguines. She asks Jacques to save her once more; he refuses: 'Look at yourself! You're breathless — your eyes are dazed — your hands are trembling - because you've seen her again, that's why! For a year I've been living with a statue and that woman had only to reappear for the statue to come to life, to become a human being capable of suffering and trembling!' (249–50). Jacques returns to his mistress, Irene to Madame d'Aiguines.

Lesbians in *The Captive* experience an ineluctable compulsion to express themselves; there is no question of changing them, and the men who fall within their orbit are doomed. We may be inclined, d'Aiguines says, to say: '"Oh, it's nothing but a sort of ardent friendship — an affectionate intimacy . . . nothing very serious . . . we all know about that sort of thing!" No! We don't know *anything* about it! We can't begin to know what it is. It's mysterious — terrible!' The man, inevitably, is defeated: 'he is alone! Alone in the face of a secret alliance of two beings who understand one another because they're alike, because they're of the same sex, because they're of a different planet than he, the stranger, the enemy!' (149–50, Bourdet's pauses). Nor should we suppose this to be a rare occurrence. It is 'the kind of story that often happens — regardless of what men think' (146).

After being performed with great success in Paris *The Captive* was banned in London in 1926, but produced in Brussels, Berlin, Vienna, Holland and Switzerland. In 1934 it received a club production in London at the Arts Theatre. On Broadway in 1926 it was received with respect, though some critics thought the subject matter 'the province of pathologists'; it settled in for a run.[15] However, press baron William Randolph Hearst took against it and used it to embarrass the liberal state governor. After four months, as part of the furore around Mae West's *The Drag*, *The Captive* was raided by the police, along with West's *Sex* and a light comedy about attempted adultery, *Virgin Man*. A new law followed, providing that a theatre could be closed for a year if a jury found that an immoral show had been presented. The police raided *The Captive* in San Francisco, Los Angeles and Detroit.

According to St John Ervine, *The Captive* 'might easily leave an audience with no other impression than that two women were unduly fond of each other'.[16] With *The Green Bay Tree*, the basic premise is that something distinctively terrible is being broached; only homosexuality will do. George Jean Nathan regarded *The Captive* as 'the most suggestive, corruptive, and potentially evil-fraught play ever shown in the American theater . . . nothing more or less than a documentary in favor of sex degeneracy'.[17] Such alternations of disavowal and acknowledgment among critics indicate that the topic is there, though contested. Also, as with Coward's plays, they suggest an informed as well as an uninformed audience. 'The audience wondered and wondered and the most sophisticated understood', one critic said at the New York production of *The Captive*. Some critics commented on the discretion of the others.[18]

While *The Captive* was running successfully, *Sin of Sins* (1926) by William Hurlbut, an experienced Broadway dramatist, was perceived as cashing in on its publicity. It culminated in the confession of a tormented lesbian that she jealously murdered the fiancé of her inamorata. *Sin of Sins* opened in Chicago to hostile reviews and closed after three weeks.[19]

Wise To-Morrow (1937) by Stephen Powys, a pseudonym for Mrs Guy Bolton, wife of an established playwright, was licensed and successful in the West End but flopped on Broadway. There is going to be a party to congratulate Joan on her first-night stage success. We see Tony, her sister; Norman, the artist who lives in the studio; Peter, her fiancé (this will be Joan's last performance because they are to marry); and Bob and Helen, who have some difficulty in Society because they live (happily) outside wedlock (Bob's wife, Diana, won't divorce him because she is a stage celebrity, though she doesn't perform any more). These people all seem genial and, by West End criteria, normal — i.e. of independent means and conservative in outlook (it is assumed that Joan can't be on the stage and married to Peter). But Diana, the actress, is flagged as a dangerous person, while Colley, her secretary, 'dresses in a mannish style, tailored suit, collared blouse with striped man's tie, etc.' (32).

Diana has conceived a passionate desire to relive her life and career through Joan: 'Here in this younger semblance of myself / I'll see my life renewed', Colley quotes. Tony calls it 'a craving for *Possession*' (35, 51). Diana will do this by coaching Joan to act, as she would have done it, a part she had reserved for herself. The play is a lurid affair out of Zola, with a climax comparable to *Salomé* — it arouses suspicions of lesbianism (48). When a one-night performance is a success the struggle over Joan becomes open: Diana wants to take the play into the West End, and to stop Joan marrying Peter. She speaks mockingly of 'Love, marriage, children! The sacred reproductive instinct before which everything else must bow' (75). But this is not a sincere love: 'It's *yourself* you're thinking of — the chance all this gives you to get back the things you've been starving for for seven years — applause — adulation — all the chi-chi that goes with being a star', Colley accuses (47). She, as a former protégée, takes a caustic view of it all, but she contrives a plot: offering to sell Peter a gushing letter written to Diana by Joan.

Diana dies from a heart attack while making a last-ditch attempt to regain Joan. But she has left her house and belongings to Joan, who moves in and takes her place. She has decided that the part of wife and mother wouldn't suit her; she inherits the devotion of Colley as well (all as in *The Green Bay Tree*, four years earlier). It's like a monstrous possession — 'as if Joan had died and Diana Ebury were looking at you out of her eyes', Tony says (108). Fortunately Tony and Peter have realised they are in love anyway, so heterosexual interests are protected. This does leave Norman, the artist, for he had thought to marry Tony. Rather oddly, he closes by promising to get on well with her children, 'especially the second boy — the little chap who draws so well, and has an odd resemblance to me'. Tony doesn't find this sinister — '*Norman*, you darling idiot' (109). But it does offer a strange reprise of queer possession.

Reviewers of *Wise To-Morrow* were divided, as with *The Green Bay Tree* which some of them mentioned, on how much lesbianism to discover. 'It has an underlying story constantly touching on homosexuality, but never quite saying so', *Variety* reported; 'Hints and situations continually recur, but a meticulous exacting censor could not legitimately raise any objection.'[20] Burns Mantle in the *New York Daily News* complained: 'There has been a more or less determined effort to read a suggestion of Lesbianism into *Wise To-Morrow* . . . . There isn't really much excuse for that. . . . It is pretty easy to read abnormality into almost any provocative drama dealing with any unconventional relationship of the sexes. If that is the way your mind runs.'[21] These two arguments amount to almost the same thing: there is this unsavoury topic that is working its way onto the agenda.

By 1945 US critics of *Trio* by Dorothy and Howard Baker (from her novel) were ready to recognise lesbianism: they compared the play with *The Captive* and *The Green Bay Tree*. It made history because after a generally moderate reception the theatre was closed by the New York License Commissioner, leading to a trimming back of the powers of that official. *Trio* (1944) is about a college student who is in thrall to an older woman — a philosophy professor who is sophisticated, fascinating and, moreover, French. A young man falls in love with the student and, after initially being repulsed by his realisation of the relations between the two women, exposes plagiarism in the professor's work and carries the student away to live happily ever after as a heterosexual. The older woman is left at the point of suicide.[22]

Manly Women

Notably, these predatory lesbians are not represented as masculine (though Colley in *Wise To-Morrow* is). Diana Ebury is gushingly manipulative; Madame d'Aiguines in *The Captive*, her husband says, 'has all the feminine allurements, every one. As soon as one is near her, one feels — how shall I say it — a sort of deep charm. Not only I feel it. Every one feels it. But I more than the rest because I live near her. I really believe she is the most harmonious being that has ever breathed' (150). In Hellman's *The Children's Hour* neither of the women is specified as of masculine appearance. Karen is 'an attractive woman of twenty-eight, casually pleasant in manner, without sacrifice of warmth or dignity'. Martha is 'a nervous, high-strung woman' (9–10, 15) — like the protagonists in *The Verge* and *Machinal*. They talk together about problems in the school, without any kind of gendered hierarchy. If any female appears masculine, it is the disturbed child, Mary, when she bullies the other girls; 'stop being such a sissy', she commands (34). It is sometimes supposed, nonetheless, that Martha should be played in a 'manly' way. Anne Revere, who took the part on Broadway, told Kaier Curtin:

I did not play the role as a lesbian, that is like gals I had seen who were slightly 'butch'. Of course, I never thought that Martha was a lesbian. She and the other girl were just good friends, in my mind, nothing more. . . .

When Hellman directed the revival in 1952 she had Patricia Neal play
Martha very 'butch', going round lighting other women's cigarettes. What
a mistake! It didn't work and the revival was a flop.[23]

Hellman's change of mind about her character suggests that the manly model
had gained ground and, in the process, had made lesbianism more audible,
clear-cut and limited.

Scholars have disagreed about how far the mannish-woman-as-lesbian was
achieved by women and how far it was thrust upon them. Lillian Faderman,
Carroll Smith-Rosenberg and George Chauncey, Jr. argue that the issue,
initially, was not sexuality, but the intrusion of the New Woman upon male
privilege. This was stigmatised as a monstrous inversion of the supposedly
natural womanly temperament. Male politicians, physicians, sexologists and
educators, disconcerted by the determination of women to enter professional
and public life, 'launched a concerted political attack condemning female
friendships as lesbian and separate female institutions — whether educational
or political — as breeding places for "unnatural" sexual impulses', Faderman
says.[24] Havelock Ellis in particular, and also Ulrichs, Carpenter and Hirschfeld,
rewrote feminists as mannish lesbians. 'The New Women — unmarried,
career-oriented, politically active, often lovingly involved with one another —
emerged within Ellis' model as "unnatural" and selfish women', Smith-
Rosenberg writes.[25]

Freud's *Three Essays on the Theory of Sexuality* (1905) switched attention
from people who manifested 'inappropriate' gender behaviour to people who
made a same-sex choice of sexual object. However Freud, like other students,
maintained an underlying idea of biological gender. This was true particularly
with regard to women: 'Freud, like Ellis and the whole turn-of-the-century
sexology, continued to assert that "character inversion" was a regular feature
of *female* inversion, although no longer maintaining that this was true of male
inverts', Chauncey notes.[26] So, while it is asserted repeatedly that object choice
need not be associated with physical, mental or social characteristics (such as
'manliness'), the notion that the lesbian will be mannish keeps recurring.

In another essay Chauncey stresses the extent to which sexual dissidents
themselves fostered the manly lesbian and the effeminate queen. After all,
Ellis and Freud based their ideas partly on observations of behaviour, and it
would be absurd to suppose that lesbian women did not form and circulate
ideas and images among themselves, informally and through nascent social
networks.[27] If those ideas and images seem suspiciously close to biologistic,

heterosexual norms, that does not mean they must be attributed to men, sexologists or heterosexuals; all of us share a great part of the dominant framework of ideas and attitudes of our time. Emergent urban queer subcultures were striving to locate themselves within the prevailing sex/gender system.

Esther Newton argues also that there were advantages for women in the notion of gender inversion. It meant they could regard themselves as biological sports, rather than as immoral, and that they would not have to marry. It was better to be a freak than to be wicked or not to exist at all. Radclyffe Hall and others 'embraced, sometimes with ambivalence, the image of the mannish lesbian and the discourse of sexologists about inversion primarily because they desperately wanted to break out of the asexual model of romantic friendship'. For their first problem was to envisage themselves as sexual at all: 'conceptually, sex could only occur in the presence of an imperial and imperious penis' – whatever Victorian women had done together, it could not be *sex*.[28] It does seem that it was the image of the manly, cross-dressing butch that enabled many people to envisage, however partially, same-sex passion among women.

The Well of Loneliness, to which Ellis contributed a preface and in which Krafft-Ebing is cited as an authority, was a crucial conduit (comparable to the Wilde trials). Not only is the protagonist, Stephen, very mannish; her 'feminine' partner, Mary, is presented as liable to revert to heterosexuality and hence as not 'a real lesbian'. But it was a start. 'By separating lesbians into a seemingly quite distinct group, the definition laid the basis for later political solidarity', Sonia Ruehl concludes. 'This enabled other women either to imitate [Hall], or to engage in a challenge to what she said.'[29]

Diana Chapman recalls: 'I sort of knew I was without knowing anything about it, because the word was never mentioned. I'd heard that there was a book called *The Well of Loneliness*, and thought, I must read it. I'd just begun to identify myself as a lesbian. . . . What I passionately wanted was to be a man, so that I could – as I saw it – fulfil my proper function. If I were a man I would be taking Jean to a dance.'[30] Jane Rule says she was 'badly frightened' when she read *The Well* at fifteen. She was a tomboy, tall and with a deep voice. 'I suddenly discovered that I was a freak, a genetic monster, a member of a third sex, who would eventually call myself by a masculine name (telephone operators were already addressing me as "sir"), wear a necktie, and live in the exile of some European ghetto.'[31] What is striking, through Rule's discomfort, is that she was already being 'recognised' as manly on the phone, and that *she did recognise herself* in Hall's image.

Of course, not all lesbians welcomed or deferred to the Ellis–Hall version. Violet Trefusis, Vita Sackville-West and Romaine Brooks disliked *The Well*.[32] Chauncey quotes an intriguing survey published in 1929, showing that a sample of lesbians evinced 'no transposition to male feeling or manifestation of male sexuality'; in fact 'the women alternately assumed various *female* roles such as child, equal, and mother in their relationships'.[33]

Sonia Ruehl remarks that the gendering of the principals in *The Well* goes well beyond what Ellis had envisaged.[34] It is interesting to note that Hall herself had not always dressed in a manly way. During 1920, after she had been accused publicly of being immoral and breaking up Una Troubridge's marriage, and had sued for libel, 'her appearance and habits underwent a conspicuous change. Her clothes became increasingly masculine. To the plain tailored jackets, ties and skirts (she did not adopt trousers until the 1930s, like most women) were added men's socks with garters, heavy, thick-soled shoes with a broad toe-cap, and (in winter) spats.' Una reluctantly agreed to cut her hair.[35] This change in appearance seems to have been an act of defiance and self-definition. Today, with transsexuals firmly on the agenda, it would make sense to regard *The Well* as a classic of gender dysphoria, as much as of lesbianism; the case is made by Jay Prosser.[36] The point, perhaps, is that in the 1920s the two were not analytically distinct in the way we now maintain.

Like the idea of the effeminate man as queer, the idea of the mannish woman as lesbian was contested. Vivie Warren, in Shaw's *Mrs Warren's Profession* (1894; banned in England until 1925), is a vigorous young woman. She repudiates marriage after learning of her mother's profession (she lives off prostitution), and dedicates herself to working for the rest of her life in a law firm run by another woman. Perhaps, Jan McDonald suggests, quoting Declan Kiberd, 'her mother's capitalist exploitation of the sexual drive has brought about in her a disgust with physical intercourse between men and women that may lead her to pursue lesbian relationships in the future'.[37] However, Jill Davis, while acknowledging that 'Vivie is at the centre of a cluster of images which are so in excess of this role that they demand further explanation', believes 'the social "persona" of the lesbian had not yet issued from the discourse of sexology into cultural reality and could not therefore be "represented"'. Davis sees the hearty manner of Vivie and the sexological model of the lesbian, both, as issuing 'from the negotiation in progressive men in this period between conscious desires, which led them to support women's emancipation, and unconscious fears of that as a threat to masculine identity'. Despite his good intentions, Shaw places 'the woman who refuses masculine prescription' — Vivie — 'beyond recognition as female'.[38] What this doesn't quite account for, as I read the play, is Shaw's evident respect for Vivie.

Davis compares Shaw's *Getting Married* (1908), in which the General has difficulty saying Lesbia's name because for twenty years she has refused his proposals of marriage. He thinks it's unnatural — not marrying; 'It may not be natural', she replies, 'but it happens all the same. You'll find plenty of women like me, if you care to look for them: women with lots of character and good looks and money and offers, who wont and dont get married' (201–2). As Davis sees it, by using the name 'Lesbia' Shaw 'conjures up the lesbian only to deny her female autonomy by subsuming her in his argument — all women are innately heterosexual and maternal and only prevented from fulfilling their destiny by absurd social laws'.[39]

In my view Shaw is indeed refusing to collaborate with the modern concept of the lesbian. However, another way of putting this would be to say that he is refusing to accept that any woman who behaves independently must be a lesbian; or, more broadly, he is refusing to grant that all feelings must be sexual at root. I have said that the dandy femininity of some of Wilde's women was hardly taken up, but there is some of it in Shaw. Other than in her self-assertiveness, Lesbia is not mannish:

> She is a tall, handsome, slender lady in her prime: that is, between 36 and 55. She has what is called a well-bred air, dressing very carefully to produce that effect without the least regard to the latest fashions, sure of herself, very terrifying to the young and shy, fastidious to the ends of her long finger-tips, and tolerant and amused rather than sympathetic. (199)

She presents her arguments cogently and with consideration for others; through her Shaw channels aspects of his principled critique of marriage.

Lesbia believes she ought to have children and would be a good mother: 'But the country tells me that I cant have a child in my house without a man it in too; so I tell the country that it will have to do without my children' (201–2). She is prepared to reconsider, if a more satisfactory contract with the man can be devised; they try to do this, but it proves difficult. As Davis says, there is a conservative biological imperative here. Shaw believes that women are designed to have offspring, and is fearful that the 'best' types of women are reluctant to undertake this under current marital legislation and assumptions. At the same time, his argument that women should be entitled to bear children in circumstances that they choose has still a progressive ring to it. In the preface to *Getting Married* he vindicates independent-minded 'old maids' who want to bear children but 'dislike the domestic habits of men' (140–1), concluding that marriage has to be changed to make women economically independent and divorce convenient. In a context where some people were interpreting the demands of women as manifestations of pathological lesbianism, Shaw was trying to recognise the former without admitting the latter. However suspicious we may feel of him, his attempts to valorise women without men – by themselves or in collaboration with other women – distinguish him from most other writers (male writers) whose work got onto the mainstream stage.

Shaw tackles mannishness head-on in the protagonist of *Saint Joan* (1923). Shouldn't she be minding her own business? the King asks. 'What is my business? Helping mother at home. What is thine? Petting lapdogs and sucking sugar-sticks. I call that muck', says Joan. 'I have a message to thee from God; and thou must listen to it, though thy heart break with the terror of it' (102). The issue, Shaw suggests, is not manliness; rather, as the Steward says at the start, some people are more positive than others, and they tend to get their way. In his preface Shaw considers the 'abnormality' of Joan's 'manliness and militarism': 'The simple answer to all these questions is that she was the sort of woman that wants to lead a man's life' (25–7). This presentation of Joan is compatible with Faderman's argument, that women who dressed as men in earlier centuries didn't necessarily have a passion for another woman and want to be a man to her; often they didn't see themselves as men trapped in women's bodies, 'but rather as women in masquerade, trying to get more freedom and decent wages'.[40]

Eugene O'Neill represents the mannish woman as independent, rather than lesbian. In *Anna Christie* (1920) Marthy 'speaks in a loud, mannish voice, punctuated by explosions of hoarse laughter', and 'wears a man's cap, double-breasted man's jacket, and a grimy, calico skirt'. That's because she works on a barge with her man (19). Hattie in *All God's Chillun Got Wings* (1923) is 'dressed severely, mannishly': this is because she stands up for her (black) race – there is no suggestion of sexual dissidence (214).

John van Druten's *The Distaff Side* (1933) also resists the thought of lesbianism, though it assumes that an authority on birth control will be a single and manly woman. The play is about the women in a family. Pairing off with the right man is the clear priority; the younger folk are less formal about it, but their values are ultimately the same as their parents'. There is an old-lady's companion, Miss Spicer; she is put upon but always cheerful. Cousin Theresa is more unusual: she is unmarried and runs a birth-control clinic. She doesn't have much of a part, but she marks out an alternative and the others want to talk about her. Mrs Venables speaks slightingly of 'women like her who've never been able to get married'. But she's 'quite an important woman', her daughter, Mrs Millward, replies, 'very highly thought of'. 'Yes, and what does she look like? Her ankles!' (611). Youth produces hardly more advanced attitudes: Roland asks his aunt.

> Was there ever a man in her life, by the way?
> LIZ: She was half engaged to a schoolmaster who was killed in the war.
> ROLAND: Oh! So, then, that's why she's turned to work as an anodyne.
> LIZ: No. She's always been that type. She wasn't meant for men. And yet, do you know, she was very pretty as a young girl? (683)

When Theresa appears, we see 'an energetic, solid, dumpy woman of about fifty', wearing 'a very sensible, unbecoming evening-dress'; she admits she has a 'bossing nature'. She doesn't 'look on marriage as the one object of a woman's life', she says; there should be 'some larger horizon. . . . Just loving someone hardly seems to me a full-time job' (654, 657). She seems to have no significant personal attachments. This representation allows Mrs Millward's opinion, that Theresa is 'of the kind that lives impersonally' — unlike other women, who have to commit their lives to their husbands because otherwise they are 'unfulfilled. I think that's what being a woman means' (673). That remark is less than clear: at first it seems that there are different kinds of women, but the last sentence claims a single normative womanly destiny for them all.

How might audiences perceive Theresa? Either as the stereotypical notion of the independent woman or as the stereotypical notion of the lesbian. Actuality was more complicated. There were two overwhelmingly prominent campaigners on birth control as precedents for Cousin Theresa: Marie Stopes in Britain and Margaret Sanger in the USA. Both were married and had other close relations with both women and men. Van Druten's forte was to raise awkward issues and then duck them.

When Miss Moffat sends her belongings on ahead of her, in *The Corn is Green* (1938) by Emlyn Williams, the locals suppose she is a man. There are so many books, the china, the furniture '*so* distinctive. The desk. And the wastepaper basket. So . . . so virile' (188; Williams' pause). And her letters were misleading: the paper wasn't scented, the hand was bold, the details about the lease were businesslike. In fact, because she used her initials ('You see, I've never felt that Lily Christabel really suited me') they thought she was a lieutenant-colonel (193). Is the play going to confront this stereotyping? Miss Moffat is certainly forceful; her purpose is to bring education to this remote Welsh village. She briskly recruits Miss Ronberry, who says she is waiting for 'the right gentleman'; 'If you're a spinster well on in her thirties, he's lost his way and isn't coming. Why don't you face the fact and enjoy yourself, the same as I do?' Miss Moffat responds. But surely, says Miss Ronberry, 'a woman's only future is to marry and − and fulfil the duties of − '. 'Skittles', Miss Moffat exclaims. 'I'd have made a shocking wife anyway.' No, she's never been in love: 'I've never talked to a man for more than five minutes without wanting to box his ears' (197).

There is no suggestion that Miss Moffat is specially attached to women; Williams' project is to make her the person who can sponsor the talented boy (played by Williams) to fulfil himself in England. This is despite his laddish sexual behaviour with the servant's daughter. In order to save the boy from a marriage that must trap him in the village, Miss Moffat will adopt the baby. She says it is against her inclinations − 'I was never meant to be a mother' (271). Yet, we may suppose, she is meeting part of her destiny as a woman after all.

In *The Distaff Side* and *The Corn Is Green*, still, it is unclear whether or not the independent woman has turned into the manly lesbian. We are looking at a classic instance of uneven development: two frameworks of understanding overlap, provoking writers to make new sense of their world. The spinster was still getting unmasked when Eustace Chesser published his book *Odd Man Out* (that includes lesbians!) in 1959. She is not what she has appeared to be: 'It is a popular fallacy to regard the lifelong spinster as a woman who has necessarily been left "on the shelf". She may prefer to remain unmarried for a very good reason, but she may not be fully conscious of it.'[41]

Nice Chap

Already in *The Apes of God* (1930) Wyndham Lewis was defining a lesbian artist as manly; she wears 'a stiff Radcliffe-Hall [*sic*] collar'.[42] Gradually the stereotypical lesbian became established on the stage. *Frolic Wind* (1935) was adapted by Richard Pryce from the novel by Richard Oke. The formidable Lady Athaliah Jeune stomps around the place; upon her death it is revealed that she kept pornographic pictures in her private tower. It is not said that they are lesbian but the consequent agitation is in excess of conventional indecency

— 'fatuous, pathetic! Poor old witch. Poor old lady. Her grubby little secret' (105). For some characters it is inconceivable. The Princess, who has a string of gigolos, says it's all because of shame and repression. General Tresmand, however, doesn't like 'all these modern explanations of everything. That man, what's his name — Frood' (38). And Miss Vulliamy, who has been jealously hostile to young love, suddenly confesses her fear: 'It's festering inside me. I'm afraid of it — I'm afraid of becoming like Lady Athaliah. There, I've said it! I . . . don't attract anyone. I never have' (122–5).

Cry Havoc (1942, Broadway) by Allan R. Kenward is about a group of volunteer military nurses in the Philippines. Stephany — 'Steve' — is 'a large, raw-boned, muscular gal who carries herself like a man' (8). When she puts her arm round the feminine Connie the others exchange looks (34); when she tries to comfort Grace, who is in pain and panicking, she is violently accused: 'Always wantin' to put your arms around people — callin' 'em "Honey" and strokin' their hair — why don't you go out there and fight with the rest of the men — you — you Freak!' (55). Steve is baffled as well as upset. Is she different from the others? No, it's a lie, Smitty says; 'If there was anything wrong with you — anything to be ashamed of, you'd know it'. But, of course, people don't always. She was brought up simply in a lumber camp, Steve says; 'Men were — well, just men, and the women raised kids and there was never any mystery about sex' (64). Probably an audience of urban sophisticates shares the suspicions of the other women. Steve has little more to do until she gets pointlessly sacrificed.

The mannish stereotype seemed unproblematically available to Jean-Paul Sartre in *Huis Clos* (1944, Arts Theatre Club; Broadway, 1946). The concept is that the three characters constitute, reciprocally, each other's hell. Garcin is too lacking in self-esteem to respond fully to Estelle; he craves the good opinion of the astringent Inez; Inez is attracted to Estelle, but Estelle will not entertain a lesbian relationship. This structure prompts pragmatic casting decisions: Estelle, the heterosexual woman, has to be frivolous and feminine; Garcin cannot believe that he is a real man; that leaves manliness for Inez. Indeed, she is forceful and honest — 'a brusque Lesbian', Maurice Cranston calls her.[43] The triangle depends on the characters occupying conventional sex/gender roles.

Agatha Christie's *The Mousetrap* (1952, West End, and still running; my mother took my brother and me to see it in the second year) includes two evident sexual dissidents (I discuss Christopher Wren in chapter 9). Among the hotel guests received by Mollie and Giles is Miss Casewell, 'a young woman of a manly type' who speaks 'in a deep, manly voice'; she's glad to see a good fire, and 'straddles in front of it in a manly fashion'. No, they won't run out of food, Giles says; anyway, they can eat the hens. 'Before we start eating each other, eh?' Miss Casewell quips, laughing 'stridently' and throwing her overcoat at Giles (293). She is on the left in politics, she says, and lives abroad. She drives the tiresome Mrs Boyle out of the room by insisting on having the radio on: 'Bloody old bitch', she exclaims (301). Mollie thinks Miss Casewell 'rather peculiar'; 'Terrible female — if she *is* a female', Giles replies (296). At the time of the first murder she was writing a letter in the library. Sergeant Trotter reads the opening: 'Dearest Jessie — h'm — a friend of yours, or a relation?' 'That's none of your damned business', Miss Casewell retorts (325). Evidently she is implicated in the cruel childhood conditions that are prompting the murderer, but she dismisses the idea that childhood events may be crucially formative. 'All humbug. Just a damned lot of nonsense. I've no use for psychologists and psychiatrists.' She thinks it's all 'a question of will power' (316–17).

In Christie's *Go Back for Murder* (1960), Carla has found that her mother, Caroline, died in prison after being convicted sixteen years ago of murdering her father. Carla sets out to uncover a more acceptable narrative. One potential culprit at first glance is Miss Williams, the governess — 'Frustration, lonely spinster, repressed love for your father'. But no, she was 'a tartar, a woman of strong character, and sound commonsense', and was devoted to Caroline and committed to her pupil, Angela, the young sister of Caroline (627). Angela was a tomboy, climbing trees, playing truant, wanting to go out to tea in jeans. Miss Williams approved: 'Angela will be a fine woman one day, and a distinguished one' (673). Indeed, Angela went on to take a first-class degree at Cambridge and has become 'one of those tough women who travel to inaccessible places and write books about it' (648). And Miss Williams still doesn't think much of men - they 'still have the best of this world' (652). When we meet Angela in the present, she is 'well-dressed in a plain suit with a mannish hat', and uses slangy expressions, such as 'carting out a lot of equipment' and 'an older child gets mad with jealousy and chucks something' (655, 657). Angela intuits that Carla is trying to find out about the murder because she has a marriageable man in view and he is uneasy about it. 'How bloody! I shouldn't marry him', Angela cries. Carla is going off him anyway, and is drawn to her young solicitor; 'Must everything be a man?' she wonders. 'Usually seems to be. I prefer rock paintings', Angela replies (659).

Of course, no one is going to suggest that Agatha Christie's popular and accomplished thrillers are about sexuality, though the thought that these women may be psychologically unbalanced is invoked in order to reinforce suspicions of them. Part of Christie's skill is the creation of a neatly differentiated bunch of characters who seem weird enough to commit murders, and easily-recognisable lesbian types come in handy for that.

Through quite casual hints, lesbians appeared on the stage as gender inverts – not just in the notorious set pieces, but in everyday chit-chat. In Coward's *Song at Twilight* (1966) Hugo refers to Hilde's friend as a 'weather-beaten old German lesbian', and suggests to Hilde that she might wear 'quite a masculine looking little hat, almost a bowler . . . as a subtle gesture to your hostess' (370, 372). And what about Rachel Stone, the journalist who interviews Hedda in *The Irregular Verb to Love* (1961) by Hugh and Margaret Williams? She is hard-headed, smokes her own Gauloises, never wears furs because she prefers the smell of tweed, has a 'manly handshake' and has written a book about her travels in China. When she leaves, Hedda's husband comments: 'Nice chap.' She reproves him: 'You're not to talk like that' (35–6). I take these sightings of manly women as strong evidence of the currency of such representations in middlebrow theatre – I know about *The Irregular Verb to Love* because I chanced to come across a copy second-hand. My supposition is that there are other lesbian representations lurking in little-regarded playtexts, and that many have never reached print.

8

Class Conscious

What About the Workers?

Roy was born in Brixton in poor circumstances in 1908; his mother took in theatrical lodgers. As a boy he worked as a messenger for dental mechanics and then at the gasworks. He realised that he liked being in theatres when he noticed the cruising. 'We were in the gallery and I realised then, my instinct. Nobody told me. I kept on looking at the back and it was jet black, and crowded, crowded full of people standing, although there were a lot of empty seats.'[1] Notwithstanding, the world of theatre was far from egalitarian. Roy got a job as 'a kind of receptionist':

> So if a Duchess had got two seats and she didn't know what to do with them because she couldn't go, she'd give them to the cook. The cook would come and I had to have the diplomatic job of directing them into the upper circle, because they wore a hat or something like that. And vice versa. Sometimes people would have a ticket and they were too well dressed to go in the dress circle or the upper circle, so I would have to say, oh I'm sorry madam, I'm sorry sir, but there's been a duplication with your tickets, and take them to either the best seat or not such a good seat. That was my job.[2]

There was a place for all classes in the West End theatre, but not on equal terms.

There were left-wing companies. The British Workers' Theatre Movement flourished between 1926 and 1935; the American Workers' Theatre for longer;

the Group Theatre produced plays by Clifford Odets, among others, in New York in 1935–51. In London the Unity Theatre took up where the WTM left off; Joan Littlewood and Ewan MacColl were active in Manchester; they planted Theatre Workshop in Stratford East (London) in 1953. These companies have been described vividly by people who were involved, but the topic of sexuality rarely figures.[3] However, the Glasgow Unity Theatre, formed in 1941 to address Scottish working class experience, presented *The Lambs of God* (1948) by Benedict Scott. It shows the meanness and corruption that threatens young people living in poor tenement conditions, focusing on the rivalry over a young man between a passionate and strong-minded woman and a lonely but powerful queer man. Tony, one of the initial actors in 1948 recalls:

> I used to take Dick's arm here, and we'd walk off the gither to have sex. I used to smile in anticipation o' that. . . . It was a difficult way to end a scene. The audience didnae know whit wis happenin', — or if they did, were appalled — so there wis this big silence. Then ma pals in the front row o' the balcony, who were roarin' throughout, wid start clappin' and that got everyone goin'.[4]

The Lambs of God was revived in London in 1949 as *This Walking Shadow*, but it didn't do well; John Binnie directed a revival in Glasgow in 1990. Scott was not asked to script another play.

In the 1950s at Littlewood's Theatre Workshop, queerness appeared in cheap, cheerful and traditional guise. Since an Irish Republican Army hostage is to be held in a Dublin brothel occupied by a bunch of eccentrics who fall to singing and dancing at the drop of a hat, it is likely enough that Rio Rita, a camp navvy and male prostitute, should be among them, and his black boyfriend as well. They co-opt a third character and sing their own song — 'We're here because we're queer' — and join in 'a dance for all the outcasts of this world' (97–8). That's all in *The Hostage* (1958; Broadway, 1960) by Brendan Behan. *Fings Ain't Wot They Used T'Be* (1959), scripted by Frank Norman with lyrics by Lionel Bart, is set in a low-life backstreet Soho shpieler (gambling den). Fred's decision 'to have this gaff done out' (this place redecorated) is the cue for Horace to appear: he is 'a queer interior decorator. He is dressed in a pair of tight-fitting white trousers, green jacket, purple pullover and bowtie. He walks and behaves mincingly' (42–3). Horace leads the song 'Contempery' and installs a new décor, but becomes fractious when the clients insist on retaining the old table. The bearing of all this was not initially apparent to the Lord Chamberlain, who heard rumours of queer goings-on during the West End run and revisited the show in February 1961. He demanded: 'The interior decorator is not to be played as a homosexual and his remark ". . . Excuse me dear, red plush, that's very camp, that is", is to be omitted, as is the remark, "I've strained meself".'[5] Both these Littlewood confections transferred to the West End, where they were patronised as full of demotic fun. I discuss *A Taste of Honey* in chapter 13.

This study has so far been preoccupied with the middle and upper classes because they dictated the terms for professional stage representation in Britain and the United States. Lower-class lesbians and gay men who found their way into theatres would presumably be able to wonder about Maugham's bachelors, to recognise a hostile treatment in *The Green Bay Tree* and *Wise To-Morrow*, and to decode Noël Coward's innuendoes. What they hardly saw is plausible representations of themselves. They saw mincing comic servants and mysteriously sinister intruders. It is not that the lower classes didn't figure in the lives of established dramatists and the classes they mainly focused on; if anything, the topic of class and sex was too central to be broached seriously.

Unsuitable Partners

A common pattern of same-sex relations in mid-twentieth-century Britain, as Jeffrey Weeks notes, was for 'middle-class, self-defined homosexuals' to take up with younger working-class men who appear to have been 'relatively indifferent to homosexual behaviour'.[6] In *Gay and After* I write of this as a subcultural myth — a collective, ongoing, lived scenario through which gays create and recreate themselves.[7] In the United States similarly, George Chauncey shows, it was middle-class men who first got the idea of '"being" a homosexual', and therefore working-class men, particularly those linked to 'masculine' milieux — sailors, labourers, hoboes and other transient workers — might engage in same-sex activity without having to categorise themselves as 'queer'.[8] After all, they might be, or appear to be, motivated largely by social deference and financial advantage; probably they were married.

This way of regarding cross-class relations was not confined to homosexuals: to a striking extent, it replicated wider class and gender patterns. It was in practice almost acceptable for a man to have as a mistress, or have casual sex with, a person of a lower class, but he was not supposed to foul up his own social stratum by forming extra marital relationships with women there; the cross-class queer liaison worked similarly. It is often remarked that some of the objection to Wilde's behaviour was that he had crossed class barriers; the furore over *Lady Chatterley's Lover* was similarly framed. Actually, the infringement was that Wilde and Lawrence had allowed cross-class liaisons to be seen. The crucial opposition was not between heterosexuality and homosexuality, then, but between legitimate and illlegitimate relations.

One way of covering was for the queer gent to take on his lower-class partner as a secretary or manservant. John Addington Symonds did this; so did Maugham and Coward. Otherwise, it was difficult for two men to live together; Terence Rattigan installed his lovers in nearby apartments. (Of course, all this cost money.) In fact, for many middle-class men lower-class people were sexy *as such*; after all servants, in very many cases, had proffered the principal affective support in infancy. The happy ending to Rodney Garland's novel *The Heart in Exile* (1953) is secured when the protagonist, a psychiatrist, finds that he is drawn to his manservant:

> I confess that the attraction was much stronger when I saw him doing the sort of work I would never had dreamed of asking him to do. When my charwoman left, he insisted on scrubbing the kitchen floor, kneeling on the rubber mat, bending over the mop in his singlet. One saw the servant's humility in the attitude. But one also saw the broad shoulders, the arched back with the freckled skin under the rebellious hair, and he would look up as I entered and give me a beautiful smile of his brown dog eyes and white teeth.[9]

By so much as the master/servant relation was sexualised, by that much it was dangerous. The opportunities for exploitation were huge, and so were the risks of exposure.

By 1932 Emlyn Williams was successful as both an actor and a playwright, and after naive beginnings (like Coward, he came from a poor family) he had located himself firmly in queer/theatrical circles. In his autobiography, *Emlyn* (1973) he tells how he meets a sexy Welsh country boy, Fess (Festiniog) Griffiths. At their third meeting Fess, who is having trouble with his rent, moves in. He can drive so he becomes the chauffeur and handyman; they take off to France, though Williams finds his conversation lacking and can't tell whether his 'wide grin' is 'honest-sly' or 'sly-honest'.[10] Months pass, and Fess' limitations are confirmed:

I had no affection for him because I knew he had none for me or for anybody else. . . . When he returned from changing, I watched him lope across the grass, settle serenely in a deck-chair and take out a packet of cigarettes. For a moment he seemed about to pick up the newspaper next to him and to open it, but he did not. I had never seen him read anything. . . . What was he thinking of? Nothing. (349)

Why does Williams retain Fess, then? I think we have to assume that he is still engrossed in him sexually. He decides to marry his friend Molly. Which of them would he prefer to see? 'If he entered now, I would feel tormented relief. If she appeared, I would be delighted by the sight of the person I loved' (347).

Matters come to a head when Fess alters an invoice for a motorbike Williams is buying him for his twenty-first birthday so that he can take cash out of the transaction; he is dismissed. Even now, Williams remains obsessed, and makes one more attempt to exorcise Fess by visiting him at his parents' home and offering to reinstall him in the London flat; it is Fess who finally says no.

The fact is, of course, that Williams experiences guilt and disgrace when he thinks of Fess, and normality and security when he thinks of Molly. 'While the protective love [for Molly] grew more secure, the other [for Fess] darkened and exulted. I felt inside me a rumbling as unmistakable as the inner disorders of the body: the sound of a battle between good and bad. To my alarm the bad, in the shape of a harmless young Welsh cousin about the house, was becoming more insistent than before' (354). These are the 'two loves' of Shakespeare's sonnets – except that Shakespeare, more distinctively, makes the woman the dark, bad love. Williams takes it for granted that his readers will disapprove of Fess and approve of his marriage.

Fess, as is usually the case with the lower-class partner, disappears from history when Williams drops him. But Williams got out of him an acclaimed play, *Night Must Fall*. He relates how he hears of a murder case and, in his fixation, imagines that the perpetrator might be the hapless Fess: 'At that moment my obsession had been strong enough for me to wonder.'[11] This leads him to recall Patrick Mahon, 'the tall blond adventurer who in 1924 killed a girl and left the body in a trunk. In a bungalow. He melted before me into a younger type, more boy than man. Welsh.' The abandoned partner is merged with a psychopathic murderer. And Williams will play the part. As it happens, he has already been trying to copy Fess' manner – 'What had my absurd aping been but an unconscious preparation?' (381).

Night Must Fall (1935) shows young Dan insinuating himself, with an uncanny sense of how to please and flatter, into the house of Mrs Bramson (she's in a wheelchair, crotchety, domineering, not as ill as she makes out). Dan has already seduced Dora, the maid. He affects a disarming alternation of naïvety and cockiness; a rough accent, more Welsh than anything else. Despite these attractions, he arouses suspicions, especially in Olivia, Mrs Bramson's unmarried niece and companion − though she too is drawn to him (another frustrated spinster). It is hard to put your finger on what's wrong with Dan; he's just too plausible in all contexts; he seems to be acting all the time. Olivia challenges him: 'You haven't any feelings . . . at all. . . . (*He looks slowly up at her. She has struck home.*) But you live in a world of your own. . . . A world of your own imagination' (58, Williams' pauses). All this is in the context where a woman from a nearby house has disappeared, perhaps been murdered. Olivia intuits that Dan is the killer, and slides into a perverse rapport with him. Her complicity is equivalent, in Williams' imagination, to his own sinister fascination with Fess. The boy must be a monstrously cunning psychopath; how else can his influence over decent folk be explained?

Peter Burton traces this pattern to guilt and self-oppression. He asks why, in *The Green Bay Tree*, Dulcimer and Leonora are so drawn to Julian, 'a callow youth, living only for sensation; almost certainly devoid of any genuine feeling or emotion'. It is, Burton suggests,

> a convention (in fiction and in real life) of homosexual men of [Dulcimer's] class and historical period: the need to act as a father substitute to a youth from the working class, often unworthy of their attentions and often maintained because of the misery they cause their keeper − this latter state indicating the level of guilt and self-loathing many gay men appear to have felt about themselves − thus, love equals suffering equals expiation of guilt.[12]

In other words, affluent men like Williams use feckless young men like Fess to punish themselves for their disgusting desires.

I would add that the circumstances of the classic cross-class liaison − the way the young man always has to be disavowed in public and often shunted to one side in private as well, perhaps in the interests of a marriage − were likely to sour the sweetest nature. I can't help reading Fess and Williams, against the grain, with some sympathy for Fess. Of course, there are plenty of sexy-but-disagreeable people around to fall in love with, but if Williams is unable to respect Fess, at least at some level, then he can always stop indulging his infatuation with him. Like others of his (acquired) class and generation, Williams seems incapable of empathising with the dependent situation of the boy; I think they simply take it for granted that wealth and position will gain them service from the lower orders. When Fess falsifies the invoice for the motorbike, Williams says he would have given him money if he'd asked. That would be begging, Fess replies. But instead of pondering whether something is not revealed here about the relation between them, Williams responds legalistically: forgery is worse (365).

Noël Coward's *A Song at Twilight* (1966) is about an ageing homosexual writer, Sir Hugo, who by concealing his sexuality behind affairs with women and marriage has blighted his life and his art. Coward allowed it to be known that he had in mind Somerset Maugham, who had died during the previous year. In pointing towards Maugham, commentators agree, Coward was seeking to deflect any sense that the play might be about himself. He had not exactly striven to camouflage his gay life; nonetheless, he had not been straightforward either. *A Song at Twilight*, therefore, was itself involved in just such an act of denial as it seemed to critique.

Sir Hugo is visited by Carlotta, an early mistress. She accuses him of having failed to acknowledge Perry, his deceased former lover, in his autobiography. This was indeed like Maugham, who in a section of his autobiography had summed up his lover Gerald Haxton: 'I had found him a very useful companion.' In fact, Coward had written and spoken in comparable manner about his lovers.[13] Carlotta means to make Hugo's letters to Perry available to a biographer. However, the project is dropped and danger eliminated when Hugo's wife (a front, of course) attacks Perry: he was not 'in any way significant as a human being'; he was not 'in any way worthy of attention on his own account, apart from the fact of his early relationship with Hugo. . . . He was a creature of little merit; foolish, conceited, dishonest and self-indulgent' (440). Of course, none of that would make the letters uninteresting to a biographer, but the argument is not challenged; to the contrary, it causes Carlotta to return the letters to Hugo. The entire critique of Hugo's inadequacy as a human being and as a writer, together with the threat to his hypocritical lifestyle, is suddenly cancelled.

What is so unpleasant about this is the way the position of Hugo (the powerful) is retrieved at the expense of Perry (the weak). But then, if you want to dump someone to whom you have made commitments, it is easier if you decide that they are worthless. Compare Wilde and Douglas (in *De Profundis*) and Ackerley and Grayle in *Prisoners of War*. To Williams, Fess is 'a foreign creature disguised, in broad daylight, as a human being'.[14] The last moments of *Song at Twilight* strive to rescue Hugo as a man of feeling: he reads the letters and is moved. However, this isn't going to make any difference to the way he lives.

The other question is the one Burton raises: why Hugo has devoted his love and his life to 'a creature of little merit'. Because he despised his own passions. Carlotta remarks that sanctions against homosexuality are out of date, but Hugo's reply represents the opinion of Coward and most of his ilk:

> Maybe so, but even when the actual law ceases to exist there will still be a stigma attached to 'the love that dare not speak its name' in the minds of millions of people for generations to come. It takes more than a few outspoken books and plays and speeches in Parliament to uproot moral prejudices from the Anglo-Saxon mind. (417–18)

Quentin Crisp elaborates: 'The fundamental predicament of homosexuals is one that no amount of legislation can improve. . . . To rob blackmail of its potency, it would be necessary to remove the homosexual's experience of shame. This no power on earth can do.'[15]

Who's for Rattigan?

By the time Terence Rattigan arrived on the scene, in the late 1930s, a small repertoire of queer effects was available to the dramatist – comic low-life stereotypes, discreetly-anguished characters, and ambiguously-drawn sophisticates. At the end of *French Without Tears* (1936) the man-hunting Diana is eager to turn her attentions to the new arrival, Lord Heybrook. He was to enter as a 'blond, swishy queer', leading a borzoi dog called Alcibiades: sexual dissidence frustrates Diana's hopes. The Lord Chamberlain accepted this. But either Rattigan or the director, Harold French – accounts vary – was unhappy. Lord Heybrook was transformed into a boy of thirteen or fourteen.[16] This episode indicates that queerness was available for dramatic deployment, and that Rattigan was ambivalent about it.

In Rattigan's *While the Sun Shines* (1943) the opening joke is that Lord Harpenden is found in bed with a US serviceman, Mulvaney, whom he brought home drunkenly the night before (this was easy to achieve during the

War). The manservant is worried, for Harpenden is to be married tomorrow, but that is when he supposes that the guest is his mistress, Miss Crum. Mulvaney does look like her, the servant says — 'the way she sleeps all curled up with her arm over her face'. Mulvaney emerges, having 'swathed an eiderdown round his otherwise naked body'. Harpenden says he found him semi-conscious outside the Jubilee, 'breathing gin fumes in my face and calling me Dulcie' — the name of his girlfriend back home, says Mulvaney (176–9). Also, of course, it was the name of the queer man in *The Green Bay Tree*. Later Mulvaney is speaking of this on the phone: 'I slept in the same bed with an earl'; he is misheard, naturally enough, as having said 'with a girl' (184–5). Queerness is not announced, but it's in the air. The mood was changing, not least because of World War II. Rattigan was himself part of that change, but he couldn't control it for long.

Rattigan's most persistent and revealing themes concern cross-class liaisons, though he transposes them into mainly straight contexts. At the opening of *The Deep Blue Sea* (1952) Hester has tried to kill herself. She left her husband, a High Court judge, because she conceived an overwhelming passion for Freddie Page, a former RAF fighter pilot, who now has no job and no money, and is drinking too much and spending time elsewhere. He doesn't love her with the same commitment, and that's why she's suicidal. He may seem a bit of a cad, but it's just not in the nature of a chap such as him to be very emotional, Freddie says. He decides to leave — he has a job opportunity in South America. 'We're death to each other, you and I', he says to Hester; she begs him to stay just the one night (343). *The Deep Blue Sea* was inspired directly by the suicide of Kenneth Morgan, an actor with whom Rattigan had had an on-off affair since 1939.[17] He shuffles the characters around and takes on the challenge of being fair to all corners of the triangle.

The play still features sexual dissidence. It was scandalous for a woman to leave her husband, outrageous for her to declare that she has done so because of an overwhelming sexual passion, and courageous for her to relinquish both men for an independent life. Freddie's confession of a countervailing lack of sexual vigour is also unusual. 'Damn it, Jackie', he says to his old RAF friend, 'you know me. I can't be a ruddy Romeo all the time' (323). As Hester says, people were 'brought up to think that in a case of this kind it's more proper for it to be the man who does the loving' (313). Rattigan even thought to make a minor character homosexual, suggesting that Doctor Miller had been struck off the medical register for this, but it was changed in rehearsal and Miller's background became merely mysterious. 'What he did wasn't — well — the sort of thing people forgive very easily. Ordinary normal people, I mean', says the salt-of-the-earth landlady. 'It takes all sorts to make a world, after all — doesn't it? There was a couple once in Number Eleven — (*She stops suddenly*)' (349). Queerness is just about audible — though one critic reported that Miller's offence was carrying out abortions.

Rattigan's *Separate Tables* (1954) is two plays, both set in a Bournemouth residential hotel among an Agatha-Christie-type bunch of diverse people (I discuss *Table Number Seven* later in this chapter). *Table by the Window* mainly concerns the relations of a left-wing journalist, John Malcolm, with his former wife, Anne, and his current partner, Pat (who runs the hotel). The marriage foundered because of divergent expectations deriving from class difference, and because John was passionate whereas Anne, who had married for security, used her attractions to enslave him. However, they have both gone downhill since they parted. Rattigan's friends, according to Geoffrey Wansell, compared Anne with Michael Franklin, his principal partner from 1952 until Rattigan's death. 'There was something about Terry that loved all that hysteria', one says — 'the threats of cutting his wrists, or throwing himself off the balcony'. In Wansell's account, 'Franklin's appetite for tantrums and deceit, his narcissism and his compulsive lying all surface in Anne Shankland's character'.[18] As with the doctor in *The Deep Blue Sea*, there is a sideways reference to queerness. Anne's second husband is described as an antique dealer who was gentle, kind and made her laugh, didn't really like women and married because he wanted a wife (112–13). Like Coward, Rattigan scatters queer inferences around the edge of his stories, either encouraging or obfuscating (depending on the audience's state of awareness) queer thoughts about his main characters.

The themes of this chapter reach a summation in Rattigan's *Variation on a Theme* (1958). Rose is beautiful and in her mid-thirties, has married four times for money, and is about to do so again — to a rather brutal German banker, Kurt. When the twenty-six-year-old ballet dancer Ron Vale insinuates himself into her life, she knows he is an unscrupulous adventurer. But, he protests, he prefers older women: 'I always say that when two people have a real *rapport* the question of disparity of age just doesn't arise — '. Rose laughs with real enjoyment: that's exactly what she said to her second husband (221). They see a good deal of each other while Kurt is away, but when he returns there is little room for Ron. The action, as ever, is from the upper-class point of view — we don't follow Ron to his lodgings. But Rattigan does express through him the situation of the kept boy:

Have you ever thought what it's been like for me, asked over here a couple
of odd evenings a week whenever there're no important people around —
because common Ron mustn't meet important people — oh dear no —
that'd never do — and then when I'm here shoved around, needled, sent up
— everyone talking about people I don't know, and things I don't understand. (248)

He arrives uninvited, gets drunk, acts up and sobs, and insists that he really
does need Rose. She is moved; they are back together again.

Ron's choreographer and mentor, Sam Duveen, persuades Rose to break it
off and return Ron to the world of ballet. For that is something he has worked
at — fighting his father to do it, and achieving true expertise. Anyway, Sam
says, a relationship with Rose would last no more than six months, because 'the
Rons of this world always end by hating the people they need. They can't help
it. It's compulsive' (267). When they break up Rose will give him money, Sam
says, but not the self-respect he could gain as a dancer. For his own good,
therefore, Rose sends Ron away and agrees to marry Kurt — which is sensible,
because she has less money than she hoped and needs to spend the winter
months in Switzerland because otherwise she will die (she's coughing blood).

Three months later, Ron returns to make another scene. But this is because
he really does love Rose. He can't understand why she dismissed him; was it
that row in the Martinez, or the pullover he bought without asking her, or 'was
it anything to do with that day when you said I always stayed in the sea too
long, and you were waving from the beach and I was on the raft pretending not
to notice — ?' (300). This is the bit that breaks Rose up. She repudiates Kurt
and concurs with Ron's analysis: 'what have we got? Just what everybody else
in the world has got — each other' (303). However, this will mean not going
to Switzerland, so Rose will die.

We see Rose's daughter Fiona rehearsing a passage from *La Dame aux
camélias* (1852) by Alexandre Dumas *fils*: 'My heart has a need — a need that
an older man cannot satisfy. Then — dear Armand — I met you — young,
ardent, happy' (227). Fiona doesn't see the relevance to Rose's situation, but
Rattigan intends that the audience should. That is the theme upon which his
play is a variation, he let it be known — like Verdi's *La Traviata*.[19]

The point Rattigan wanted to make was that Armand, the upper-class man,
gets off too lightly in Dumas' account. This is because Marguerite, as a kept
woman, cannot be taken seriously (though there is no disgrace for the man); it
is assumed that a liaison with such a woman will not last, and it doesn't.

48

Rattigan valorises the lower-class partner. Although Ron is, explicitly, an adventurer, he and Rose fall in love. Whatever his friends said, Rattigan and his boyfriends genuinely needed each other. On the opening night, Franklin sent Rattigan a telegram − a reshuffle of the dedication Rattigan could not announce: 'From Michael, without whom this play would never have been written.'[20]

Variation on a Theme includes explicit queer elements: the Lord Chamberlain had begun to permit serious references to homosexuality. Ron is elaborately coiffured and has been living with Sam; Rose assumes that they have a gay relationship. Kurt asks if Ron flies across the stage on wires 'like Peter Pansy' (250). But Ron insists to Rose that he does 'go for women'. 'You girls never give us the benefit of the doubt', he exclaims; 'Sam Duveen's just a good friend of mine and that's that − ' (212−13). Later on, this is confirmed by Sam: 'Would you try to get this into your Wolfenden-conscious mind? Feelings can't sometimes be helped, but the expression of them can. They can and are' (268). In other words, Sam may have sexual feelings for Ron, but he has not been trying to satisfy them. Queerness is disavowed, but it is there.

The 'Wolfenden-conscious' atmosphere exposed Rattigan to comment. The critics knew that *Variation on a Theme* was about Rattigan and Franklin, and also about Margaret Leighton and Laurence Harvey, who was being kept and promoted by a male film producer when Leighton fell for him. Since Rattigan's dénouement turned on sincerity, it seemed unsatisfactory that his treatment was so oblique. Kenneth Tynan in the *Observer* mockingly suggested that Rattigan had switched the genders round.[21] Alan Brien in the *Spectator* said that he agreed for once with Harold Hobson of the *Sunday Times*: 'the play really was about something not its ostensible subject' − namely 'a homosexual relationship between a bored and ageing rentier and a sharp, oily male tart'. Of course, this was quite wrong; what Rattigan had meant to say is that the young man might turn out to be a good, caring person, and a true love after all. But his indirection crucially undermines that theme, suggesting, inevitably, that the subject must be sordid. 'As with some of Proust's women', Brien said, 'the heroine here should have five o'clock shadow bristling through her make-up'.[22] The drawback with discretion, always, is that it colludes with the notion that there is something disgusting and contemptible to be concealed. Only T.C. Worsley, in the *New Statesman*, stood up for the play − but then, he was Rattigan's friend and the central situation was not unlike that of Johnny Luscombe and himself. I suspect *Variation on a Theme* is better on the page than it was in a sumptuous production by H.M. Tennent (Binkie Beaumont's company) with gowns by Norman Hartnell, where it must have been hard to believe that anything important can happen to such social butterflies.

Cause Célèbre (1977) was Rattigan's last shot at all this, and it discloses the playwright stuck at a point not all that far from where Emlyn Williams had been with *Night Must Fall* in 1935. That was the year of the event Rattigan chose to dramatise: the Rattenbury trial. Alma Rattenbury had been having an affair with George Stoner (George Wood in the play), whom she had employed as an odd-job boy and chauffeur. They had carried this on under the nose of her husband, who was elderly and deaf and perhaps didn't care. One or both of them had beaten him to death with a wooden mallet; the play indicates that George did this, in a fit of jealousy that Alma might discard him and return to her husband. Like Rose, Alma had been married several times and just wanted a bit of fun and, if possible, love; like Ron, George was impressed with her lifestyle but eventually became passionately in love.

The scandal in *Cause Célèbre* centres, once more, upon differences of class and age. 'If one starts trying to think of it seriously', a bystander exclaims, 'one would go mad. I mean, it being with a servant! To me that's the real horror' (373). Even Alma's defence counsel feels obliged to condemn her: 'How could any one of you fail to feel disgust and nausea at the ensnaring and degradation of a helpless youth by a middle-aged woman of licentious and degenerate habits?' he asks (430). The difference from *Night Must Fall* and most other versions of this story, again, is that Rattigan wants to justify the feckless and dangerous young man: at the trial, Alma and George try to shield each other. However, all this is within a class structure which Rattigan, by using a setting in the 1930s, can still present as inevitable − much of the play is taken up with the manoeuvrings of barristers within their old-boy network. The murder is precipitated by George's unhappiness because they are going to visit friends and Alma will sleep with her husband, while he will be quartered with the servants.

Censorship and the Closet

In another strand of narrative in *Cause Célèbre*, Mrs Davenport (one of the jurors) and her husband mishandle their son, Tony, who is the same age as George. She dislikes sex and refuses her husband's advances; he has been unfaithful to her. Tony strives for freedom from his mother and attention from his father. He is engaging in same-sex practices at school and is probably growing up queer. What has this to do with Alma and George? We may infer a cross-identification, in which Rattigan is both Tony, the boy he once was, and Alma, the consequent grown-up who desires boys such as George.

It is frustrating that Rattigan shrinks from articulating such themes in the dialogue; he broaches them but seems to lose his nerve. He did want to write serious drama about such topics, but he didn't want to lose his middlebrow audience (whom he figured as 'Aunt Edna'); consequently, his treatments were confused and weakened by what he regarded as an appropriate indirection.

In *Table Number Seven*, the second play in *Separate Tables*, the residents of the hotel are thrown into conflict over the revelation that Major Pollock has been convicted of 'insulting behaviour' – harassing women in a cinema. Pollock explains himself: 'You wouldn't guess, I know, but ever since school I've always been scared to death of women. Of everyone, in a way, I suppose, but mostly of women. . . . I'm made in a certain way, and I can't change it. It has to be dark, you see, and strangers, because – ' (181). Rattigan had in mind the conviction and hounding by the press of John Gielgud (recently knighted) for 'importuning' in 1953. Courageously, Gielgud chose to carry on with his performances, and received standing ovations in the theatre and at the stage door.[23] This was to be Pollock's offence; to get past the censor it was changed to nudging a woman in a cinema.

For the Broadway production Rattigan had the opportunity to restore Pollock's queerness, but another set of pressures changed his mind. The producer, Bob Whitehead, said he didn't want *Table Number Seven* to become 'a play about homosexuality' – there had been several such on Broadway lately, it had 'almost become a cliché'. Eric Portman, who was to act the part, didn't like the idea either; 'he had always conducted that side of his life with great discretion', Wansell says. Rattigan backed down. After all, he declared in an interview in the *New York Times*, 'the play might have been construed as a thesis drama begging for tolerance specifically of the homosexual. Instead it is a plea for the understanding of everyone.'[24] This seems not to be logical: it becomes a plea for men who harass women. Heterosexuals are not 'everyone'.

What is extraordinary is that Rattigan believed that audiences actually knew that homosexuality was the issue. He said:

They fully realised that the Major's peccadilloes (in the cinema) were in fact only symbolical of another problem of which, at that time (just after several prominent cases), they were most sensitively conscious. An English audience knew my problem and accepted the fact that I had to skirt around it. They got the full impact of the play, as I subsequently learnt from many conversations.[25]

Of course, Rattigan was getting this feedback from a rather limited circle. As throughout this study, we have to ask which audiences 'knew'. However, reviewers were beginning to refer openly to the matter, as we saw in the case of *Variation on a Theme*. Tynan wrote his review of *Table Number Seven* in the *Observer* from the viewpoint of an imaginary 'young perfectionist', who regrets 'that the major's crime was not something more cathartic than mere cinema flirtation. Yet I suppose the play is as good a handling of sexual abnormality as English playgoers will tolerate.'[26]

Rattigan's expectation, that audiences know about homosexuality and that he has purposefully obscured it, suggests how the conditions governing queer representation in theatre had changed from those which pertained when Wilde wrote *A Woman of No Importance*, Maugham wrote *Our Betters*, Shairp wrote *The Green Bay Tree* and Coward wrote *Design for Living*. Those playtexts disclose a movement from general scandal, through bohemian repudiation of Society, to subcultural innuendo – with audiences divided over their ability and inclination to decode queer references. By the time of *Separate Tables* and *Variation on a Theme* the cat-and-mouse game with censorship and decorum has become not an occasional awkwardness but a structural factor in many significant productions. In a very real sense, it becomes what those plays are about – almost what theatre is about. What they represent, beyond their ostensible subject, is what the succeeding generation was to call 'the closet'.

Because Rattigan believed in gentlemanly discretion, this suited him well enough. Yet he is not so far from us. He died shortly after the première of *Cause Célèbre*, in 1977, at the age of 66. Michael Franklin was then about fifty, having been with Rattigan for twenty-five years. He died thirteen years later in 1990, of AIDS.

9

Queer Thrills

Persistently, the plot of West End and Broadway drama in mid-century hinges upon an anxiety about the stability of bourgeois society. From J.M. Barrie's *Admirable Crichton* and Maugham's *Jack Straw* in the first decade of the century, through to Coward's *Relative Values* and Rattigan's *Separate Tables* in the 1950s, respectable characters meet a threat to the security of their group. Either a plausible impostor is making his or her way into Society, or one of their own number has 'gone wrong'. More challenging authors suggest that the intruder or misfit manifests a superior ethic or wisdom. Consider *Lady Windermere's Fan*, Shaw's *Saint Joan*, Coward's *Easy Virtue*, *The Chalk Garden* by Enid Bagnold, *Orpheus Descending* by Tennessee Williams. But usually in West End and Broadway theatre the danger is adequately, though perhaps not entirely, contained at the final curtain.

Such anxieties had a wide purchase; this chapter finds instances among beleaguered subordinate groups as well as the upper classes of England and the United States. They had distinct resonances for leisure-class homosexuals who had made theatre their special space. Such men, I showed in chapter 8, were likely to be engaging in cross-class liaisons — inviting in the class enemy. At the trial of Lord Montagu of Beaulieu and his friends in 1954, the prosecution counsel made much of the crossing of class barriers: 'It is a feature, is it not, that inverts or perverts seek their love associates in a different walk of life than their own?' Peter Wildeblood replied defiantly:

The homosexual world knows no such boundaries — which is precisely why it is so much hated and feared by many of our political diehards. The real crime of Lord Montagu, for example, in the eyes of some 'Society'

167

people, was that he became acquainted − on no matter what basis − with
a man who (to quote the prosecuting counsel) was 'infinitely his social
inferior'.[1]

This was all very well, but the lower-class man was a risk. He might exploit
you and bring you into disrepute.

Further, queer men were, themselves, an unacceptable presence: they were
the enemies within. J.R. Ackerley remarks, almost in passing, that he and his
friends were 'outcasts and criminals in the sight of the impertinent English
laws'; Wildeblood said he would be 'the first homosexual to tell what it felt like
to be an exile in one's own country'.[2] Because queerness was scarcely spoken,
but had to be inferred from a generally mysterious, and probably pathological,
unease, any intruder or unacceptable presence was liable to trigger consternation about it. Harry M. Benshoff has shown how monster movies 'might be
understood as being "about" the eruption of some form of queer sexuality into
the midst of a resolutely heterosexual milieu'.[3] This chapter explores how
thriller, detective and mystery plays, through into 'Pinteresque menace', fed
off queer anxieties.

Psychodramas

All the most interesting murders are among the most seemingly ordinary
people. That's the queer thrill of it.

He took some − it was in little white tablets − while I was there, and it
had a horrible effect on him. I can see him now. His eyes were queer. Oh −
he really wasn't sane.[4]

The Drag (1927) by Mae West features psychological disturbance in a respectable
family, a murder and a police inspector, and thus marks out the ground for
queerness as a component in the thriller. The action is framed by a doctor who
has been reading Ulrich's 'third sex' theories and believes homosexuals should be
cured if possible; these are new ideas, we gather. A relevant patient immediately
presents himself: David, although accompanied by his campily happy friend
Clem, is distraught because he is 'one of those damned creatures who are called
degenerates and moral lepers for a thing they cannot help'. He had a partner, but
this man left him to marry, and is also in love with 'a normal man' (102–3).

It rapidly emerges that this ex-partner is the doctor's son-in-law, Rolly. He is a nasty piece of work: he has married merely as a cover and is very unsympathetic to David. He spends his time with Clem and other camp friends, and mooning after the 'normal man', Grayson — who, it transpires, is disgusted at Rolly's treatment of his wife and ready to console her. Rolly hosts a drag party which is broken up by the police. After the guests have left a shot is fired: Rolly is dead. Police enquiries focus at first upon Grayson, but the murderer is 'the poor abnormal creature', David. The doctor and Rolly's father agree to report the case as suicide, protecting the family name and recognising that David and Rolly were two of a kind — 'Little did we know that a fine, strong boy, like Rolly, was one of them' (139–40). The enemy was already within the gates.

Patrick Hamilton's thriller *Rope* (1929) had a try-out performance on a Sunday night and then a West End run; it was filmed by Alfred Hitchcock in 1948. Brandon and Granillo have murdered a fellow-student just for the hell of it: 'I have killed for the sake of danger and for the sake of killing', Brandon declares (14–15). They serve supper for friends on the chest in which they have placed the body. Are they a queer couple? The story looks very like the notorious Leopold and Loeb case in which the homosexuality of the two murderers had figured; it is the basis also of Meyer Levin's *Compulsion: A Play* (1957; see chapter 11), and of Tom Kalin's 1991 film *Swoon*. Hamilton, who was not gay-identified, denied that he took the story from the Leopold and Loeb case.

D.A. Miller develops through the film of *Rope* an argument about how queer connotation works (I draw on this in chapter 1). However, the most notable signs of queerness that he quotes from the film are not in the playtext. It exhibits no 'post-coital nuances of the dialogue' ('How did you feel — during it?' 'I don't remember feeling much of anything — until his body went limp, and I knew it was over, then I felt tremendously exhilarated'). And there are no mentions of bedrooms in the apartment and the intimacy they may imply.[5] Sean French suggests that the film (which Hamilton strongly disliked) discloses the gruesome basis of the story: 'The unspoken story behind Hamilton's play is that of forbidden sexuality and the forbidden act of violence, the complicity of lovers and the complicity of criminals.'[6]

In my view neither Miller nor French addresses the queerness of the play (however, Keith Howes registers it as 'unusual in that it dealt fairly explicitly with a gay relationship').[7] Hamilton depicts a notable intimacy between the murderers; at one point Brandon puts his arm around Granillo as he shares a match for his cigarette. Also, their appearances correspond, far more than in the film, to gender stereotyping. Brandon has the build of a boxer, whereas Granillo is slighter and 'rather ornately dressed', with an 'enormously courteous' manner, 'something between a dancing-master and a stage villain'; at school Brandon was good at games, Granillo not (19, 26). One of the most startling moments in the play is when Granillo enters the darkened room, unaware that Brandon is already there. As he moves to the chest which contains the body, he emits 'a horrible, shuddering, muffled scream': 'He has touched the other's body' (51). He has touched the body, that is, of his partner, but imagines it to be the murder victim, rising somehow from the chest. At this moment, the horror of murder coincides with the horror of same-sex contact. A corpse is equivalent to a live partner. The queer energy here is not just between the two murderers (only same-sex complicity can account for terrible crimes), but between the murderer and his victim (having sex with a man is akin to murder).

The most strikingly queer figure in the play is Rupert, the fellow-student who intuits and exposes the crime. He is 'a little foppish in dress and appearance' and 'enormously affected in speech and carriage'. He carries a 'very exquisite walking-stick'; 'His affectation almost verges on effeminacy' (31). The equivalent character in the film (played by James Stewart) has nothing at all of that. Rupert, in the play, is being deployed as the detached Wildean dandy who, like Lord Goring in *The Ideal Husband*, emerges at the end as the man of principle. Hamilton was uneasy later on when his brother played the part of Rupert because, he said, it 'is really cut out for a pansy'.[8] What does Rupert's effeminacy do for the putative queerness of Brandon and Granillo? We may think that it inoculates the text against any such perception – his manifest queerness seems to close off the topic. Alternatively, we may think that it puts sexuality on the agenda. *All* these young men may be queer – not only those who commit murder, but the victim and the man who has the insider intuition to detect it. That is how queer murder is, and how it has infested Society.

J.B. Priestley's *Dangerous Corner* (1932), produced in the West End and Broadway, shows another bourgeois group (directors of a family publishing company) infiltrated by queerness. The key figure is absent: Robert's brother Martin. He is supposed to have committed suicide, but no one altogether understands why; also, some money was missing. The action of the play uncovers a good deal about all of them. By the end, Robert says, his entire world has changed:

I began this evening with something to keep me going. I'd good memories of Martin. I'd a wife who didn't love me, but at least seemed too good for me. I'd two partners I liked and respected. There was a girl I could idealise. . . . Don't you see, we're not living in the same *world* now. Everything's gone. My brother was an obscene lunatic. . . . And my wife doted on him and pestered him. One of my partners is a liar and a cheat and a thief. The other — God knows what he is — some sort of hysterical young pervert. . . . And the girl's a greedy little cat on the tiles. (403)

All uncontrolled passions are dangerous in this play, but in two cases they are specially so. One is Martin, whose bisexual appeal facilitates the ingenious density in the relations of the group. 'He seemed to think that everybody young, male or female, ought to be falling in love with him. Both Freda and Gordon were involved with him, and they dispute which of them he really liked. He saw himself as a sort of Pan.' Martin is rather like the generally-dissolute Wildean dandy, but in a psychological age dandy detachment is perceived as a front: 'All that stuff about his merely being amused is nonsense. That was just his bluff. Martin hated anybody to think he was really moved or alarmed by anything' (393, 389). The other danger point is Gordon, whose confession of love is made 'hotly and scornfully' — hysterically: 'Friend of mine! He wasn't a friend of mine. You talk like a fish. Martin was the only person on earth I really cared about.' He concludes: 'And now you can call me any name you like, I don't care' (384). But 'there is a silence'; nobody calls Gordon anything until Robert attempts it in his final speech: 'God knows what he is — some sort of hysterical young pervert' (403). James Agate remarked: 'Mr Priestley has treated with skill and understanding a matter which on the stage is usually a subject for facetiousness, and I congratulate the Censor on having passed what must have been a difficult play.'[9]

The word 'queer' rings through these thrillers. I discussed in chapter 5 the emergence of 'gay' through its more general connotations of leisure-class and theatrical frivolity. In London in 1924, according to Michael Davidson, 'The word "queer", then, hadn't been invented; the cryptic designation was "so", corresponding to *comme ça* in Montparnasse', and there was 't.b.h.' ('to be had').[10] William Stewart reports 'queer' in the 1920s in the UK, and Chauncey finds it among US homosexual men in the 1910s and 1920s.[11] In recently published diaries of a man born in 1899, working as a government clerk in Washington, the editor notes: 'The reader may find pleasure in observing in

Jeb's diaries how the word "queer" changes its meaning from "odd" to "homosexual".' During the 1920s the sexual meaning emerges through the general meaning, then in 1928 Jeb says clearly, of gossip and intrigue among his friends, 'All that queer stuff. It makes me sick to think of it.' From then on 'queer' is customary for 'homosexual', on into the 1950s. 'Gay' is not thus used, though it appears in other contexts.[12]

These plays, in London and New York, use the indeterminacy of 'queer' to connote the moment when something mysterious, ominous and perhaps pathological hoves into view. Something is not quite right, in a way you can't quite pin down; perhaps because of eccentricity, or someone being 'not all there'. The situation is generally perverse, so homosexuality may be present in latent or covert form. To Robert in *Dangerous Corner* it is queer that Freda gave Martin a cigarette box: 'I don't mean it's queer your giving him the cigarette box − why shouldn't you? But it's queer your never mentioning it' (361; Wilde gave cigarette cases to his partners). To Rupert in *Rope* 'This is a very queer, dark and incomprehensible universe' (88). Queerness sometimes shades, to modern ears, into sexuality. Was Martin afraid of Robert? − No − or 'Yes, he was, in some queer way' (*Dangerous Corner*, 382). Talk with Brandon about rotting bones in chests is 'rather queer', and Rupert is a 'queer lad' (*Rope*, 47–50; 73). The word is used repeatedly in this significant-but-not-quite-specific way in Rose Allatini's novel, *Despised and Rejected* (1918).

John van Druten's West End thriller *Somebody Knows* (1932) is a lower-middle-class murder mystery framed by barristers, actresses and authors who profess to be intrigued by it, I think, as a way of claiming a boulevard audience's attention for the ordinary people who perform the main action. The slightly-too-plausible actor, Lance, has established himself in the affections of a retired opera singer and her daughter and hero-worshipping son, Harcourt. He has brought in Lily, a prostitute, and is excited by the idea that she has been used by men and now belongs to him. She is murdered and Lance is suspected. The family try to shield him, but is he worth their devotion? Lance feels 'a bit queer'; but then, he was 'a queer chap. You'd get so far with him and then you couldn't get any further' (98, 87). Harcourt feels queer as well, and dreams that Lance dies and returns to sit on his bed and talk to him (93).

Gayden (1949) by Mignon and Robert McLaughlin is in this vein. The eponymous protagonist is indulged by his mother; his disciplinarian father is dead. He seduces people, scandalously, and drops them; we see him bullying and cajoling a young family friend until she breaks her engagement; boys also are at risk. 'Look what's happened to the people around Gayden. Elisha was one. He hanged himself. Ellen Pritchard was another. She was found in a gas-filled apartment — just in time. The Tremaine boy this summer. He had a bad fall' (46). This is very like the accusations levelled at Dorian Gray by Basil Hallward.[13] According to Gayden's uncle Ned, a doctor, his misdeeds may extend to murder: 'He has no conscience. No moral sense. . . . He's a *constitutional psychopath*. You can't handle him. Neither can science' (47–8). There are three choices for his mother, Ned says: Gayden should be abandoned, locked up in an asylum, or suddenly killed. She hasn't the strength to do any of these, so the play ends inconclusively (compare *The Vortex*).

As with other enemies-within discussed in this section, Gayden's queerness is not just a matter of same-sex passion. In fact the authors want to have it both ways. Gayden has an indulgent mother, is involved with boys, did the décor of the house, knows about art, music and philosophy, and edits an intellectual magazine. However, they insist, he must be played 'very, very attractive, physically; virile, rather, and not at all a "pretty-boy". . . . There must be about him no touch whatever of the sinister or the queer.' They want the informing idea of queerness without the full stigma. For that would spoil 'the tragic sense of waste; it is a truly remarkable and appealing young man who turns out, alas, to be sick, and beyond redemption' (4).

Agatha Christie's mysteries were popular because they evoked and tamed the danger that may be lurking in any drawing room — especially, perhaps, in the most amiable and attractive young man. In *The Mousetrap* (1952) snow has blocked communications with the house where Mollie and Giles are starting out as hoteliers. They are joined by Police Sergeant Trotter, who says there is a murderer among them. Once, such people would all have been vouched for, but Mollie doesn't really know anything even about her husband, Trotter points out:

You'd be surprised, Mrs Ralston, if you knew how many cases like yours we get. Especially since the war. Homes broken up and families dead. Fellow says he's been in the Air Force, or just finished his Army training. Parents killed — no relations. There aren't any backgrounds nowadays and young people settle their own affairs — they meet and marry. It's parents and relatives who used to make the enquiries before they consented to an engagement. That's all done away with. Girl just marries her man. Sometimes she doesn't find out for a year or two that he's an absconding bank clerk, or an Army deserter or something equally undesirable. (331)

Indeed, no one in the play is who they initially seemed to be, and each of them entertains suspicions about the others.

Christie doesn't use 'queer'; probably by this date it would be too direct. But at least two guests in *The Mousetrap* show signs of queerness, and this is germane because the murderer is said to be mentally unstable — seeking to avenge, sadistically, the cruelty and neglect that he and his siblings experienced as foster children. One of them is Miss Casewell: as I show in chapter 7, she instances the availability of a lesbian stereotype in middlebrow theatre. The other, Christopher Wren, is rather wild looking and neurotic, finds the house 'heavenly', and can tell a genuine antique from a fake; he fancies the room with the fourposter and chintzy roses. Molly's cooking sounds distinctly unambitious, so Wren insists on donning an apron and taking over. 'I don't think your husband is going to like me', he says; but then only artists really understand people. Giles indeed despises Wren: 'He liked the pretty fourposter. Twerp! . . . I've got no use for that kind' (296).

Wren is notably impressed with Sergeant Trotter when he arrives: he's 'terribly hearty', 'very attractive' — 'I always think that policemen are very attractive' (308). But when he falls under suspicion of the murder he goes to pieces, and confesses to Molly that his mother died when he was young, that his name actually is Christopher Robin and it was hell at school, and he has always been persecuted. However, while I don't want to give the plot away, I have to reveal that neither of these queer people is the murderer. Casewell turns out to be a responsible person who has handled her difficulties well and who contributes significantly to the satisfactory conclusion of the plot. And Wren is entirely irrelevant. The point, of course, is that their sexual dissidence makes them plausible red herrings. (Christie's detective Hercule Poirot is effeminate, as Alison Light points out, but 'as a foreigner, he is forgivably cissy'.[14])

Servants and Masters

Servants were always a danger point. When Strindberg's *Miss Julie* (1888) was banned in 1925 the Lord Chamberlain found it 'objectionable from two points of view'. First, 'the sordid and disgusting atmosphere . . . makes the immorality of the play glaring and crude'; second, 'there is the very questionable theme in these days of the relations between masters and servants, which this play tends to undermine'.[15]

Robin Maugham's novella *The Servant* (1948) was based on his own experience, he says. His mother installed him in a flat together with the unsettling manservant who was to become Barrett in the book. One night Robin passed Barrett's room and glimpsed a naked boy on the bed; Barrett offered to send him up later. Terrified of a blackmail set-up, Robin pretended not to hear, and soon got rid of Barrett when he was arrested for trying to pawn his clothes. In the novella, the boy became a girl, as in the film of 1963, scripted by Harold Pinter and directed by Joseph Losey; *The Servant* was tried out also as a play, in Worthing (1958). Actually, Barrett was not off the mark: Robin preferred his partners 'to be men who looked and behaved in a masculine manner, came from the working class, were educationally inferior and had a low income or none at all so that he could play benefactor'.[16] It is the fact that Barrett had understood his master's predilections correctly that made the situation perilous.

Mel Dinelli's thriller, *The Man* (1950), was well received on Broadway and in the West End in 1952. Mrs Gillis believes she lives in a world of reason and compassion. When she hires a casual worker to clean her house she thinks she knows what she's doing — 'He was *not* a tramp. He was very nicely dressed' (8). But Howard turns out to be very odd. He is dark and frail and has a simple likeable quality about him, but he has an intense, serious expression on his face. He has memory lapses, it emerges, perhaps he harms people. Mrs Gillis tries everything — being patient, understanding, stern, crafty, apologetic — but Howard becomes more and more threatening. Either she dislikes him, like everyone else, in which case he seems likely to attack her, or she is different, in which case he wants to stay with her.

Further, there is something queer about Howard. He has trouble with masculinity. He was rejected for military service: 'And that room full of men . . . all of them capable, with their strong naked bodies. . . .' He felt belittled; 'While the others were signing up, I had to sit like a tired old woman and sip coffee . . . ' (30–1, Dinelli's pauses). When Mrs Gillis' niece comes on to him, he freezes; she taunts him: 'I don't see many *men* around polishing floors . . . it's a woman's job . . . seems to me there're better ways for a *man* to make a living' (53, Dinelli's pauses). W. David Sievers in *Freud on Broadway* finds here an illustration of 'the close relationship between homosexuality and paranoia'.[17]

These anxieties generally cluster around men. The predatory lesbians discussed in chapter 7 might be regarded as instances of outlaw-intruders or enemies-within, but the danger constituted by women is usually seen in heterosexual terms: they will seduce the father or the son of the house, producing illegitimate offspring and messing up class and patriarchy. Part of the perversity of Jean Genet's *The Maids* (1947, *Les Bonnes*) is that it focuses anxieties about class and sexual intrusions through women.

The Maids was performed at club theatres in London in 1952 (in French) and 1956, and Off-Broadway in 1963. It derives from a historical event in Le Mans in 1933, in which Madame and her daughter died at the hands of their maids, two sisters. It was a disputed question, why these women should brutally slaughter their employers. For a left-wing newspaper in September 1933, the humiliations of servility were a sufficient explanation: 'This trial should not have been only that of the sisters, but also that of the sacrosanct bourgeois family in whose heart developed a baseness and a wickedness, and a scorn for those who earn their living by serving them.'[18] In Genet's play the maids' role-play is a vehicle for their resentment of authority. 'I'm tired of being an object of disgust. I hate you, too. I despise you. I hate your scented bosom. Your . . . *ivory* bosom! Your . . . *golden* thighs! Your . . . *amber* feet! I hate you', Solange says to Claire/her mistress (12, Genet's pauses). As the women reverse roles, they foreshadow a revolutionary overthrow of the upper classes. 'Madame thought she was protected by her barricade of flowers, saved by some special destiny, by a sacrifice. But she reckoned without a maid's rebellion', Solange says (12).

For other commentators, the issue is not class revolt but a perverse sexual relationship between the sisters. In the view of the Lord Chamberlain's reader, 'running through the whole play is the suggestion of Lesbianism, not easy to follow, not directly described and in the main left to be inferred; none the less it appears to be the essential background to the plot', and this creates 'a depravity which makes the play unsuitable for public performance before mixed audiences'.[19] Certainly sexuality is everywhere in the text. The role-play dialogue weaves obsessively around Madame's clothes and body – her gowns, her furs, her jewels, her bosom, her throat, 'her satiny skin, and her little ears, and little wrists' (38). As Solange gets 'right into the transformation' her sensations are orgasmic: 'I'm quivering, I'm shuddering with pleasure. Claire, I'm going to whinny with joy' (34). Eroticism is the glue between the maids and between them and their mistress.

It is not, I think, that anyone is having an actual lesbian affair, though at one point Solange comforts and caresses Claire. Rather, as Solange says, their love has become inseparable from their servitude. 'Filth . . . doesn't love filth'; 'I'm repulsive to you. And I know it because you disgust me. When slaves love one another, it's not love' (16, 21). Their sexuality is dangerous *because* they are dominated by Madame; Solange calls herself 'The monstrous soul of servantdom' (39). As in *Rope*, queerness both completes and compromises the act of murder.

Yet the action of *The Maids* results not in the death of Madame, as in the historical case, but of the servant who has been imitating her. The dominant reading of this, for instance in Martin Esslin's influential *Theatre of the Absurd* (1961), is that revolt is locked inevitably into a fantasy repetition of the power that it tries to oppose, and will consume itself; that political action towards purposive change will be futile.[20] What is reductive, indeed sinister, about this interpretation is the implication that significant social change would occur if individuals got up and murdered the nearest powerful individual. Very few revolutionaries have believed that. Leo Bersani apprehends the question more subtly.

> The maids' dilemma is that there is nothing they might do to Madame that would not confirm their identity as maids. Even to kill her — though it is not an intrinsic part of the social scenario within which they are inscribed — would transgress their maid-subjectivity in a way determined by that scenario. Transgressiveness is part of their identity.[21]

It is the structure that must be changed. The insight that might be derived from this (though it is not quite Bersani's point), as from Bertolt Brecht's *Good Person of Szechwan*, is that individual violence is indeed pointless; the way forward must lie in political analysis and collective action.

Nations and Aliens

The danger of the same-sex intruder is greater in an already-beleaguered community, as may be seen in two Jewish plays. *God of Vengeance* (1907) was written in Yiddish by Sholem Asch and produced in German by Max Reinhardt in Berlin in 1911, and also in Polish, Russian, French and Italian.[22] Yankel Chapchovich believes he can buy religious and marital respectability for his daughter although he has made his fortune by running a brothel. But the daughter, Rivkele, is passionately attached to one of the prostitutes, Manke. There is virtually no analysis of the sexual situation, but it is entirely explicit. Manke says:

That's right, press your face against my breast. Like that, that's the way. And let your body caress me. So cool, like water running between us. (*Pause.*) I uncovered your breasts and washed them with the rain water that ran into my hands. So white and firm, your breasts, and the blood in them cools under the hand like white snow, like ice. And their fragrance is like the smell of grass in the meadows. (98)

However, the offence resides not in the lesbian relationship, but in the fact that it leads Rivkele too into prostitution: the play ends with the father distraught, believing she is no longer suitable for a decent marriage. Yankel has brought danger, but also love, into his own house. Probably much of the lesbian dialogue was cut when *God of Vengeance* was produced in English at the Provincetown Theatre in Greenwich Village in 1922. When it transferred to Broadway the complaints of Christian and Jewish religious leaders caused its indictment for obscenity.

Rose Franken's play *Outrageous Fortune* (1943, Broadway; banned in the UK) is set in a Jewish family; the extent to which Jewish people should be putting up the shutters against people and practices that apparently do not belong to their tradition is a running question. Kaier Curtin dislikes *Outrageous Fortune*, perhaps because he had an unpleasant telephone interview with the now elderly and homophobic author. However, the play is quite complex and demanding. If critics were confused, it is probably because there turns out to be not just one queer man but two, and because the focus is partly upon intimacy between a gay man and a straight-identified woman.

The first queer, Barry, is familiar enough: 'He is tall, slender and good to look at. If he were a woman, he would exude a kind of inherent fragrance. In a male it must be marked against him as an extreme fastidiousness, and a sensitivity easily mistaken for a lack of virility' (x). *Outrageous Fortune* is friendly towards Barry, insofar as hostility is evinced by people who are unhappy and is repudiated by wise characters. He is allowed to explain himself: 'No, Kitty, I didn't play with dolls. But I did housework and cooking, because after my father died there wasn't any money, and my mother, who had never worked before, had to get a job. The boys on the block used to call me sissy. Maybe I was. Maybe I am, according to the way you see things' (128–9). However, there seems no prospect of Barry finding a boyfriend.

A further note to Barry's character is interesting: 'It is easy to understand a woman falling in love with him, for he has tenderness, intuition and polish' (x). In fact, two women are in love with Barry: Crystal, the enigmatic celebrity, and Madeleine, the quietly married woman. At the end of act II, after confessing all to Crystal, he is invited up to her bedroom. I don't agree with Curtin that this indicates that Barry will 'escape the gay underworld', even though the author suggested forty years later, in a phone conversation, that she had meant that.[23] It is Crystal who who makes the clearest statement about Barry: 'No mystery about it. You were born with a few too many F cells in your body' (146). This hardly suggests that she means or expects to change his orientation. As I read *Outrageous Fortune*, Crystal is a sophisticated woman, likes Barry, and doesn't regard queerness as an ineluctable barrier to intimate pleasure.

The second queer, Julian, Madeleine's brother-in-law, is not lovable. Despite his engagement to Kitty, he is having some kind of affair with his more famous and notorious collaborator (they are writing a musical). He makes a pass at Barry, and when he is rejected denounces him. So queers are their own worst enemies. However, even Julian has to be acknowledged as part of the Jewish community. His conservative brother, Bert, would 'rather see him dead than the thing that he's become', but he is defended by Crystal: 'If he were ill or crippled, would you turn against him?' Jewry has to cope with irregularities among its own. 'A part of you is responsible for Julian' (195).

South (1953, Paris; Arts Theatre Club, 1955) by Julien Green is set at the moment when gentlemen had to choose whether they would fight for the beleaguered South in the Civil War. However, perhaps because of the intensity of this moment, the young men and women are preoccupied by intimate passions. Lieutenant Wicziewsky is the outsider. As he points out, America is peopled by men and women from elsewhere. Yet he is different, he is told: 'they end by having a family likeness. But in your case, it's not so. You remain a stranger, in spite of your uniform' (112). His strangeness includes an inability to accept the love of any of the women, and heavily meaningful remarks suggest that he is tragically doomed to an unrequited passion. Finally, as each is about to leave for the army, Wicziewsky achieves an enigmatic conversation with another young man, Mac Clure, who is evidently the person he loves. Mac Clure almost understands that he is being wooed; he responds by recalling 'a sudden affection for a classmate' (188). But he is in love with the young woman of the house — though not, Wicziewsky accuses, with a passion such as he himself feels. Wicziewsky abruptly provokes a duel with Mac Clure, in which he gets himself killed. Kenneth Williams saw the Arts production:

> It's about a young homosexual in love with a normal young man; of course he commits suicide. Really, this is the kind of thing that seems inevitable

in all the homosexual writing. They're always killing themselves. Totally misleading & distorted picture of life, for there are a great number of happy homosexuals – at least as happy as heterosexuals. I'm sick of this 'persecuted queer' stuff.[24]

Differences of ethnicity and nation aggravate and are aggravated by sexual passion in Jean Anouilh's *Becket* (1960, Broadway; Royal Shakespeare Company, 1961). The Saxon Becket is the favourite of the Norman King Henry, but speaks of his father as a collaborator and of the Normans as the master race and tries to protect Saxon people from Henry's rapaciousness. As Kenneth Tynan remarked, 'something here smacks less of pre-Renaissance England than of post-war France'.[25] It all takes a homoerotic inflection from the opening flash-forward, where Henry is submitting to a flogging as penance for the murder of Becket. The main action then begins as the King comes from his bath, and Becket dries and dresses him: 'Nobody rubs me down the way you do, Thomas' (*Becket*, 8). Henry makes a point of taking women from Thomas. As Anouilh presents it, Henry experiences the defection of Becket when he becomes Archbishop not as a political difficulty but as a personal loss. The Queen Mother accuses Henry of being 'neither healthy or manly. . . . If Thomas Becket were a faithless woman whom you still hankered after, you would act no differently' (107). 'I loved him! Yes, I loved him! And I believe I still do!' Henry proclaims, 'sobbing hysterically'. That is why he calls for someone to rid him of this priest – not because Church and State cannot agree, but because he can't stand the pain of lost love (110). Tynan added: 'His Henry was devoured by a passion that confused him even as it consumed him: the actor implied what the character never suspected, namely, that his attachment to Becket was homosexual.'[26]

It would not be sensible to derive a pattern from four plays from such diverse times and places. They show the potential, largely untapped on the stage, of the theme that queerness is even more threatening in contexts of racial and ethnic dominance, where patterns of intrusion, subversion and belonging are distinctively violent and contorted.

Pinteresque Menace

The encroachment of a menacing outsider upon a purportedly secure but actually fragile situation is the staple stuff of early plays by Harold Pinter. Rose and Bert's tenure is jeopardised in *The Room* (1957); Goldberg and McCann winkle Stanley out of his retreat in *The Birthday Party* (1958); Aston invites in the ungrateful Davies in *The Caretaker* (1960); Teddy's return with Ruth destabilises the family in *The Homecoming* (1965). In *A Slight Ache* (1959) Edward challenges the Matchseller, who has been standing mysteriously outside his house, threatening his boundary: 'God damn it, I'm entitled to know something about you! You're in my blasted house, on my territory, drinking my wine, eating my duck!' (34–5). These themes bear a striking resemblance to the anxieties about queer intrusion that we have been observing. To be sure, Pinter's concern is not social propriety, but an uncertain compound of metaphysical vacuity and sexual challenge, whose ultimate residence may be the psyche. However, the inhibitions on speaking queerness on the stage mesh conveniently with the thought that the answer may lie in the silences. There are intense male relations in all the plays I have mentioned, and also in *The Dwarfs* (1960) and *The Dumb Waiter* (1960); Stanley in *The Birthday Party* and Lenny in *The Homecoming* are discomfited at the prospect of sexual relations with women.

In *The Collection* (1961, Royal Shakespeare Company; Off-Broadway, 1962) Pinter makes sexuality central, depicting tension in the households of Harry and Bill and James and Stella. The question is whether sexual congress has occurred between Stella and Bill; we never find out what 'actually happened', of course. Homosexuality is to be inferred from the usual cues – the 'artistic' décor of Harry and Bill, Bill's occupation as a dress designer, the proprietary attitude of the older and wealthier Harry. According to Harry, Bill has 'a slum mind'. That is 'perfectly all right in a slum, but when this kind of slum mind gets out of the slum it sometimes persists, you see, it rots everything' (43). Esslin deduced that Bill may have wanted to sleep with Stella because he 'may have been made into a homosexual by an older man who offered him social advancement, a good job, life in a middle-class milieu'.[27] Bill's 'alleged bisexuality', John M. Clum remarks, 'makes him dangerous to all the characters, because it makes him an unstable force'.[28] At the end, the two couples are still there, but each of them has a far stronger sense of their vulnerability.

For other writers too, the customary indirection about homosexuality combined with a Pinteresque blend of obliquity and menace. *The Zoo Story* (1960, Off-Broadway) by Edward Albee was widely regarded as establishing an American version of absurdist writing (it was produced in a double bill with *Krapp's Last Tape* by Beckett). The characters have difficulty making communication — the most intense relationship is between Jerry and the landlady's dog, and he succeeds in reducing that to sadness and suspicion; Jerry insists on fighting Peter for his place on a park bench. As well as intruding upon Peter's solitary reading, Jerry mocks his female-dominated household. So what is going on? The theatregoer may recognise the idea of the plausible psychopath, as in *Night Must Fall* and *The Man*, as well as the possibility of a guarded gay pick-up. The latter dimension is denied: Jerry distances himself from the colored queen who lives in the next room and admits to only an adolescent queer phase; 'And now; oh I do love the little ladies; really I love them. For about an hour' (396). 'You won't find a policeman around here', he says, because 'they're all over on the west side of the park chasing fairies down from the trees or out of the bushes' (410). However, the denial does not erase the possibility — Jerry may be dangerously confused or intentionally misleading Peter. The conclusion, in which Jerry engineers his own death at Peter's hand, resembles that of *South*.

The Ballad of the Sad Café (1963, Off-Broadway), adapted by Albee from Carson McCullers' novella, is partly in this vein. Lymon, a mysterious dwarf, gets taken by Miss Amelia into her home and business, but when her violent husband returns Lymon displays sexual interest in him — 'small, involuntary spasms of excitement, little jumps from the ground, strange jerks of his hands' (114). He transfers his affections to the husband and contributes, treacherously, to Amelia's defeat and the destruction of the café.

In my view Pinteresque menace had rapidly became a trick, perhaps even for Pinter, whereby, with sectors of the audience becoming more intellectual and libertarian, basically traditional elements of the queer thriller could be loaded with new 'significance'. However, at a time when some people were campaigning courageously on the agenda of the Wolfenden Report, it was hardly progressive to use queers as images of obscure menace.

In *The Trigon* (1963, Arts Theatre Club; Off-Broadway, 1965) by James Broom Lynne, the mysterious intruder, Charles, expels Arthur and Basil from their flat. There is no indication of sexual passion as such between Arthur and Basil, but there are gross hints. For instance, as the play opens Arthur is wearing Boy Scout uniform and playing a record of 'Dance of the Sugar-Plum Fairy'. Their intentions towards their friend Mabel are evidently half-hearted (compare Stanley and Lulu in *The Birthday Party*): it is said that if they both addressed her 'She wouldn't know which way to turn' (106). One explanation of Charles' intrusion might be the stereotypical one that homosexuals gain satisfaction from breaking up the relationships of others. However, it is suggested that Arthur and Basil will be better for the self-knowledge Charles has produced: 'It's no good either of us thinking of Mabel. Or any other woman for that matter. We'll make plans for each other. No third party' (152). This ought to mean Arthur and Basil coming to terms with their sexual relationship, but since conventional discretion prevented that question from being broached, it could hardly be answered. To the reviewer in *Theatre World* (July 1964) the characters were 'inexplicably bound together emotionally'. Probably *The Trigon* is best regarded as a spoof.

The Killing of Sister George (1965, West End; Broadway, 1966) by Frank Marcus depicts the encroachment of the sinister and manipulative Mrs Mercy upon the ménage of June and Alice. I try to account further for this intriguing play in chapter 14. The difficulty that is relevant here, I have always thought, is working out where Mrs Mercy is coming from. Is she a predatory lesbian who sees a good prospect when she meets Alice, or a career woman who discovers her lesbianism through her engagement with June and Alice, or a controlling person who likes to make mischief? Marcus indicated the last of these. He told Eileen Atkins, who played Alice: 'Mrs Mercy isn't looking for a lover, she's looking for a slave. In a woman like that every normal physical instinct – what I call normal – has long been sublimated into a power complex and she'll keep you impotent, but there won't be anything overtly sexual between you at all.'[29] I don't know whether that is altogether plausible or quite realisable on stage. The film introduced a steamy bedroom scene between Mercy and Alice (Marcus loathed it). As with other plays discussed in this section, I think *The Killing of Sister George* relies on the vogue for Pinteresque menace, wherein the enigmatic stance of the intruder is part of the trick. The role of Madame Xenia, a fortune-teller, seems designed to fit with this. 'The BBC is very Kafkaesque with all those corridors', Marcus added.

Pinteresque menace found its way to the Dublin Theatre Festival. In Thomas Kilroy's play *The Death and Resurrection of Mr Roche* (1968) the party after the pub is at Kelly's. Things take a nasty turn when, at Kelly's instigation, Roche, who is queer, is bundled down the stairs to the basement and has a fatal seizure. They try to get rid of the body. It is Kelly's own queerness, it appears, that has made him anxious and aggressive. However, Roche returns: he is not dead after all, or perhaps he is a ghost – compare J.M. Synge's *Shadow of the Glen*. As Kelly and the others go to mass, Roche installs himself in the flat. This is either a sinister move – he is blackmailing Kelly – or the stirring of Kelly's conscience.

This genre culminates in Joe Orton's *Entertaining Mr Sloane* (1964). Already in the unproduced *Fred and Madge* (1959) Orton was drawing absurdist techniques towards a realist critique of English mores. There is a rather half-hearted attempt to reinflect the subversiveness of 'queer' when the characters voice their suspicions about a youngster called Brian: he hates organised games, goes on protest marches, and wears jeans on all occasions. 'Oh, there's definitely something queer about Brian' (67). A Pinteresque air gives an edge to *Ruffian on the Stair* (1964), which was written before Orton's better-known plays and produced on radio, and then at the Royal Court Theatre in 1966. Wilson menaces the home of Joyce and Mike; it is hinted that the disturbance stems from Mike's forays into a queer world and Wilson's love for his good-looking brother; Wilson manipulates Mike into killing him.

In *Entertaining Mr Sloane* Orton makes a new break: he deploys oblique dialogue and an enigmatically destructive intruder not to invoke a mysterious menace which might be queer, but as discreet manoeuvrings in a plausible queer liaison. The middle-aged Eddie is evidently homosexual: that is the only way to make sense of his toleration of Sloane, his interest in Sloane's physique and sex life, and his horror of heterosexuality. The obscurities in his dialogue occur, as Orton explained to Alan Schneider, the US director, because 'he thinks he can get Sloane. Sure he can. But it may take a bit of time − cause Sloane is such a nice kid.'[30] However, Sloane is not the innocent of Eddie's fantasy − he reads Eddie's indirection very well. He teases him by suggesting that he is 'sensitive'; Eddie is flustered: 'I seen birds all shapes and sizes and I'm most certainly not . . . um . . . ah . . . sensitive' (113, Orton's pauses). Sloane plays him along:

> A couple of years ago I met a man similar to yourself. Same outlook on life. A dead ringer for you as far as physique went. He was an expert on the adolescent male body. He's completed an exhaustive study of his subject before I met him. During the course of one magical night he talked to me of his principles − offered me a job if I would accept them. (135).

'Sloane knows Eddie wants him', Orton added. 'He's been in bed with men and women in the past. But he isn't going to give in until he has to.'[31]

Entertaining Mr Sloane revises the received terms of queer theatre in two ways. First, where earlier writers had written discreetly, Orton deploys Eddie's indirection as the inhibitions and manipulations of a discreet homosexual. Sloane's obscure responses are a plausible reaction to that. It is the characters who are oblique, not the play. Second, although Pinteresque motifs, deriving from the thriller, contribute an air of menace, the violence in this case is not arbitrary, pathological, paranoid or metaphysical. Sloane, the attractive young man invited in, has killed a man who wanted to photograph him; it is a danger experienced all the time by cruising gays. Simon Shepherd argues that Orton's plays 'end with a negotiated settlement that fixes the youths into their place'.[32] However, by the end of this play Sloane has killed a second man, and Kath and Eddie may be rash to assume that he won't kill again.

10

Reading Tennessee Williams

Queer Genders

Never for a moment are Gwendolen and Cecily persuasively 'female'. They
are creatures of indeterminate sex who take up the mask of femininity to
play a new and provocative role. (Camille Paglia).

[*Private Lives*] uses a heterosexual relationship to dramatize a camp
sensibility. (John Lahr)[1]

Gay men cannot create women characters; either they use them as surreptitious versions of themselves, or they caricature them as a way of expressing
their misogyny — that is the charge. Molly Haskell accuses Tennessee
Williams of making woman 'the repository of certain repellent qualities which
he would like to disavow. He projects onto her the narcissism, the vanity, the
fear of growing old which he is horrified to find festering within himself' (as if
heterosexuals were not narcissistic, vain and frightened about growing old).
Williams' women are products of 'his own baroquely transvestized homosexual
fantasies', Haskell avers.[2] Through such arguments, any prospect that gay men
might have a noteworthy perspective upon the sex/gender system is set aside.
Peter Hall, directing Williams' work, found it helpful to bear in mind that he
'was a woman right through'.[3]

It is not reasonable to attribute all such comments to homophobia; many
gay men have said more or less the same thing. For Jack Babuscio, Williams'
'crypto gayness found relief in the form of female guise: Blanche, Alma, Karen.
These characters do express their creator's own "unacceptable" emotions as a

gay man. They do all declare the nature of Williams's own fantasy life at the time of their creation.'[4] John M. Clum is aware of the dangers in this approach, but summarises:

> *A Streetcar Named Desire*, though without a living homosexual character or overt gay theme, depicts in a codified fashion a paradigmatic homosexual experience. It is the quintessential closeted gay play, and Blanche DuBois is in many ways the quintessential gay character in American closet drama. Williams himself was quoted as saying, 'I am Blanche DuBois.'[5]

Clum elaborates this by pointing to Blanche's preference for magic and theatre over realism, her knowingness and her promiscuity; throughout *A Streetcar Named Desire*, he says, 'a homosexual code is operative' (151). Mark Lilly is uncomfortable with such readings of Blanche, but observes nonetheless: 'many gay students whom I have taught find her sympathetic, tend to withhold their condemnation, and are, indeed, even attracted by her doomed status'.[6] Recently Ian Lucas has written of Blanche as 'a projection' of Williams' 'own homo-sexual desires' — an instance of coding used by 'homosexual playwrights attempting to conceal their own sexuality'.[7]

Williams did not entirely discourage such ideas. He said he had to have physical desire for at least one character in any work he wrote, that he was hysterical like Blanche, and (referring to her famous line) that 'chance acquaintances, or strangers, have usually been kinder to me than friends'.[8] 'The reason that I have no difficulty at all in creating female characters is because, in my psyche, there is a little congregation of panicky ladies and/or tramps', he declared in a letter to *Gay Sunshine*, in 1977.[9] This could be simply the invocation of androgyny that many authors make, within the prevailing romantic idea of creativity. But Williams continues: 'Why panicky? Because they are confined there': this sounds like the restraints placed upon male femininity in modern Western cultures. Indeed, Williams flourished in the 1950s, when the idea of a female soul in a male body persisted. 'It is found that the cycle of these individuals' homosexual desires follows the cycle closely patterned to the menstrual period of women', congressman A.L. Miller asserted in 1951. 'There may be three or four days in each month that the homosexual's instincts break down and drive the individual into abnormal sexual practice.'[10] However, Williams also declared that he'd never been drawn to drag, that '"swish" and "camp" are products of self-mockery, imposed upon homosexuals by our society', and that he was against gay men behaving like 'a travesty of the other sex'. His own sexual preferences seem to have been what is conventionally known as 'active'.[11]

Imagining a woman as a gay man, or vice versa, is intrinsically demeaning to neither. The ramifications may be conservative or radical, depending on the context and quite how it is done. Nor does reading gay men into Williams' women have to involve a sentimental merging of the world and fantasy. Such readings may be developed critically. Williams' plays bear upon the whole pattern of relations in the sex/gender ideology, in which there are both analogues and differences in the situations of women and gay men. I have broached these matters in my books *The Wilde Century* and *Gay and After*; it is not an ambition of the present study to resolve them.[12] I would add, though, that they are implicated in the persistent confusion, in our cultures, of sexual orientation (object choice) and gender identity. A transsexual in Kate Bornstein's play *Hidden: A Gender* (1989) insists: 'My gender identity has nothing to do with my sexual preference. Gender identity for me answers the question of who I am. Sexual preference answers the question of who do I want to be romantically or sexually involved with' (191). Assumptions that are made about Williams, his female characters, and the relation of audiences to them mainly concern gender identities, but they are presented as if they were to do with object choice. No wonder we cannot get the issue sorted.

Yet, having separated these matters analytically, their practical entanglement in the lives of men and women as they apprehend themselves must be acknowledged. Stephen Maddison, in an original study of gay identification with women in the work of Williams, Pedro Almodóvar, and the televsion series *Roseanne*, concludes: 'in as far as transsexualism seems to represent a radical engagement with the kinds of damage and punishment experienced by those who cannot reconcile their identity with the expectations of a hostile gender system, then perhaps we could see homosexuality and transsexualism as alternative responses to similar conditions'.[13] Briefly, all of us, gay, straight and other, are trying to manage our genders and sexualities in unpropitious circumstances.

Along with Alexandra del Lago in *Sweet Bird of Youth* (1959), Blanche DuBois has been welcomed into the pantheon of courageous-distraught women with whom gay men have often felt a sympathetic identification. Her line, 'I have always depended on the kindness of strangers' has become one of the great affirmations of a cruising culture that resists both the intensity and the banality of the committed relationship (418). Neil Bartlett is asked in an interview: 'But this is 1991. Is drag really important to gay men?' 'I think it's a really important part of British gay men's culture', Bartlett replies. 'Almost all the things that are now traditionally gay are very important for that fact alone, and they represent gay space. They are a cultural space which we can inhabit.'[14] I think this means: drag and female identification are among the sites where gay men have constituted themselves, and such subcultural myths cannot and should not lightly be discarded.

Where, then, do we stand with Stanley, Blanche's tormenter? 'The modern Queer was invented by Tennessee Williams. Brando in blue jeans, sneakers, white T-shirt and leather jacket. When you saw that, you knew they were available' – so Derek Jarman.[15] The irony there, however, is that Stanley, as Williams has written him, would be a dangerous man with whom to risk a sexual advance; he is not likely to be 'available'.

Violence Against Women

The blatant scandal of *A Streetcar Named Desire* (1947), initially, was its depiction of female desire. The gaze which Blanche and Stella direct at Stanley seemed to exude an extraordinary, even perverse, energy. Hence, in part, the supposition that this gaze must come from a gay man; women, it is (or was) imagined, are modest. While we may want to read Blanche as a way of elaborating gay subcultural experience, I think it important to observe that transposing her too rapidly out of heterosexuality elides an important theme of male violence against women.

Donald Spoto and Lyle Leverich reveal in their biographies that Williams' father was frequently drunk and violent. Regarded in this light, the absence of the father in *The Glass Menagerie* (1944) is understandable and significant, and Stanley becomes a candidate for his embodiment. That makes Blanche not Williams, but Williams' sister, Rose. Further and crucially, the event that immediately preceded the hospitalising of Rose, we know from Spoto, was her shouting 'hysterically that her father had come to her room drunk and had spoken and acted in a lewd, provocative way: she insisted, wildly, that Cornelius [the father] wanted her, his own daughter, to go to bed with him. This was something unthinkable, unutterable' for the mother, *and hence the lobotomy*.[16] Leverich adds that when Rose was admitted to the State Hospital in 1937, the report did not say that Cornelius had made improper advances toward Rose, but it did say that she had 'delusions of sexual immorality by members of the family'.[17] Both Spoto and Lyle are inclined to go along with the parental and official line: Rose said such things because she was crazy. However, it is entirely unsafe to suppose that Rose's version was substantially untrue. She was prevented by the lobotomy from announcing such an awful situation.

Williams, evidently, believed Rose. The sexual violence attributed to their father is echoed in the rape of Blanche by Stanley in *Streetcar*, and the decision of Rose's mother to have her incarcerated and eventually lobotomised is echoed in Stella's response to the rape. 'I don't know if I did the right thing', Stella says; 'I couldn't believe her story and go on living with Stanley.' Eunice concurs: 'Don't ever believe it. Life has got to go on' (405–6). The women cannot afford to recognise what Stanley is like. 'Don't let them do that to her', Stella cries at the last minute, but she stands aside (416). Blanche is lobotomised in order to protect a dreadful truth about family violence.

Williams then may become Allan, the queer boy who loved Blanche (Rose) ineffectually and wrote poetry, and was unable to intervene (Williams was far away when Rose was lobotomised). However, my aim is not to propound a biographical allegory for *Streetcar*, but to bring into focus the network of family, sexual and gender violence that may be read through it. The play embodies a powerful instance of male oppression in heterosexual relations, and displays some of the pressures on women to collude in that. In *Growing Up Gay in the South* James T. Sears records similar instances of sexual harassment: 'I told my mother about the incidents with my father three nights before she died. We cried together. She told me she had been sent to reform school for running away after being raped by her stepfather and accused by her mother of lying — to get out of reform school she ended up marrying my father.' One study suggests that the likelihood of a US female being sexually abused before the age of eighteen is one in four.[18]

Stanley may be sexy, then, but he is also violently abusing. He presents, as Blanche says, a primitive model of masculinity: he brings home raw meat from the jungle and his woman is waiting, hoping for a friendly grunt. Even Stella says he's being 'stupid and horrid'. 'We've had this date with each other from the beginning', he tells Blanche (275, 402). But it is not true that she wants to be raped. Certainly she has been flirtatious and snobbish — but pathetically, as Stanley well knows. He exploits her weakness, sadistically. She tries to defend herself with a bottle.

One of the initial reviewers, Harold Clurman, felt that Stanley's 'mentality provides the soil for fascism', and that the audience is likely to collude with him. He perceived 'an American parable', a drama of 'sensibility crushed by a brutishness so common' that the audience may take Stanley as hero.[19] Sears locates Stanley as a 'redneck bully'.[20] If he has not often been regarded in this way, it is partly because of the casting of Brando in the film − a younger man, Williams said, than he had anticipated: 'It humanizes the character of Stanley in that it becomes the brutality or callousness of youth rather than a vicious older man.'[21] Also, as Clurman suggests, Stanley's behaviour may seem only right because it is in line with the prevailing ideology of manliness. 'Having sensed a challenge to his robust manhood', John Gassner says, Stanley 'must [sic] even violate her while his wife is giving birth in the city hospital. It is his awesome, earthy health, which will defend itself at any cost, that destroys Blanche.'[22] In such readings, Stella's deference to her husband is the proper attitude. To Signi Falk, Stella is one of Williams' few 'normal characters . . . happy with her husband.'[23] Again, to a psychoanalytic commentator, Sievers, Stella is 'a healthy housewife, adjusted to reality, expecting a child, and serenely happy in her physical relationship with Stanley'. He sees in Stella's collusion in Blanche's lobotomy merely 'a technical injustice': 'Though she does Blanche a technical injustice, it cannot alter her psychological destiny. Blanche is too psychotic now to be helped by the Kowalskis.'[24] That is rich − actually it is the 'healthy' Kowalskis who ruin Blanche. Her sleeping with boys was gentle and loving; it is her family who violate her, body and mind.

Williams sought to generalise his critique, as I see it, by encouraging audiences to regard Stanley as the real 'American' male; 'what I am is a one-hundred-per-cent American, born and raised in the greatest country on earth and proud as hell of it', he is made to say (374). He resents allusions to the Polish origins of his family; he appeals to the right-wing populism of Huey Long. The other men offer no tenable alternative. Mitch has 'a sort of sensitive look' and loves his sick mother (292). Stanley's other buddies defer to him; he keeps them complicit, exerting homosocial pressure to prevent them from showing sympathy or respect for Blanche.

And, almost out of the frame, almost beyond the scope of American manhood, there is Blanche's late husband. He is a different kind of man − gentle, sensitive, vulnerable, and queer. Initial critics seized upon Allan as the crucial factor in Blanche's 'tragedy'. 'Her marriage to an attractive boy who looked to her for spiritual security was doomed from the start; and even if she had been a superwoman she could not have saved it' (Brooks Atkinson); 'Mr Williams names an outside cause for the unhinging of her mind − the fact that Blanche's husband, whom she loved dearly, had turned out to be a homosexual' (John Mason Brown).[25] For John T. von Szeliski, this was a flaw:

'Her psychological difficulties date back to the suicide of her boy-husband and, while it may be that this trauma was sufficient to bring Blanche to her eventual promiscuity, its importance in her character limits her tragic stature.'[26]

Blanche's abuse of Allan, leading to his suicide, occurred because she was under the sway of the customary notions of manliness. When it is too late she cherishes his sensitivity, but for the critics that is part of her sickness. In fact it is not Allan's queerness that dooms Blanche: she functions, more or less, for years after his death. Belle Reve is lost not through feminine weakness (hers or Allan's) but 'as, piece by piece, our improvident grandfathers and father and uncles and brothers exchanged the land for their epic fornications' (284). Imperious and irresponsible male sexuality has doomed the house.

The silencing by the mother of the young woman who speaks the dreadful truth about sexual exploitation appears again in *Suddenly Last Summer* (1958). Mrs Venable wants to believe that her son, Sebastian, was a celibate; she herself was 'the only one in his life that satisfied the demands he made of people' (362). However, Catharine knows that Sebastian, her cousin, sought homosexual experience, using Mrs Venable, and then herself, to attract young men: 'I was PROCURING for him!' (412). Mrs Venable is determined to prevent Catharine from telling this story. Her scheme is to bribe a doctor to silence Catharine by operating on her. He is specialising in the new technique of lobotomy.

Williams and Queerness

Suddenly Last Summer is also Williams' most homophobic play. Sebastian's desire is presented as an uncontrollable appetite which leads ineluctably to his death from the cannibalistic attack of the street boys he has been courting. None of this is subtly rendered. Catharine says Sebastian was 'Fed up with dark ones, famished for light ones: that's how he talked about people, as if they were – items on a menu' (375). To be sure, some misty symbolism suggests further dimensions. 'If homosexuality is just one more of the perversions of civilizations', David Bergman observes in his helpful discussion, 'it is also the source of Sebastian's salvation'; he is something of a Christ-figure.[27] But projecting homophobia onto the universe is no way to critique it.

Suddenly Last Summer was a critical success, and filming did not arouse the protests that *Streetcar* and *Baby Doll* had, or require the adjustments that were thought necessary for *Cat on a Hot Tin Roof*. The Catholic Legion of Decency was happy with the punishment of Sebastian: 'It is a stark and horrifying lesson', said their spokesman. Gene D. Phillips attributes the film's success to the fact that 'audiences were now ready for genuinely adult subject matter tastefully presented on the screen'.[28] I'd say they were ready for misogyny and homophobia. Williams had spent twenty years as a writer, trying to comprehend and get into the public domain an analysis of the harassment suffered by sexual dissidents in that society. The strain was telling.

Gore Vidal pointed out to Williams that sexual taboo is one of the ways a ruling class manages to stay in power, but Williams, he says, 'had been too thoroughly damaged by the society that he was brought up in to ever suspect that he had been, like almost everyone else, had. He thought he was wrong and *they* were right.'[29] Certainly, Williams was sometimes unhappy about being queer. In *Camino Real* (1953) the Baron de Charlus requires for a sexual encounter 'An iron bed with no mattress and a considerable length of stout knotted rope. No! Chains this evening, metal chains, I've been very bad, I have a lot to atone for' (464–5). However, there is no reason to suppose this reflects Williams' attitude. Even gay critics interpret Big Daddy's bowel cancer in *Cat on a Hot Tin Roof* as 'the wages of sodomy', though it seems to me that Big Daddy has thrived in the wake of his early experiences, and his current illness signifies a current (social) sickness.[30] Anyway, I don't think Williams was mystified in the way that Vidal suggests. He knew we have been had.

Nor is it altogether right to envisage Williams' love life as disastrous. After an initial shyness, he was very successful at making pick-ups. He had three major affairs, one of which lasted for fourteen years, and, in between, a series of medium-term relationships. Only by the criteria of family ideology was this a failed love-life. Commentators have suggested that sexual indirection in the plays should be attributed to self-oppression; Sarotte, for instance, says most of the overt homosexuals in the plays are dead before the start because of 'the author's own guilt complex, his inability to show himself on the stage as he truly is'.[31] True, they are dead in *Cat on a Hot Tin Roof* and *Streetcar*, and in *Camino Real* we are offered a self-hating stereotype who is immediately killed. However, there are equally good grounds for arguing that an unusual determination to set queerness on the stage led Williams to risk his career by alluding to it at all.

Many of the stories published in the collections of 1948 (*One Arm*) and 1954 (*Hard Candy*) indicate that Williams was keen to handle queer themes. See, particularly, 'The Angel in the Alcove', 'Mysteries of Joy Rio', 'Hard Candy', 'Two on a Party', 'One Arm', 'Desire and the Black Masseur'. Where the stories resemble the plays, the stories are notably more straightforward. 'The Night of the Iguana' (1948) features a settled gay couple, for whom there is no equivalent in the play of the same name (nor in any other US play produced before Mart Crowley's *Boys in the Band*). 'The Resemblance between a Violin Case and a Coffin' (1950), which partly anticipates *The Glass Menagerie*, elaborates fully on the narrator's interest in the boyfriend of his withdrawn sister. 'How on earth did I explain to myself, at that time, the fascination of his physical being without, at the same time, confessing to myself that I was a little monster of sensuality?'[32] This story was not published surreptitiously. It was printed first in the magazine *Flair*, where it gained sufficient notice to be selected for *Best American Short Stories of 1951*, before being included in Williams' collection of 1954.

Contrary to popular belief, theatre was not a supportive place for a gay man to work. At the time of *The Glass Menagerie* and on through *Streetcar*, the powerful critic George Jean Nathan was hostile to Williams because he knew of his queerness; he referred to him as 'a Southern genital-man'.[33] Donald M. Kaplan noted in 1965 'complaints of directors that they were unable to get adequate performances out of this or that actor because the actor was queer and therefore possessed a shallow emotional repertoire'.[34] The reason for these unfortunate effects, in Kaplan's view, may be discovered in psychoanalytic theory: the homosexual is unable to move beyond 'an autoerotic, infantile experience' (32). It is the same with the gay playwright, especially if he propounds a critique of the dominant ideology: 'when he sides with the victim against the oppression of God or society, the homosexual's ideologic style does not champion humanity, but merely himself', Kaplan says. He is 'actually seeking the restoration of the spoilt child', because he lacks 'intelligence, discrimination and reason − the dawnings of the post-Oedipal child' (36–7).

'It is the *last* play I will try to write for the *now* existing theatre', Williams said in 1944, of *Glass Menagerie*.[35] The plays are oblique not because Williams couldn't handle gayness, but because he had to negotiate prevailing theatre institutions. He was subject to others' decisions over direction and casting, and then to endless textual compromises with directors and censors. On the first night, more often than not, he was waiting for make-or-break notices of a production that represented huge emotional commitment but which he himself regarded as seriously flawed. He accepted Elia Kazan's revisions of *Cat on a Hot Tin Roof*, he said, because 'a failure reaches fewer people, and touches fewer, than does a play that succeeds'. It is to this work pattern that he attributed 'the long, long slide towards a crack-up'.[36] Perhaps he should have tried harder to find or create alternative opportunities, but the little theatre movement was not very effective in the 1950s. Probably minority theatre seemed unAmerican — wanting to go off and do something by yourself (open-plan houses became *de rigueur*). And, despite a personal identification with Hart Crane, who had been driven to drink and death by the literary establishment, Williams hoped for mainstream approval. He thought of it ultimately as a way to appease his father: 'he knew that my mother had made me a sissy', he said; but 'I had a chance, bred in his blood and bone, to some day rise above it, as I had to and did.'[37] A writer had more difficulty than most in being manly, but if he was successful enough it was all right.

What is true is that Williams adopted demeaning Freudian notions about gayness. At the age of eight he was kept in bed for a year by diphtheria, he explained: 'During this period of illness and solitary games, my mother's overly solicitous attention planted in me the makings of a sissy, much to my father's discontent. I was becoming a decided hybrid, different from the family line of frontiersmen-heroes of east Tennessee.'[38] As Henry Abelove has shown, Freud deprecated the moralism of his US followers. In 1909 he wrote: 'Sexual morality as society — and at its most extreme, American society — defines it, seems very despicable to me. I stand for a much freer sexual life.'[39] But US analysts paid little attention to such criticism; upon the death of Freud in 1939, as we will see more fully in chapter 11, reactionary figures asserted with fervour that homosexuality was pathological.

Like many gay men, including his friend William Inge, Williams submitted himself to analysis; this was in the late 1950s, when he was distressed by the failure of *Orpheus Descending* (1957) — which he believed had had the wrong cast and director. A 'strict Freudian' urged him 'to attempt a heterosexual life', and Williams did not repudiate him: 'He taught me much about my true nature but he offered me no solution except to break with Merlo, a thing that was quite obviously untenable as a consideration, my life being built around him.'[40] Frank Merlo had been Williams' lover since 1948. The relationship did break up, because, Williams says, he was impatient with the moodiness resulting from Frank's illness. But Williams was distraught at his death: 'As long as Frank was well, I was happy. He had a gift for creating life and, when he ceased to be alive, I couldn't create a life for myself. So I went into a seven-year depression.'[41] The analyst's assault on the relationship was based on a stupid and prejudiced theory.

Psychoanalytic ideas influenced Williams' representations of women. They are given to hysterical sexual repression, which renders them alternately frigid and nymphomaniac. They cling on to their children, blighting their sexual potential, and, given a chance, try to humiliate their men. *The Glass Menagerie*, *Baby Doll* (1956) and *Summer and Smoke* (1948) depend on such notions.[42] In *Suddenly Last Summer* Mrs Venable insists that she was the 'natural' companion for her (queer) son: 'He was *mine*! I *knew* how to help him, I *could*!' Only at the age of forty, at the point of his death, was Sebastian breaking 'that string of pearls that old mothers hold their sons by like a − sort of a − sort of − *umbilical* cord' (408–9). I discuss 'Momism' in chapter 11. However, Williams never supposed that women were finally in charge. It is not they who castrate in *Orpheus Descending* and *Sweet Bird of Youth*.

In later plays Williams deals with gayness in a scarcely-veiled autobiographical manner. *Small Craft Warnings* (1972), *Vieux Carré* (1978) and *Something Cloudy, Something Clear* (1981) present more or less derelict people clustered round a bar or living on a beach. The gay characters are no more lonely or dissipated than the straights, but a particular pain is ascribed to them: 'There's a coarseness, a deadening coarseness, in the experience of most homosexuals', Quentin says in *Small Craft Warnings* (260). Yet the young man is always decent, a beacon of hope. If Williams didn't like himself very much, he remained true to his ideal love object.

Buddies

The Freudian climate which thwarted and, in a way, sustained Williams infected what had been the most innocent and illustrious region of US life − the classic fiction which had contributed to the very idea of America. Leslie Fiedler stirred up controversy in 1960:

> We can never shake off the nagging awareness that there is at the sentimental center of our novels, where we are accustomed to find in their European counterparts 'platonic' love or adultery, seduction, rape, or long-drawn-out flirtation, nothing but love of males! What awaits us are the fugitive slave and the no-account boy side by side on a raft borne by the endless river toward an impossible escape; or the pariah sailor waking in the tattooed arms of the brown harpooner on the verge of some impossible quest.

Emerson, Melville, Thoreau and Whitman all seemed questionable. Fiedler's formulation of this theory, he said in a later preface, 'met with a shocked and,

I suspect, partly willful incomprehension. I have been accused of impiety, grossness, a contempt for the classics of childhood, even of a disturbing influence on private lives.'[43]

Male buddying was a key part of the story the USA told itself about World War II. A non-gay veteran says: 'among men who fight together there is an intense love. You are closer to those men than to anyone except your immediate family when you were young.'[44] This is the relationship that is violated in Arthur Miller's *All My Sons* (1947), when Joe acts on behalf merely of his own family. Of course, buddies were likely to be strenuously heterosexist. Stanley in *Streetcar* gives as his reason for destroying Mitch's relation with Stella: 'Mitch is a buddy of mine. We were in the same outfit together – Two-forty-first Engineers' (365). But the relationship could easily become sexual, or be subject to fears that it was latently sexual. In *Third Person* by Andrew Rosenthal (1951: see chapter 1) Kip moves in on Hank and his family on the basis of their wartime experience. The relationship is sexual for Kip but not (ostensibly) for Hank; the idea of buddying enables them to live at cross-purposes. Finally Hank is reconciled with his wife but (as at the end of *Women in Love*) insists that he and Kip had something valuable. In Gore Vidal's *The Best Man* (1960) and Loring Mandel's *Advise and Consent* (1960) the War and buddying help to explain how an otherwise decent American might come to behave in an unAmerican way sexually – away from the good influence (or, we might say, the policing) of his family and neighbourhood (I discuss these plays in chapter 11). Williams exploited this faultline.

In *Cat on a Hot Tin Roof* (1955) Brick claims the innocent manly love of the pioneer tradition: 'Not love with you, Maggie, but friendship with Skipper was that one great true thing' (57–8). But Brick is immature: he has problems with work and women, and is trying to hang on to his athletic youth. 'Was it jumping or humping that you were doing out there? What were [you] doing out there at three a.m., layin' a woman on that cinder track?' Big Daddy asks (73). Brick seems to have been over-mothered (Big Mama speaks of him as her 'only son': 142) and doesn't get on with his father ('Communication is – awful hard between people an' – somehow between you and me, it just don't – ': 90). A Cold War audience, on the lookout for unAmerican tendencies, may well be suspicious. After all, Skipper couldn't make it in bed with Maggie and went to pieces. And now Brick won't sleep with Maggie.

As I show in chapter 11, the prominence of the concept of latency makes it pointless to debate whether Brick or Skipper is *really queer*. Maggie insists:

'Brick, I tell you, you got to believe me, Brick, I *do* understand all about it! I — I think it was — *noble*! Can't you tell I'm sincere when I say I respect it?' But the more she insists, the more anxious Brick gets. That is the double bind of latency: the more straightness is asserted, the more doubtful it becomes. Maggie is 'naming it dirty', he says. She replies: 'I know, believe me I know, that it was only Skipper that harboured even any *unconscious* desire for anything not perfectly pure between you two!' (57–8). The critic Walter Kerr complained of 'a tantalising reluctance . . . to let the play blurt out its promised secret'.[45] That demand misses the point precisely: '*unconscious* desire' signifies not a secret but anxiety that there might be a secret. Cleverly, Williams extends the provocation by making Brick declare that the relationship with Skipper was *not normal*. 'No! — It was too rare to be normal, any true thing between two people is too rare to be normal'; though when they were touring and shared rooms perhaps 'we'd reach across the space between the two beds and shake hands to say goodnight, yeah, one or two times we — '.[45] Williams makes Brick tease himself, and anxious men in the audience.

Cat on a Hot Tin Roof confronts the 1950s by showing that self-oppression and social constraints are the problem, not dissident sexuality. For Big Daddy — the unassailable patriarch who is both a pioneer and a successful business-man — the pioneering spirit has not been incompatible with queerness. 'I knocked around in my time. . . . Slept in hobo jungles and railroad Y's and flophouses in all cities . . . I seen all things and understood a lot of them' (115–16). But times have changed. Such casual involvement in queer practices is no longer possible, and Brick is profoundly frightened. 'Big Daddy, you shock me, Big Daddy, you, you — *shock* me! Talkin' so — [*He turns away from his father.*] — casually! — about a — thing like that' (119). And Brick has reason to be frightened: 'Don't you know how people *feel* about things like that? How, how *disgusted* they are by things like that?' When in their fraternity a boy '*attempted* to do a, unnatural thing with . . . We told him to git off the campus, and he did, he got!' (119). He was last heard of in North Africa (which is about as unAmerican as you can get).

Meanwhile, the older son, Gooper, is presented as mature, responsible and qualified — but a dummy, and dominated by his wife. Bear in mind that Big Daddy's and Maggie's concern for Brick is not merely personal: they need him to stop drinking and sire children to secure the patriarchal line and the family business. But in this play no one is going to achieve an unproblematic manliness. Brick finds it suspicious that Big Daddy put him in the bedroom of 'that pair of old sisters', but they were the men — queer men — who built up the plantation. As Williams says in a stage direction, the point is not 'one man's psychological problem', but 'a common crisis' (114–15).

The changes to the script that were necessary to get *Cat* performed show the extent of that crisis in US society. It was successful because it touched a contemporary nerve, but its critique had to be muffled. Kazan, the first stage director, thought that Brick should 'undergo some apparent mutation' as a result of the exposure of his anxieties. Hence the change in the stage directions at the end, whereby Brick seems to incline towards renewing sexual relations with Maggie. Williams was unhappy at this: he did not 'believe that a conversation, however revelatory, ever effects so immediate change in the heart or even conduct of a person in Brick's state of spiritual disrepair'.[47] Of course, Williams was right: if the problem derives from the prevailing family and social structure, it won't be solved by interpersonal adjustments, even on a more sustained basis than occurs here. Williams wanted to refuse a central bourgeois literary tenet − that people gain empowerment through reflection on personal experience. Even the published version was not all performed.[48]

The film of *Cat on a Hot Tin Roof* (1958) required even more fixing: the project was, quite starkly, 'writing the homosexuality out of Brick's character', said the director, Richard Brooks. The script was designed to retain immaturity as an explanation while suppressing the link between it and latent queerness − emphasising 'Brick's basic immaturity, his refusal to grow up and meet the responsibilities of adult life'. This might appear sufficient to motivate his rejection of 'manhood as understood by Big Daddy, by a sensual wife, by most of middleclass America'.[49] However, the attitudes of Big Daddy and Maggie were not that straightforward either, so they too were changed. In the play, Maggie says she and Skip wanted to sleep together to get closer to Brick, but he couldn't make it with her (55–6, 59). In the film, Maggie approaches Skip because she is jealous that they pay so much attention to football (!), and Skip is very keen, but she draws back in case she loses Brick. The result is confusing. One reviewer declared Brick 'the best dramatized study of homosexuality I have seen'; another thought the film 'played down the deviation motif'.[50]

There were other changes designed to suppress queerness. Brick is shown burying his face in Maggie's slip and caressing it in agony. And in the introductory scene with Maggie, Brick is made to 'wield his crutch in a series of phallic positions', implying, to Maurice Yacowar at least, 'that he has a sexual disability, rather than a deviance'.[51] Trivial as this may sound, it was the key to the project: Brick's limb is fractured temporarily, and sensitive treatment should work a cure (this, of course, was the psychoanalysts' line).

Williams' *Period of Adjustment* (1960) takes these issues more gently. Ralph and George were buddies in World War II and the Korean War, and settling into the approved model of relations with women is proving difficult. Dorothea has just left Ralph after six years of marriage, and Isabel's husband George abandons her on their honeymoon. There is scarcely a suggestion of queerness, but Harold Clurman was distressed by 'something disturbingly ambiguous, not "quite straight"'.[52]

Both the men and the women are in trouble. For the women, the problem is, alternately, frigidity and nymphomania — twin misogynist terms which blame women for any mismatch with the sexual agenda preferred by straight men. Ralph explains to George that men come on too strong, and 'That rouses resistance. Because a woman has pride, even a woman has pride and resents being raped. . . . You got to use — TENDERNESS! — with it, not roughness like raping, snatch-and-grab roughness' (210). With such coaxing, the women turn out to be homely types with a healthy liking for sex, committed to helping their husbands to make good in the world. At the end, unlike Brick and Maggie, the appropriate couples get to bed. This doubtless pleased an audience that wanted to be cheered up about the family. But, as with a Shakespearean comedy, the closure may not altogether eliminate the faultlines exposed in the course of the play.

Love-making, Ralph says, 'ain't a thing every Tom, Dick and Harry has got a true aptitude for' (209–10). His most rewarding sexual experiences have been during the War, with prostitutes; he doesn't find his wife attractive, and feels guilty when he can't satisfy her. George has a 'nervous tremor'; it started in Korea, and is related to sex. Ralph tells Isabel:

> I happen to know he didn't come on as strong with those dolls in Tokyo and Hong Kong and Korea as he liked to pretend to. Because I heard from those dolls. . . . He'd just sit up there on a pillow and drink that rice wine with them and teach them *English!* Then come downstairs from there, hitching his belt and shouting, '*Oh, man! Oh, brother!* — like he' laid 'em to waste. (159, Williams' pause)

The two men are happiest being buddies again. 'I might as well not be present!' Isabel complains — 'For all the attention I have been paid since you and your buddy had this tender reunion!' (169). Ralph is fatherly, George is young and very good looking but rather wild. They hug, chuckle shyly together a good deal, put their arms around each other's shoulders, talk intimately, squabble and make up. They could set up as cattle ranchers: 'There's dignity in the agrarian, the pastoral - way of existence! A dignity too long lost out of the − American dream − ' (197). The new twist is that they will breed buffalo and Texas Longhorns for western movies. According to Williams in this play, the American male is suffused with nostalgia for lost manhood. Ralph perceives in TV westerns a national homesickness for the old wild frontiers; he would like to be a coloniser in space, the Adam on a star in a different galaxy. But, astronauts apart, there seems little scope for manliness at the moment. Indeed, it is hard enough to make 'that long, long, dangerous walk between "His" and "Hers"' − the twin beds (242).

Despite his calm wisdom about how George and Isabel should adjust, Ralph is obsessed with the idea that Dorothea is turning their son into a sissy. 'Just last week, I caught the little bugger playin' with a rag doll.' This is dangerous: 'a sissy tendency in a boy's got to be nipped in the bud, otherwise the bud will blossom'. Then the boy won't be fit for the modern world, 'Because in this world you got to be what your physical sex is or correct it in Denmark. I mean we got a *man's* world coming up, man! Technical! Terrific!' (177–8). Denmark was notorious as the country of Christine Jorgensen, whose sex change operation in 1952–53 'most titillated and unsettled the fifties' public complacency about the absoluteness of gender roles'.[53] For Christmas Ralph has bought his son a miniature of the rocket-launching pad at Cape Canaveral (it explodes in George's face), a cowboy outfit, and a train-set with a tunnel to push the train into. The writing of *Period of Adjustment* signalled, among other things, Williams' disillusion with his psychoanalyst.

There is a reference to queers in *Period of Adjustment*. Isabel strays into the neighbouring Spanish-type cottage, and that is worrying because it is occupied, Ralph says, by a 'bachelor decorator and you know how they destroy wimmen'. How do gay men destroy women, audience members might ask themselves − by marrying them and being sexually unrewarding? That would be a question for the characters in the play. But no: 'He is running a sort of unofficial USO at his house. Service men congregate there' (203). So Williams' favourite types − derelicts, prostitutes, queers, alcoholics, young men on the loose − lurk just around the corner, offering an alternative to the family and organised by a local full-blown un-American. These lines were cut from the film.

The Great American Tragedy

I believe I have shown *Streetcar*, *Cat on a Hot Tin Roof* and *Period of Adjustment* to be radical in their dwelling upon faultlines in the sex/gender system. David Savran makes a further case. Relating the constructedness of gender to the Brechtian principle that dramatic form should expose the constructedness of ideology, he argues that Williams' plays are revolutionary in their rejection of domestic realism. They undermine 'the hegemonic and hierarchical structure of masculinity itself by disclosing the contradictions on which its normative formulation is based'. They do this primarily, Savran says, through 'a process of *desubjectification*, an unbinding and deconstruction of the sovereign subject'; through 'a profligacy of words that disrupts traditional notions of narrative continuity and dramatic forms'.[54] Arthur Miller has often been regarded as the radical dramatist of the 1950s, but his 'dramaturgy remains strictly teleological, moving towards a future that has already happened, a peripety that is always a disclosure of the past', Savran says (31). The structure of Williams' plays, conversely, 'is adamantly plural, strewn with multivalent symbols, and reluctant to provide the interpreter with a master perspective or code' (98).

The problem with this formulation, as Savran acknowledges, is the general critical acclaim that has attended Williams' best-known plays. Of course, most of these critics do not take him as a Brechtian writer — that would make him even more unAmerican. I suspect that the non-realistic manoeuvres of Williams are better understood as *expressionist* — in other words, as tending to intensify theme, symbol and atmosphere, rather than disrupt them. Perhaps, as Alisa Solomon argues, we should be looking to directors to 'move Williams out of relentlessly realistic scenery, into a theatricalized space that talks back to the plays. In more presentational productions than we're used to, we might be able to hear new overtones in familiar speeches.'[55] I discuss in chapter 17 a radical rewriting of *Streetcar* — *Belle Reprieve* (1991) by Split Britches and the Bloolips.

The question we should ask of Williams' career is not why he was often received with hostility, but why he was successful. After all, he held radical views on matters other than sexuality; for instance, he knew the evils of the Batista regime in Cuba and believed the US Government should have cultivated Castro.[56] As Spoto suggests, *Camino Real* was rejected in 1953 not 'because it was vague, but because it was all too clear in its denunciation of the fascist demagoguery then spreading over the country in the voice, especially loud, of Senator Joseph McCarthy'; for the Broadway production references to 'fascism in America, and to brotherhood and love were cut, since they were thought to be ringing cries of Communist sympathy'.[57] *Orpheus Descending*, a critical failure on Broadway in 1957, is a tremendous indictment of gender and racial bigotry and repression. *Baby Doll, Streetcar, Cat*, and *Orpheus Descending* all trace individual disturbance, in Marxian manner, to social, political and economic disturbance.

Nonetheless, US critics and the theatregoing public did want a powerful 'American' playwright to celebrate, particularly as O'Neill came to seem rather old-fashioned, and they were prepared to put up with some authorial temperament if that was the price. Indeed, with a bit of manipulation things might not look too bad. Marion Magid in an essay of 1963 remarked, rather nervously, the strange image a European would have of America if Williams' plays were the only source. Yet 'Williams is American in his passion for absolutes, in his longing for purity, in his absence of ideas, in the extreme discomfort with which he inhabits his own body and soul, in his apocalyptic view of sex.'[58] Magid is negotiating between Williams' plays and a (just) plausible America, adjusting one to the other. Introducing a collection of essays on *Streetcar* in 1971, Jordan Y. Miller declares that Williams was 'never one to make the headlines, never marrying, an artist dominated by the powerful forces of the tragic spirit'. If something untoward is lurking round that failure to marry, it is quickly absorbed into 'the tragic spirit'. On such terms, Miller can venerate 'the truly classical tragic outlook in what is now a "classic" American play'.[59] He quotes Joseph Wood Crutch's comment to his students on the morning after he first saw *Streetcar:* this 'may be it. This may be the great American play' (11).

Declaring texts and humanity tragic or 'absurdist' is usually a reactionary move, because it refuses the first premise of political action: that significant change is possible. Kazan, the first director of *Streetcar*, stressed its classic, 'universal' potential, in terms which illustrate very well how conservative this move is likely to be:

This is like a classic tragedy. Blanche is Medea or someone pursued by the Harpies, the Harpies being *her own nature*. . . . she is a heightened version, an artistic intensification of all women. That is what makes the play universal. Blanche's special relation to all women is that she is at that critical point where *the one thing above all else that she is dependent on: her attraction for men, is beginning to go*. Blanche is like all women, dependent on a man, looking for one to hang onto: only *more so!*[60]

For Benjamin Nelson, Williams' plays are about 'the loneliness of human existence'.[61] On seeing a revival of *Cat on a Hot Tin Roof* in 1974, Stanley Kauffmann found he didn't much like it (the 'articulation' was 'clumsy'). But he was happy to begin his article with a confirmation that Williams is 'one of the two American dramatists of enduring substance' and that *Streetcar* 'is truly an American tragedy'.[62]

So Williams could be celebrated as flawed and dangerous, but nonetheless a great, tormented, 'American' playwright. In fact, to be tormentedly unAmerican was to affirm America – first as a site where profound, 'universal' passions might be enacted, and second as the implicit healthy norm for the majority who do not aspire to tragic stature. Sacvan Bercovitch avers: 'all our classic writers (to varying degrees) labored against the myth as well as within it. All of them felt, privately at least, as oppressed by Americanism as liberated by it.'[63]

Other queer plays seem to have got through under cover of the classic muse. Sievers heard 'the unmistakable hint of homosexuality' in a dramatisation of Herman Melville's *Billy Budd* (1951) by Louis O. Coxe and Robert Chapman.[64] Claggart, the master-at-arms, acknowledges the attractions of Billy, the foretopman: 'Your messmates crowd around, admire your yellow hair and your blue eyes, do tricks and favours for you out of love.' Surely recognising the feeling he has aroused, Billy approaches the older man: 'Yes, sir. I was wondering . . . could I talk to you between watches, when you've nothing else to do?' he asks. 'Thank you, sir. That would mean a lot to me' (20–1, the authors' pause). Claggart, though evidently drawn to Billy, is unable to respond positively (there is no equivalent to this scene in the Forster–Britten opera, also performed in 1951). However, Melville was a great American writer, so *Billy Budd* could be accommodated as about good and evil: none of the New York dailies, Curtin says, acknowledged a sexual theme.[65]

A classical aura may also have sheltered the free adaptation by Ruth and Augustus Goetz of André Gide's *The Immoralist* (1954, Broadway). Michel has been expelled from school for 'a sin of the flesh, an offense against yourself and the other boy', and is unable to make love with his patient and devoted wife, Marcelline.[66] Bachir, his Arab houseboy (played by James Dean), knows the score: 'The first time I saw you with Madame – the day you took this house – I knew what you were' (II-3-25). Bachir introduces Michel to Moktir, a former university professor who has chosen to live as an acknowledged homosexual. Michel is the immoral one, Moktir says, because he is deceiving himself and hence his wife. As Marcelline is progressively demoralised by the situation, Michel comes to agree: 'I will never be silent again! Whoever knows me will know that about me first' (II-4-34). After sending Marcelline back to France Michel plunges into debauchery: 'I have scavenged through the back streets of every town I have passed through — There is no loneliness like that! I have been exploited by those who are like me, and shunned by those who are not' (III-2-15). To save him from such a life, Marcelline and he decide to stay together.

This is hardly a progressive outcome, but the entire treatment is far more positive than Gide's novel of 1902, in which Michel's self-awareness is far slower to develop, there is no frank conversation between him and any of the characters, and Marcelline pays for his self-deception with her life. The Goetzes' version of *The Immoralist* does accomplish their stated intention of getting the topic out into the open; Michel really is gay, and he is not an unworthy person. Critics tended to dismiss the play as too much of a study, rather than condemn its theme. It was shown in London at the Arts Theatre Club in 1954 and revived successfully in a more liberal Off-Broadway climate in 1964.[67]

In discussion after a talk at Northwestern University in 1997 I was asked whether I had any thoughts on the success of Tony Kushner's *Angels in America* (*Part 1: Millennium Approaches*, 1991; *Part 2: Perestroika*, 1992). I replied, hesitantly, that I was cheered by Kushner's socialist pronouncements, but felt that the mode of these plays was too much influenced by aspirations to be 'art' (perhaps like some of Edward Bond's work), and hence unhelpfully mystifying (angels, for instance). Some critics and audiences may like that because they believe they are in the presence of 'significance'. (Leo Bersani takes this view.[68]) I was reproached, almost angrily, by a kind and courteous colleague: who was I to question a work of art whose relevance would be felt for generations?

Angels in America is probably the first play since *Streetcar* and *Death of a Salesman* to gain classic 'American' status. Savran notes that commentators have cited in its elucidation Sophocles, Brecht and Shakespeare (*Richard III*, *Richard II*, *King Lear*, *Macbeth*, the romances). An operatic treatment has been commissioned from Peter Eötvös by Glyndebourne and the Châtelet in Paris.[69] To be sure, Kushner's plays are witty, inventive, shrewd, and take on large issues. They build on motifs from earlier successes (*Torch Song Trilogy* has split scenes, the discarded female partner, and mother flying in to sort things out; *Death of a Salesman* includes a character with delusions about pioneering, to flute/oboe accompaniment; *The Boys in the Band* has everyone doing Jewish humour regardless of whether they are Jewish). But what renders *Angels in America*, with such explicit attention to gay sexuality, self-evidently valuable?

Sometimes it seems that only one theme is prized in US writing: the history, condition and destiny of 'America'. This is Kushner's pitch from the start of *Millennium Approaches*, where the Rabbi says that Jewish people have made great voyages across Europe and the Atlantic. Prior claims WASP lineage; one of his forefathers captained ships bringing Irish people to the new world.[70] Joe, Harper and Hannah are specified as Mormons, whose forebears made an epic journey across the continent. Harper imagines she is at the last frontier, in Antarctica. African American people, Belize reminds us, were taken to America by force.

Kushner means not to be complacent about America. Through the crooked lawyer, Roy Cohn, he links President Ronald Reagan in the 1980s and Senator Joe McCarthy in the 1950s, and requires liberal-minded US people to confront their knowledge that major assertions of America have been reactionary and corrupt. The theme is broached by Louis, who is Jewish and 'Left' (he can scarcely endure a Republican sexual partner). He wants to believe that 'ultimately we're different from every other nation on earth', and that for Americans race is not a real issue, just a political tactic (I, 68–9).[71] He is challenged emphatically by Belize, who is black; the two men descend into racist recriminations.

Yet, the plays suggest, Amerca does have a spiritual destiny: heralded by Prior's WASP ancestors, the Angel descends. She declares that the world is spinning out of control and that Prior must deliver a new prophecy: migration must cease, Americans must stop moving. He rejects this admonition, but not America's destiny. In *Perestroika* he concludes:

> The world spins only forward. We will be citizens. The time has come.
> Bye now.
> You are fabulous creatures, each and every one.
> And I bless you: *More Life*.
> The Great Work Begins. (II, 99)

That last sentence was first uttered by the Angel at the end of *Millennium Approaches*. There is to be a 'Great Work'; the dispute is about its nature – whether America should stand still or press on. Kushner says in an interview that the image of the angel is designed to suggest that 'America is in essence a utopian and theological construction, a nation with a divine mission.' This might be regarded as an ideology, the main effect of which has been to legitimise conquest and oppression. Kushner interprets it as an opportunity for the Left: 'I really believe that there is the potential for radical democracy in this country.'[72]

Gays then come in as one of the minorities who will be generously accommodated by change. They too have been pioneers: 'Across an unmapped terrain. The body of the homosexual male. Here, or the Ramble, or the scrub pines on Fire Island, or the St Mark's Baths. Hardy pioneers. Like your ancestors', Louis tells Joe. 'And many have perished on the trail' (I, 43). Further, the apocalyptic location of US gay men in the AIDS crisis makes them authorities at the millennium. Cohn's reactionary stance is evident in his refusal to admit that he is homosexual and has AIDS. It is Prior who has the energy to resist the Angel's ordinance and to resume the 'Great Work'. The bearer of rootedness and recipient of the prophecy is a gay man with AIDS; America has to get used to that.

There is much here that is strong, subtle and demanding for various kinds of audience. My misgiving is that *Angels in America* slides into the cloudiness of irony, symbolism and profundity at moments where clear elucidation would be valuable. Is there any plausible congruence between US pioneer ideology — which, arguably, is a version of unregulated exploitative capitalism — and a peaceful and prosperous future for humankind? At one point Louis acknowledges that there were angels in America before: 'I mean Native American spirits and we killed them off so now, there are no gods here, no ghosts and spirits in America' (I, 69). It must be a question, whether a State that has depended on extreme violence in its founding, consolidation, continental expansion and global hegemony can realise, from within the ideology that has shaped it, a future that will be harmonious as well as purposeful. The role of the American classic is to permit (though not necessarily to affirm) a hard-won but ultimately positive answer. And sexuality and race become indices of the obstacles that have been, prophetically, overcome.

11

The All-American Family

Witch-Hunting

Since bohemia, radicalism has been tainted with queerness. In George O'Neil's play, *American Dream* (1933), produced by the Theatre Guild in New York, the first two acts, set in 1650 and 1849, display business in conflict with idealism in the American pioneer tradition. The third act takes the family through to the present day of 1933. Daniel is trying to devote himself and his inherited wealth to the Communist Party, but he is neurotic and the social circle around him is trivial and insincere; it is maintained by his wife, Gail, with whom he is on poor terms. Finally she tries to seduce Schwarz, the Communist leader. When this fails and she is confronted by Daniel, she accuses him of a homosexual attachment to Schwarz: 'Am I in the way? Wouldn't you two come to an arrangement if I left the room? You're both so sensitive and shy. It's just lovely to watch. . . . If you ask me, it's rather excessive, isn't it − this attachment between you two?' Daniel is distraught: he does depend on Schwarz. 'That makes me a homo-sexual hero-worshipper, I guess. Yes, I'm a fairy, then. A pansy! In your stinking mind, I'm in love with Jake Schwarz! (*He laughs hysterically, turns to* SCHWARZ.) Would it be remarkable?' (156). Daniel shoots himself with the gun with which his great-grandfather killed Indians.

Now, these are not just personal failings. 'They've all been yapping about America here tonight − this house − the great American epic.' Daniel is, he says, 'the American story. I'm the end of a family that helped to build the whole damned business. I'm here fully equipped to revel in the Utopia produced by those relentless idealists of the plast. And that's what we've got'

208

(155–7). W. David Sievers comments: 'In the bleak thirties O'Neil could see only neurosis and disintegration as the legacy of the American dream.'[1] As in so many of the US plays in this book, personal sexuality is taken as a reflection upon the condition of the US male. Yet what is striking in *American Dream*, in 1933, is what is not said. Homosexuality is presented as a sign of weakness but not, in itself, as subversive.

The adventures of US gays in World War II have been valuably recounted. Allan Bérubé observes: 'the military had reinforced their gay identity by beginning to manage them as homosexual persons in its screening, antivice, and discharge policies, as well as the practice of utilizing them in stereotyped jobs, sending them to the fighting fronts, and tolerating them where necessary'. Many men and women got a sense of themselves as gay (the word spread across the country for the first time); bars became important, contributing the beginnings of gay subcultural cohesion. 'They were teaching each other important defensive tactics – "camping", blending in, secret slang and signals, and most important of all, a stronger sense of camaraderie and mutual respect.'[2] Equally important, the war had freed men and women from their customary, regulatory, social contexts, and encouraged them to take risks (when you are likely to be killed you tend to live for the moment). In the late 1940s the denial of rights generally available to ex-service personnel stimulated gay people to organise, though none of the established civil rights groups would acknowledge their case.

A conservative reaction followed in matters of family, sexuality and personal intimacy. A narrow selection of the attitudes and practices that had featured historically in the United States was declared 'American' – necessary to maintain the strength of US business and to justify US world hegemony in the face of an alleged threat from Communism. (I now drop the quote marks around 'America'. However, I regard it as an ideological expression, claiming to subsume the continent into the nation state – as if one said 'Britain' to mean 'England' or 'Europe' to mean 'Germany'.)

The immediate framework for this reaction was the Cold War – which was itself an ideological strategy, and should not be invoked as if it were a prior historical fact. It was a means for justifying overseas interventions and, above all, delegitimising dissent at home. Bertrand Russell wrote in 1963:

> The elimination of dissent was achieved by identifying dissent in the popular mind with support of the 'enemy', the 'devil', the inconceivably wicked Russians. The nice thing about this was that it also became

impossible to question the power-struggle itself. . . . the struggle for power with Soviet Russia has enabled American politicians to sanctify every oppressive act in the name of national security. . . . The sole criterion for support [of tyrannical regimes] has been subservience to American military needs and willingness to allow the resources and peoples of the respective countries to be exploited by American industry.[3]

The harassing of lesbians and gay men was a small cog in this wheel.

Homosexuals were not supposed to fight in World War II because they weren't manly. In the Cold War, the stakes were primarily ideological: whether the US had the resolution to confront an 'evil empire'. This seemed to require the purging of unAmerican enemies from within; like Communists, gays were dismissed from jobs in government, municipalities, business, education and medicine, often on suspicion and without appeal. They were supposed to endanger security, both because subject to blackmail and because the supposed homosexual personality type was inherently immature and emotionally unstable. Newspapers felt encouraged to publish scandals and scare-stories, and to withhold news of oppressive policies; the *New York Times* reported not a single word of the Senate hearings in which charges of sexual perversion were made against State Department employees. Police made wide and arbitrary sweeps of bars and cruising grounds in major cities and small towns. By the mid-1950s, one in five of the workforce had been required to sign an oath of moral purity in order to get or retain employment.[4]

'You can't hardly separate homosexuals from subversives', Senator Kenneth Wherry told journalist Max Lerner in 1950, adding: 'Mind you, I don't say every homosexual is a subversive, and I don't say every subversive is a homosexual. But a man of low morality is a menace in the government, whatever he is, and they are all tied up together.'[5] Indeed, founders of the homophile Mattachine Society, in 1951, were or had been Communists, and derived an understanding of oppression and organisation from the Party. However, their stance could not survive the climate of opinion, and a new, respectable leadership took over the society. They actually proposed a loyalty oath: 'I believe it is my duty to my country to love it; to support its constitution; to obey its laws; to respect its flag; and to defend it against all enemies.'[6] Even unAmericans had to be American.

In Loring Mandel's play *Advise and Consent* (1960, Broadway, from the novel by Allen Drury) the President's nominee for Secretary of State is accused of Communist sympathies. However, the chair of the Senate committee handling the appointment, Anderson, comes under the more severe pressure when a rival senator blackmails him over a gay affair during the War. The nomination of the secretary is lost, but nothing less than suicide is the proper fate for Anderson. *Advise and Consent* was produced as a major film by Otto Preminger in 1962. Again, when Gore Vidal needed a personal failing that would, if known, discredit a presidential candidate, it just had to be a report of homosexual experience in the military during the War. *The Best Man* (1960) ran for more than 500 performances on Broadway in the orbit of the Kennedy/Nixon presidential campaign. For today's reader, casual references to Adlai Stevenson, Joseph McCarthy and J. Edgar Hoover, all of whom have been thought to have queer leanings, may prompt an awareness of just what a precarious issue sexuality was in US public life.

William Inge mocked these obsessions in *The Tiny Closet* (1962) − which, Clum believes, he did not mean to stage.[7] Mr Newbold's private closet arouses intense suspicion in his landlady; her first thought is that he is a Communist: 'You can't tell, he might have a bomb in there he meant to destroy us with. I'm not gonna set idly by while someone is plotting something, Mrs Hergesheimer. I pride myself, I'm a real American, and I say, if anyone's got any secrets he wants to keep hid, let 'em come out into the open and declare himself' (194). It transpires that Mr Newbold keeps there ladies' hats, which he makes and likes to wear before the mirror. 'Why, I'd rather be harboring a Communist', the landlady exclaims (197).

In this context, sexual dissidents scraped together what subcultural support they could on the Broadway stage. William M. Hoffman registers John van Druten's comedy, *Bell, Book and Candle* (1950) as one of the 'hidden gay plays' that 'gay theatregoers interpreted'; Michael Bronski concurs.[8] A coven of modern witches − who could well be a queer clique − is disturbed when one of them falls for a non-witch. The author remarks, surely tongue in cheek, that his mind was running on magic, fairy-tales and good and bad fairies.[9] There is *I Am a Camera* (1954), van Druten's adaptation of Christopher Isherwood's Berlin stories (and the origin of the musical *Cabaret*, 1966), although you'd have to have sex on the brain to get much queerness out of that. Bronski also mentions *Harvey* (1944) by Mary Chase, in which the gentle and eccentric bachelor Elwood P. Dowd is attended by a partner who causes respectable people to shun him and psychiatrists to try to cure him; the partner is a big, invisible rabbit. All these stories received wider circulation in the cinema.

Latency

World War II had helped the psychiatrists to get a hold on both the official and the popular imagination in the United States. Traditionally, the military had depended on the prevailing medical language of degeneracy and brain disease; 'sodomists' was the word, and vigorous handling was the answer. The army would 'make a man' of you. Psychiatrists introduced the concept of the 'personality type', and a new Freudian language involving tendencies, proclivities, stages of development, maturity, deviance, normality, regression, adjustment, latency, active and passive, homosexual panic. The victimised men and women were moved from prisons to psychiatric wards.[10] Psychoanalytic ideas were widely influential among an intelligentsia which swung hard to the right in the Cold War; scores of playwrights, W. David Sievers and Donald L. Loeffler find, went that way.[11]

In 1929 Patrick Hamilton had allowed only subliminal hints of queerness into *Rope* (see chapters 1 and 9 above). The treatment of the Leopold and Loeb story by Meyer Levin, *Compulsion: A Play* (1957, Broadway), encourages the inference that homosexuality may be at the heart of a criminal personality. At first the heterosexual interests of the two murderous boys are stressed, but queerness increasingly supplies the imaginative energy of the text. We learn that, three years ago, another boy walked in when Judd and Artie were 'frigging around' (33). One of the boys in their fraternity speculates, 'What if [Judd] was fooling around with that poor kid?' (56). Once they are arrested, psychologists and Freudian analysts quiz them, disclosing more and more queerness. Judd is persuaded to divulge his childhood fantasies: he imagined himself as the slave of a king − 'my ideal type, like I wanted to be − tall and blond, and athletic'. Like Artie, in fact. 'I wanted to be Artie!' Judd admits. 'I completely identified myself with him. I would watch the food he ate, the drink going down his throat, and be envious' (89–90). Artie admits that he was initiated sexually by the chauffeur and had liaisons with other men. According to the psychiatrist, 'his emotional development is arrested there, he remains raging, six years old, and his guilt, his sense of inadequacy, of impotence if you want, forces him to take out this rage on other victims'. 'Symbols! Death wishes! These are the teachings from Vienna', the prosecutor protests. 'Everything is sex, the sex drive is an excuse for perversion and murder' (113). That is indeed how it appears. Unsatisfactory psychic development, with queerness at its centre, equates to all kinds of malfunction and explains everything.

The task of purifying America appeared far greater when the Kinsey Report, *Sexual Behavior in the Human Male*, was published in 1948. It stayed twenty-seven weeks on the bestseller list and sold 250,000 copies; it argued that sexuality depends on learnt behaviour and varies with the mores of the culture, and that all kinds of illicit sexual activity were far more widespread than the dominant ideology had acknowledged. Two particularly disconcerting factors in the report were the number of homosexuals, and the proportion of males who took part in same-sex practices at some point in their lives. Fifty per cent of males admitted erotic responses to their own sex, 37 per cent said they had had at least one post-adolescent experience leading to orgasm, 4 per cent were exclusively homosexual throughout adulthood, and same-sex eroticism had predominated for at least a three-year period in one male out of eight. Kinsey proposed a seven-point scale, ranging from exclusive heterosexuality (0) to exclusive homosexuality (6). Some gays spoke of themselves as 'a Kinsey 7'.

The implications were decidedly unAmerican. Edmund Bergler, a leading psychoanalyst, declared in 1954: 'Kinsey's erroneous conclusions pertaining to homosexuality will be politically and propagandistically used against the United States abroad, stigmatizing the nation as a whole in a whisper campaign, especially since there are no comparable statistics available for other countries.'[12] Bergler's stance was awkward because psychoanalysis also might support the idea that homosexuality is widespread. Freud had thought there was an initial disposition towards bisexuality in every child: 'Analysis shows that in every case a homosexual object-tie was present and in most cases persisted in a *latent* condition.'[13]

Latency was all too appropriate for Cold War paranoia. Donald Webster Cory, in his book *The Homosexual in America* (1951), noted that Freudian analysis may reveal 'the homosexual character − latent, repressed, sometimes sublimated and driven into the unconscious − of even the most perfectly adjusted and most "normal" of men'.[14] The trouble was, with latency it became hard to see how anyone could be securely exonerated. In an article first published in 1954 Norman Mailer acknowledged, as a result of reading Cory's book, that he had been wrong to be so prejudiced against homosexuals. He experienced another benefit too: 'There is probably no sensitive heterosexual alive who is not preoccupied at one time or another with his latent homosexuality, and while I had no conscious homosexual desires, I had wondered more than once if really there were not something suspicious in my intense dislike of homosexuals.'[15] Such preoccupation with homosexuality was indeed regarded as a sign of latency. Mailer's new self-analysis seemed to guard against this: now he was so *un*-bothered that he could contemplate the possibility of his own latent proclivity. This pleased him: he found he was 'no longer concerned with latent homosexuality. It seemed vastly less important, and paradoxically enabled me to realize that I am actually quite heterosexual.'

And yet . . . why is Mailer so keen to tell us all this? That is the double bind of latency: the more you think you haven't got it, the more you might have it. And so might others around you; the more straight they looked, the more they might be latently queer.

In *Homosexuality: a Psychoanalytical Study* (1962) Irving Bieber and his associates assessed a group of homosexual patients alongside a comparison group of patients who had been 'exclusively heterosexual' in their adult lives. Their cardinal project was to repudiate Kinseyite theories which 'hold homosexuality to be one type of expression of a polymorphous sexuality which appears pathologic only in cultures holding it to be so'.[16] However, they were troubled when they found that many of the ostensibly straight comparison group had suspicious symptoms: they feared homosexuals and homosexuality and had experienced fantasies and dreams. Other disconcerting factors were the frequency with which they reported advances 'by known or suspected homosexuals' and wishing, at some time, to be a woman. Adding it all up, the results were disconcerting. Although 41 per cent of the heterosexuals surveyed had 'no problem', 17 per cent reported a 'mild problem', 15 per cent a 'moderate problem' and 27 per cent a 'severe problem' (257–8). Bieber et al. were studying homosexuals because they were sick, and it turned out that more than half the heterosexuals had a problem — a 'severe' problem in a quarter of the cases.

So many Americans couldn't be unAmerican. The only answer was to defy Freud: 'Since the concept of homosexual latency is one that assumes a universal tendency present in all men, we prefer to discard the term entirely.' It would be better, Bieber averred, to say that the 'heterosexual' men had 'homosexual problems' (318). Thus he could conclude that 'heterosexuality is the *biologic* norm and that unless interfered with all individuals are heterosexual'. And therefore they could be re-interfered with: 'We are firmly convinced that psychoanalysts may well orient themselves to a heterosexual objective in treating homosexual patients rather than "adjust" even the more recalcitrant patient to a homosexual destiny' (319).

US culture wanted latency — that is why it went on about it: it was the most far-reaching way of worrying about the American male. But that culture also did *not* want it — it came too close to home.

Latency fascinated dramatists. It enabled them to write about queers without any actual homosexuality, and suited very well the bourgeois realist convention that the action will involve progressive revelation of the truth about the characters. In *The Small Hours* (1951), by Broadway playwrights George S. Kaufman and Leueen MacGrath, Laura has lost confidence in her loveless marriage and is out of touch with her children. As she rebuilds her life Peter, her son, feels able to confide why he goes to low dives and smokes dope: 'I'm a latent homosexual, that's what's wrong with me.' He has fought against it, and believes he has met a doctor who can help him, and now he and his mother will help each other (69). In *The Bad Seed* (1954) by Maxwell Anderson (a Broadway hit) Monica's experience of psychoanalysis enables her to assert, by way of conversation after lunch, that her brother Emory is a 'larvated homosexual' – 'covered as with a masque – concealed'. The evidence? He's fifty-two, unmarried and hasn't had affairs, and he likes male company and mysteries in which housewives are dismembered. Emory replies: 'If I'm a homosexual, they'll have to change the whole concept of what goes on among 'em' (17–18). There seems to be no point to this, other than to establish a lurid context in which a psychopathic child murders people (Leopold and Loeb are adduced in passing).

Rodolpho in Arthur Miller's *A View from the Bridge* (1955, Broadway) seems straight insofar as he is courting Eddie's daughter. But although Eddie doesn't have the word for latency, he thinks Rodolpho 'ain't right'. He sings and has 'wacky hair; he's like a chorus girl or sump'm' (35); he doesn't want to box; he knows how to cut material for a dress. 'I mean he looked so sweet there, like an angel – you could kiss him he was so sweet' (47). Maybe. Yet is not Eddie himself suspiciously preoccupied with queerness? And when he forcibly kisses Rodolpho, is that the insult due to an unmanly man, or a frustrated attraction? 'Doubt arises in the spectator's mind', writes Georges-Michel Sarotte for one, about Eddie's 'true, unconscious motives'.[17] Dennis Welland, conversely, doesn't see the kiss as necessarily proving that Eddie is sexually attracted to Rodolpho and yet horrified to realise it: his hostility to Rodolpho is adequately explained by Catherine's affection for him and by his apparent effeminacy'.[18] Yet Welland has to disavow the latency interpretation (and why is Rodolpho so sensitive to effeminacy?). The point, I think, is not to decide what Eddie was really doing, but to observe that once latency is in play, there is no getting it out of the system. That is how Brick is trapped in *Cat on a Hot Tin Roof* (see chapter 10).

There is actually another interesting theme trying to break through *A View from the Bridge*, concerning the drawbacks of conventional stereotyping of sex and gender roles. All the characters in the play assume that there are right and clearly known ways for men and women to relate. This conservative notion is endorsed by the good and authoritative lawyer, Alfieri: 'I'm warning you — the law is nature. The law is only a word for what has a right to happen. When the law is wrong it's because it's unnatural, but in this case it is natural' (66). The play seems not to question this ideology of law and nature, but a radical reading might ascribe to it the confusions and frustrations which the characters experience. However, we have to read against the grain to get this thought. As Clum argues, the 'rightness' of the play's denouement depends on Eddie's opinion about Rodolpho being mistaken; it is not all right for the boy actually to be gay.[19]

The project of Robert Anderson's *Tea and Sympathy* (1953) is to calm fears about latency. It was produced on Broadway, and in England in 1958 when the censor's embargo on homosexuality was partly lifted. The action begins with a witch-hunt: a junior master is reported as having bathed naked with a boy. That is sufficient evidence that he is 'a fairy. A homosexual'; he is dismissed (261). And what about the boy who was with him? Tom is accused of having feminine manners. He sings winsome folk songs and is to play Lady Teazle in the school play — we see him try on the dress; last year he was Lady Macbeth. His father doesn't like it. He took him away from his mother when he was five and wants to know why his boy isn't 'a regular fellow'. True, he wins at tennis, but he doesn't even play that like a man: 'No hard drives and cannon-ball serves. He's a cut artist' (257). 'Grace', the boys call him; he reads poetry, objects when they use his room to spy on a nursing mother, and doesn't bring girls to dances. The boys refuse to shower with him; his friend Al is persuaded not to room with him. No one accuses Tom of doing anything queer, but the presumption of latency is enough to make him a pariah.

As in *Young Woodley* (see chapter 4), Tom is harassed by his housemaster, Bill, and rescued for heterosexuality by Bill's wife, Laura. In a showdown between Laura and Bill, she accuses him of marrying because he was ribbed by others and because an aspirant headmaster has to have a wife, and of being more interested in going climbing with the boys than in her. She finally comes to the point: 'Did it ever occur to you that you persecute in Tom, that boy up there, you persecute in him the thing you fear in yourself? . . . This was the weakness you cried out for me to save you from, wasn't it[?]' (308–9). So there probably is a latent queer around: if it's not Tom (and that's never quite certain) then it's Bill.

Tea and Sympathy makes some shrewd points about witch-hunting. Attempting to get Al to see Tom differently, Laura asks what would happen if she put a rumour round about him. It would 'show you how easy it is to smear a person, and once I got them believing it, you'd be surprised how quickly your . . . manly virtues would be changed into suspicious characteristics' (Anderson's pause). Al notices that he has been standing with his hands on his hips, and thrusts them quickly down by his side. So you shouldn't jump to conclusions. However, to support this argument Laura adds that she's come across men 'who weren't men, some of them married and with children' (272). There are queers at large, then, and they may be so hard to spot that most people don't suspect them. The difference between her and Bill is that she is better informed about what to look out for. The casualty is still the gay man.

Clum emphasises the evasive language in *Tea and Sympathy*, suggesting that homosexuality is here 'unthinkable'.[20] That is indeed how it was in the 1920s, in the time of *Young Woodley*: there queerness, if it crossed your mind, was quickly repudiated, romantic friendship was exonerated, the house-master's wife had to contribute only embraces, and the father assumes his natural authority. The film of *Tea and Sympathy*, released in 1956, is like that. The action is framed in a flashback: Tom returns to the school a few years later, having married and having written a successful novel about it all; he reads a letter from Laura, dwelling on the ruin of her life and Bill's. However, Laura (Deborah Kerr) does not suggest that Bill himself is queer. So the cure did work, no one is queer, and adultery is punished. But in *Tea and Sympathy* – the play – queerness is by no means 'unthinkable'. On the contrary, the dialogue depends on the audience being alert to the nuances, silences and evasions of latency. This is a culture obsessed with queerness, not one that cannot think it. Eric Bentley commented, in respect of *Tea and Sympathy*: 'In the thirties you felt the reassuring presence of the "real" at the mention of a Worker. Today you feel it at the mention of a Homosexual.'[21]

The opportunities for gay representation were more dissimilar in New York and London during the 1950s than at other times. In England, activists and progressives were making homosexuality a prominent cause for reform, while the Lord Chamberlain was trying to close down the topic altogether, at least in serious drama (see chapter 12). In New York, with US manliness at stake, law reform was hardly contemplated and queerness figured prominently as an anxiety. Discreet plays about it were acceptable, so long as they showed it either not to be occurring after all, or to be confined to despicable characters. In brief, gayness was more present on the US stage, but more progressively handled in England. At the end of the 1950s these two modes suddenly cross-fertilised. In 1958 West End managements persuaded the Lord Chamberlain to change his policy, and *Cat on a Hot Tin Roof*, *Tea and Sympathy* and *A View from the Bridge* were performed. And new British plays, showing gay youngsters sympathetically, were produced on Broadway in 1959–60. In Peter Shaffer's *Five Finger Exercise* and Shelagh Delaney's *A Taste of Honey*, the important thing is not so much whether the young people are gay or straight as whether they can retain their sensitivity amid the cynicism that prevails in their milieux.

The writer who tried hardest to shift the atmosphere on Broadway was Hugh Wheeler. In *Big Fish, Little Fish* (1961) William, a bachelor, is surrounded by male as well as female devotees − 'the lonely and the misfits' (5) − and no one regards it as surprising. Basil, a lonely eccentric who arrives for a dinner party campily carrying his cat ('Kitty' or 'Pussikins'), says he loves William; 'Sometimes I can't understand', Edith says, 'I mean, one man being so fond of another man' (70). And Jimmy declares his love: 'William, I know you know how fond of you I've been. And I am. Of course I am. But it isn't just that. It's more. William, we've never talked about this and I never thought I would, but . . . but. . . .' William is not surprised. 'Jimmie, do you think I didn't know? . . . Who am I to mind? People are the way they are' (106, Wheeler's pauses). There is also casual talk of lesbianism, inspired by a novel about a girls' reform school in Canada, enabling Basil to suggest, jealously, that Hilda might be one. *Big Fish, Little Fish* achieved 101 performances.

Wheeler followed up with *Look: We've Come Through* (1961), which presents young Bobby's dissident sexuality sympathetically and as an unresolved question. Among a sophisticated New York set he is perceived at once as gay: 'That divine Mr Onopolis *did* pick up a boy' − 'At least he's Greek, and the Greeks invented all that, didn't they?' (11–12). His rather vague and naive gentleness renders Bobby vulnerable. He admits to Belle that he visits an older man who gives him money for sexual favours: 'Mr Millington's always been a real gentleman. And if he wants something . . . okay. What you got to lose?' he asks. 'Ain't nothing like hustling' (20, Wheeler's pause). His mother approves: they are on to a good thing. Bobby has an excessively-admired best mate called Skip (echoing *Cat on a Hot Tin Roof*). He returns from the navy with coarsely macho attitudes, and believes he knows what Bobby has been wanting. He locks the door and commands him to have sex. 'Who d'you think you're kidding? Little faggot. Goddam little son-of-a-bitch faggot. (*He continues ominously toward BOBBY as BOBBY picks up a beer bottle.*).' The curtain protects the audience from knowledge of the outcome (55–6). It is as if Stanley in *Streetcar Named Desire* encountered Blanche's husband Allan. Bobby's sensitivity appears preferable, even if he is gay.

The person who gets along with Bobby is another youngster, Belle, who is intelligent, knowledgeable and idealistic. She too has difficulties working out her emotional and sexual life among a group of young people who are selfishly engrossed by the false gods of media success. The closing moments suggest that Bobby might make it with Belle after all: 'Belle? (*Pause.*) You and me? (*He takes her in his arms. He kisses her.*) Wow! What do you know? Live and learn, don't you?' (62). Does this mean that Bobby wins through into normality, as in *Tea and Sympathy*? Perhaps the title, *Look: We've Come Through*, supports that idea, but in context it is ambiguous. It alludes to a poem by D.H. Lawrence, which Bobby reads from a book of Belle's: 'If only I am sensitive, subtle, oh, delicate, a winged gift, / If only most lovely of all, I yield myself . . .' (48, Wheeler's pause). I think the conclusion says that Bobby and Belle are good young people: even if he doesn't succeed in wooing her, they may be good friends and help each other to have rewarding lives.

In an article called 'Not What It Seems: Homosexual Motif Gets Heterosexual Disguise', Howard Taubman of the *New York Times* protested that the conclusion said that Bobby would change, 'but everything about him said that he would not'.[22] New York critics could not tolerate the thought that a sympathetic, unreformed and unpunished gay boy might hold the stage at the end. *Look: We've Come Through* ran for just five performances in a largish theatre; the producer panicked after mixed notices dwelt upon the gay issue. However, the play has found admirers; I have been quoting from a collection entitled *Broadway's Beautiful Losers*. Wheeler went on to write the book for *A Little Night Music* (1973) and other Stephen Sondheim musicals.

Family Values

The ultimate model for US manliness was the pioneer. The west opened her bosom and bestowed her treasures upon him as he hacked his way through the virgin continent, Frederick Jackson Turner says in his 'frontier thesis'.[23] In William Carlos Williams' account, Daniel Boone sought 'with primal lust . . . the ecstasy of complete possession of the new country . . . there must be a new wedding'.[24] These notions were applied to US expansionism after World War II when, as Michael S. Sherry says, war and national security became consuming anxieties and provided the memories, models, and metaphors that shaped broad areas of national life.[25] Well before President Kennedy used the phrase in 1960, Godfrey Hodgson points out, 'the new frontier' meant that

'American influence and American corporate business would spread around the world'.[26]

Yet questions were being raised about the relations between the pioneer tradition and the demands of corporate business. Already in *Childhood and Society*, published in 1950, Erik Erikson was worrying about 'bossism' and the individuality and autonomy of the US male. 'How can our sons preserve their freedom and share it with those whom, on the basis of new knowledge and new identity, they must consider equals?' Erikson asked, with the global expansion of US influence in view.[27] David Riesman in *The Lonely Crowd* (1950) said that business culture was making middle-class men too concerned about what others thought, too pliable; in fact, as Barbara Ehrenreich remarks, they seemed to be becoming as women were reckoned to be.[28] Herbert Marcuse argued that when individual development had been determined by the family, rivalry with the father had left scope for non-conformity; but now socialisation was being conducted by a whole system of depersonalised agencies, and you can't revolt against anonymity.[29] Business didn't need pioneers, or hardly; it needed smooth cogs.

These arguments underly *All My Sons* (1947, Broadway) by Arthur Miller, where the culture of business is set against the autonomy in comradeship that Chris experienced in the military. He found there 'A kind of − responsibility. Man for man.' Business seems phoney in comparison, but Chris' father, Joe, who stayed at home producing aircraft parts, is claimed as manly too, though he did make money out of it: 'Your father put hundreds of planes in the air, you should be proud. A man should be paid for that' (121–2). When it has to be admitted that Joe was responsible for supplying faulty aircraft parts, he tries to justify it as manly: 'You're a boy, what could I do! I'm in business, a man is in business' (157). Even in the face of such a failure of US ideology, Miller has nothing very different to offer. Chris has discovered nothing beyond his initial position. 'If I have to grub for money all day long at least at evening I want it beautiful. I want a family, I want some kids, I want to build something I can give myself to' (102). Manliness is still the goal, and there is no assessment of its exclusions. Women are seen merely as prizes for warriors, valued according to their capacity to support their men through thick and thin.

Even so, Miller had broached a critique: business might be bad for your integrity as a man. The conformist response dismissed such objections as 'immature'. That meant not measuring up to responsibility − which was defined as holding a decent job and maintaining a family. The stakes were raised by an alleged link between immaturity and homosexuality.

Freud had posited a sequential psychic development, which in the homosexual was 'arrested'.[30] This allows the inference not only that lesbians and gay men have not grown up properly; also, they have not properly grown up. For Gustav Bychowski, 'the first striking feature of the development of the ego of homosexuals is the persistence, almost unaltered, of infantile attitudes'. This was ineluctable, Bychowski declared: 'We may conclude that the solipsistic attitude of primary narcissism can be completely abandoned only when there is a normal development of the ego. If this process is hampered, then neither ego-feeling nor the feeling of reality can reach full maturity.'[31] Inge accepts this notion, even in a play which he probably did not expect to get produced, *The Boy in the Basement* (1962). Spencer cannot raise the nerve to leave his strong mother and invalid father. 'I bet in some ways you never grew up', says the delivery boy whose visits are the light of his life (173). The boy dies in an accident and Spencer, a mortician, has his most intimate moment when he prepares the body for burial; so much for gay love. Immaturity did not have to displace the older idea, that male homosexuals were feminine, because the immature man was reckoned to be like a woman − emotional, unreliable, dependent, and rather pathetic. Kenneth Lewes summarises: 'Homosexuals were seen as deeply flawed and defective because they shared certain psychic characteristics with women.'[32]

By definition, then, gays would be at odds with the demands of business in the Cold War. They 'envy the female as a way of escaping the difficulties and responsibilities of maleness', Abram Kardiner declared. 'They cannot compete. They always surrender in the face of impending combat.' According to Betty Friedan, 'homosexuals often lack the maturity to finish school and make sustained professional commitments'.[33] Conversely, it was easy to stigmatise hostility toward business as queer. This notion is active when Signi Falk complains, of Williams' plays: 'The poet-itinerant-outsider − the male who is often closely identified with his creator − seeks to avoid the full responsibilities of a job and of family life.'[34] Above all, this sounds like Biff in Arthur Miller's *Death of a Salesman* (1949, Broadway).

Once, it was possible to be a salesman and a pioneer; Willy's father would 'toss the whole family into the wagon, and then he'd drive the team right across the country; through Ohio, and Indiana, Michigan, Illinois, and all the Western states. And we'd stop in the towns and sell the flutes that he'd made on the way'; flute music haunts the play (38). Willy's Brother Ben still claims this lineage − he walked into the jungle at seventeen and walked out again rich at twenty-one. However, his achievement was not quite classic. He had been making for Alaska, but got rerouted from the last American wilderness into the jungle of capitalism. Anyway, Ben is only a vision; nowadays it's more difficult. Willy is struggling to hold on to the territory he has.

His sons, Biff and Happy, are notably immature: both are in their early thirties, neither has a wife and family, and Biff has been through twenty or thirty jobs. He feels happiest herding cattle, in Nebraska, the Dakotas, Arizona, Texas. This might seem a manly occupation, but no, Biff is immature; it would be all right if he could raise money and buy a ranch, then he would be in business. 'Maybe I oughta get married. Maybe I oughta get stuck into something. Maybe that's my trouble. I'm like a boy. I'm not married, I'm not in business, I just − I'm like a boy' (17). 'You never grew up', Willie confirms (48). To be sure, Biff was an excellent ball-player, and Bieber and his colleagues regarded this as a good indicator for sexual maturity.[35] But that was for boys − compare Bill's climbing in *Tea and Sympathy* and Brick's hurdling in *Cat on a Hot Tin Roof.* Sarotte expounds the normative pattern: 'youth is devoted to team sports and to various experiences with girls; it is a condensed version of the youth of American civilization itself. Once tribute has been paid to the country's ideal, maturity is devoted to building a family and a career. The first phase represents the dream; the second is the reality.'[36] Biff's continuing attachment to ball games is mature only if it is a way of selling sports goods.

Nothing is said in *Death of a Salesman* about queerness, but Biff's boyish masculinity may appear over-assertive. He annoyed the math teacher by imitating his lisp; he whistles in the elevator at work; he takes time out to go swimming. He and his brother talk a lot about girls, but Happy makes all the running: 'I think I got less bashful and you got more so. What happened, Biff? Where's the old humour, the old confidence?' (15). Biff has no girlfriends and doesn't make it with the girl Happy arranges for him ('all we did was follow Biff around trying to cheer him up!': 98). He is hung up on an adolescent trauma: the revelation of Willy's betrayal of Linda, his mother, which occurred at the moment when Biff was telling his father how he mocked the lisping math teacher. As David Savran says, it is not a matter of Biff being homosexual, though there is 'certainly enough material in the text for an actor' to play him that way. But we may perceive 'the constitutive role that the dread of a feminine male plays in the construction of the authoritative Cold War masculinity for which Miller's protagonists yearn'.[37] In *Death of a Salesman* effeminacy is at the boundary of permissible thought.

Biff's final perception is surely right: Willy was not cut out to be a salesman. But, as in *All My Sons*, members of an audience may remark that Willy's confusions and treacheries are not just individual. They occur on the faultline between the manly-pioneer notion, and the mature-family-responsibility notion. The pioneer presumably took his sex where he could; the family man is expected to bring his earnings home and provide a secure basis for the sexuality of his sons. It is the same with Biff's stealing. Miller suggests no way out of this impasse. And, as in *All My Sons*, the women are not envisaged as presenting any kind of alternative; the men's quest for selfhood is conducted among themselves.

What is finally striking in all these plays is the extent to which consumer capitalism is predicated on a satisfactory attainment of manliness; it seems a very American preoccupation. It is active still in Paddy Chayefsky's play *The Latent Heterosexual* (1968), where Morley, a flamboyantly effeminate writer who has made a lot of money, is advised to turn himself into a corporation and marry a call-girl to get a tax break. He and Christine are 'enchanted' with each other at first sight, and a psychiatrist doubts that Morley ever was really queer:

> In America, a country whose national lunacy is virility, where a man's measure is the multiplicity of his erections − and where a high officer of our government is said to have interrupted councils of state to unzipper his pants, unleash his beef and flop it on the conference table, saying: 'Has Mao Tse-Tung got anything like that?' − in such a society, impotence is far more of a stigma than homosexuality, and the patient might well have fancied himself a homosexual all these years just to maintain his self-respect. (393).

Morley becomes ultra-masculine and obsessed with the corporation − dehumanised. Queerness thus correlates with humanity, but Chayefsky nonetheless allows Morley's partner, Richard, to be no more than an off-stage cipher.

Casting around for the origin of these male anxieties, many laid them at the door of women. The ideology of domesticity that had developed in the nineteenth century was double edged. Mother was celebrated as the instiller of religious, moral and social virtues into the young, and as the guardian of morality generally. In return for this power, she was expected to accept economic and political subordination. The drawback, as Michael Rogin observes, is that 'sons and husbands whose intimate needs women served felt dependent for their freedom on the women who attended to them'.[38] The answer, of course, was that Mom should let go, but this still left the initiative with her.

World War II exacerbated such anxieties: families had been broken up, women had taken on additional tasks, and men had been resocialised into male bonding and prostitution; gayness came into view. In 1942, shortly after Pearl Harbor, Philip Wylie put 'Momism' into circulation through his bestseller, *Generation of Vipers*. Mom had become an untouchable national myth, he said; but she was drenching the nation in selfishness and sentimentality, dominating her husband and making her son dependent. By 1950 Erikson was writing, of the typical American boy:

> His mother is somewhat of a 'Mom'. She can be harsh, loud-voiced, and punitive. More likely than not she is sexually frigid. His father, while exhibiting the necessary toughness in business, is shy in his intimate relationships and does not expect to be treated with much consideration at home. Such parents in our case histories are still noted down as pathogenic, while it is clear that they represent a cultural pattern.[39]

The boy, as a consequence, suffers from lack of imagination, inability to take on big questions, and excessive deference to the autocratic boss who wants men like machines. This was not a good training for democracy in an age of US world hegemony, Erikson observed. In fact, Mom might be unAmerican. In the Rosenberg spy trial her dominance was blamed: 'Julius is the slave and his wife, Ethel, the master', insisted Morris Ernst. President Eisenhower repeated the argument as he refused to commute the death sentence.[40]

'You men think you can decide on who is a man, when only a woman can really know', Laura warns in *Tea and Sympathy*. She is as determined as the males in the play that a gay boy shall not emerge among them; she transfers the stigma to her husband, Bill, choosing to sleep with Tom instead. Bill accuses her of wanting a boy to mother: 'You were more interested in mothering that fairy up there than in being my wife' (307–8). Her first husband was indeed sensitive and little more than a boy when they married (compare Blanche's husband in *Streetcar*). Perhaps Laura doesn't want a real man; she says she is drawn to that 'heartbreaking time . . . no longer a boy . . . not yet a man . . .' (253, Anderson's pauses). Making women responsible for the sexual maturation of their menfolk compounds the problem of manliness, rather than resolving it. In *Cat on a Hot Tin Roof*, even if Brick experiences some kind of 'cure' at the end, it depends upon Maggie cajoling and dominating him. And compare *The Vortex*, where Nicky pleads with his mother to help him become more independent. You can't get out of Momism through Momism.

What Wylie did *not* say in 1942 — and it indicates how the preoccupation with queerness was to gain momentum in the Cold War — was that Mom was making her son into a fairy. He remarks that homosexuality is increasing and that this may herald national decline, but 'to treat it as a fiendish manifestation, like ax-murdering, is silly'. Actually, it is 'thoroughly normal in the young, although its continuance in maturity may be regarded as infantile'. Wylie discusses homosexuality not in the Momism chapter, but in the one about how US people delude themselves about sexual morality. The problem is not sexuality, but repression: 'The fact that it goes on all the time means only that millions of people have dangerously guilty consciences.'[41] For Erikson likewise, in 1950, homosexuality was not the danger. On the contrary, it was a sign of inadequacy in the American boy that he was excessively concerned about appearing 'a "sissy"'.[42]

But Bieber and his associates insisted that Moms were producing homosexuals. They 'overstimulated their sons through seductiveness', 'sexually inhibited' them, discouraged 'masculine attitudes and behavior patterns', and interfered with their 'peer group participation'.[43] Bieber's big problem, once more, was that dysfunctional families were experienced not only by the homosexuals. Just over 80 per cent of them said their mothers were dominating and 57 per cent said they were seductive. But 65 per cent and 34 per cent of the heterosexual comparison group said this too! Again, while 62 per cent of the gay patients said their mothers tried to ally with them against their fathers and 58 per cent said their mothers openly preferred them to their fathers, 40 per cent of the comparison group gave the same reply to the first question, and 38 per cent to the second (45). The difference was one of degree: the homosexuals were only an intensified version of the US family.

Finally, Bieber believed, it is down to the father to rescue his smothered and inhibited offspring: 'a constructive, supportive, warmly related father *precludes* the possibility of a homosexual son; he acts as a neutralizing, protective agent should the mother make seductive or close-binding attempts' (310–11). Indeed, 44 per cent of the gay patients said their fathers humiliated them, and 56 per cent said they feared physical injury from their fathers. However, of the comparison group, the heterosexual patients, 40 per cent said their fathers humiliated them, and 43 per cent that they feared physical injury from their fathers (86–7). All over the United States, innumerable boys were being humiliated and beaten by presumptively heterosexual men, putting at risk their sexual adjustment. The queer panic which had been instigated to root out inadequate men and reinforce the rest was disclosing a general faultline in family and gender ideology.

Emergent feminists, as well as conservatives, sought to eliminate Mom, and often gays with her. 'The role of the mother in homosexuality was pinpointed by Freud and the psychoanalysts', Betty Friedan confidently declares in *The Feminine Mystique* (1963). The obligatory modern role of housewife-and-mother is so unfulfilling that she 'attaches her son to her with such dependence that he can never mature to love a woman, nor can he, often, cope as an adult with life on his own'. Hence 'the homosexuality that is spreading like a murky smog over the American scene'. Strangely, Friedan complains that 'the man-eating mother' as portrayed in texts such as Williams' *Suddenly Last Summer* amounts to 'an agonized shout of obsessed love-hate against women'; but then herself accuses Mom of producing homosexuals according to the Freudian recipe.[44] In my view Momism was largely an attempt to scapegoat women for the difficulties men experienced in living up to a contradictory and oppressive ideology of masculinity. I have shown how Williams opened out these ideas in *Period of Adjustment* (chapter 10).

Edward Albee's *The Zoo Story* (1960, Off-Broadway), as I indicate in chapter 9, may be regarded as establishing an American version of absurdist writing and as a Pinteresque flirtation with the mysterious menace of queerness. What is also American is the way Jerry activates Peter's anxieties about domesticity, his wife, girl-children and unmanly pets. The conclusion depends on a challenge to Peter's manliness: 'fight for that bench; fight for your parakeets; fight for your cats, fight for your two daughters; fight for your wife; fight for your manhood, you pathetic little vegetable. [*Spits in* PETER'S *face.*] You couldn't even get your wife with a male child' (413). Thus Albee contrives to suggest both that American manhood is undermined by Mom and that it is male insecurity that is the real issue. In *The American Dream* (1961) Albee makes Grandma resourceful, being of pioneer stock, but Daddy is feeble, despite Mommy granting that he was really masculine – 'Oh, Daddy, you were so masculine; I shivered and fainted' (34). Mommy is dominating and has a rather basic idea of marriage: 'I have a right to live off of you because I married you, and because I used to let you get on top of me and bump your uglies' (31). Being incapable of producing children of their own, Mommy and Daddy have emasculated their first adoptive son physically. His twin, 'the American Dream', is incapable of emotion and subject to Mommy's seductive attentions.

The principal rationale for the internecine taunting that constitutes the dialogue of Albee's *Who's Afraid of Virginia Woolf?* (1962, Broadway) is anxiety about the American family. George is not successful in his occupation;

Martha's alleged over-mothering of their son has included 'climbing all over the poor bastard, trying to break the bathroom door down to wash him in the tub when he's sixteen' (126). Above all, the climactic admission of the play is that George and Martha couldn't have children. The point about this revelation is not a supposed human tendency to prefer fantasies to uncomfortable truths, or the supposedly therapeutic benefits of facing things squarely; those are traditional preoccupations of bourgeois drama. What is revealed is a hysterical terror of not siring and bearing offspring, and hence of failing to become fully American. At the same time, the other, younger couple, Nick and Honey, are spoken of as the children, so the audience can see how the new generation is shaping up. They manifest their own failures of femininity and masculinity (baby doll and houseboy), and without even the intensity of George and Martha. The ultimate source of consternation, running through the play, is male dependency. 'I am the Earth Mother, and you're all flops', Martha proclaims (111). Nick has to beg for a validation of his sexual prowess: '[to MARTHA, *quietly with intense pleading*]: Tell him I'm not a houseboy' (119). There is no way out of such dependency.

Get the Gays

Albee allowed it to be known that the destructive family in *Who's Afraid of Virginia Woolf?* is intended to be representative. The names of the principals, George and Martha, allude to the first President of the United States and his wife, and their fantasy child is 'the revolutionary principles of this country that we haven't lived up to yet'.[45] George reads aloud: 'And the west, encumbered by crippling alliances, and burdened with a morality too rigid to accommodate itself to the swing of events, must . . . eventually . . . fall' (104, Albee's pauses).

Critics didn't like this at all. Richard Schechner, editor of *Tulane Drama Review*, complained that *Who's Afraid?* is a misrepresentation of 'American society'; 'The lie of his work is the lie of our theatre and the lie of America. The lie of decadence must be fought.' And without quite accusing Albee, he traced the corruption to 'morbidity and sexual perversity which are there only to titillate an impotent and homosexual theatre and audience'.[46] Tom F. Driver asserted explicitly that the four characters make better psychological sense if regarded as homosexual men — because although 'heterosexual couples engage in *some* of the same behavior and show *some* of the same psychology', such an orgy 'most aptly refers' to homosexual liaisons.[47] Gay men not only misrepresent decent, straight Americans; they attribute to them their own perverse behaviour.

Once theatre critics had broken the taboo on talking about these queer slurs on American manhood, there was no holding them. I have touched elsewhere on the thought that artistic writing was a problem in principle: it was only doubtfully manly, doubtfully American. Even writers who seemed to have contributed crucially to the idea of America seemed problematic in a Freudian age.[48] As I showed in chapter 1, theatre had always been queer space; now a massive uneasiness emerged about established playwrights.

The dramatist who was usually placed alongside Williams and Miller was William Inge — a friend of Williams and a discreet homosexual who was absorbed in Freudian notions. He had been widely regarded as commendably American: the film *Splendor in the Grass* (1961) was praised by *Newsweek* as 'one of the richest American movies in years', and 'as American as apple pie' (it hinges on frigidity and hysteria).[49] Nonetheless, the idea began to circulate that unAmerican attitudes were being infiltrated through Inge's work. Actually this was unfair: Inge's strategy in plays produced up to that date was to pick up anxieties around Momism and manliness, and make it all come right in the last act. *Dark at the Top of the Stairs* (1957, Broadway) has the salesman whose job is going downhill, and who cheats on his wife; he doesn't pay appropriate attention to his children, so the girl is hysterical and the boy is a sissy. However, at the end the husband re-establishes himself in a better-paid job in a more forward-looking line of business, and suddenly asserts a warm but manly stance towards his wife and children, who are duly appreciative and snap into place as the good American family.

This was not entirely persuasive. In a review of *Dark at the Top of the Stairs*, entitled 'The Men-taming Women of William Inge', Robert Brustein attacked Inge as 'the first spokesman for a matriarchal America'. The theme of his plays was the emasculation of the male; he was following Williams 'in writing she-dramas, in giving to women if not the leading role then certainly the pivotal (and most insightfully created) role in his work'. In part, Brustein was conducting a familiar negotiation around Momism, but a distinctive slant was added by the accusation that the heroes of Inge and Williams belonged to 'a new theatrical type' — the 'male impersonator', who wears blue jeans, cowboy boots and T-shirt and is credited with athletic prowess, but 'hides fundamental insecurities behind an exaggerated show of maleness'.[50] Actually only *Bus Stop* (1955), among Inge's plays, approximates to that theme.

In 1963 Inge, with uncharacteristic boldness, gave critics the play they had been accusing him of writing. *Natural Affection* (1963, Broadway) depicts two couples where the man lacks the confidence to dominate his woman and affection between the men is beset with uneasiness about faggotry. The handsome outlaw-intruder, Donnie, is Sue's illegitimate son: he's been in reform school where he was badly beaten by a warder whose advances he repelled. His friend proposes making money out of rich queers: 'You're not bein' a queer. You're just doin' it for the money' (31). But Donnie is unstable and desperate for his mother's love, and it all ends violently. The critics didn't approve. Howard Taubman in the *New York Times* offered in his column a 'Primer' – 'Helpful hints on how to scan the intimations and symbols of homosexuality in our theater'. One should look out for handsome young male characters, baneful women, and other signs of 'total disenchantment with the possibility of a fulfilled relationship between man and woman'.[51]

Theatre people must have known all along that Inge was gay, and, of course, Williams. So what happened around 1960 was not news. Nor was there much of a change in the conditions of discretion; these accusations were still oblique. The new factor, I think, was the prospect that US theatre, like contemporary British theatre, might be developing a more stringent social analysis.

These critics were onto Albee from the start. *The Zoo Story*, Brustein said, 'embodies the same kind of sexual-religious claptrap we are accustomed to from Allen Ginsberg. . . . I will not elaborate on the masochistic-homosexual perfume which hangs so heavily over *The Zoo Story* except to say that Mr Albee's love-death, like Mr Ginsberg's poetry, yields more readily to clinical than theological analysis.'[52] Resentment accrued to the notion that Albee was cultivating an effete, European, avant-garde manner. Philip Roth attacked such features in Albee's *Tiny Alice* (1964) – 'Its tediousness, its pretentiousness, its galling sophistication, its gratuitous and easy symbolizing, its ghastly pansy rhetoric and repartee'. Only covert queerness could account for an American male writing like that: ' – all of this can be traced to his own unwillingness or inability to put its real subject at the center of the action'.[53] *Tiny Alice* was produced on Broadway in 1964, and by the Royal Shakespeare Company in London in 1970.

Stanley Kauffmann took over the *New York Times* slot, and argued in January 1966 that gay writers should be able to express themselves without disguise. Commentators have doubted the quality of Kauffmann's concern, perhaps without realising that he lost his job as the *Times* critic because of his liberal stance in this article. Even so, he was not prepared to allow that gay writers might have a relevant critique of family ideology: 'Because three of the most successful American playwrights of the last twenty years are (reputed) homosexuals and because their plays often treat of women and marriage, therefore, it is said, postwar American drama presents a badly distorted picture of American women, marriage, and society in general.' This is because gays are bitter and twisted: 'there is every reason to expect their plays to be streaked with vindictiveness toward the society that constricts and, theatrically, discriminates against them'.[54]

The strategy is precisely focused. Albee says the recommended US version of heterosexual relations is corrupt and corrupting; hostile critics reverse the charge, alleging that gays don't like the American dream because they are unAmerican and can't join in. All this was still within the Freudian orbit – Bychowski had made the same point. One of his patients actually wanted to 'fight for equality of rights for himself as identified with other wronged, frustrated and exploited individuals'. This is pathological and needs explanation: 'Thus he used not only to gratify his narcissistic grandeur but also to better his own feelings of weakness and frustration.' 'Incidentally', Bychowski adds, 'it is curious to observe that among many homosexuals a more or less overt admiration for Fascism prevails'.[55] So a commitment to freedom is turned first into a sickness, then into fascism.

Unspoken Lesbians

A radical view of queerness, dramatic creativity and sexual politics was taken by the black writer, Lorraine Hansberry. In her Broadway play *The Sign in Sidney Brustein's Window* (1964) a playwright (David) is gay, but the larger problem – larger than race or sexuality – is how the person of radical instincts is to locate political commitment in the wake of Soviet suppression of the Hungarian Revolution. Sidney supports a 'Reform' candidate in city elections but finds that he is corrupt like the others. In this bohemian setting David's gayness doesn't cause much problem; what Sidney complains of is his absurdist stance (his new play – a substantial critical success – has two characters, male and married to each other, and is set in a fridge). 'You have now written fourteen plays about not caring, about the isolation of the soul of man, the alienation of the human spirit, the desolation of all love, all possible communication. When what you really want to say is that you are ravaged by a society that will not sanctify your particular sexuality!' Absurdism may be an understandable product of gay oppression, but why not write positively about that? Sidney will support a campaign for changes in the sex laws, but he resists 'the notion that your particular "thing" is something that only the deepest, saddest, the most nobly tortured can know about' (150). David's sexuality, like all the important things in this committed play, is implicated in the system.

Hansberry's work prompts a question about lesbian representation in theatre of this period. Where was it? Two plays which I discuss elsewhere — Sartre's *Huis Clos* and Genet's *The Maids* — received New York productions in the 1940s and 1950s. But they came with the cachet of Parisian avant-garde chic, and did not produce local offspring. *The Children's Hour*, which now seemed to be about McCarthyism, was revived on Broadway in 1952 and in San Francisco in 1957; a faithful film, with Audrey Hepburn and Shirley MacLaine, was made in 1961. *The Captive* was revived in 1957. Kaier Curtin draws on three doctoral studies to support his assessment that very few plays with lesbian roles of any kind were presented in New York between 1950 and 1975 (though he has Broadway mainly in view).[56] He suggests that the topic was choked off by the sudden closure of *Trio*, by Dorothy and Howard Baker in 1945. Eventually, after a lot of dispute, City Hall backed off but, even so, the dominant producer, Lee Shubert (like Binkie Beaumont in the West End) was not inclined to take further risks.[57]

Ed Bullins sets a lesbian scenario among the black people of South Philadelphia in his play *Clara's Ole Man* (1965, San Francisco). Big Girl (aged twenty-five to forty) is not pleased that Clara (aged eighteen) has invited a young man, Jack, to the house. She treats him to a boisterous and domineering — Falstaffian, perhaps — display of humour. Evidently Clara is under her sway (compare *The Killing of Sister George*), but Jack doesn't catch on to the lesbian relationship until he asks Clara when her 'ole man' will be home from work. Big Girl got the afternoon off: 'Clara's ole man is home now' (280). For his presumption Jack suffers expulsion, a beating, maybe death; you mess with these people at your peril. Then, suddenly in 1966, after its West End success, *The Killing of Sister George* ran for 205 performances on Broadway.

Hansberry is described by Nina Rapi as a playwright 'now known to us to have been lesbian' who 'produced no lesbian texts at all'.[58] It is worth looking again at her successful play, *A Raisin in the Sun* (1959, Broadway), for an indication of where the lesbian issue went in the 1950s. There are social problems enough here; each member of the family nurtures a proper discontent with what is available to black people — income, accommodation, family cohesion, social dignity. Each of the answers that presents itself proves either unsatisfying or dangerously idealistic. For instance, space is so limited that a pregnancy has to be terminated, but the alternative is moving to a house in an aggressively whites-only district. It is a kind of black *Death of a Salesman*: the factors that make the American Dream unworkable in Miller's play are exacerbated grossly for African Americans.

The women have to be strong, especially Mama, though this makes her conservative on gender. Beneatha, her daughter, struggles to find a radical Africanist vision. But what is different here is Beneatha's discontent with her options as a woman. The sensible choice would be to marry George, who is good-looking, affluent and truly attached to her; the idealistic choice would be marrying Asagai and discovering a new future in Nigeria. In many a story of the period, two such choices constitute the scope for the individual. But Beneatha is drawn to neither of them. She is impatient with George's wish to kiss at the end of an evening out, and tries to get Asagai to see that there is 'more than one kind of feeling which can exist between a man and a woman'. No, he says, there is only one kind. 'I know', Beneatha replies, 'because that's what it says in all the novels that men write' (81–2, 68). She wants to be a doctor; 'go be a nurse like other women', her brother tells her, ' – or just get married and be quiet'. 'I'm not worried about who I'm going to marry yet – if I ever get married', she remarks. '*If!*' Mama and Ruth exclaim (59, 64). *A Raisin in the Sun* hovers on the edge of a perception of lesbianism as one of the issues in African American culture, but it is not quite focused. Maybe, as many women were to find in the 1970s, there was so much to deal with in the ordinary lot of women that lesbianism seemed too much to take on. Hansberry died in 1964.

Yet lesbianism was not unrepresentable. Sonya L. Jones refers to the 1940s as 'ripe with lesbian pulps'.[59] Valerie Taylor averred in the lesbian campaigning magazine *The Ladder* that she was finding 'more books about female homophiles than about males'.[60] Ann Bannon's tough romances (five were published between 1957 and 1962) flourished in the bestseller lists, chronicling the passionate adventures of Laura, Beebo and their friends in New York. Some pertinent features are: Laura's initial ignorance of lesbianism; her reliance on Jack, a gay man, to guide her onto the Greenwich Village scene; a general sharing of lesbian and gay male space; the gradual emergence of the word 'gay'; an assumption that a violent and abusive father has something to do with becoming lesbian; and an open attitude toward butch/femme roles (some do, some don't).[61] There is a good deal of doom and angst, but also some positive thinking. At no point in the chronicles do the women have anything to do with a theatre.

Bannon's novels are not written in a private language, but they were most illuminating for the lesbian reader. Carol Ann Uszkurat endorses Diane Hamer's view: 'The fictional fantasy world Bannon created through her novels was not separate from, but formed part of the reality of being lesbian in the 1950s. Bannon herself was swamped with requests for help and advice about lesbianism from isolated women desperate for information.'[62] Perhaps, as we saw with Tennessee Williams, fiction was less of a public mode, and hence more negotiable, than the stage. Nevertheless, according to Jann Miller, reviewing the 1957 production in *The Ladder*, *The Children's Hour* was heartening: 'there were many in the audience the night I was present, and there will be many in innumerable future performances to come, who will read into the drama a certain deadly but ever-present self-identification'.[63]

It may be, as Faderman suggests, that lesbian subculture had become closed off and they just didn't make it happen. 'Perhaps because they could "get by" they were less motivated to organize and protest, even during the civil rights movements of the 1960s.' By 1970 both the lower-class bar scene and the more respectable and campaigning Daughters of Bilitis 'were, each in their own way, more conservative than heterosexual society had become during the era of flower children, unisex, sexual revolution, and the civil rights movement'.[64] If anything, lesbians became harder to envisage as the women's movement became more vigorous. In Friedan's *Feminine Mystique* 'the problem that has no name' was the bored and frustrated housewife. Perhaps what she wanted was a lesbian relationship, but commentators were not inclined to see it that way.

Tennessee Williams mocks at the silence around lesbian sexuality in *Something Unspoken* (1958), which was presented on Broadway as a curtain-raiser to *Suddenly Last Summer*. Grace (widowed) is companion and secretary to the tyrannical Cornelia (single). The latter, in between phone calls through which she conducts her campaign to become regent of the Confederate Daughters of the city, demands of Grace: 'Don't you feel there's − *something unspoken* between us?' (290). Today she has given Grace fifteen roses, one for each year of their association. 'How blind of you not to see how desperately I wanted to keep you here for ever', she exclaims (295). Grace is terrified: 'I do know some things are better left unspoken. Also I know that when a silence between two people has gone on for a long time it's like a wall that's impenetrable between them! . . . Or maybe *you* can break it. I know I can't' (292). The person in the stronger position makes the terms. Florence Conrad, writing about *Something Unspoken* and *Suddenly Last Summer* in *The Ladder*, saw little to attract her into the theatre. She was 'repelled by the ugliness and horror in these plays. . . . the deviant *need* not be the predatory'.[65]

12

The Problem of the Problem

Social Problem/Problem Plays

In Britain nervousness about gay activity was specially marked in the early 1950s. The idea of a witch-hunt of well-placed homosexuals, instigated to appease US fears about the passing of atomic secrets to the Soviets, has been disputed by Patrick Higgins.[1] Indeed, it has never seemed entirely plausible that the British establishment could accomplish such a focused intervention. It should be remembered also that it is not just queerness that was taboo: conception outside wedlock was regarded as a family disaster, virtually across the class spectrum, and divorce was very difficult to accomplish and heavily stigmatised.

What is plausible, though, is a climate of opinion, running through various institutions and tending to the belief that a homosexual threat had to be countered. Probably this was an anxious reaction to the War, which had weakened inhibitions about sexual expression by moving people around and freeing them from the monitoring gaze of significant others (upheaval on the home front in Britain had been far greater than in the United States). 'I think the war led to a sort of breaking down of old inhibitions and customs and family ties', says one oral history respondent; 'I think the introduction of the American queens over here during the Second World War changed a lot of people's attitudes towards sex', says another.[2] There are many such accounts. I would just add that, afterwards, World War II was presented as a general fun time by many British people, but there was also misery and desperation. Some of the sexual emancipation derived from the thought that one's friends, partners and oneself were likely to die.

Between 1938 and 1952 sodomy convictions rose from 134 to 670 per annum; recorded attempts to commit 'unnatural offences' from 822 to 3,087; and gross indecency offences between males from 320 to 1,686.[3] How far this nervousness reflected an increase in activity among sexual dissidents is hard to say. More significant than the figures, with all their toll in ruined lives, is the fact that the victims extended beyond the usual – the powerless – to the discreet, cultured gentlemen who had seemed to have achieved a moderately successful accommodation with the system, especially through the cross-class liaison, and who set the tone for West End theatre. They felt their class privileges generally to be under threat, as the State moved to meet the lower-class expectations of a better world which had been raised in order to win the War.

In *The Life For Me* (1952) the author Rupert Croft-Cooke writes of his distaste for postwar London: everything is run on the cheap, one's money no longer stretches to restaurants, theatres and thoughtless pleasures, and one is confronted continually by petty officialdom. Croft-Cooke has moved to the country, he says, setting up a leisured household with his young Indian (male) secretary.[4] His account is discreet, but haughty and unfraid; Croft-Cooke didn't really expect anyone to question his lifestyle, secretary included. However, two years later they were arrested – in the country retreat – solely on evidence extracted by the police from two naval cooks who had been picked up in the Fitzroy Tavern by the secretary and invited to stay for the weekend (they had been arrested on unconnected charges of assault and drunkenness). Croft-Cooke wrote up his case in a further book, *The Verdict of You All* (1955), displaying open outrage that a person of his station should be treated like a common criminal.

The most notorious case since Wilde occurred in 1954. Lord Montagu of Beaulieu, Michael Pitt-Rivers and Peter Wildeblood were tried on charges of indecency with two young airmen. They had not risked public visibility; they had not sought to flout the law. They were convicted of committing and conspiring to commit indecent acts with consenting adults in private houses; the evidence consisted entirely of statements obtained by the police from the young men involved, on the promise of leniency in respect of other offences. All the accused were sent to prison. In his book about the trial, *Against the Law*, Wildeblood, like Croft-Cooke, stresses that they had not expected the law to be used in this way: 'We always supposed – and the cases reported in the newspapers appeared to bear this out – that if we behaved ourselves in public, the police would leave us alone.'[5]

A surprising wave of sympathy arose among the public, in parliament and in the press, even the popular press. Wildeblood quotes the *Sunday Express*: 'We have been encouraged to believe [the need for a search warrant] to be the vital difference between a Police State and a democracy. Have we been deluding ourselves?' (112). A perverse, medium-term benefit was enhanced visibility and a great increase in public discussion. 'I don't think I was really made aware of the law until years later when the Montagu case came up', says an oral history informant.[6] As Higgins argues, these high-profile trials, together with the conviction of Sir John Gielgud for soliciting in 1953, allowed the press to write about homosexuality. The Kinsey Report of 1948 was also important, though Wolfenden and his colleagues doubted how far American findings would be relevant to the less troubled social system of Britain.[7]

Homosexuality was discussed, increasingly, *as a social problem*. A Church of England pamphlet, published in 1954, was called *The Problem of Homosexuality*. The Wolfenden Committee on Homosexual Offences and Prostitution was set up in 1954 after a minister for home affairs declared: 'Quite clearly, this is a problem which calls for very careful consideration on the part of those responsible for the welfare of the nation.'[8] The sociologist Richard Hauser was asked by the Home Secretary to write a follow-up report, which he was pleased to do because he wanted to study 'the most intractable social problems'.[9] Gay activists adopted the social problem. By the end of the decade Gordon Westwood believed that his 1952 objective, of bringing 'the problem of homosexuality . . . out into the open where it can be discussed and reconsidered', had been achieved.[10] Antony Grey, who was to become secretary of the Homosexual Law Reform Society in the 1960s, wrote to the *Sunday Times* in 1954: 'As you rightly say, it is a social problem'; 'Here is a sizeable social problem', he told the Wolverhampton *Express and Star* in 1963; addressing the Rural Deanery of Westminster in 1965 he declared homosexuality 'a widespread social problem'.[11]

The idea of the social problem is, in my view, a major conceptual development. Commentators have often observed that during the twentieth century homosexuality came to be considered less an evil or a sin, and more a clinical condition. That is true; the social problem appears alongside, as a third framework of understanding. *The Wolfenden Report* (1957) altogether ignored the question of sin, and explicitly set aside medical interpretations. Homosexuality presented 'social rather than medical problems'; courts should not call for medical reports in most cases, and 'therapeutic measures' were likely to be effective not in producing 'change in sexual orientation' but in promoting 'a better adaptation to life in general'.[12] Of course, the medical model remained strong, and the idea of sin has been reactivated lately by conservatives. The three explanations still jostle for interpretive authority, alongside those preferred by lesbian and gay people.

It wasn't just homosexuals; in the 1950s there was suddenly a swathe of social problems – juvenile delinquents, unmarried mothers, latch-key children, the elderly; there were shortages of housing, teachers, nurses, engineers; there was gambling, divorce, prostitution and the colour bar. It is not that there were suddenly more problems; nor was the social problem a new construct (it goes back to Chadwick, Rowntree and the Webbs). But as a way of apprehending social instability it was suddenly central to the self-understanding of social democratic societies in the postwar period. It was supported by the rise of sociology as a discipline and of social work as a profession.

The social problem is a welfare-capitalist formation. Let's locate that, briskly. In the 1930s, there had seemed to be three kinds of future: Fascism, Communism and a rejigging of capitalism to make it fairer – welfare-capitalism. These three fought it out between 1939 and 1945. Welfare-capitalism won in Western Europe: on the right as well as the left, it was agreed that there should be no return to prewar conditions. Now all the people were to have a stake in society, an adequate share of its resources as of right: a job, a pension or social security, a roof over your head, healthcare, education. These promises were to be sustained by government management of the economy in the manner proposed by John Maynard Keynes. The social problem flourished within this framework: the State intervenes to ameliorate injusticies, smooth over inequalities, and secure steady general progress. The sequence is standard: a social problem is nominated and the State declares its readiness to respond to parliamentary and media concern; a committee of the wise and the good is set up, and further public discussion is invited; the committee reports, more discussion follows, and the State passes laws to improve matters. That is the consensus which broke down in the late 1970s, allowing Thatcherism to confront it, declaring that there are no social problems, only personal and family difficulties – taking us back, in theory and in effect, to the 1930s.

The Wolfenden Report on male homosexuality was a textbook instance, though it took ten years for the change in the law. The key proposal was to locate homosexual practices in a private realm where, though immoral, they might not require the attention of the law. At the same time, penalties for public soliciting should be retained (it may still be unlawful in the UK to propose to someone a sexual act that is, in itself, lawful). This public/private binary model has often been analysed. While seeming to demarcate our subjectivities from a public realm of ideological and official interference, it actually constitutes those subjectivities. For the idea of private space might seem to free an autonomous zone for self-expression, but the effect, rather, is a focused policing of the border between the two. As David T. Evans puts it, 'by concentrating on public manifestations of sexual deviance in the buffer zone between moral and immoral communities, this policing has effectively penetrated all "private" territories with immanent self-regulating material forms of power/knowledge'.[13]

Gay Liberation, as lesbians and gay men conceived it after the Stonewall riot, has sought to refuse the traditional public/private binary structure. For despite the legalising of same-sex acts in many contexts, lesbian and gay occupation of public space still has to be confirmed — the cruising ground, the gay village, holding hands in the street. And our privacy has remained problematic — for instance, the police in England have assumed that they may invade our homes and clubs merely on suspicion that certain kinds of queer activity may be taking place. So David Bell writes: 'The quest for sexual adventures in heteronormative environments is part of the mission to rearticulate both public and private spheres. But equally important is the campaign for a queer private sphere that is out of sight and reach.'[14] This seems right as an agenda for today: for both public and private, we need to set our own terms.

At the same time, we need to bear in mind that attempts to position sexual dissidence, or this or that aspect of it, as either a private or a public matter have been ideological mystifications. In practice, its characteristic location is *on the boundary*. In part, that is where the surveillance may most effectively be sustained, facilitating orchestration of our internalised apparatuses of desire and guilt. Yet not all of this is hostile manipulation. The subculture that we have made for ourselves is poised equivocally on the public/private boundary. Because we can pass in the midst of straight society, crucial sites for us have been shops, art galleries, churches, schools, organised sport, cinemas, public transport.[15] And, of course, theatres. In these mixed spaces, typically, we have customs but no rights; that is how we have existed — partly accommodated, partly controlled. Hence the emphasis on Pride demonstrations: there, for once, we seem to be disambiguated — though, in fact, the demarcation between those in the parade and those watching on the sidewalk is far from plain.

During the Wolfenden interim — the decade between the Report and the Sexual Offences Act of 1967, which decriminalised much gay behaviour — all kinds of representations of male homosexuals were canvassed. As Gregory Woods puts it, despite the reputation for 'rigorously enforced conformity', the 1950s afforded 'a virtual festival of queer self-assertion'.[16] And the gay problem play flourished. Since Ibsen, theatre had often been a place where the boundaries of public and private power and morality might be disputed. The Lord Chamberlain found himself faced with many more plays about homosexuality: Christine Fox's valuable summary of the reasons for the refusal of licences to plays between 1903 and 1968 indicates a notable spurt of gay cases.[17]

As well as the plays to be discussed in this chapter, work from other times and places was drawn into London. The Arts Theatre Club showed *The Immoralist* by the Americans Ruth and Augustus Goetz in 1954, and *South* by the French author Julien Green in 1955. *The Green Bay Tree* was revived at the Playhouse in 1950, and *The Prisoners of War* at the Irving Theatre in 1955. The dramatisation of Melville's *Billy Budd* by Louis O. Coxe and Robert Chapman was presented at the Lyric, Hammersmith under the title *The Good Sailor* (1956). The Royal Shakespeare Company performed Jean Anouilh's *Becket* in 1961. In 1957 Binkie Beaumont and other impresarios, aware that they were being left behind by the changing mood, broke ranks with the Lord Chamberlain and combined to produce 'club' presentations of *Cat on a Hot Tin Roof*, *A View from the Bridge* and *Tea and Sympathy*, three US plays which had been banned in London. This action by his customary allies led the Chamberlain in 1958 to admit homosexuality as a topic when the treatment was 'sincere and serious'.[18]

Lesbians, meanwhile, were scarcely admitted as a problem. They were not perceived as causing embarrassment around toilets, breaking the law or as dominating the literary, artistic and theatrical establishment. Even so, there were more lesbian representations on the postwar London stage than has been supposed. I invoked in chapter 7 Sartre's *Huis Clos*, plays by Agatha Christie, and *The Irregular Verb to Love* by Hugh and Margaret Williams. *The Children's Hour* was performed at the Boltons in 1950 and at the Arts in 1956. *Two Loves I Have* by Dorothy and Howard Baker was denied a licence and performed at the Arts Club in 1952; I assume this is *Trio* (1944) retitled (see chapter 7). *The Lonely Heart* (1951) by Judith Warden was refused a licence and performed at the New Lindsey Club. Judy in Robert Bolt's first play, *Flowering Cherry* (1957), is very attached to Carol, another student, but there's little more to go on. Lawrence Durrell's verse play *Sappho* (1961), performed at the Edinburgh

Festival, is about everything but lesbianism; as Joan DeJean puts it, Durrell belongs among 'a few scattered examples of authors who exploit the name "Sappho" without reference to the sexual sensationalism generally associated with it'.[19] However, I discuss two substantial ventures, Ronald Duncan's *The Catalyst* (1958) and David Mercer's *Ride a Cock Horse* (1965), in chapter 13, and *The Killing of Sister George* in chapters 9 and 14.

The more progressive of this work appeared in little theatres, most of which were clubs: this helped them to cultivate a constituency of enthusiasts and allowed them to serve alcohol outside the hours otherwise allowed. Above all, clubs were regarded as *private*, and therefore not subject to the Lord Chamberlain's regulation. This manifest loophole was indulged explicitly by the Chamberlain. Thus these theatre clubs were curiously like the discreet pubs and clubs which lesbians and gays were gradually claiming for themselves, which also were more-or-less allowed. Both venues licensed deviance in private while facilitating surveillance. As we will see in chapter 13, the public/private boundary as it pertained to both theatre and homosexuality was contested in the 1960s. Before that we have a swathe of problem plays.

Coming Clean

Philip King was the author of *Sailor Beware* (1955), a farce hit organised around the ancient figure of the nagging mother-in-law. The sailor-boy fiancé puts his foot down, while relations with his buddy are strictly homosocial. King was also involved in three campaigning plays which revised many of the existing terms of queer drama — the bachelor of suspect sensibility and occupation, the buddy relationship which might be sexual, the boy who might be going wrong, the sinister intruder, the rough lad, the false accusation, social ostracism, the confrontation with moralistic authority, the damaging consequences of self-repression, the risk of police attentions.

In *Serious Charge* (1954) Howard, an unmarried vicar, is embarrassed by the attentions of a thirty-year-old spinster of the parish, Hester. Indeed, she comes on strongly to Howard's mother as well: 'I like you. I admire you tremendously and I envy you' (509). When she becomes too pressing and Howard rebuffs her, she supports, somewhat hysterically, the assertion of good-looking, seventeen-year-old Larry that Howard tried to interfere with him. Larry is a bad lot: when Howard confronts him with seducing a village girl and contributing to her death, Larry smashes ornaments and pushes over furniture so that Hester thinks he has been resisting assault. What is striking, in comparison with earlier false-accusation scenarios such as *The Children's Hour*, is that everyone, of all classes, genders and ages, at once knows what is meant. To be sure, it is not quite said: 'I don't know how to tell you. He tried to . . . tried to . . .' (563, King's pauses). But the meaning is plain. Furthermore, they are all ready to believe it. 'After all, Vicar', Granger, the schoolmaster, observes, 'it wouldn't be the first time that this sort of thing has happened — if it *has* happened. You've only to read your Sunday papers — well, some of 'em. Not only your profession, of course; mine as well. (*Slight pause.*) And you're a bachelor (*His eyes wander round the room.*) with an artistic flair' (583).

Indeed, Granger is not the first to question Howard's 'flair for interior decoration'. Hester finds the sitting room 'so cosy, and yet so . . . artistic — if you know what I mean. What you might call a real woman's room'. She is startled to find that Howard is the designer; 'one would never think of it — meeting him', she exclaims. 'One usually thinks of artistic men as being rather . . . well you know what I mean' (500, 504, King's pauses). We do indeed; and, after all, Larry's accusation does contain plausible elements. Howard did summon him to the vicarage when everyone else was away, and perhaps he has been watching, unconsciously, for opportunities to catch him out. When Howard says Larry made 'quite an impression' at an inquest, 'with your soft voice; your golden hair; your angelic face', Larry remarks: 'That's sissy talk. (*After a long curious look at Howard.*) Isn't it? Not that I . . .' (554, King's pause). *Serious Charge* teases the audience, challenging it to ponder whether there can be so much smoke without the glimmer of a fire. Perhaps a generally good man does have gay impulses. The problem is not so easily dealt with.

Serious Charge started out in Worthing in 1954 and moved into the West End in 1955 (a film appeared in 1959). The Lord Chamberlain thought it would do 'no great harm', though he was 'not convinced by the retort that because the accusation was untrue no question of propriety can arise'.[20] In King's next play in this vein, co-written with Robin Maugham, the accusation of homosexuality is true, though the accusation of sexual activity is false. Probably for that reason, *Lonesome Road* (1957) was refused a licence, so it was presented at the Arts Club. Martin is a writer who seeks a new identity in a remote village following a prison sentence for a homosexual offence. He is 'thirty, good-looking, but with a pale, rather strained face'; he does the décor nicely (1, 46). Trouble takes a pleasant guise when Jimmy, the seventeen-year-old son of the vicar, falls in love with him. Jimmy doesn't get on with his father, and 'though he looks healthy enough, there is something nervous about his movements and an odd look of yearning in his eyes' (16). He comes to Martin's cottage a lot. As in *Serious Charge*, that is enough to produce a presumption of homosexuality: 'It has been suggested to me that in view of the differences [*sic*] in ages, your friendship is, perhaps — how shall I put it . . . ?' says the vicar (50, King's pause). He works out who Martin is and assumes that sexual activity has occurred: 'Filthy. Filthy. When I think of what has been going on between you.' Further, Jimmy left school not because of a heart condition, as has been given out: he was expelled 'in disgrace for the very same thing' (60).

Jimmy appeals to Martin to help him, but he can't do this without attracting scandal and a second blow to his career. Alex, his agent, insists that people don't want to see plays and films scripted by queers — even Wilde was vulnerable. Martin wants to see Jimmy once more, whatever the risk, because it's his own story over again: 'if only I'd had someone I could talk with about it, if only there'd been someone to help me along that lonesome road' (65). But it's too late to help Jimmie: he has driven his bike over a cliff. Martin concludes: 'I've been a cheat and a coward. You start by deceiving a few strangers and you end up by deceiving your friends and your very own self. But I'll never pretend again so long as I live' (71). Discretion is part of the problem, not part of the solution. Dan Rebellato invokes *A Lonesome Road* as a register of changing perceptions in the 1950s:

> Critics in the early part of the decade either thunder against the 'nauseous matter' and 'repulsive odour' of the plays, or simply do not mention homosexuality at all. But only a few years later, when *A Lonesome Road* was produced, critics complained that the play was too hesitant; the *Daily Mail* opined that 'the authors have approached their subject honestly, and, if anything, a little too discreetly'.[21]

Wolfenden was gaining ground.

Five years later, in '*How Are You, Johnnie?*' (1962, Worthing), King depicts a wider spectrum of attitudes to homosexuality. Johnnie (twenty-five), a lorry driver, is not much bothered that Les, his mate (twenty-four), is gay. Johnnie's mother, Mary, likes Les a lot; queerness never enters her head, even though he knows more about cooking than she does. Roberts, Johnnie's bullying step-father, is in the police and recognises Les. He wants to get him fired, but Johnnie says Les' private life is his own business. As well as this explicit contest over attitudes to homosexuality, '*How Are You, Johnnie?*' is notable for its references to gay subculture. Johnnie knows, unawares, at least a couple of other gays, Les remarks; the homosexual doesn't have to be lonely. He is vulnerable, though. Roberts, the policeman, knows the scene as well, he warns. Also, Les gets Johnnie to break their journey so he can call on one of his gentleman friends. Sexual activity within the time-span of a play is extremely unusual at this date.

Roberts is brutal to Mary; Johnnie, who is something of a boxer, kills him with a blow to the jaw. Les realises that Johnnie is the killer and uses the knowledge to work his way into the family. For four years he has endured Johnnie's indifference; all he has wanted is to be treated as a human being. But Johnnie fears that Les is going to use his advantage to establish an emotional and sexual hold over him. Come to think about it, there is something a bit queer about Johnnie: the only person he cares for is his mother, and he seems in no hurry to marry.

An unpublished script discloses two versions of the last moments of the play. In one, Johnnie breaks down under aggressive police questioning, calls for Les, clings sobbing to his hand; this is Les' moment of supreme happiness. He may love Johnnie, but there is always something narcissistic, corrupt and untrustworthy about the passions of these queers. In a second version, Les urges Johnnie to remain staunch. But how can Les be so calm? He's used to being questioned and having to lie. One version shows the predatory queer winning out; the other shows persecuted outsiders sticking together. That spectrum represents the range of alternatives, from *The Green Bay Tree*, virtually to Gay Liberation. Unfortunately '*How Are You, Johnnie?*' has not been published and I have been unable to gain a response from the agents, Eric Glass Ltd, to my requests to quote from this interesting play.

The Creeper (1964) by Pauline Macaulay, which was produced at the Nottingham Playhouse and achieved a transfer to the West End, takes on *The Green Bay Tree*, *Night Must Fall* and *The Man*. A Pinteresque air of obscure menace seems at first to issue from Edward, a wealthy gay man very like Dulcimer (the parasitic creeper of Macaulay's title has killed a tree by twining round it). Edward has advertised for a companion, and is interviewing Maurice, a former shop assistant, about twenty-five years old, for the post. Maurice meets his departing predecessor, Michel — a highly camp number, beautiful but sulky. As in *The Green Bay Tree*, there is a faithful manservant as well, though this one is very old: he has been in the family since, as it were, the earlier play. But now there is no attempt to mask the matter of queerness. Edward draws attention to his mauve silk socks and adds that the colour is all over the house, specially in the bedrooms. Maurice's pay will not be very high, he explains, but the perquisites will be luxurious: 'I will also buy your clothes . . . everything down to your . . . (*He smiles.*) You see I want you to be dependent upon me. I don't want you opening a savings account behind my back' (206, Macaulay's pauses). Maurice is not very smart but he can read the signals. He attempts to retreat: 'it seems perfectly clear that . . .' Edward picks up the inference: 'That I'm an old queen? I'm not actually. Nor am I anything else. I lost interest in sex many years ago in the physical sense . . . aesthetically I find it quite interesting . . . the performance bores me. It's much more exciting in my head if you know what I mean' (207, Macaulay's pauses). As in earlier plays, the audience is preserved from imaginative engagement with a practising homosexual, but at least it is clear what we are all talking about.

It becomes apparent that Edward is basically kind and caring. He describes his disturbed childhood and gets Maurice to do the same; Maurice is blooming, idolising Edward. As in other plays discussed in this chapter, the predatory queer and the mutual resentment of the cross-class liaison are replaced by the caring adult who tries to save the boy from repeating his own mistakes. There is to be trouble nonetheless. In a weird episode Maurice 'strangles' a balloon with a tie in his sleep. Michel reappears: he has found out that Maurice tried to strangle a customer with a tie in a shop where he worked before. It was nothing, Maurice says; the customer was very demanding. He demonstrates to Michel what happened; without realising what he is doing, he strangles Michel. The lower-class psychopath strikes once more. Edward and the manservant dispose of the body. The police come round asking questions. Edward encourages Maurice to talk – it would be therapeutic – but he is unable to do that. The police get closer to Maurice; Edward wants to give him a big cheque so he can go abroad and never return. But Maurice is very distressed: he wants to be with Edward: 'You were my friend. And you were my father too', he says. 'I love you' (289–90). As Edward gazes out of the window at the tree and the creeper, Maurice shoots him dead with a bow and arrow. *The Creeper* exonerates the Dulcimer figure from *The Green Bay Tree*, though at the expense of reincriminating his lower-class partner.

Schools Again

The schoolboy wrestling with his sexuality was the most prominent of the pre-existing queer scenarios to be revisited with new ideas and attitudes in the postwar problem play. In *The Hidden Years* (1947) by Travers Otway (a pseudonym for Edward J. Miller) Digby, a house captain in a public school, becomes enamoured of young Martineau after admiring his physique and prowess at diving. They meet on Sundays in an out-of-bounds wood. Their situation is not helped by a school dispute about playing rugby or soccer, in which Johnstone, Martineau's housemaster, has taken the other side. Johnstone finds the boys together and wants Digby at least to be expelled. However, partly through the intercession of the chaplain, it is acknowledged that their affair is innocent. Indeed, it was a good thing: they both tried harder at games, and Digby was transmitting to Martineau his enthusiasm for Shakespeare (*The Tempest*).

In a foreword Otway says he was attempting to deal 'with a problem, the existence of which is known to all who have been at a public school'. *Young Woodley* ducks it, for 'in ninety-nine cases out of a hundred it would have been more natural for a boy in Young Woodley's position to have centred his affections, not upon his Housemaster's wife, but upon another boy'. However – according to an article in *The Lancet* – this would be only 'a normal phase associated with adolescent development', on the way to 'what will ultimately become mate love' (8–10). So there isn't a problem after all. In fact *The Hidden Years* is more interesting than this, because Otway chooses to establish the attractiveness of a boy such as Martineau. The chaplain enthuses: 'I shall never forget the . . . look of innocence in his eyes . . . the awful purity in them. . . . I don't think I ever realized before quite what Wordsworth meant: ". . . *trailing clouds of glory do we come / From God, Who is our home*"' (47, Otway's pauses). If this is what you get with a boy, one might wonder whether it is so much better to move on to 'mate love'.

The Hidden Years was produced first at the Boltons Club and then, since the Lord Chamberlain had no objections, in the West End. Roger Gellert's public-school play, *Quaint Honour* (1958), despite approving reviews, couldn't get beyond the Arts Club. In the opening moments Park, the puritanical head boy of the house, tells Hallowes, the housemaster, that he has 'a bit of a problem' (13). There is no obscurity about what this is: Tully, the deputy head boy, discusses liaisons among the boys openly with Turner, his flirtatious fag (young boy servant); they view it all as a bit of a lark. Even the mousiest of boys – young Hamilton, for instance – may have some potential. Turner challenges Tully to seduce Hamilton – he would be a real problem (24). In a brilliant scene, Tully auditions Hamilton for the part of Lady Anne in Shakespeare's *Richard III*, impressing him with techniques very like those deployed by Richard. Tully and Hamilton become lovers; Park notices this and reports it to Hallowes.

Tully and Hallowes have a long and generally constructive discussion about the ethics of same-sex liaisons. Hallowes' best argument is that Tully has damaged Hamilton, but the boy seems to have become 'more alive, more of a person' (40). But perhaps Tully has made him queer, Hallowes says: 'Surely you know the sort of pathetic half-men that are the logical development of that situation — men with painted faces and womanish gestures? I've seen them if you haven't. Ruined human lives, a misery to themselves and a joke to others.' Tully replies, angrily, that there doesn't have to be a male and a female; indeed, why may Hamilton not 'be the active one and me the passive? Well, if you want to know, when Hamilton and I lie together, there's no submitting, there's no top dog and substitute bitch — ' (41). As I showed in chapter 6, many mid-century gay men were keen to repudiate the conventional implication of queerness with effeminacy.

Quaint Honour still allows the adolescent-phase argument. Turner doesn't want to be one of those who get 'stuck with it'; Tully reasssures him: 'I think they might if they'd wanted it at school and not had it' (45). When Hamilton insists on going off by himself to sort out his own ideas (like Nora in *A Doll's House*), Tully concedes, somewhat awkwardly: 'You're absolutely right. The whole point is that it was an emergency measure; and now the state of emergency's over, and the grenadiers can go home' (48). However, alongside this uneasy claim that the problem will go away is another, far bolder one: that relations between a boy and a mentor are beautiful and worthwhile in their own right. Tully never accepts that he has done wrong; 'It's just as if you were to show me, oh, a ripe apple, or a warm fresh loaf, and tell me they were foul and disgusting. I shouldn't believe you' (40).

As censorship relaxed, Christopher Hampton's *When Did You Last See My Mother?* (1966, West End; Off-Broadway, 1967) was able to challenge the notion that public-school boys grow out of same-sex interests as they leave. Ian and Jimmy, who are between school and university, share a flat and bicker continually; there is emotion between them that is not finding expression. Part of the trouble is that Ian was in love with Dennis, a younger boy, and Jimmy slept with him. Now Jimmy is dating girls, but Ian is both unimpressed and excessively involved: 'You don't fool anybody, you know, with all your fake virility. All this shaving yourself every other day when there isn't a hair on your face, all this devoted attachment to birds, however crummy they are. It doesn't take me in one bit.' This accusation makes Jimmy 'almost hysterical'

(31). They wrestle and Ian kisses Jimmy, who leaves, though perhaps not for good. As in *Tea and Sympathy*, Ian has the benefit of loving sexual experience with an older woman, but now it proves fatal to her and doesn't straighten him out. Gays are here to stay, this play says, and repression is dangerous.

A Fashionable 'Gimmick'?

The gay problem play has had a mixed press. In an article of 1959 Angus Wilson disparaged 'social debates disguised in play form', while granting that male homosexuality might be 'a litmus of truth or falsity in contemporary England'.[22] In 1961, in the radical theatre magazine *Encore*, Rogert Gellert defined the problem play as 'a sincere but minor play using some topical, and preferably, rather clinical issue as its mainspring'. And why should the gay problem play be so prominent? 'The obvious dramatic potential of the homosexual problem has tempted many dramatists to use it, some with power and insight, others merely as a fashionable "gimmick"' (notice the quote marks − a new buzzword). Gellert wonders why, given the reputation of gay men as 'witty, frank and audacious', most dramatic treatments are 'entirely social and tragic' and not 'personal and comic'.[23]

In my view the reluctance of sexual dissidents such as Wilson and Gellert to endorse purposeful subcultural work (a reluctance that persists: see chapter 17) is unfortunate. It is often said that writing for and on behalf of lesbians and gay men is limiting − as if writing for heterosexuals were not. To be sure, the problem play may be stodgy, or stodgily presented. *'Now Barabbas . . .'* (1947) by William Douglas Home was printed with a recommendation from H.M. Commissioner of Prisons: 'This play will do good because it will enlist the sympathy and interest of a wide circle of intelligent people, and will make them think and ask questions' (ix). *'Now Barabbas . . .'* is a lot better than that. But was it not merely sensible, after decades of being someone else's problem in straight-oriented plays, and vilified or mocked for it, that gay men should give their side of the story? The social problem was equally important in British cinema, and several of the plays discussed in this chapter and the next were filmed.[24] The depiction in the film *Victim* (Basil Dearden, 1961) of the dangers of blackmail, alongside some of the thrills of the cross-class liaison, was very influential in Britain. It was not licensed for general distribution in the USA because of 'an implicit approval of homosexuality as a practice', *Time* magazine explained.[25]

John M. Clum, from a mainly American point of view, defines the problem play as one where 'a social or psychological aberration that threatens a community is introduced only to be, in the end, expunged. In the history of this genre, homosexuality is all too often presented as the "problem" that must be solved or eliminated by the final curtain.'[26] This is broadly true of *Tea and Sympathy*, *The Small Hours* and *The Immoralist*, for the gay problem play was differently oriented in the USA. Welfare-capitalism, and hence the concept of the social problem, was weaker there; pioneer ideology encouraged people to impute problems to individuals. With US manliness at stake, I suggested in the previous chapter, queerness figured as an anxiety to be exposed and worried at. However, in the British plays discussed in this chapter and the next, even ostensible closures fail to contain the problem of homosexuality. The overall message is that it cannot be suppressed and that it is the social framework that needs to change. In November 1958 Jim Kepner noted London club productions of *The Catalyst*, *Quaint Honour* and *Lonesome Road* with some envy, in the Los Angeles homophile *ONE Magazine*.[27]

Above all, gay problem plays should be assessed in a context where hostile representations still predominated. *Look on Tempests* (1960) by Joan Henry attracted a quality West-End cast (including Gladys Cooper, Vanessa Redgrave, Ian Hunter, Brewster Mason and Gwen Williams). Rose's husband Philip is on trial for homosexual practices; unlike *Victim*, with which there are some resemblances, we neither see nor hear the gay man. Philip is probably guilty; Rose always knew he was a bit that way. The only evidence is his love letters, but no one says this is an unreasonable prosecution; rather, they take frequent opportunities to declare how disgusted they are. The central dilemma is Philip's mother's: his barrister says he will probably avoid prison if he pleads guilty, but he won't do that without her approval, which would mean her admitting to herself that the accusation is true. She and other characters grow into redemptive self-knowledge, and so on. In fact, *Look on Tempests* is about the problem of everyone other than the unfortunate gay man. The Shakespearean sonnet which provides the title is actually quoted:

> Love is not love
> Which alters when it alteration finds,
> Or bends with the remover to remove;
> O, no! It is an ever-fixed mark,
> That looks on tempests and is never shaken.

'Do you know to whom those words apply, Alice?' Philip's stepfather asks the mother. The answer we get is not 'Shakespeare and his boyfriend', but Rose, Philip's wife.[28] She is indeed courageous, but the peculiar application of the quote indicates the extent to which *Look on Tempests* scorns the predicaments of sexual dissidents. The critic of the *Bournemouth Evening Echo* declared it 'an interesting study, treated as a family affair, of a social problem'.[29]

13

Politics and Anger

New Wave

As well as enabling a social-problem approach to dissident sexualities, British welfare-capitalism promised universal access to the arts. Like healthcare, education, housing and social security, they were to be available not just to the privileged but to people generally. To this end the Arts Council was set up in 1945 and the BBC Third Programme in 1946; the extension of secondary education through the Butler act of 1944 was understood partly in the same terms. A key postwar assumption was instituted at this point in the 1940s: that the condition of culture is in substantial part a responsibility of the State. It persisted into the 1980s, when it was confronted by the Thatcherite demand that the arts be subjected to market forces — i.e. made more conservative.

Theatre was not perceived immediately in the postwar period as in need of State support. But what was the West End offering to the new Britain? In 1954 Kenneth Tynan was appointed critic at the *Observer*, where he complained, insistently, that the set-up was moribund: 'apart from revivals and imports, there is nothing in the London theatre that one dares discuss with an intelligent man for more than five minutes'.[1] Neither the economics of stage production nor the temperament of dominant figures encouraged innovation. The English Stage Company was founded in 1955 to remedy this; the idea was to discover new British playwrights. It took over the Royal Court Theatre (in Chelsea: outside the West End but still posh) and gained support of £7,000 from the Arts Council; this rose to £20,000 in 1962, £50,000 in 1965 and £100,000 in 1967.

The key point is that this was a change of principle: the State undertook to subsidise a certain kind of theatre as a social good. This was generally interpreted as meaning (a) abstruse plays that might make demands upon an audience comparable to those made by contemporary music and painting (Beckett, for instance); (b) plays that engaged with social and political issues (there was much talk of Brecht). Funding for the Royal Shakespeare Company to extend its scope into contemporary writing began in 1961; the National Theatre began work in 1963 and the South Bank complex was designed to house it; fifteen regional theatres were built with public money between 1958 and 1970.

The catalyst which confirmed that something new was afoot was John Osborne's *Look Back in Anger* (1956, Royal Court). Reviewers generally took exception to the class hostility expressed by Jimmy Porter: the *Daily Mail* called him an 'oaf', the *Manchester Guardian* a 'boor', the *Financial Times* 'blatantly loutish', the *Birmingham Post* 'self-pitying, uncouth, cheaply vulgar'.[2] Maybe he is all that, but Tynan saw something else: a spokesman for a new social group – a new potential audience. He began his review by quoting Somerset Maugham on grant-aided students: 'They are scum.' The postwar extension of State education was producing a new, class-mobile intelligentsia; by 1955 the number of university students had doubled from the 1939 figure, and three-quarters of them received grants. Tynan relates Jimmy Porter to this group: he is 'all scum and a mile wide'. *Look Back in Anger* 'presents post-war youth as it really is, with special emphasis on the non-U [non-upper-class] intelligentsia'. This potential audience defined itself partly against the world of Rattigan – who remarked on the opening night that Osborne was saying, 'Look, Ma, I'm not Terence Rattigan.' Tynan glossed: 'The Porters of our time deplore the tyranny of "good taste" and refuse to accept "emotional" as a term of abuse; they are classless, and they are also leaderless.'[3]

This new social grouping may be regarded as a class fraction, effecting, like bohemia (of which I wrote in chapter 3), a kind of middle-class dissidence. Its members derived their opportunities and their confidence not from wealth or social background but from educational attainment. Surveys conducted at theatres showed that they were hugely over-represented at new-wave plays. In the late 1960s at the National Theatre, the Glasgow Citizens, and a 'serious' West End production (*The Man in the Glass Booth* by Robert Shaw, about the trial of a Nazi for crimes against Jews), between 55 and 80 per cent of the audience were under thirty-five. Between 18 and 35 per cent were students;

and between 23 and 48 per cent had completed higher education (whereas this latter group amounted to 3.7 per cent of the population as a whole).

These eager young people enjoyed 'difficult' plays because they could be discussed afterwards in the pub — in an informal seminar as it were — like, say, Kafka and Joyce. They had every reason to adopt a leftist stance, and to attack the ethos and credentials of what got to be called 'the establishment' — which seemed to be sustaining extremes of wealth and poverty, stifling creativity with snobbery, oppressing imperial subjects around the globe, and endangering humankind by playing war games with nuclear weaponry. They regarded themselves as an oppositional cultural and political formation. Their typical milieux were the peace movement, the left wing of the Labour Party, higher education, folk song and jazz, and subsidised theatre. They entered into contest with, and gradually displaced, the traditional leisure-class elite that had controlled culture, and theatre in particular.[4]

Insofar as members of this youthful intelligentsia were earnestly progressive, they would be opposed to laws against homosexuals. In 1966 it was found that between 75 and 94 per cent (depending on social class) of supporters of the Campaign for (unilateral) Nuclear Disarmament supported the decriminalisation of male homosexual acts.[5] They believed that gayness was primarily a social problem, and welcomed the broaching of such matters in the theatre. They cultivated a general political theory, within which homosexuals figured not just as an unreasonably harassed minority, but as victims of an oppressive family and social structure. In plays such as *Look Back in Anger*, *Five Finger Exercise* by Peter Shaffer and *A Taste of Honey* by Shelagh Delaney, grown-ups are represented as selfish, hypocritical and emotionally damaging to the young. These plays entered into a developing mood of inter-generational resentment.

In Shaffer's *Five Finger Exercise* (1958, West End; Broadway, 1959) problems in an affluent family are exposed by the arrival of Walter, a young German who is to tutor Pam, the daughter. The parents, Stanley and Louise, don't get on; he is the bluff businessman, she aspires to refinement. Clive, the son, a student, calls it a split between the saloon and the salon. Walter is in flight from a childhood under the Nazis and is desperately seeking a new family; he tries to engage himself with each of them, but falls victim to the tensions between them. 'You've got a crush on our family that's almost pathetic', Clive tells him. 'Can't you see how lucky you are to be on your own? Just because you never had a family you think they're the most wonderful things in the world' (70).

Clive is drawn to Walter. Already his father is complaining that he is involved with a 'pansy set of spongers. . . . Arty-tarty boys. Going around London, giggling and drinking and talking dirty; wearing Bohemian clothes' (17). Increasingly, the play becomes about what is wrong with Clive − he is rude, sulks, drinks, cries, has had no girlfriends; he responds with desperation to Walter's invitation to intimacy. Louise says Clive is 'sensitive'; Stanley says she has 'turned him into a snivelling little neurotic. A mother's boy' (76–7). The parents are presented as the source of the problem, and particularly Louise, who positions Clive as if he were courting her, replacing, as it were, the uncultivated Stanley (there is more than a hint of *The Vortex*). The play ends inconclusively; perhaps Clive will go away to find himself, as Walter has urged.

Five Finger Exercise was produced in the West End. *A Taste of Honey* (1958; Broadway, 1960), set in shabby, lower-class Manchester, claimed a production by Joan Littlewood at Stratford East (though it transferred to the West End and played widely in repertory). Publicity featured Delaney's announcement that she had written it in a fortnight because she was annoyed by Rattigan's representation of gayness in *Variation on a Theme*.[6] In fact, *A Taste of Honey* conducts a round-up of social problems: we have a lower-class, one-parent family with housing and educational difficulties, an irresponsible black youth and an unwanted teenage pregnancy, all in a run-down northern industrial town. When Geof, a gay boy, befriends Jo at the start of act II he seems less of a problem than a solution. He's just like a big sister, she says; they get on and gain in confidence. Geof has problems of his own, however: he is bashful about his sexuality, and becomes dependent on Jo; he tries, briefly, to go straight with her (she won't have it). He gets called to his face 'this pansified little freak' and 'Bloody little pansy' by Jo's foolish mother and 'that little fruitcake parcel' by her bullying stepfather (63, 79, 68). These painful insults surely produce a gay-friendly response in other than homophobic audience members. Jo tries to defend and retain Geof, but he is intimidated into giving way to her mother.

As Michelene Wandor sees this conclusion, 'the two generations of women are together, living without men and not particularly bothered by that fact'.[7] I never read it that way. Apart from anything else, the play actually ends with Jo on her own and expecting the return of Geof, whereas the mother, after expelling Geof, has fled to the pub upon realising that Jo's baby will probably be black. The alternative ménage of Geof and Jo would have been better; the older generation threatens further harm to Jo and her child. *A Taste of Honey* points towards emergent lifestyles − art students were to spearhead the inventive 1960s subcultures. Geof has some stereotypical mannerisms, but he is in quest of emotional reality, is hardly discreet, and shows no signs of wanting a leisure-class protector. He knows about drawing because he is an art student, not an aesthete. Compare John van Druten's *I Am a Camera*, which also has a rather limp young man living with a rather unstable young woman who gets pregnant and is 'rescued' by her mother. *A Taste of Honey* finally gets to name in public discourse the kind of life the Isherwood figure was actually leading in 1930, while moving the entire topic into an unwonted social class.

The attitude of British new-wave writers and their audiences towards homosexuality was more ambivalent than these two plays might suggest. They believed in emotional authenticity and meaningful personal relationships (D.H. Lawrence was much invoked), and in serious, frank discussion of social and personal problems. However, they distrusted the most prominent mode of queer relating – the discreet cross-class liaison, with its reliance upon concealment, class, money and deference. For while homosexuals were plainly discriminated against, they seemed to be well placed in the cultural establishment. Indeed, they might be thought to dominate in theatre – and the progressive, social-problem climate allowed this to be said. In October 1953 the *New Statesman*, alongside liberal articles by Kingsley Martin and E.M. Forster, carried a warning by J.B. Priestley about the dangers of 'Block Thinking':

> there are some aesthetic enterprises that are hardly likely to succeed without some assistance from the Inverts' Block – called by a sardonic friend of mine 'the Girls' Friendly Society' – which enthusiastically gives its praise and patronage to whatever is decorative, 'amusing', 'good theatre', witty in the right way, and likely to make heterosexual relationships look ridiculous: all of which is probably the stiff price we are paying in London for our stupid laws against inversion.[8]

Discreet leisure-class homosexuals seemed responsible for the dominant ethos in theatre and literature, which was perceived (like the establishment generally) as effete – 'effeminate' – and hypocritical. This concatenation of class and gender was like a red rag to a movement whose members liked to cultivate what they imagined to be a no-nonsense, working-class attitude to sexuality. In effect, this often meant misogyny and homophobia.

The sneer at the queer occurs repeatedly in new-wave novels. The predatory homosexual is introduced to be rejected by the hero, purportedly in no doubt about his own virility, in John Wain's *Hurry On Down* (1953) and John Braine's *Room at the Top* (1957). On the last page of Kingsley Amis' *Lucky Jim* (1954), Dixon's rivals, Professor Welch and his artistic son Bertrand, have 'a look of being Gide and Lytton Strachey', and at least three times Welch's other son is referred to as 'the effeminate writing Michel'. Doris Lessing makes the heroine of *The Golden Notebook* (1962) complain that there are no more 'real' men, just little boys and homosexuals. The mentors of these rising younger writers were F.R. Leavis and George Orwell, both of whom had expressed distaste for leisure-class queers in literary culture. Leslie Fiedler, with the freedom of a stranger, got to the point: the young British writer 'is able to define himself against the class he replaces: against a blend of homosexual sensibility, upper-class aloofness, liberal politics, and avant-garde literary devices'.[9]

The representation of gays in generally progressive productions by the English Stage Company at the Royal Court was uncertain, therefore. In Arnold Wesker's *Chips with Everything* (1962) the Pilot Officer seems to make a sexual advance to an airman – he 'places hand on McClore's knee', the airman says 'Don't do that, please, sir', and the officer sharply changes his mood: 'Don't ever rely on this conversation.' The incident seems to typify the exploitative attitude of the officers. It appears that Wesker came to regret this stereotyping of class power as queer, for in a later edition he changes the stage directions: the officer 'places hand on McClure's knee in a friendly gesture' and when McClure says 'Don't do that, please, sir' the officer's response is 'contemptuous that his friendly gesture was misread'.[10] In *The Knack* (1961) by Ann Jellicoe the aggressive Tolen challenges Tom: 'Are you homosexual?' Tom replies: 'No. Thanks all the same' (52). That is a smart put-down, but it depends on the assumption that gayness is demeaning.

The Royal Shakespeare Company pursued a similar policy to the Royal Court at its London venues. In *Afore Night Come* (1962) by David Rudkin, Johnny Hobnails takes a shine to young Larry and protects him from atavistic violence. However, Johnny is more of a holy fool than a practising gay man. In *After Haggerty* (1970) by David Mercer the protagonist's flat is being decorated by a camp, out-of-work actor who is abused by the other characters, including his fellow-worker who amiably declares: 'His sort – you can't deal with them. Know what I mean? He makes me wish I was prejudiced. If I let him yap he bores the arse off me. And if I spell out the odd home truth, then what? He's *hurt*! . . . But at least I can take anything, can't I? Fairies, blacks, dykes, students – ' (16). While none of these representations is progressive, even in the terms of their decade, they do indicate that the topic was becoming almost casual in progressive circles.

Yet there was plenty of queerness among the new wave — at the Royal Court for instance. I have been striving to unravel my topic in historical and thematic sequence, but it should be remembered that most of the attitudes I have described in the course of this book were present *simultaneously* in Britain in the late 1950s and early 1960s. There was a preoccupation with Wilde (two films of his life appeared in 1960); Coward was still writing new plays; Rattigan appeared to be safely in mid-career; new productions of *The Children's Hour* and *The Prisoners of War* were stimulated by the vogue for problems; *Night Must Fall* and *Rope* were staples of repertory companies; *Tea and Sympathy* (1953) was attacked for its boldness and its timidity; Tennessee Williams' vigour of utterance was still overwhelming. If the new wave didn't have gayness sorted, it is hardly surprising.

Lesbians and Men

I listed briskly some lesbian stage representations of the post-war period in chapter 12. Generally, though, lesbian images were pushed to the margins. Comments appeared from time to time in the *New Statesman*, Elizabeth Wilson reports, but 'there was an inexplicit feeling that it was only an aspect of female sexual frustration and would fade away as women learned to enjoy heterosexuality and now that there was a sufficient supply of men'.[11] When the *Sunday Pictorial* in 1958 purported to describe the experience of a girl drawn into lesbianism, this was, in Patrick Higgins' view, an exceptional exposure.[12]

'This book deals primarily with male homosexuality, because in men the condition causes more obvious social problems and has been studied more intensively by psychiatrists', D.J. West wrote in his study, *Homosexuality* (1955).[13] Dr Eustace Chesser in *Odd Man Out* (1959) devoted 24 pages out of 192 to relations between women. He attributes their relative invisibility to the fact that 'for two women to kiss and hug each other causes no comment. They are free to accompany each other to the toilet or sleep in the same bed. Society not only tolerates such acts but regards them as entirely natural.'[14] While there is some sense in this, Chesser's grossly Freudian and normative account also illustrates why women might be reluctant to present themselves publicly as lesbian. For instance, he says that when a girl takes her mother's side against a violent father 'she continues to identify herself with her mother instead of outgrowing this infantile dependence' (98). Nor should she look for subcultural opportunities to meet other women: 'In its more bizarre forms Lesbianism degenerates like male homosexuality into vice. There are Lesbian clubs in all the great cosmopolitan cities where similar perversions to those found in male brothels are practised' (116).

Maureen Duffy suggests in an essay of 1967 on London lesbian subculture that professional women did go in for theatre evenings, but this was part of a conservative lifestyle – sticking to an established circle of friends and avoiding 'extremes of dress' and demeaning contact with lower-class women. It was hardly the ground for radical interventions.[15] Oral histories rarely mention theatre: that is a notable point of difference with gay male accounts. Harriet Gilbert in the early 1960s knew several out gay men in her year at drama school, but no lesbians; gayness 'had a kind of glamour associated with camp and style whereas dykedom then certainly wasn't'.[16]

Two other plays by men may fairly be considered as new-wave ventures into lesbian territory; they display the gamut of current attitudes. Ronald Duncan had been associated with the flurry of Christian verse drama around 1950, but he was also one of the founders of the English Stage Company – where he became increasingly ill-at-ease as the agenda became more socio-political. His play *The Catalyst* (1958) was refused a licence and produced at the Arts Club, where it was well received. It managed to 'deal seriously at heart, and with some truth, with the subject of sex', according to Philip Hope-Wallace (*Manchester Guardian*); the *Observer* thought it 'the first serious English play about sex for many years'.[17] In 1963 a new Lord Chamberlain granted a licence, and *The Catalyst* was performed in the West End.

Charles is having an affair with Leone, his secretary; when Therese, his wife, finds out, Leone leaves. However, they are all lonely, and Therese encourages Charles to invite Leone back – in fact, she takes the initiative. As the feeling between the two women develops, Leone becomes fearful and asks Charles to take her away; it seems that we are getting into the predatory lesbian syndrome. However, Leone decides that she was running from her true self. The catalyst is not (as commonly) the queer intruder, who illuminates the scene at the price of his or her expulsion from it; it is Charles, the heterosexual male. His advances to the two women have brought them together. The outcome is not that the women will leave and take on a conventional lesbian lifestyle. 'Don't you start trying to see me in brogues or Leone in tweeds', Therese tells Charles (79). They are going to form a threesome, she declares, and he, since he has been maintaining that he is able to love both women, can hardly protest. In the closing lines they revise the conclusion of Sartre's *Huis Clos* ('Hell is other people'): their new life 'will often seem sheer hell', Therese says. 'I know', Charles agrees. 'But the hell we accept / Is the only heaven we'll ever know' (82).

David Mercer was significant for his dramatic treatments of the disappointments of Marxist commitment, for his success in bringing such themes to television, and for *Morgan − A Suitable Case for Treatment*, filmed in 1966. He had been working with anti-psychiatrist and counter-culture guru, R.D. Laing, from whom he derived a combination of careful interpersonal analysis and the thought that everyone is probably crazy anyway. In *Ride a Cock Horse* (1965, West End) Peter, finding that he isn't getting on well with Nan, his wife, attributes this to her lesbianism. She is made partly to collude with this. She did have a lesbian affair when she was sixteen, she says, and she doesn't feel like having sex with Peter; therefore she is ready to tolerate him having affairs with other women. But he is not appeased. When she changes into slacks he taunts her: 'You never feel quite yourself in a suspender belt do you? Are you sure your mother and father *wanted* a daughter?' Again: 'When you started menstruating and your mam realised you weren't a boy, she − '; Nan screams and rushes at him with clenched fists (15, 65).

Peter has told Myra, one of his mistresses, that Nan is a lesbian; Myra seeks to reassure herself by referring to 'that ugly little lesbian of yours'. 'If your kinky wife won't let you reproduce yourself, you'd better stick a kid inside somebody else', she says (30, 41). Fanny, Peter's other mistress, has dreamt that she was taken as a casualty to the hospital where Nan is a doctor, and that Nan kissed her. 'Did Nan like it?' Peter asks. 'Why do you go round telling everybody your wife's a lesbian?' Fanny rejoins. 'Well you see, I'm a repressed queer, and that fantasy expresses my unconscious desires. Nan and I were made for each other' (48). There is no reason, of course, why Nan should not be a lesbian, but as the play is arranged she is plainly an extension of Peter's fantasies. She doesn't do anything lesbian; the outcome of their rows is always her reassertion of how much she loves Peter.

Mercer was following a prominent motif in 'angry' writing, deriving from *Look Back in Anger*. In it the protagonist is allowed to be as horrible as he likes, to women in particular, because he is witty and vital, suffering more than they, and ultimately committed to life. This motif adapted very well to anguished (crypto-)queers as they began to assert themselves, for instance in *The Killing of Sister George*, Christopher Hampton's *When Did You Last See My Mother*, John Hopkins' *Find Your Way Home* and Simon Gray's *Butley*.

John Osborne

When the *Daily Express* averred in 1959 that evil queers dominated English theatre, Osborne was moved to respond. Sexual preference is a private matter and homosexuals have been good for art, philosophy and literature, he says; the idea of driving them from the theatre is 'detestable'. Nonetheless, he adds, homosexual artists are responsible for the current West End mode of 'unreal, chintzy plays, gorgeous decor and a glamorous selection of theatrical lords and ladies glittering over all'. They have made theatre 'over-traditional, conservative, narrow, parochial, self-congratulatory, narcissistic'.[18] Osborne's divided attitude is typically new-wave.

Yet, from the start, there was something excessive about Osborne's concern with gayness. Jimmy Porter in *Look Back in Anger* goes out of his way to talk about Webster. He is the only one of Alison's friends (i.e. upper-class and feminine) that he likes, and offers the exception to Jimmy's famous complaint that there are no good brave causes any more − 'old Gide and the Greek Chorus boys'. Webster makes too much of it, though: 'he keeps thrusting it in your face because he can't believe it doesn't interest or horrify you particularly' (35–6). And what about that *ménage à trois* − Jimmy, Alison/Helena, Cliff? The homosocial relationship between Jimmy and Cliff is interesting and sometimes moving in its understatement. 'You've been loyal, generous and a good friend. But I'm quite prepared to see you wander off, find a new home', Jimmy says when Cliff decides to leave. 'And all because of something I want from that girl downstairs, something I know in my heart she's incapable of giving' (84). Perhaps it is something that Jimmy is incapable of receiving. The initial critics maintained a discreet distance from such thoughts but, Osborne records, Gilbert Harding 'grabbed my knee in almost fatherly affection and demanded, in front of the company of floppy bow-tied waiters, I admit that Jimmy and Cliff were in love with each other'.[19]

In his first volume of autobiography, published in 1981, Osborne discloses that he and his wife had shared a flat with his friend Anthony Creighton, and that Creighton was gay and attracted to Osborne. As well as *Epitaph for George Dillon* (produced in 1958 at the Royal Court), Osborne and Creighton had written together *Personal Enemy*, a play about McCarthyite smearing of liberals with queerness (it was performed at Harrogate in 1955 after being cut by the censor). After Osborne's death in 1995 Nicholas de Jongh, drawing on letters from Osborne to Creighton and conversations with Creighton, showed that the two men had a passionate, loving and lengthy relationship, apparently sexual, before, during and after the time of *Look Back in Anger*.[20]

The immediate reaction to such a revelation must be indignation — not because Osborne preferred to keep aspects of his life private, but because he often wrote dismissively of gays. My guess is that we have here a curiously residual pattern. One of Osborne's remarks about Creighton is that 'he was one of those luckless homosexuals, like J.R. Ackerley, who only fall in love with heterosexuals'.[21] I suspect Osborne thought of queers as invariably effeminate, and of himself as a straight man who consented to be tended upon by Creighton, for whom he had considerable affection. In 1955 this was a residual but not implausible way of maintaining the idea that, whatever you did, the queer was someone else. Yet it was, of course, precarious, and Osborne's gay characters are always both distanced from and close to himself. Hence, we might surmise, his abiding anxiety about the relation between emotion and manliness. 'That voice that cries out doesn't *have* to be a weakling's, does it?' Jimmy Porter demands (94).

Through these tense confusions, Osborne put his finger upon some of the key predicaments of sexual dissidence in his generation. In *Inadmissible Evidence* (1964, Royal Court; Broadway, 1965) the world of Bill Maitland, a solicitor, is collapsing. He's drinking too much and people are edging away from him (taxis won't stop for him). His practice is failing because he fantasises his clients — three women seeking divorce — into his own complications with his wife, mistress, secretary and receptionist; he becomes distracted and the clients lose confidence in him. The fourth client is a young man, Maples, facing an indecency charge. We hear of his best friend at school, his unsuccessful marriage, how he was picked up on a train, his consultation with a doctor; of Denis whom he loves but has given up to sustain the marriage. He describes how a policeman flashed his torch on him and his partner and 'made me meet him the next night. Only about three times' (99). And he tells how the police trapped him and forced him to make a statement by threatening to involve Denis. These topics had rarely been broached in the first person before the British public. The censor wanted to cut them, but the Royal Court insisted: 'Mr Osborne's intention is to show, as seriously and trenchantly as possible, the extent of sordid furtiveness and guilt to which a man of this sort is drawn.' And episodes like the policeman meeting him the next night 'are well known to have happened' (in fact Gordon Westwood reports two of them).[22]

Formally, as the play is structured, Maples' predicament should have resonances in Maitland's psyche comparable to those evoked by the women; indeed, Maitland has a recurring dream in which he is the wicked, bawdy and scandalous object on trial. More or less jocularly (he may be charged with unprofessional conduct), he puts Maples and himself in the dock together: 'I should think Sir Gwatkin Glover Q.C. is sure to apply the full rigour of the law and send the both of us down' (99). In his autobiographies Osborne deploys key speeches by Maitland as indicators of his own state of mind and prints without comment John Betjeman's assessment of the play as 'an agonizing self-analysis'.[23] Osborne is trying, almost, to tell us something.

In *A Patriot for Me* (1965, Royal Court; Broadway, 1969) Osborne articulates sexuality with nation and empire. The play offers an ambitious analogue of the contemporary British situation, as critics immediately noted: the declining years of the Macmillan–Home Conservative governments had been marked by sex-and-spy scandals, at least one of which (the John Vassall case) involved the blackmailing of a homosexual.[24] The Austro-Hungarian pre-1914 officer corps is portrayed as snobbish, racist, incompetent and in terminal decline. It is, of course, about to be destroyed in World War I. Many of its members cultivate discreet cross-class homosexual liaisons.

The central figure, Redl, is an officer from the lower middle class; as the Royal Court intelligentsia were supposed to do, he makes his way through ability and commitment rather than wealth, background and influence. He therefore has no ready access to a leisure-class pattern of same-sex relations; he makes a long and anguished discovery of opportunities that are taken for granted by other officers. Even then, he is baffled and frustrated in the cross-class liaisons which his advancing status facilitates. The young men to whom he is attracted do not assume a gay identity and do not stay with him; his violent reaction against effeminacy in the ball scene indicates self-hatred. He has heterosexual relations as well and they are equally tangled (a parallel with Osborne gets more and more inviting); indeed, the Countess is more treacherous than the boys. Redl succumbs gradually to the ethos of the class he has joined, taking on its coarse attitudes (such as anti-Semitism). The ruling elite is not only inefficient and obsolete, the play said to its Royal Court audience, but its characteristic patterns of sexual relations are unsatisfying and brutalising. Redl betrays his country, but Osborne makes it seem scarcely worth preserving.

Up to the point where Redl discovers how to be a homosexual, the dialogue colludes with the discretion which is excluding him. The audience is invited to watch out — as Redl is doing — for hints that might open the secret of queer subculture. His first experience occurs at the end of the first act, when he is attacked and robbed by soldiers: 'Don't be too upset, love. You'll get used to it', one of them says (69). Westwood reports almost the same words spoken to a man robbed of his watch by a guardsman: 'When I protested he said, "It's no use being upset about these things. You'll just have to get used to it."'[25] From the start of act II, the dialogue moves decisively inside the closet, with a drag ball for leisure-class gays and lower-class objects of their attention. From this point almost all the characters are in the know, but the price of this development is that Redl (now a counter-intelligence officer) becomes the object of surveillance. The ball, its host says, is for 'People who are very often in their everyday lives, rather lonely and even miserable and feel hunted. As if they had a spy catcher like the Colonel [Redl] on their heels' (85).

Of course, the censor was not going to pass all this: *A Patriot for Me* had to be presented in a club production. This is usually read as general establishment prudery, nannying and failure to turn on to the Swinging Sixties, but the Lord Chamberlain actually did attempt to accommodate the play. He wanted to cut the bedroom activity and bits of explicit language – which might still today not be allowed on television before midnight (the required changes are listed in the published text). But he was prepared to allow the theme, characters, and general action. What he was determined to cut is the whole of the drag ball.

Now, there is no specifically sexual action in that scene. The dialogue is not especially explicit – mostly camp backchat, with a sharp wit and some shrewd points about oppression. And the scene concludes with Redl aggressively dissociating himself from all of it. But the Chamberlain did not discriminate details, he found the drag ball unacceptable. The point, I believe, is that it is organised – collective. Here gayness is not all solitary anguish, as it appears generally for Redl and in the social-problem dramas of the mid-century. The Baron asks: 'Don't you think we should all form an Empire of our own?' (83). In effect, they already constitute an alternative social structure – virtually all Redl's acqaintance is at the ball and it parallels another occasion at the royal palace. And, despite everything, it is confident and it is fun. The Baron calls it 'the celebration of the individual against the rest, the us's and the them's, the free and the constricted, the gay and the dreary, the lonely and the mob' (77).

The ball raises the prospect of an effective gay subculture. This was not as remote as might be supposed. In fact, in 1965 drag was the principal form through which a new visibility was already being asserted. There was revue and pub drag; Danny La Rue's club in Hanover Square had become fashionable after a visit from the Queen's sister.[26] Semi-private balls started up in London in 1964, and were regarded as a big advance in gay subcultural expression. A revue called *Sh* . . . included a mock-up of a grand Venetian ball, and featured Douglas Druce, to great acclaim, as Queen Elizabeth II. But on the second night 'we were just about to go on stage when the Lord Chamberlain came down in person and stopped the show'.[27] Dan Rebellato examines the report of an official sent in 1958 by the Lord Chamberlain to reassess another drag revue, *We're No Ladies*, at a small London venue; it had passed censorship but was giving rise to complaint. Not very much had been added to the script, the officer found, but he was alarmed that the whole audience were immediately 'familiar with the phraseology of the perverted' and feared the theatre was becoming 'a focal point for pederasts'.[28]

A Patriot for Me did excellent business, and no one complained that it was merely indecent. Some said it was boring; B.A. Young (a friend of Rattigan) found the drag ball distasteful − it displayed 'all the clichés of camp backchat in the hope, I suppose, that there will be someone in the house to whom they are a novelty'.[29] Of course, he was wrong: there were many who knew nothing of the alternative gay culture disclosed in the ball and hardly any who had seen it represented in any kind of public context. The ball was censored because it represents the possibility that the closet will prove not only a way of isolating gays, but a basis from which they might gain confidence and organise their own demands. It is characteristic of Osborne that this positive potential should be accompanied by Redl's self-hating rhetoric.

Osborne's later work edged back to the discreet, leisure-class showbiz world of Rattigan − the world from which he had never altogether severed himself. The three men in *The Hotel in Amsterdam* (1968, Royal Court) are drawn together by professional and personal commmitments to and resentments of a film producer, K.L.; the three women are affiliated to the men. Laurie is the one with the Osborne tendency to speechifying, and he doesn't disguise his fixation on queerness. He recalls an 'English faggot' whom K.L 'picked up in Hollywood'; Laurie called him Sybil − he had a crown of sibillants [*sic*] over his head'. He ponders how if K.L.'s name had been Young or Yeo or Yarrow they could have called him 'K.Y'. He initiates a discussion about whether he or Gus is the more 'effeminate' (112, 97). In *West of Suez* (1971) the central character tells the story Osborne liked to tell about Noël Coward and himself: the older author asks 'How queer are you?' In the autobiography the younger − Osborne − replies, 'Oh, about twenty per cent.' In the play the reply is 'Oh, about forty-five per cent.'[30] Osborne didn't really know.

Making It Legal

We have traced through this book the tangled conjuncture of restrictions upon homosexuality and the stage, and the decline of the leisure-class accommodation with those restrictions. It is no accident, then, that the English legislation governing both theatre and homosexuality was reformed when the Labour Party was elected with a big majority on a modernising platform in 1966. Harold Wilson and his colleagues did not introduce socialism, but they facilitated progressive changes on the social problem agenda — on capital punishment, divorce, abortion and race relations. The Wolfenden proposals were enacted in 1967 and theatre censorship was abolished in 1968.

Among gay activists, it is customary to remark the limitations of the Sexual Offences Act of 1967. Male homosexuality was decriminalised only in private, and only when there were no more than two people present, they were over twenty one, and not in the armed forces, the merchant navy, the prisons, Scotland or Northern Ireland (the Scottish and Irish laws were changed later). 'In private' was to be interpreted narrowly in the courts, and accompanied by a stringent policing of 'the public'.[31] Nonetheless, it was a victory for progressive thinking and for 'the non-U intelligentsia', as Tynan had called it in his review of *Look Back in Anger*. It enabled many gay men and lesbians to refuse the discreet spirit of the law, and, with varying degrees of flamboyance, to come out.

Meanwhile the efforts of the Lord Chamberlain appeared increasingly anachronistic. In *Inadmissible Evidence* Osborne was not allowed 'Do you have it off with that girl of yours?' but the line became acceptable when 'off' was deleted (26). The issue, really, was not which was the ruder utterance, but whether the ordinary speech of a large part of the population might be heard on the public stage. Henry Livings complained that he had been required to change 'bugger' to 'bleeder'. However, in Manchester, where he came from, the former had 'friendly rather than offensive connotations', whereas the latter was 'sharply vituperative'.[32] In *Afore Night Come* Rudkin was permitted 'firk' but not 'fuck'; however, in a Worcestershire accent it sounded the same.[33] The Lord Chamberlain's function was premised on the assumption that West End theatre would speak, or aspire to, the language of the leisure class. Now serious artists, a confidently vocal audience, and the more prestigious part of the cultural apparatus, wanted something else. At some moments the State was both subsidising (through the Arts Council, the British Council, theatre in education groups) and restraining (through the Lord Chamberlain) the one stage production. This kind of asymmetry — the State at odds with itself — is likely to pertain only for a while; the disorderly institutions soon attain a new equilibrium.

Matters came to a head when, in order to evade the cutting of *A Patriot for Me*, the Royal Court theatre turned itself into a private club; you joined when you bought your ticket for the play. The Chamberlain didn't like this at all, and tried, unsuccessfully, to get support from government law officers. The next play presented in this way at the Royal Court, Edward Bond's *Saved* (1965), which shows Len trying to forge personal-sexual relationships among a family of damaged people, presented a softer target. Its author was unknown and its offence was more to do with violence than sexuality. The police prosecuted, and the magistrate determined that theatre clubs had in fact never been private: properly interpreted, they had always been within the censor's jurisdiction.[34] The private club had been a collusive device, enabling dissidents to let off steam in a controlled way. As I have suggested, it had been remarkably like the gay or lesbian club.

The closing of this loophole meant that something had to be done about stage censorship. Under the Theatres Act of 1968 plays can still be prosecuted on the grounds of obscenity, but only by the Director of Public Prosecutions. In fact, no case has been brought under this legislation. Mary Whitehouse's attempt to prosecute Michael Bogdanov and the National Theatre for presenting Howard Brenton's play *The Romans in Britain* (1980) was made under the statute against 'gross indecency' — as if the actors on the stage had actually performed the same-sex rape that they were simulating.[35]

Another way of describing these legal changes, linking back to earlier concerns of this book, would be to say that arrangements which had suited the cultivated leisure elite lost credibility when that class fraction lost influence generally. Such diverse men as Quentin Crisp, Terence Rattigan and Joe Orton had learned how to live with the cross-class liaison, the private secretary, the discreet bar, the private party, the thrill of cottaging, the overseas holiday; they felt they had little to gain from legal reform. Remember the assumption of Wildeblood and Croft-Cooke in the early 1950s (see chapter 12) — that prosecutions would be provoked only by activities in public places. In effect, the 1967 Act merely restored that situation. In typical welfare-capitalist manner, it extended to the rest of the population a semblance of what had been upper-class privileges.

In similar fashion, the leisured elite, in its heyday, had colluded happily enough with the Lord Chamberlain. Stage censorship was abolished when they lost control to a new group of producers, writers, critics and audiences. The youthful, leftist intelligentsia had reshaped theatre to suit its concerns, and had developed supportive institutions and resources – mainly with the State support promised under welfare-capitalism. This is the structure which Thatcherite governments were to unpick during the 1980s, by demanding that theatre defer to the market.

14

'The Sixties'

Zany Humour

The 'whole subject' of lesbianism was 'shunned during the permissive sixties', Elizabeth Wilson says. 'It was the one "problem" about which *Nova* never ran an article.'[1] In fact, lesbians were beginning to organise. In the USA the Daughters of Bilitis had been active since the mid-1950s and a mixed group, the Homophile League of New York, engaged in more confrontational campaigning from the early 1960s. In Britain Esmé Langley and Diana Chapman started the Minorities Research Group in 1963. *Arena Three*, its magazine, canvassed many issues, engaging a community of perhaps 9,000 British lesbians. The drawback with this activity, Emily Hamer suggests, is that it became more difficult than before 'to be a lesbian pillar of the community without feeling at risk of exposure'.[2]

We need another kind of explanation for the sudden lesbian visibility in Frank Marcus' play *The Killing of Sister George* (1965, West End; Broadway, 1966). Indeed, by the time of the film, released in 1968, the public was deemed ready for a sex scene between Alice and Mrs Mercy. Equally important, they got a scene of lesbian subcultural organisation, shot actually in the Gateways Club; it looks cheerful, friendly, unthreatening.

In an interview with Jackie Forster in *Sappho* in 1980, Frank Marcus says he thought of his play as about 'oppressive paternalism', with the BBC as an instance, and lit upon lesbianism as the kind of thing that would make the George character vulnerable. I believe this is broadly true. 'Did you know any lesbians?' Forster asks. 'I suppose I must have done', Marcus replies.[3] What I want to establish is that *Sister George* and other prominent plays owe far more to what we call 'The Sixties' than to the high-minded concern with queerness of so many of the plays discussed in this book, from *The Prisoners of War* to *A Patriot for Me*.

I argued in chapter 9 that *Sister George* exploits fashionable Pinteresque menace, as it emerged out of the queer thriller. The mysterious invasion of the home of June and Alice by the sinister and manipulative Mrs Mercy, the gesture toward metaphysical realms in the clairvoyant, Madame Xenia, and the general air of aggression link the play with Pinter and with Orton's *Entertaining Mr Sloane*. Also, *Sister George* develops the grotesque, comic potential of all that, drawing on another strand in absurdist theatre writing, from N.F. Simpson (*One Way Pendulum*, 1959, Royal Court) through Tom Stoppard. Marcus taps this vein in incidents such as the filtering of aggression through the routines of Laurel and Hardy, and in the running juxtaposition of scenes from the mawkish soap opera with the erratic and boisterous actress: Sister George opens church bazaars, whereas June engages in a surreal (Ortonesque) tussle with nuns in a taxi.

After writing the foregoing paragraph, I read Jill Dolan's essay in which she considers *Sister George*, alongside *The Children's Hour*, as written in a realist mode: 'Once again the lesbian is positioned as external to the discourse of dominant culture by the realist structure.'[4] I have never seen the play that way. First, although the text does not use standard Brechtian techniques, I think the playful juxtapositions I have just described discourage audience members from relaxing into realist assumptions about the inevitable, natural, *thereness* of the world. Indeed, the commuting of June between her roles invites an awareness of the narratedness of social and sexual conventions. The part was created by Beryl Reid, a major comic performer.

Second, I read Mrs Mercy's intrusion quite differently. In Dolan's view, 'the dominant culture, represented by the BBC's Mrs Mercy Croft, intervenes in June's personal life to reclaim her infantilized lover Alice − called "Childie" − back into the bosom of the family life that the BBC radio program enshrines' (166). I see no prospect of family life for Alice. She may believe she is escaping, but Mercy is installing her as her private secretary, living and working in her London flat. 'You're my little girl. You're going to be − my little girl' (68). Alice moves from one subjection to another; she will remain materially and emotionally dependent. And I can't imagine any British theatre audience in 1965 that would regard *The Archers* (the radio soap on which George Applethorpe is modelled) as enshrining a model for intimate relations. Of course, I am drawing here on personal recollections as well as historical study of the context in which *Sister George* was produced. The question, perhaps, is how well the play makes sense beyond that initial context. It is unfortunate that lesbian commentators, pursuing lesbian writing rather than lesbian representation, have said so little about such an influential text.

What was and remains controversial is the gendered hierarchy, established near the start when June makes Alice eat the butt of her cigar. Alice is not a mere victim: she is smart enough to know that she can spoil June's fun by pretending to enjoy it. And lately we have had important reassertions of the viability of the butch/femme model, both historically as a way of existing in the 1950s and in principle as a valuable lesbian mode that got sidelined by some kinds of feminism.[5] Nonetheless, *Sister George* is troubling, because not all of June's behaviour can be positioned as role-play. According to Marcus, June and Alice are playing 'sado-masochistic games . . . among themselves', rather than being 'destructive' and 'fuelled by hate'.[6] This is, of course, the distinction often made in S/M theory. But when June says, '(*with disgust*) Look at you: whimpering and pleading. Have you no backbone, can't you stand up like a man?' (70) she is not playing. Her contempt for 'feminine' weakness is comparable to that of Jimmy Porter.

Overall, *Sister George* depicts the (apparently) necessary failure of a lesbian relationship founded in a masculine/feminine hierarchy which it cannot operate successfully. Marcus might have gleaned this thought from contemporary Freudians, such as Eustace Chesser: 'There is a distinctively homosexual temperament in which jealousy, possessiveness and sado-masochism predominate. The overt Lesbian suffers from a basic insecurity and a constant fear that the loved one may be seduced into heterosexuality. She enters into competition with men and often compensates for her sense of inferiority by imitating the dress and mannerisms of men.'[7] 'I'm not married to you, you know', Alice says when June threatens her because she says she fancies the man downstairs (36).

The fact that there are problems with *Sister George* doesn't make it historically ineffective, any more than the fact that it was written by a man. In a dearth of lesbian representation it was bound to be significant, for lesbians as much as for others. Harriet Gilbert says it was from *Sister George* that she learned of the Gateways club.[8] 'It had absolutely no relationship to either of the affairs I'd had', Jackie Forster remarks – the cigar-eating scene 'was like do lesbians use dildos?' But, Forster adds, 'it was how I imagined lesbians to be and that was still very powerful while I was watching the play'.[9] That's how representation works: we make our cultures by negotiating more and less satisfactory images.

Finally June, monstrous though she is, has far more life and emotional integrity than the other characters. And her gender-bending is undeniably funny — she wants a 'man-to-man' talk with Mrs Mercy, and tells Alice to serve the tea because she can't be doing with 'all that pansy stuff' (8, 9). *Sappho* magazine presented a pub reading of *Sister George* in the 1970s, 'to be rewarded by cheers, laughter and applause which erupted throughout the performance'.[10] In 1998 the woman-only Wonder Bar in Victoria (London) was renamed The Sister George. My contention is that a sequence of plays featuring lesbian and gay characters was produced mainly through a Sixties vogue for 'zany' humour. At the same time, this visibility did bring notions of queerness, however inadequate, into everyday popular interest.

From *The Goon Show* (BBC radio, 1952–60) to *Monty Python* (BBC television, 1969–74), via Beat writing, Pop Art, *Private Eye*, the Beatles and the Liverpool poets, irreverent mockery seemed the most effective stance from which to upset established institutions. Sex was an easy topic around which to organise such mockery, since the prevailing norms — it was suddenly obvious — were so stodgy and ridiculous. 'Kinky' humour was cultivated, along with kinky boots and PVC. I have mentioned the gay sketch in *Beyond the Fringe* (chapter 6): effeminate actors film an advertisement for 'Bollard', 'a *man's* cigarette' (30). 'Camp', which had been part of queer subculture all through the century, came to general notice. Susan Sontag picked it up in her 'Notes on Camp' (1964); even while co-opting, extending and anaesthetising camp, she infused every kind of tasteful excess with gay potential.[11] In 1968 the comic actor Kenneth Williams was asked to define camp for television viewers of *Moviegoround*: 'To some it means that which is fundamentally frivolous, to others the baroque as opposed to the puritanical (classical), and to others — a load of poofs'.[12] *Monty Python* was often awkwardly camp. 'Some of the attitudes now make me cringe. Especially towards women and homosexuals', Terry Jones admitted in 1991. 'We were six men who found it difficult to write for women. We didn't really think a lot about homosexuality. We weren't anti, just very camp. Which I don't think we would do now.'[13]

In 1960 Peter Burton registered the homosexual slang 'Polari' as 'our own camp secret language with which we could confound and confuse the naffs (straights)'.[14] But from 1965 Polari expressions such as 'bona' (attractive), 'varda' (look at), 'omee' (man) and 'polonee' (woman) featured regularly in the dialogue of two very camp men in the BBC Light Programme comedy series *Round the Horne* by Barry Took and Marty Feldman (1965–69), with Hugh

Paddick as Julian (Jules) and Kenneth Williams as Sandy. In a typical exchange from March 1967 they are journalists:

PADDICK: Can we have five minutes of your time?
HORNE: It depends what you want to do with them.
WILLIAMS: Well, our editor said, Why don't you troll off to Mr Horne's
    lattie . . .
HORNE: Flat or home − translator's note.
WILLIAMS: And have a palare with him. . . .[15]

For regular listeners, as well as for gays, the 'translation' would be unnecessary; the offer was part of the joke. Often all this is recalled with great affection by gay men, but there is actually not much that is liberatory about it. You don't have to hide in the closet, it says, you can come out and be a grotesque for the amusement of straights.

In the late 1960s the television comedy series *Steptoe and Son*, written by Ray Galton and Alan Simpson, produced a gay episode (broadcast again in 1996). Harold (the son) is courted by a Dulcimer-type exquisite (Timothy) who is promising to set him up in a shop; Albert warns that he'll end up in a drag show down the Skinners' Arms. But it's platonic, Albert insists, invoking 'the beauty of the Homeric union between two cultured minds'; 'he don't wear scent, he wears after-shave lotion'. After dinner Timothy changes into something more comfortable − a smoking jacket − and seats himself close to Harold on the sofa. Isn't it warm? Wouldn't you like to take something off? May I feel your hand? You have sensitive fingers; do you play the piano? I've grown very fond of you, I'm a very lonely man. As Harold flees, his terror is augmented by a policeman at the door. But he has not come to arrest anyone. 'Hello Edgar, you're home early': the policeman (compare E.M. Forster's liaisons) is Timothy's partner! The predatory queer and his bit of rough translate beautifully into a popular idiom.

The hippie musical *Hair* (1967, Broadway; West End 1968) by Gerome Ragni and James Rado includes a brief number, 'Sodomy':

Sodomy, fellatio, cunnilingus, pederasty,
Father, why do these words sound so nasty?
Masturbation can be fun.
Join the holy orgy, Kama Sutra, everyone.

In 'Lola', a hit single by the Kinks (1970), that stunning woman you meet in a club turns out to be a transvestite.

> Well, I'm not the world's most masculine man,
> But I know what I am, and I'm glad I'm a man,
> And so's Lola.[16]

Lou Reed was a cult hero in 1969; by 1972 Alice Cooper and David Bowie were making gender-bending conventional; Richard O'Brien's long-running *Rocky Horror Show* ensued in 1973.[17]

In theatre comedy, the effeminate gay man became a standard ingredient. Kenneth Williams queened it as a private detective, to the amazement of a bullying client, in *The Public Eye* (1962, West End) by Peter Shaffer. 'And such a *gorgeous rug*! Real Bokhara! I can tell. I used to sell them once, door to door, wearing a fez and a stick-on goatee. Some dreadful gimmick of my employers. I looked like an extra out of "Kismet" and sold nothing at all *ever*, not even a welcome mat' (87). Shaffer's *Black Comedy* (1965, National Theatre) is a very ingenious farce, in which darkness and light are reversed so that for most of the action the characters blunder around in full view of the audience when a fuse causes a blackout in their world. The characters include Harold Gorringe, a bachelor owner of an antique shop, given to emotional blackmail, and 'hysterical when slighted, or (as inevitably happens) rejected' (140). The fiancée of a sculptor claims that his work will be famous and she will be like Mrs Michelangelo; 'There wasn't a Mrs Michelangelo, actually', says Harold. '*He* had passionate feelings of a rather different nature' (175). Harold ends up like Ernest in Coward's *Design for Living* – rebuffed, furious and spiteful. The National also produced Shaffer's *Royal Hunt of the Sun* (1964) and *Equus* (1973). Both are in more spectacular mode, and have homoerotic aspects: the Inca god Atahuallpa appears with few clothes on, and the boy Alan talks about his disturbed sex life with no clothes on.

Charles Dyer had been successful with *Rattle of a Simple Man* (1962, West End; Broadway, 1963), in which a football fan, who is also a Scout leader, fails to rise to the occasion when he visits a good-hearted prostitute. 'I'm afraid I'm not a man; I'm afraid I'm effeminate or something', he finally bursts out. 'There's nothing different about you, love, I'm the expert', she reassures him, but the play ends inconclusively (93). In Dyer's *Staircase* (1966) Harry Leeds and Charlie Dyer, a couple of barbers, score camp points off each other. Didn't

Harry get his Brothel Badge in the Scouts? – 'It's worn on the left arm between the one for getting knotted and the one for rubbing sticks together. Lovely! Sort of field of azure with a pair of discarded knickers on a tent pole' (25). The element of grotesquerie/absurdity is enhanced when it is pointed out that the names of all Charlie's acquaintance are anagrams of his own – including even Harry's. Indeed, Charlie's name is also the author's, so we may ponder, as Dyer invites us in a note, whether perhaps the whole story exists only in Charlie's mind – whoever he is (89). This might be either profound (critics thought Beckett's *Endgame* might be a monodrama), or Sixties silliness.[18] *Staircase* was produced by the Royal Shakespeare Company.

Plot and dialogue in *Staircase* enact the inevitable humiliation of queerness. Harry would prefer it if people had antennae rather than sexual organs - they could be folded away so as not to get tangled in the rush hour on the tube. Charlie is proud of his straight credentials: 'I was married, mate. That's me. Nothing puffy with me, mate. *I'm normal. I* was married *with a baby*' (32). However, little of this turns out to be true – Charlie has a court case hanging over him (importuning in female attire). He is made to confess his dependence on Harry, so the two silly old things make the best of it and soldier on together. When *Staircase* reached Broadway in 1968 Walter Kerr nominated it 'the simplest and most honest treatment of homosexuality I have come across in the theater', and Martin Gottfried hailed 'the first play that I have seen deal sensitively and adroitly with homosexuality'.[19]

The commuting of writers such as Shaffer and Dyer between the West End and the major subsidised companies bespeaks the ideological confusion of the Sixties. It had always been alleged that the youthful, leftist intelligentsia, which emerged around *Look Back in Anger* and claimed State subsidy for its culture (see chapter 13), was vague in its political agenda. Now it was swept into the Sixties project of combating dreary conformity. The Royal Shakespeare Company (RSC), the Royal Court and the National Theatre responded with brilliant and innovative programmes – though sometimes it seemed that more or less any bizarre farrago might be on the right lines – 'radical' and 'challenging'.

By 1964 the powerful impresarios Emile Littler and Peter Cadbury were objecting that the RSC was abusing its privileges with such 'dirty plays' as Peter Weiss' *Marat, Endgame, The Birthday Party* and David Rudkin's *Afore Night Come* in its season.[20] However, Orton's *Entertaining Mr Sloane*, which they also condemned, was being produced commercially in the West End by Michael Codron. Suddenly, the standard, middlebrow product appeared grossly out of touch with The Sixties, and a new generation of commercial producers saw that a fair return might be had from showcasing innovative work – the more surreal and kinky the better. As well as *Sloane*, Codron produced *The Killing of Sister George* and plays by Pinter and Charles Wood. Michael White produced *Oh! Calcutta!* (1967) and brought in Brecht's *The Resistible Rise of Arturo Ui* (1969) from Nottingham and Jean-Claude van Itallic's *America Hurrah* (1966) from Off-Broadway. The protests of Cadbury and Littler were plastered outside the theatre to publicise *Sloane*; compare the arrest of Wilde – his name was taken off the hoardings for *An Ideal Husband* and *The Importance of Being Earnest* and the plays soon closed. Perhaps there is a contemporary implication in Tom Stoppard's *Rosencrantz and Guildenstern Are Dead* (1967, National Theatre) when the players, having fallen on hard times, make Alfred, the boy actor, sexually available. Kinkiness was in vogue.

Wise Child (1967), produced by Codron in the West End (Broadway, 1972), was Simon Gray's first success. It presents Sir Alec Guinness (Artminster) in drag; ostensibly this is a disguise – he is on the run from the police. But that would be as likely to draw attention to him as to camouflage him, and gender confusion seems more than a convenience for his young and pretty companion, Jerry. He refers to Artminster as 'Mum' when they are alone, and contrives to lose at stone, paper and scissors so that he can be punished. The hotel owner, a figure like Eddie in *Entertaining Mr Sloane*, demands that Jerry accede to his advances in order to finance Artminster's escape. 'And what does that matter? He's got needs like everybody else and he's got other feelings on top of them', Artminster says (128–9). At the end, when Artminster abandons his disguise to leave, Jerry cross-dresses. They stare at each other in silence as the curtain falls. This exuberant/sinister farrago threw the Lord Chamberlain's office into confusion. Despite the reluctance of one reader, it was decided that 'the audience would know from the start "Mrs Artminster" *is* a man, and that there really is no element of homosexuality'.[21] This peculiar interpretation shows how baffled they had become.

For much of the century addressed in this book, the question is: Who would hear such queer nuances? By the mid-1960s the split was hardly over decoding competence – nearly everyone knew what was being talked about. Now there was an explicit contest, over what could be said in public. When *The Killing of Sister George* was playing at Wimbledon in 1967, Joe Orton prophesied: 'I don't suppose they'll understand what the play is about.' 'Don't you believe it', Kenneth Halliwell replied. 'They'll know very well what it's about.' Orton acknowledges: 'He was right. It became clear, from the opening scenes, that they understood and weren't amused.'[22]

On the Beatles' *Sergeant Pepper* (1967) 'Lovely Rita, Meter Maid', is 'sitting on the sofa with a sister or two'. Representations of lesbianism, few as they were, were also surreal, and tended even more toward the grotesque and threatening. In David Pinner's *Fanghorn* (1967), Joseph King is First Secretary in the Ministry of Defence and averagely complacent and patronising with Jane, his (second, younger) wife, and Jackie, his daughter. The mysterious Tamara Fanghorn, a friend of Jane, is the predatory lesbian intruder, whose purpose is to dominate the wife and humiliate the husband. She is distinctly kinky, and obliges Jane to join her in an experiment of which Joseph is to be the subject: 'Men have got to pay in kind. Have I trained you for nothing[?] Put up with your ridiculous loneliness and professional virginity? Your little perversions? Rubber and wetness? What we did, eh? We did. You swam in it. To the mouth' (40). Tamara knows an uncanny amount about Joseph's personal history: perhaps she is working on unsolved accidents for the police — what happened to his first wife? And is he really who he says? (Pinter again). Amid a lot of bizarre business, Joseph is stripped and humiliated with his own fencing sabre, and threatened with his own bullwhip; it looks like he is going to be castrated, but it is his bushy moustache that is cut off.

Fanghorn was produced by Charles Marowitz, an American who at this time was the principal fringe director in Britain, at the Traverse Theatre in Edinburgh and briefly in the West End. It attracted a news story in the *Times*: 'Lord Chamberlain's Change of Mind'. John Johnston, the Chamberlain's reader, was persuaded to visit a performance and to agree that it was a fairly light-hearted spoof — 'a purple comedy, that is, a mixture of blue and black elements'.[23] The point, I think, is that it was not regarded as a serious account of lesbian sexuality — that might have been difficult to countenance — but as a zany fantasy about the danger of the unregulated female.

Edward Bond's *Early Morning* (1968, Royal Court) had to await the ending of the Lord Chamberlain's veto. It seeks to expose the violence and oppression of the State through a nightmare vision of the Victorian ruling elite. The princes Arthur and George are Siamese twins; Prince Albert and Disraeli plot revolution; Gladstone is a trade union leader; the Lord Chamberlain is ineffectual (his modern counterpart held up the play until censorship was abolished). And Florence Nightingale reports: 'I'm changed. Queen Victoria raped me. I never dreamed that would happen. George will know. I'll disgust him . . . I've started to have evil thoughts. Her legs are covered in shiny black hairs' (28, Bond's pause). The presentation here seems designed to repel, but the development is quite amiable. 'Call me Victor', the Queen says; 'I've never had a girl with such deep feelings — you've seen my maids of honour. You cried when you came.' Florence appears in the Scottish costume associated with Victoria's faithful servant, John Brown: 'If they knew you were a woman there'd be a scandal, but if they believe you're a man they think I'm just a normal lonely widow' (71).

Notoriously, The Sixties were best for young, heterosexual men — women were encouraged either to display a lot of thigh, or to cover their legs entirely and masquerade as earth mothers. Compatibly, most of the lesbian and gay presence was created for the amusement of straights and had little to do with (what was to become) Gay Liberation. Indeed, the joke depended on lesbians and gay men staying more or less where they were. It is easier today, I think, to understand why *The Captive* in 1926, *The Green Bay Tree* in 1933, or *Serious Charge* in 1954 was assessed as a profound psychological study, than it is to see how *Staircase* and *Fanghorn*, in 1966–67, could be thought significant and funny. Gays working in theatre and popular culture remained discreet for a decade or two longer. At the same time, these plays did act as a route through which gayness, and other broadly irreverent matters, could get into popular discourse without the solemn agonies of the problem play. Though theatre made little attempt to take lesbians and gay men seriously, it did suggest that we were there and having fun some of the time.

The Moment of Orton

I discuss Pinteresque menace and 'angry' and political plays in other chapters because they manifest different kinds of impetus and different kinds of awareness of queerness. Nonetheless, these modes jostled together with the Sixties spirit of 'zany' exuberance, for instance in writers as different as Edward Albee and David Mercer. This overlap is nowhere more complex than in Joe Orton's plays.

I described in chapter 9 how in *Entertaining Mr Sloane* Orton achieved a realistic deployment of oblique, menacing dialogue and the sinister intruder. Also, the play presents a challenge for a progressive audience — not around homosexuality, but in the psychopathic violence of Sloane. Plays such as *A Taste of Honey* and *Five Finger Exercise* presented the young person as a victim of the grown-ups, and Sloane is in part such a victim — at the end Kath and Eddie are able to force him into their 'family'.[24] But he is also the unsocialised hoodlum whom conservatives were invoking as grounds for clamping down on all youthful self-expression. He is set up in some ways as the attractive character among the four — he looks good. But kicking old men to death is carrying intergenerational conflict a bit far. Alan Schneider, the US director, had difficulty with Sloane's murder of Kemp: it was too capricious, too amoral. He coped with it by making the old man unattractive, so that it might seem to serve him right![25]

Loot (1966, West End; Broadway, 1968) is certainly in the zany mode, but it was also well attuned to a leftist audience. The play is on the side of the boys, Hal and Dennis, and attacks officialdom and moralism. Some of the dialogue is in a discreet manner, but deployed so as to expose hypocrisy and bogus formality ('And even the sex you were born into isn't safe from your marauding': 200). However, the treatment of sexuality was not the main excitement of *Loot*. This, for the youthful intelligentsia, lay in its treatment of the police and the law. During the relative social harmony of the 1950s, the image of the friendly 'bobby' was hardly challenged (though homosexuals always had reason to distrust it). But repressive attitudes to political demonstrations from around 1960, and then to recreational drugs, shifted liberal opinion. In 1965, while Orton was writing *Loot*, the case of Detective Sergeant Harold Challenor came to prominence. He had arrested, beaten, and planted a brick and an iron bar on people demonstrating against the Greek monarchy (because it sponsored right-wing governments). Orton became 'obsessed with Challenor', says Kenneth Williams, disapprovingly.[26]

Orton's critique of police malpractice goes far beyond anything previously seen in the theatre, or indeed other media.

TRUSCOTT (*shouting, knocking* HAL *to the floor*): Under any other political
    system I'd have you on the floor in tears!
HAL (*crying*): You've got me on the floor in tears.

    .   .   .   .

TRUSCOTT: And you complain you were beaten?
DENNIS: Yes.
TRUSCOTT: Did you tell anyone?
DENNIS: Yes.
TRUSCOTT: Who?
DENNIS: The officer in charge.
TRUSCOTT: What did he say?

DENNIS: Nothing.

TRUSCOTT: Why not.

DENNIS: He was out of breath with kicking. (235, 245–6)

Challenor's sanity had been in question even before the planted brick. In the closing moments of the play McLeavy tells Truscott 'You're mad!' He replies: 'Nonsense. I had a check-up only yesterday.' Orton even worked into the text Challenor's actual words, as reported in court: 'You're fucking nicked, my old beauty' (273–4). Hilariously, the Lord Chamberlain would not allow 'fucking'.[27] With the repressive State apparatus starkly displayed, he was still chasing after naughty words.

While all this was exhilarating for progressive audiences, *Loot* provoked walk-outs during its pre-London tour: 'Bournemouth Old Ladies Shocked', reported the *Times*.[28] For them, lugging Hal's mother's body round the stage was shocking, and so was the casual way with Christian imagery. Simon Trussler remarked the difference between 'kinds of audiences': one kind 'may understand *Loot* because they share its moral assumptions', the other will prefer Whitehall farces and 'either ignore *Loot* or hate it'.[29] The play crystallised the stand-off between old and new audiences.

Orton's affiliation with progressive theatre was, in my view, temporary and fortuitous — deriving mainly from his suspicion of authority as a gay man. *Ruffian on the Stair* and *The Erpingham Camp* were presented by the Royal Court in 1967; when *Loot* wasn't going well Orton doubted whether it was right for commercial theatre and thought of approaching the Royal Court or the National. But he had studied at the Royal Academy of Dramatic Art in the early 1950s; he had few links with the student culture of the peace movement and subsidised theatre. And his commercial success helped to keep him among the older type of discreet, leisure-class queer. Orton's diaries show virtually no interest in other gay plays, or in the new 'fringe' companies, or in moves to abolish stage censorship, or even in the legalisation of male homosexuality. Rather like Osborne, who shared much of the same background, Orton makes a poor fit with the progressive movement he helped to initiate.

Orton's preferred garb was remarkably like that worn by Sloane: initially, at least, he imagined himself as the outlaw-intruder, pushing his way into an affluent, stylish and effeminate theatrical milieu through audacity and cuteness while remaining insolent, dangerous and masculine. The theatre queens were queer, he was a lad putting it about. 'I'm from the gutter', he said to Oscar Lewenstein. 'And don't you ever forget it because I won't.'[30] However, as Orton himself became a successful theatre queen the outlaw role became increasingly implausible, though no less necessary.

What the Butler Saw (1969, West End; Off-Broadway, 1970) has been Orton's most widely praised and performed play. I believe, notwithstanding, that he lost his way between the two audiences. The play includes notable satire against medicine and psychiatry, and creates continuous gender confusion, with cross-dressing and 'inappropriate' sexual advances. But it was not too disturbing for Orton's discreet friends. They were very enthusiastic about it, and encouraged him to have it produced at the Haymarket by Binkie Beaumont with Sir Ralph Richardson in the star role − in other words, in the heart of traditional West End theatre. Orton said he was setting a trap: he wanted a conventionally 'lovely' set so that 'When the curtain goes up one should feel that we're right back in the old theatre of reassurance.'[31] But it wasn't the censor (by then defunct) who would not allow Churchill's 'missing part' to be produced on stage, but Richardson, the Beaumont star. I fear it is Orton who was trapped − in the Sixties assumption that throwing the pieces in the air will, of itself, be challenging.

Albert Hunt admires the way *What the Butler Saw* destroys 'the sexual stability on which the mechanics of bedroom farce depend'.[32] But such stability presumes a 1950s farce audience. By 1969 very many people no longer believed that it is important to conceal adultery, that Christian imagery is sacrosanct, even that female sexual desire is shocking and/or funny. Brian Rix, sponsor of the Whitehall farces, had remarked in 1966: 'with the more tolerant climate there now is, we could put on a farce about adultery and our audience wouldn't bat an eyelid'. He attributed 'the more liberal attitude' partly to Royal Court plays. Orton was not unaware of the change. In the same article he is quoted as complaining: 'A lot of farces today are still based on the preconceptions of a century ago, particularly the preoccupations about sex. But we must now accept that, for instance, people do have sexual relations outside marriage.'[33] Quite.

Things were moving faster than he realised. Earlier in the decade Giles Cooper's *Everything in the Garden* (1962, RSC and Michael Codron) was powerful when it showed conventional middle-class people making money from prostitution, disposing of the body of a murdered witness, and getting used to the idea. By 1969, for many people, the fuss in *Butler* about adultery and nakedness was merely quaint. Simon Shepherd in his important book observes that instead of a return to order at the end of *What the Butler Saw*, incestuous desire is revealed. Shepherd believes the audience, 'like any comedy audience . . . sees itself to be like the characters in expecting an ending to disorder; but discovers that ending to be alien and uncomfortable. Thus trapped the audience is driven wild. The first performances succeeded: people stormed out or barracked the players.'[34] Part of the audience did that. But suppose one did not find incest between consenting adults so very terrible? Already Osborne had worked it over in *Under Plain Cover* (1963, Royal Court).

To be sure, the play upset Richardson's admirers in the preliminary week at the Theatre Royal in Brighton ('They should burn that joint down. They think it's 1950': Pamela in John Osborne's *Time Present*; 1968, 49). And it was booed and jeered on the opening night in London, though this was not an innocent response but an organised campaign by the group of traditional gallery first-nighters that had recently disrupted Colin Spencer's *Spitting Image*.[55] But was it important to taunt those people in 1969, at the price of framing *Butler* in terms they would react against? The play's title, which refers to ancient seaside machines showing 'sexy' pictures of knickers and suspenders for a penny, was of course meant to be ironic, but it binds Orton to the framework of attitudes that he wants to oppose. He enjoyed watching audiences upset by *Loot*, and believed his 'authentic voice' was 'vulgar and offensive in the extreme to middle-class susceptibilities'.[56] He seemed not to realise that those susceptibilities were already on the run and that there was enthusiastic support for his stance. He thought Kenneth Tynan wouldn't dare include 'Until She Screams', the sketch he submitted for *Oh! Calcutta!*, but this piece had basically been written in 1960. Shepherd observes: Orton 'had a rather inflated idea of his own shockingness: they did dare do his sketch. Orton's underestimate of the sexual "liberation" of others is a mark not just of his vanity but of his isolation.'[37]

Finally, Orton's representations of gayness are disappointing. There is the closeted Eddie in *Entertaining Mr Sloane*, but his devious exercise of power makes him unattractive. Hal and Dennis in *Loot* are said to be indifferent to the gender of their partners ('You scatter your seed along the pavements without regard to age or sex': 244). This is intriguing, but gay men and lesbians at this time were struggling to be gay, not to be indifferent to or vague about sexual orientation. In *What the Butler Saw* gayness is not developed after the initial interview between Prentice and Nick. Orton insisted that there should be nothing 'queer or camp or odd' about his characters: 'Americans see homosexuality in terms of fag and drag. This isn't my vision of the universal brotherhood. They must be perfectly ordinary boys who happen to be fucking each other. Nothing could be more natural. I won't have the Great American

Queen brought into it.'[38] We all believe we should get away from stereotypes, but these are not arbitrary, external inconveniences; they are historical realities, implicated in the whole construction of sexuality in the modern world. You dislodge them not by trying to jump clear but by engaging with them. Clum concurs: Orton 'rejected the queen stereotype of traditional farce but had no positive vision of homosexuals with which to replace it'.[39]

Jonathan Dollimore reads *Butler* as 'a kind of black camp', composed of irony, parody and pastiche, held together by 'a stylistic *blankness*'. He argues that the play insinuates 'the arbitrariness and narrowness of gender roles, and that they are socially ascribed rather than naturally given'. So we may see that sexual relations are not essentially thus or thus, but are based on manners, convention, custom, ideology, power. This is indeed what *Butler* does some of the time. It 'becomes a kind of orgy of cross-dressing, gender confusion and hierarchical inversion', and the dialogue calls into question the 'natural' − in circumstances where the speaker is in fact mistaken, because of cross-dressing, about the 'naturalness' of the very example he is using.[40] But the comedy works against such postmodern insights. The jokes assume, first, that these attitudes and situations are outrageous (rather than utopian visions of the dispersal of gender conventions); and, second, that whatever their clothes, Nick is really a boy and Geraldine really a girl.

The contest between progressive and reactionary attitudes permitted Orton's notoriety. Earlier, he would not have been tolerated; later he would not have mattered. We might call it the moment of Orton. He wanted to scandalise Aunt Edna, the 'middlebrow' follower of theatre invented by Rattigan. But Rattigan put money into *Sloane*, remarking: 'Orton thought it very funny that I, of all people, should have thought his play so good'.[41] Actually, they were not so far apart, for Orton's revolt depended on Rattigan's world. The disturbance that helped make him a celebrity also set a limit to his moment.

Repression

I have depicted The Sixties initially as frivolous and tending to deploy gay representation as an amusing way of being disruptive. However, in chapter 13 we saw earnest work by John Osborne, David Mercer and others running on from the social and political concerns of the late 1950s. And, alongside a knock-about attempt to shock people by lugging a corpse about the stage, *Loot* fed a current vein of criticism of police practices. As it became evident that the social order was not going to respond to a spirit of fun, the mood became increasingly intense and politicised. 'And what's the point of a revolution without general copulation[?]' the imprisoned lunatics demand in Peter Weiss' *Marat* (1964, Royal Shakespeare Company: 98). Political repression was interpreted through sexual repression.

The Freudian mainstream had supposed that people are born violent and have to be tamed through socialisation. Insofar as this suggests that people are fundamentally uncooperative, it tends to legitimate right-wing policies — that for our own good we need to be controlled, and that capitalistic striving is for the good of the race. The radical thinkers who became influential in the 1960s turned it all around: people would be decent and fulfilled were it not for the repressive impositions of the State and the capitalist system. Sexuality, then, appears not as the sign of our underlying animal nature, to be tamed and channelled, but as a potential source of human revolt against a stultifying system. In *The Sexual Radicals* (published initially in the USA in 1969 as *The Freudian Left*) Paul A. Robinson identified current gurus — Wilhelm Reich, Geza Roheim and Herbert Marcuse — as 'radical Freudians', because of 'their unqualified enthusiasm for sex, their belief that sexual pleasure is the ultimate measure of human happiness, and their pronounced hostility to the sexual repressiveness of modern civilization'. Further, they regard 'sexual repression as one of the principal mechanisms of political domination'.[42] Norman O. Brown, also, was often invoked. This group of thinkers was said to be inspiring a 'counter-culture'. In a way, this is just another manifestation of the ongoing dispute between romantic individualism and social order — there was much quoting of William Blake. Yet the particular formulation — that sexuality *will and should* assert itself — was radical.

An approximate translation of these ideas into theatrical terms was available in the theory of Antonin Artaud. Charles Marowitz, in his work with Peter Brook under the auspices of the Royal Shakespeare Theatre and as manager of the Open Space Theatre, was a crucial mediator to the English: 'How valuable, asks Artaud, is a theatre that elegantly, excitingly and wittily reiterates the clichés of our lives — compared to a theatre that suddenly opens up, like a mountain crevice, and sends down a lava that scours the lies, half-truths and embedded deceptions of our civilization?'[43] In fact Artaud afforded an imprecise fit with the radical Freudians, since he tended to suggest that the breaking down of repression, though a necessary transformative experience, would reveal our savage proclivities. But this didn't matter too much — it was a time for passionate commitment rather than lucid thinking.

Queerness merges with Artaudian attitudes in Christopher Hampton's dramatisation of the relationship of Rimbaud and Verlaine, *Total Eclipse* (1968, Royal Court; Off-Broadway, 1974). Verlaine hesitates to leave the security of his marriage, but Rimbaud has found it 'valuable' to be sexually assaulted by drunken soldiers:

> It clarified things in my mind which had been vague. It gave my imagination textures. And I understood what I needed, to be the first poet of this century, the first poet since Racine or since the Greeks, was to experience everything in my body. I knew what it was like to be a model pupil, top of the class, now I wanted to disgust them instead of pleasing them. I knew what it was like to take communion, I wanted to take drugs. I knew what it was like to be chaste, I wanted perversions. It was no longer enough for me to be one person, I decided to be everyone. I decided to be a genius. I decided to be Christ. I decided to originate the future. (23)

Verlaine and Rimbaud could be just the traditional cross-class liaison, with its dangers and discretions, but Rimbaud proclaims a new set of priorities.

In large part, the counter-culture took heterosexuality for granted. Reich ignores everything, Charles Rycroft remarks, 'that can be related to the homosexual component of human nature'.[44] However, Robinson notes, William Burroughs and Allen Ginsberg 'fused Reichian rhetoric with a most un-Reichian apology for homosexuality and hallucinatory drugs'.[45] Peter Brook, the most prominent Artaudian director, showed little interest in sexual dissidence. As David Savran points out, even Julian Beck, the bisexual leader of the resolutely experimental Living Theatre, makes little reference to queerness in his work.[46]

Marcuse, the most systematic, informed and flexible of the gurus, argued that heterosexuality had been co-opted by capitalism, such that 'the societal organization of the sex instinct' places a taboo on 'practically all its manifestations which do not serve or prepare for the procreative function'. Were it otherwise, the body would become 'an instrument of pleasure. This change in the value and scope of libidinal relations would lead to a disintegration of the institutions in which the private interpersonal relations have been organized, particularly the monogamic and patriarchal family'. Marcuse located homosexuality and 'the perversions', therefore, as modes of 'rebellion against the subjugation of sexuality under the order of procreation, and against the institutions which guarantee this order'.[47] So lesbians and gay men come in alongside blacks, women, third-world peasants, draft-resisters and students, as potential replacements for the working class as a revolutionary force.

It is hard to overstate the significance of the radical Freudians for Gay Liberation. They provided the impetus for a sudden and total reversal of priorities, converting shame into defiance, stigma into pride. The task is no longer to negotiate social niceties, however cunningly, but to proclaim your true sexuality – the queerer the better. And if that disconcerts people, it shows you are on the right lines.

It became important to perform Frank Wedekind's *Spring Awakening* (1891), which is about the difficulties resulting from ignorance and repression at the onset of puberty among a group of naturally good and decent schoolboys and -girls. Wedekind had published the play at his own expense in Zurich in 1891; after a heavily bowdlerised production fifteen years later by Max Reinhardt in Berlin, it became a classic of the German-speaking theatre. It was banned in Britain, and Eric Bentley was aware in 1974 of just a single Broadway matinée performance, sponsored by the *Medical Review of Reviews* in 1917; Bentley's translation was produced at the University of Chicago in 1958. In London the National Theatre and the English Stage Company tried to secure a licence for *Spring Awakening* in 1963–65, but the best they could get was the Royal Court production of 1965, in which boys kissing and masturbating were not allowed (they had to spit instead – much nicer).[48] When the National eventually did the play in 1974 (in a translation by Edward Bond) a passage from Reich was printed in the programme.

As well as scepticism about religion and morals and excruciating anxiety about school assignments (leading to a suicide), the youngsters in *Spring Awakening* experience sexual dreams and sado-masochistic arousals. Hänschen lusts over women in reproductions of classic paintings: as he puts them back in their box he quotes Othello murdering Desdemona. In a hilarious and tragic scene Wendla's kind mother just can't manage to tell her where babies come from, so she becomes pregnant and dies after an illicit abortion. Homosexual practice appears to be the consequence of a bad system when boys in a reformatory attempt to hit a coin as they masturbate together. However, Ernst and Hänschen have a touching and erotic love scene – they talk about eating grapes in a vineyard: 'When I bend the spray, it swings from my mouth to yours. Neither of us need move – just bite the grapes off and let the stalk spring back to the vine.' They kiss; 'I wouldn't have known contentment if I hadn't met you. - I love you, Hänschen, as I have never loved a living soul'. In thirty years they will be respectable or rich and will look back in wonderment; perhaps this will remain their most intense experience (153–5).

New plays were organised around the need not to be bashful about queerness. John Hopkins was an experienced television writer (he had developed the Z-*Cars* police series) and in his much-admired sequence of four overlapping television plays, *Talking to a Stranger* (1966), he had displayed the consequences of repression in a family. His powerful *Find Your Way Home* (1970, Open Space; Broadway, 1974) addresses a key motif of the discreet tradition: the married man discovering his repressed queerness. Alan (aged forty-seven) returns to the flat of Julian (aged twenty-three – Julie for short, as in *The Green Bay Tree*); they have been lovers, but Alan has withdrawn for twelve months to his wife and family to decide where his commitment really lies.

> I ran away, Julie – mostly from myself.
> [*Silence.*]
> If what you are disgusts you – the man you are – how can you live with any hope of being – knowing – happiness – or peace? . . . I thought it was meant. I thought – this is the man you are – the life you've made – and now – accept it. . . . I lived ten years – and every day lies, deceit, pretence – and endless little insincerities. (36)

Correspondingly, Alan's wife – Jackie – has colluded in a marriage in which she has been unable to express herself sexually. 'How could you accept – how could you do that – to yourself?' Alan asks (64). Repression has become the sin against oneself.

Jackie follows Alan to Julian's flat, becoming the intruder in a fight for territory and appearing, even, as the straight predator who wants to break up a gay relationship. She is scornful: 'It isn't – er – fucking – what you do together. You want to think it is – all right – you want to call it that – it isn't', she tells Julian. 'He – uses you'. Julian accepts this: it is 'the truth of what we do together' (55–6). The responsibility to express your ultimate sexual desires is complicated by Julian's masochistic response to Alan's absence: he has fed his sense of worthlessness by allowing himself to be exploited sexually. Does this make him a worthless person? No, authenticity is the only criterion. 'I shall have trouble sometimes, when I think about it', Alan says; 'I may want to hurt you.' Julian can be guilty for both of them, and Alan can punish both of them. 'Please – don't hurt me more than you have to', Julian says as they draw together (91).

Simon Gray's *Butley* (1971, West End; Broadway, 1972) is more amiably pitched, but also consists largely of people goading each other to acknowledge the truth of their sexuality. Ben, a university teacher, and Joey, his protégé, share an office (in which the play is set) and a flat (Ben's wife has left him after a year of marriage). Ben assumes proprietorial rights, but these are now irking Joey. He is gay, and has taken up with Reg, toward whom Ben is laboriously and homophobically offensive − he tries to trap him into acknowledging a special investment in the word 'queer'. However, Reg has the upper hand because Joey is going to move in with him; Ben becomes desperately abusive: 'you're just a lucky parvenu fairy old fig, and to tell you the truth you make me want to throw up. Pardon, ooop! All over your characteristically suede shoes' (60–1).

A passage that was cut in performance conveys, Gray says in a note, 'a great deal of useful information about Butley's relationship with Joey and about his sexual nature'. Butley prefers friendship to love and sex with women, he says. But 'it's the sort of friendship people used to have with me at school', Joey replies: 'Abuse, jokes, games . . .' (65, Gray's pause). Now immaturity is attributed not to gays, but to people who can't enjoy a sexual relationship of any kind. Even so, the question of Ben's sexuality remains somewhat mysterious. Alan Bates, who had played the part, referred to Ben as 'the alcoholic homosexual', whereas Gray expressed amazement at 'the assumption that Butley is homosexual'.[49] We are still on the territory of Pinter, who directed these plays. But whatever it is that inhibits Ben, it is plain that Reg and Joey, as gays who are expressing themselves, have the better prospects.

Although the tendency of Sixties counter-cultural thought was deeply sexist, a Marcusean analysis could be applied to women and a feminist agenda. Germaine Greer in *The Female Eunuch* (1970) explores 'how it is that women's energy is systematically deflected from birth to puberty, so that when they come to maturity they have only fitful resource and creativity. . . . what happens to the female is that her energy is deflected by the denial of her sexuality into a continuous and eventually irreversible system of repression'. Hence the term 'female eunuch'.[50] Further, because 'the permissive society' has tended to neutralise and contain heterosexual revolt, there is an opportunity for lesbians: 'Homosexuality in many forms, indeed any kind of sex which can escape the dead hand of the institution − group sex, criminal sex, child-violation, bondage and discipline − has flourished, while simple sexual energy seems to be steadily diffusing and dissipating' (45). Anything out of the ordinary is on the right lines, in fact. One should be able to 'choose lesbianism in an honourable, clear-eyed fashion, rejecting shame and inferiority feelings as a matter of principle' (294).

Such a principle was worked out in practice in *Trevor* (1968), a genial play by John Bowen (Hampstead Theatre Club and then the West End; part of a double bill called *Little Boxes*). Sarah and Jane are upper-middle-class women in their late twenties, living together as a lesbian couple (they give no sign of gendered roles). A visit from Jane's parents causes them to rearrange the flat into two bedsits, and to pick up in a pub a young actor to impersonate her supposed boyfriend, Trevor. He does his best, but when Sarah's parents turn up at the same time, also expecting to find a boyfriend called Trevor, the project becomes impossible. One mother is traditional about sex ('She doesn't want me to become a dried-up spinster': 67), the other trendy ('I brought Sarah up on D.H. Lawrence': 106). But both sets of parents expect the young women to have boyfriends, and both are distinctly unhappy with Trevor. He has tried out Sarah's scent and likes cooking: they think he looks gay. The masquerade collapses; Sarah declares herself sick of deception and tells her mother how she and Jane became lovers, made love. But the parents would rather delude themselves with Trevor — you must bring him down, they say. 'They do know, you know', Trevor says. 'It's just that they don't want to put it into words' (110).

The effect for the audience is to validate Jane and Sarah. They are true to themselves, have a loving sexual relationship, try to face the truth. They even cope with the landlord who makes heavy-breathing phone calls. They are confident and modern; the parents are quaint. The term 'coming out' was not available to these characters, but they show how important it was going to be.

Maureen Duffy's novel *The Microcosm* (1966) was 'one of the very few books during this period to confront lesbianism openly and to describe the social life of lesbians', Elizabeth Wilson says.[51] In her play *Rites* (1969) Duffy questions the new Artaudian/Marcusean orthodoxy, by reassessing the dangers of atavistic regression in the release of repressed instincts. In a public lavatory (what private spaces did women have?) the supervisor, the cleaner, and users — typists, lifelong housewives — chat about men and this and that. A Pinteresque air of menace is generated around a boy-child who is brought in; his trousers are dropped to see what he's made of (he is represented by a doll). At this point audience members may think of Euripides' *The Bacchae*, but the boy is not to be the object of the women's fury. Nor is a woman who tries to commit suicide in one of the cubicles; she is the victim of men, and provokes the women to declarations of independence. They dance together and chant: 'Don't need them, don't need them.' Yet they turn upon an elderly bag-lady. 'Knees up Mother Brown', they sing, joining hands and dancing round her, until the dance 'reaches a frenzy of menace'. Suddenly, their attention is drawn away from her by what they take to be a man – spying, as in *The Bacchae*, upon their rites. In a frenzy, they fall upon the creature and kill it; only to discover that it was a woman. The mistake was understandable – she was 'suited and coated, short-haired and masculine': the intruder was a lesbian (23–4). Ruefully, the women dispose of the body.

In her note to the text of *Rites* Duffy comments: 'In the very moment when the women have got their own back on men for their type-casting in an orgasm of violence they find they have destroyed themselves and in death there is certainly no difference' (27). Once women claim space (territory) of their own – initially only the space of the women's lavatory – they too, like male-dominated groups, may find themselves disconcerted by sexual dissidence. The scope of female sexuality was to be an abiding issue in the women's movement, along with questions about how far different strategies and lifestyles might be replicating the narrowness and aggression of patriarchy. Duffy believes experiencing these things in the theatre might be purgative but, as Jane Rule remarks, this involves her in displaying women in an unattractive light.[52]

The way *Rites* got written and produced is interesting. A group of women writers met under the auspices of Joan Plowright and Laurence Olivier, Duffy explains, to develop an evening of one-act plays that would be produced under the auspices of the National Theatre. Such were the beginnings of women's and lesbian theatre in Britain.

Revolution

While the theory of the damage done by sexual repression aspired to account for the entire social order, its immediate bearing was often individual and personal. The other strand of Sixties earnestness was collective and activist. What Marcuse had been describing as 'repressive tolerance' was seen as having given way to direct repression, initially in places remote from the centres of capital – Vietnam most grossly; and then, quite suddenly, in North America and Western Europe, among draft refusers, blacks, people who proclaimed an intellectual or imaginative critique of capital, and those who merely preferred an alternative lifestyle (using cannabis, for instance). Edward Bond's early plays are dominated by the idea that repression is both the means by which the State maintains control and the source of violence generally (see the preface to his *Lear*, 1971). In the USA the Vietnam War and resistance to racial integration moved young people especially to rage. In 1967, despite tensions between them, hippie counterculture and left activism discovered common ground. 'On the verge of the 1967 "Summer of Love", many were the radicals and cultural revolutionaries in search of convergence, trying to nudge the New Left and the counterculture together, to imagine them as yin and yang of the same epochal transformation', Todd Gitlin recalls.[55] In London the Grosvenor Square demonstrations of 1967–68 drew in many who had supported the Campaign for Nuclear Disarmament in the early Sixties, together with a new generation who were disappointed that giving flowers to policeman did not mollify them.

The conjunction of race and homosexuality was worked through urgently by LeRoi Jones (after the death of Malcolm X in 1965 he renamed himself Amiri Baraka). By 1960 or so, in the latter days of the Beat movement, Jones had become a significant figure in avant-garde New York. *The Baptism* (1964) is a typical Sixties product, exposing in ludicrous manner the hypocrisy and self-repression in a pastor and his female congregation (a boy is taken to be Christ because he has masturbated more than a thousand times in the year). The critical voice in *The Baptism* comes from 'The Homosexual'. Throwing coloured confetti over the assembly, he sings: 'The pride of life is life. And flesh must make its move. I love my mind, my asshole too. I love all things. As they are issued from you know who. God. God. God. God. Go-od. The great insouciant dilettante' (15). The Homosexual is to be played as a stereotype – 'Elegant, 40-ish, priggish, *soi-disant* intellectual. Growing fat around the middle and extremely conscious of it. Very queenly' (9) – but then, the other characters are stereotypes too.

Jones' *The Toilet* (1964) is more substantial. A group of boys collect in a school washroom with the purpose of beating up another boy, Karolis. Their language is violent and sexualised. The immediate stimulus is disclosed towards the end: a letter from Karolis to Foots, who is a leader among the boys but yet sensitive and intelligent, telling Foots he is 'beautiful' and that Karolis 'wanted to blow him' (56). Because of this, Foots is expected to fight Karolis. However, Karolis reveals that the letter followed upon an encounter with Foots in this toilet, in which first names were used: 'You put your hand on me and said Ray! . . . No, no, his name is Ray, not Foots. You stupid bastards. I love somebody you don't even know' (60). The boys beat Karolis again, despite his courageous resistance and Foots' evident reluctance. In the final moments, Foots returns to cradle Karolis' head in his arms.

As *The Toilet* was produced, all the boys are black save two, of whom Karolis is one; as in *West Side Story*, we have an ethnically divided *Romeo and*

Juliet. In this instance, however, all the aggression comes from one side — from the blacks. The conclusion thus seems to illustrate the potential of gay love — even interracial gay love — as against the homophobic mob pressure apparently indigenous to black culture. Of course, that was and is a controversial theme; Baraka subsequently showed himself to be embarrassed by it. Langston Hughes suggested that white and black performers might alternate roles from night to night.[54]

As Werner Sollors remarks, it is possible to read the play differently — as critical of assimilation: Foots' liaison with Karolis is of a piece with his more respectful attitude toward the school and both might indicate that he is tempted by corrupt white values to sell out his black community.[55] This reading seems to underlie Ron Simmons' argument, that gays are portrayed 'constantly' in Baraka's plays as 'degenerates and cowards. They are weak, soft, and unmanly. Gay men are the antithesis of what [Baraka] idealizes as the "Black Man".'[56] However, the violence and self-repression of the black boys, the courage of Karolis, and the affection between Foots and Karolis at the end make it hard to justify such anti-assimilationist readings of *The Toilet*. In fact, as Sollors and Simmons point out, the theme of sexual love between boys from different backgrounds being destroyed by hostility from within black youth culture seems to have had personal resonances for Jones. *The Eighth Ditch (Is Drama* (sic, 1961), an earlier poetic-dramatic piece, has a scenario not unlike *The Toilet*: love between a middle-class black youth and a lower-class boy is corrupted when they are discovered by others.

Meanwhile, during 1963–64, inter-racial violence spread from the southern states to the northern cities, and black militants became increasingly impatient with nonviolent protest and sceptical about the role of white activists. It was not a period for the working out of interpersonal subtleties. If in Jones' early plays gay love affords a human and bohemian corrective to the crudeness and violence of aspects of African American culture as he initially experienced it, in subsequent writings homosexuality becomes synonymous with whiteness and weakness. *The Slave* (1964) is set during a future race-revolt. Walker is a black activist; he confronts Easley, his erstwhile English professor: 'You never did anything concrete to avoid what's going on now. Your sick liberal lip service to whatever was the least filth. Your high aesthetic disapproval of the political' (88). Easley, though his wife Grace is on-stage, is repeatedly called a faggot and a fairy. Walker is the father of Grace's children, he claims. Baraka is repudiating both gayness and the white liberal/bohemian context that had facilitated his initial escape from the restrictions of the traditional African

American middle class. Now anti-white/anti-queer violence is re-envisaged as revolutionary.

At about the same time, Eldridge Cleaver was attacking black gays through the instance of James Baldwin, as acquiescing in a 'racial death-wish' and 'frustrated because in their sickness they are unable to have a baby by a white man'. However, homosexuality was not inevitably at odds with black power. In 1970 Huey Newton, leader of the Black Panthers, declared that gays 'might be the most oppressed people in the society'; indeed, they 'could be the most revolutionary'.[57]

Overall, this book has had little to say so far about imperialism, race, ethnicity and faith groups – but see the discussions of Maugham (chapter 2), *God of Vengeance*, *Outrageous Fortune*, *South*, and *Becket* (chapter 9), *Angels in America* (chapter 10), *Clara's Old Man* and *Raisin in the Sun* (chapter 11). I just haven't come across many plays that broach it in implication with same-sex passion. Obviously this is mainly because non-white people have only rarely been welcomed in British and US theatre (as in other middle-class cultural institutions), or only as performers. Also, black and white people, alike, have found interracial sex too hot to handle. From about 1960 there is an opportunist tendency, if you are putting in a queer character, to make him black just for the ride – like the colored queen who has bad teeth and wears a kimono and plucks his eyebrows in *The Zoo Story* (1960). In Donald Kvares' *Mushrooms* (1967, Off-Broadway), in which a sinister group of American zealots conspires to distribute chemical weapons, one of the incidental victims is 'a Negro queen'. He is vain, exploitative, and makes money out of shares in chemicals (168–70). Mona, the effeminate boy in *Fortune and Men's Eyes*, was played as black. At least Bernard in *The Boys in the Band* is serious, if cautious. Since, the late Eighties playwrights have explored the distinctive circumstances of sexual dissidents of diverse ethnicities. I discuss *Chiaroscuro* by Jackie Kay and *Giving Up the Ghost* by Cherríe Moraga in chapter 15; *Men on the Verge of a His-panic Breakdown* by Guillermo Reyes in chapter 16; *Cloud Nine* by Caryl Churchill, *Gorilla Queen* by Ronald Tavel, *M. Butterfly* by David Henry Hwang and *Porcelain* by Chay Yew in chapter 17.

As Martin Duberman's study *Stonewall* conclusively shows, much of the work and inspiration for the development of gay activism in the wake of the Stonewall riot came from people who had been active in the civil rights and anti-war movements; some had already begun to stir up the reformist 'homophile' movement. They brought with them campaigning language and strategies; in 1966 the North American Conference of Homophile Organizations

adapted the slogan 'Gay Is Good' from 'Black Is Beautiful'.[58] Adrienne Rich
records how she was engrossed by the civil rights movement (with all the
complexity that entailed among Jewish people) and early feminism; 'And there
was, of course, a third movement, or a movement-within-a-movement: the early
lesbian manifestoes, the new visibility and activism of lesbians everywhere.'[59]
The appellation of the Gay Liberation Front in 1970 (short-lived as it was)
signalled the decisive arrival of a group that had been ignored in the activist
politics of class, race, empire and gender, but which had learned from those
engagements.[60]

These connections are displayed in C.P. Taylor's *Lies About Vietnam*
(1967), which was commissioned for commercial television. The Head of
Programme Clearance required that there should be a warning: 'Something
like e.g. "The delicate relationship of Cyril and Tom is nearly upset by the
intrusion of Frank" should do the trick' (quoted with the playtext, 55). Note
the assumption that everyone will understand what this means; it is, more or
less, a description of most of the plays considered in the latter part of this book.
Lies About Vietnam was performed live at the Traverse Theatre, Edinburgh, in
1969. The title is from Adrian Mitchell's angry war poem, 'To Whom It May
Concern'. Cyril, an experienced campaigner, is travelling the country
addressing anti-war meetings with the support of Tom, who has served as a
pilot in Vietnam. They are lovers, as the hotel manager, Frank Graham,
realises – 'I've seen this kind of thing time and again in the army' (65). He
tries to get them to leave. But Cyril inveigles Graham into believing that they
think alike, after all – indeed, that fighting Communism means fighting
homosexuality: 'one of the nastier elements of this communist conspiracy to
take over the world is the way it exploits such sexual deviations as
homosexuality'. In fact, Cyril says, their business is weapons manufacture: he
shows Graham pictures of burned Vietnamese children (from the anti-war
campaign) as examples of the effectiveness of their new rocket. Graham is
visibly shaken – he thinks of his grandchildren – and falls back on the
thought that God 'works in strange ways' (68–9). In conclusion, Cyril remarks
how God is associated, for Graham, more plausibly with death and destruction
than with peace and gay love. Sadly, he and Tom go to bed together.

Cyril's determination to engage Graham on both gayness and Vietnam
foreshadows the political impetus of early-1970s lesbian and gay campaigning.
Where gay rights were not acknowledged, leftist audiences and performers
began to demand them – including in fringe work. In Howard Brenton's
Fruit (1970, Portable Theatre) queerness is, yet again, the dreadful secret: it

might be used to expose the hypocrisy of the Prime Minister. The play shows the political system overriding the accusation, illustrating, for Brenton, the Situationist thesis that public life is a fraudulent spectacle. However, some in the audience were not pleased; they did not accept the premise that the Prime Minister's sexuality was disgraceful. In 1970–71 the Bradford Marxist theatre group The General Will produced a sketch in which Prime Minister Edward Heath was being taught French by a very camp French master, inviting audience mockery of Heath's imputed gayness. This precipitated a split in the group and its realignment with the local Gay Liberation Front.[61]

Colin Spencer's *Spitting Image* (1968, Hampstead and West End; Off-Broadway, 1968) culminates in a prototype of a Pride march. To general astonishment and fear, one partner in a male homosexual couple, Gary and Tom, conceives and bears a child (Andrew – he calls them Daddy One and Daddy Two). The situation is, of course, ridiculous:

DOCTOR: Yes, yes, any other symptoms, Mr Dart?
TOM: Oh, just the normal ones, you know.
DOCTOR: Normal?
TOM: I mean, well, morning sickness in the first two months and then . . .
(28, Spencer's pause)

The play misses no opportunity to get the language of patriarchy, family and heterosexuality to entangle itself. When a girl friend tries to kiss him Gary retreats: 'It's wrong. I'm a mother . . . I can't go around kissing girls' (37, Spencer's pause). The authorities decide that their tactic should be to break up the family unit: they use the term 'family' for Gary, Tom and Andrew, even as they plot against them because they are not a family.

Gary and Tom are not sentimentalised; most of the time they are bickering because of the strain of the situation ('Doctor Spock says that parents often find it difficult to adjust': 33). John Russell Taylor found them 'an entirely believable married couple, living and growing together and apart. Few heterosexual plays have done this so well.'[62] While *Spitting Image* appropriates straight concepts, it never allows them to settle down. All this is in the vein of *Sister George* and *Staircase*, but it is oriented so as to make best sense to a gay audience eager for its own theatre. At the West End opening, *Spitting Image* received 'loud boos from the gallery and sustained applause from the stalls'.[63] This is the split in the audience that we saw in relation to Orton. Michael Billington in *The Times*, Philip French in the *New Statesman* and Hilary

Spurling in the *Spectator* liked it, but Milton Shulman's review in the *Evening Standard* was headed 'Ugh!' Old-fashioned moralists were upset, progressives were supportive, and gays were energised. A psychiatrist asks: 'and would you say that you are the active partner of this relationship?' Tom replies: 'Eh? No, not really. I mean, it comes and goes. Sometimes one thing, sometimes another' (28). I recall people in the audience applauding this challenge to one of the gendered myths that aspire to organise gay sexuality. This is a new break: *Spitting Image*, though in a public mode and at a public venue, is written for gays.

It transpires that many children are being conceived by gay couples. Daddy One responds by organising a national movement, though Daddy Two is apathetic. 'But don't you see? Before we were alone, utterly alone, a freakish development. Now we are stronger. . . . At first we're bound to be a deprived minority. The Government will be trying to hush the whole thing up. Well I'm not going to let it' (40). Their tactics recall those of the Suffragettes, but allude also to current peace demonstrations – Andrew is distressed by the Vietnam War.

Of course, the triumphant ending is even more of a fantasy than the rest – 'Funny how people's attitudes have changed' (45). But fantasies are important: they signal the boundaries of the plausible. Nancy K. Miller has noted the way women writers are accused of falling prey to implausibilities in their fiction. But such 'improbable' plots may be read as commenting on the pressures that women experience; they manifest 'the extravagant wish for a story that would turn out differently'.[64] That is, the wish of women for power over their lives cannot be expressed plausibly within dominant discourses, only as fantasy. The implausibility of *Spitting Image* is utopian, but it also alludes to that fact, and to the scale of social change that would have to occur for gays to become acceptably empowered.

Spitting Image has continuing resonances for gay subculture. An obvious analogue for its main situation is discrimination against lesbian mothers, whose children are often taken from them in the way that is attempted in Spencer's play. And the government's attempt to place the gay parents compulsorily in an 'enclosed colony', telling them they have 'a rare disease' (39), has an all too familiar ring.

15

Subcultural Work

The Boys on the Stage

After *The Immoralist* in 1954, Curtin says, 'only five plays with unmistakably gay male roles were seen on Broadway during the 1950s'. In fact, of these five neither *A Hatful of Rain* by Michael Gazzo nor *The Bad Seed* by Maxwell Anderson ventures more than a passing reference.[1] I discuss Meyer Levin's *Compulsion* in chapter 11. As I have noted, lesbian representations were even scarcer. This chapter is about how gay people, on either side of the Stonewall riot, changed this, in US alternative work up to and beyond *The Boys in the Band*, and in UK work by and around Gay Sweatshop.

Of course, gayness was not the only topic which Broadway was reluctant to treat in the 1950s. 'We were not alone', Robert Patrick remarks. 'Atheists, socialists, intellectuals, artists, and any member of a non-white race who was neither an entertainer nor a Nobel Prize winner were essentially culturally invisible.'[2] The pressure for an alternative ethos supported the Beat writers (who, according to David Savran, were a further symptom of the US crisis in masculinity provoked by Cold War ideology) and underground film by Kenneth Anger and from the Andy Warhol Factory.[3] This work was shown in improvised venues, with no promise of safety (compare the club theatre in London). A printing of LeRoi Jones' poetic play *The Eighth Ditch (Is Drama* in *The Floating Bear* (circulation 300) was intercepted in the mails, and when the New York Poets' Theatre scheduled a performance Jones' home was raided. He was charged with sending obscene materials through the mail and the theatre was charged with licensing infringements. Jones successfully defended his play, but the production was not pursued.[4]

From the late 1950s, alternative theatre spaces were conceptualised as Off-Broadway and then, when this came to seem too tame, Off Off-Broadway. Here, mainly in lofts and cellars in Greenwich Village, theatre workers were not trammelled by the financial priorities and consequent timidity of conventional theatre. 'If Off-off signifies anything', Charles Marowitz writes,

> it is the sense of encroachment that artists feel in the presence of the Broadway monolith. Not simply the existence of commercial playhouses from 42nd to 59th Streets, but the all-pervasive influence of the commodity culture these theatres represent. As with the early Provincetown Playhouse and the Washington Square Players, American artists feel the need to affirm their opposition to, and difference from, the Broadway state of mind, and all it represents.[5]

Nonetheless, as with the little theatres earlier, the idea of showcasing material that might be taken up by the establishment was rarely out of sight.

Most Off- and Off Off-Broadway work was trivial, Marowitz says. However, the fact that it was brief, ephemeral and informal in style − not massive like Eugene O'Neill − does not mean it wasn't significant: 'If you are dealing with fugitive insights in a high-speed society which is constantly changing focus, you do not naturally construct a full-scale permanent edifice. It would be like building a block of flats during a safari instead of throwing up a tent' (11). Arguably, this was one of the last avant-garde formations in the West, for as cultural revolt spread across the social and spectrum through the 1960s and 1970s, culminating in punk, bourgeois society discovered that its smart move was not to be shocked but to buy up and aestheticise dissident movements. Today the most startling formal and cultural juxtapositions are to be seen in television advertising.

Like the bohemia I discussed in chapter 3, the alternative scene of the early 1960s was hospitable to sexual dissidence. By 1966 *Time* magazine was complaining that 'Homosexual ethics and esthetics are staging a vengeful, derisive counterattack on what deviates call the "straight" world.' *Time* noted this in Pop Art and 'the "camp" movement, which pretends that the ugly and banal are fun', and in writers who 'delight in explicit descriptions of male intercourse and orgiastic nightmares. It is evident in the theater, with many a play dedicated to the degradation of women and the derision of normal sex.'[6]

Joe Cino's Caffe Cino was the crucial Off-Broadway venue for gay work between 1964 and 1967. Plays by Inge, Williams, Wilde, Genet, Lanford Wilson,

Robert Patrick, Doric Wilson and William Hoffman were produced there. In *The Haunted Host* by Robert Patrick (1964) Jay (a writer and gay) has Frank (young, straight and naive) billeted on him. Frank has studied psychiatry and has one great line: 'people and homosexuals should try to understand one another' (315). Frank and the scenario uncannily resemble Jay's earlier experience with Ed, who committed suicide. They smoke dope; Jay reads from his work; Frank is very impressed. He doesn't move in, but he does enable Jay to exorcise the ghost of Ed. The innovation here is in the dialogue − Jay is bohemian, camp, witty, candid and confident − and in the assumption that in this context gayness is the norm and it is Frank who has to explain himself. Jay in *The Haunted Host* is probably the first comic representation of a gay character that is not patronising.

Gayness is spiritually authoritative in Robert Heide's play, *Moon* (1967, Caffe Cino). A straight couple are edgy and perplexed as humans land on the moon; another couple are violent and distressed − the man is accused of repressing his homosexuality; a gay man, Christopher, is calm and fruitful (he and his partner paint and make bread). The play's editor comments: 'Only with the arrival of Christopher, the Parsifal figure, does the space-age moon regain its reflective power to light the heart' (47).

The Madness of Lady Bright (1964) by Lanford Wilson was also a Caffe Cino play. Leslie Bright is forty and a 'screaming preening queen, rapidly losing a long-kept "beauty"' (178). On the walls of his room he has the signatures of hundreds of his partners; prompted by a boy and girl, who seem to represent both aspects of his personality and a more confident heterosexual coupledom, he recalls the partners and laments his loneliness. 'Old hustlers never die, they just start paying it back!' (188). *The Madness of Lady Bright* was a hit; today, although the dialogue is verbally inventive, it seems to lack pride − in comparison, say, with Arnold as drag queen in Harvey Fierstein's *Torch Song Trilogy*. Perhaps the play knows this: Leslie does describe himself as the creature of a passing era: 'You are a very rare specimen that should be saved for posterity', he tells his mirror reflection, 'in a time capsule as a little piece of the twentieth century that didn't quite come off. Along with an Olivetti type-writer and a can of − cream of celery soup' (184). A tendency not to emerge from the tragic doom of gay sex appears also in John Herbert's undeniably powerful *Fortune and Men's Eyes* (1967, Off-Broadway; see chapter 6).

The Caffe Cino plays I have mentioned offer representations of contemporary gay men. Director John Vaccaro and playwright Ronald Tavel formed

the Playhouse of the Ridiculous in New York in 1965, specialising in extrava-
gantly transvestite performances – pop, multi-media, loosely plotted, impro-
visatory, obscenely punning, frenetic, psychodelic, Artaudian, often alluding to
old movies. This work may be regarded either as looking back to the drag
shows of the 1940s and the notion of the gay man as a feminine soul in a
masculine body, or as anticipating 'queer' performance theory of the 1990s (I
discuss Tavel's *Gorilla Queen* in the latter context in chapter 17). In 1967
Charles Ludlam broke away from Vaccaro (who teamed up with the writer
Kenneth Bernard) to found his own Ridiculous Theatre Company. His *Turds
in Hell* (1969) abruptly juxtaposes infernal scenes of capricious perversion; in
Bluebeard (1970), based on a horror movie, a sex-crazed doctor is experi-
menting to develop a third sex.[7]

Ludlam is most famous for his cross-dressed versions of classic films and
plays, in which burlesque occurs alongside unaffected feeling. His *Camille*
(1973) is a version of *La Dame aux camélias*, which had moved Rattigan in
Variation on a Theme, now viewed through the Garbo film of 1937. Where
Rattigan had allowed a queer liaison to be inferred through a story that
remained ostensibly straight, Ludlam, by playing the lead part in drag,
transposed it to a gay man's point of view. He wore an elaborate costume but
his chest hair was fully visible. 'Wanting to look like a woman was not the
point. Wanting to create the illusion of Dumas' heroine was', he said. He
was committed to the emotional truth of the story: 'Sometimes, at the
farewell scene with Armand at the end of the play, just before I died in his
arms, I became so totally wrapped up in Marguerite that my mascara ran
down my cheeks in my own tears.'[8] Yet the incongruity was simultaneously
present: the deathbed scene is capped by the line, 'Toodle-loo Marguerite.'
Audiences, reportedly, found *Camille* spell-binding; Ludlam claimed
something more: 'You believe in the gender of the character beyond the
gender of the actor, and no one who has experienced that can go back.'[9]
Back, presumably, to the assumption that we know a woman, or a man,
when we see one. 'There are only two ways a woman may rise from the
gutter' Camille says: 'prostitution or the stage. And believe me, Nichette, I'd
rather peddle my coosie in the streets than become an actress!' (236).
Ludlam is indeed not an actress, we may say, though s/he is acting; s/he is
playing on gender – peddling the coosie s/he doesn't actually have. Thus,
Everett Quinton says, the play foregrounds the self-oppression which
persuades Marguerite to believe that 'she has no right to love as herself'.[10]
In the time of AIDS, and since Ludlam's death from the condition in 1987,

Camille has seemed to be a play about that, especially when performed by Quinton, Ludlam's surviving partner.

After Stonewall, Off-Broadway-style venues and companies specialising in lesbian and gay material grew up in US cities. Doric Wilson formed TOSOS (The Other Side of the Silence) in New York in 1972. There was a late 1970s explosion of work in San Francisco and Los Angeles. The achievement of such innovative productions (even where scripts have survived) and such transient companies is difficult to chart. Theodore Shank evokes performances by Hibiscus and the Cockettes from around 1970: 'intended primarily for the gay community of San Francisco, [they] were anarchic and aggressively amateurish as they celebrated fun, dress-up, drag, exhibitionism, and sexual freedom'.[11] The Gay Theatre Alliance was formed in 1978 and had twenty-eight associated companies by 1981.

Two full-length plays stand out from this vivid body of alternative US work. Mart Crowley's *The Boys in the Band* (1968) started life Off-Broadway at Theatre Four. The critic Clive Barnes recalled how Stanley Kauffmann had alleged that *Who's Afraid of Virginia Woolf?* was a displaced account of gay life; *The Boys in the Band*, he said, was the true version we had all been waiting for.[12] It ran for three years and was filmed in 1970. Many gays dislike it. Merle Miller wrote in 1971: 'What a pity that the first really popular play about homosexuals was such self-pitying kitsch as *The Boys in the Band*, although maybe the kitsch accounts for its popularity. Maybe some people want to think that's the way homosexuals are, and, of course, some of them are, none that I have known, though, not for long anyway.'[13] The standard psychoanalytic tropes are invoked: Donald is said to be a casualty, purposefully weakened in his mother's war against his father; Mom refused to let Michael grow up, and his father 'stood by and let her do it' (13). But at least we can see, here, that this is *a theory* of homosexuality; it does not emerge, implicitly, through character and action, as if it were a pragmatic truth. Gays object specially to the concluding gesture: 'You show me a happy homosexual, and I'll show you a gay corpse' (102). However, Larry and Hank are happy, and the movement between them, whereby Hank gets to see that they don't have to replicate the pattern that he expected when he was married, points the way toward distinctive and sensible kinds of relations among gay people.

Above all, *The Boys in the Band* is important for its studied reprise of almost all the standard motifs of gay representation. Cowboy, for instance, is the figure complained of by Robert Brustein in the plays of Williams and Inge — the 'male impersonator', who wears blue jeans, cowboy boots and T-shirt and is credited with athletic prowess, but 'hides fundamental insecurities behind an exaggerated show of maleness'.[14] 'He looks right out of a William Inge play', Michael says (43); his character note matches exactly that of Bo in *Bus Stop*. In this instance, though, there is no discreet ambivalence: Cowboy is hired for the night as Harold's birthday present.

For audience members who have been scraping together a gay subculture out of scraps from the Broadway theatre of the 1950s and 1960s, the references are precise. 'You have just eaten Sebastian Veneble', Michael announces as they consume his lasagne — 'A character in a play', he explains to Cowboy — 'A fairy who was eaten alive' (this is *Suddenly Last Summer*, of course). 'Jesus', Cowboy exclaims, unwittingly echoing Williams' religious symbolism. 'Did Edward Albee write that play?' Hank asks. 'No. Tennessee Williams. . . . Albee wrote "Who's Afraid of Virginia Woolf?"' (61–2). Michael's sexual restlessness mimics Sebastian's in *Suddenly Last Summer*: 'Bored with Scandinavia, try Greece. Fed up with dark meat, try light' (*Boys*, 12). The truth game, calling up your one great love and telling him about it, recalls 'Get the Guest' in *Who's Afraid of Virginia Woolf?*, and Blanche's idea that she can save herself by phoning her long-lost beau. Michael doubts that Harold will have the nerve to kill himself: 'It's not always like it happens in the plays, not all faggots bump themselves off at the end of the story' (65; one almost hears 'The Zoo Story'). Crowley's characters camp and bitch like Albee's, but less spitefully. My favourite is Emory's response to Cowboy's explanation of how he hurt his back: 'I lost my grip doing my chin-ups and I fell on my heels and twisted my back.' 'You shouldn't *wear* heels when you do chin-ups' (43).

To my mind, Crowley's reprise of these familiar motifs points to their constructedness, and opens the possibility that we might reconstruct ourselves. Doric Wilson in *Street Theater* (1982) picks up the tactic and continues it by having Michael and Donald witness the Stonewall riot. They deplore such rocking of the boat: 'The way some of them behave, they're asking for trouble' (72).

The main disturbance in *The Boys in the Band* is the one that haunts the US plays discussed in chapters 10 and 11: whether manly American manners guarantee conventional sexuality, or whether it may all be undermined by latency, repression, business, Mom, and so on. This question is actualised on the stage by Hank and Alan, both of whom appear straight, are married and have children. Hank now prefers to live with Larry instead, but Alan, the intruder, seizes on him as the one person with whom he can engage in man-to-man talk: 'I would have taken you for an athlete of some sort' (34). Indeed, they both play tennis, though, we have seen elsewhere, that is not a secure sign of manliness.

Alan becomes increasingly distressed as he realises he is at a gay party; he abuses and assaults the effeminate Emory: 'Faggot, Fairy, pansy . . . queer, cocksucker! I'll kill you, you goddam little mincing, swish! You goddam freak! FREAK! FREAK!' (45). Of course, this could be the hysteria of latency — it is the language of Brick in *Cat on a Hot Tin Roof*. Still Alan thinks Hank is straight and that he can draw him away from the others: 'Just the two of you together. The pals . . . the guys . . . the buddie-buddies . . . the he-men', Michael mocks (73, Crowley's pauses).

So is Alan a latent homosexual? It is not a new question. The climax of the truth game is Michael's attempt to trap him into admitting sexual involvement with another college friend. Alan holds the same line as Brick: 'It is a lie. A vicious lie. He'd say anything about me now to get even. He could never get over the fact that *I* dropped *him*. But I had to. I had to because he told me about himself . . . he told me that he wanted me to be his lover. And I told him that he made me sick . . . I told him I pitied him.' Michael reasserts: 'You ended the friendship, Alan, because you couldn't face the truth about yourself' (96–7, Crowley's pauses). However, it remains unresolved. The gay audience member may wish Alan's closeted hypocrisy to be exposed but, courageously, Crowley doesn't allow this. Not everyone whom we might want to be gay is.

By making explicit the familiar tropes of gay representation, *Boys in the Band* draws a line under the most significant gay theatre writing of the time. The tradition of discretion and innuendo is reviewed, item-by-item, reoriented, and rendered obsolete. To be sure, the sickness and quasi-tragic models that gay men are supposed to inhabit are still in place at the end. But the outcome of the play is not limited to its explicit statements. As a public theatre event, it helped to dislodge the discreet conditions that had determined those models.

La MaMa Experimental Theatre Club had been producing work in the Artaudian vein since 1962. Harvey Fierstein, who began acting there with Warhol in 1971, developed the three parts of *Torch Song Trilogy* in 1979; it reached Broadway in 1982 and the West End in 1985, and was filmed in 1988. Again, gay commentators complained that the characters are stereotyped. 'Arnold is exactly the kind of gay man that straight audiences (and critics) like to see on stage', Peter Burton wrote in *Gay Times*. 'He is everything that is freakish yet safe — "feminine", "witty", . . . "warm" . . . and, basically, so outlandish as to represent no kind of threat to anyone.'[15]

Burton's view can't altogether be denied, but there are novel elements in this story of how Arnold, a camp but very sincere gay man, eventually gets it together with Ed, despite Ed's attempts to go straight, and creates an alternative family by fighting off his mother and adopting a gay teenager. Arnold isn't just 'feminine', he builds a career — manfully, we might say — as a drag artiste. His transparent attempts to manoeuvre Ed into a commitment and Ed's covert attempts to form a straight liaison (the opposite way round from usual) are insightful as well as funny. Arnold's struggle to impose a personal significance on a back-bar incident is a new and comical way of talking about the limitations of anonymous six. The link between queer-bashing and Nazism is well made; teenage gayness and adoption are still controversial. True, Arnold and his partners seem to be aping straight marriage, but their contract is different: 'We, Arnold and Alan, being of sound mind and social-diseaseless bodies, hereby swear to take equal responsibility for walking and feeding the dog' (46). Above all, perhaps, the sequence of *Torch Song Trilogy*, starting from traditional preoccupations around drag, loneliness, sexual frustrations and tragic loss (or is it self-indulgence?), enacts a movement towards independent personhood, responsibility and community — though without abandoning camp. Thus Fierstein records not just what befell one man, but the progress of many gay men through the 1970s. (I discuss misogyny in *Torch Song Trilogy* in chapter 17.)

History and Politics

In London, meanwhile, *The Boys in the Band* had considerable impact in 1969, as did *Fortune and Men's Eyes* (Open Space and West End, 1968). *The Madness of Lady Bright* was presented by the American Theatre Project at the Mercury theatre in 1968. *The Haunted Host* was in the first season of gay plays in London at the Almost Free theatre in 1975. While the West End and subsidised companies thrived on reputations derived from the 1960s, fringe theatre became the place where lesbian and gay issues were confronted.

Gay Sweatshop was formed in London in 1975, on the model of the Women's Theatre Group and Monstrous Regiment.[16] It was invited to perform *Mister X* (1975) at a Campaign for Homosexual Equality conference in Sheffield; Roger Baker and Drew Griffiths wrote material which was worked on by the cast in rehearsals. The play is a series of challenges to 'Mister X' to discard his pseudonym and 'come out'; it concludes with the actor abandoning his role and declaring his own name and address. This was an incredibly powerful moment for people who had never, hitherto, been allowed to recognise themselves on a public stage, or indeed in any public context. The audience at Sheffield stood and cheered, many of them in tears, and the company was inundated with requests to tour − for which it obtained an Arts Council grant. Around the country, nothing remotely like this had been seen before. Local bigots raised various kinds of furore, but the effect was to incite gay people to attend − a brave thing to do in their home town. The discussions between the cast and the audience after the show disclosed isolation, distress, courage and exhilaration.

Maureen Duffy's *Rites* (see chapter 14) had produced no immediate offspring. 'I've written several others', Duffy said in 1972, 'but the theatre is sheer hell. It's so difficult trying to get things put on, unless you're constantly in the theatre and chatting people up.'[17] Sweatshop was started by men, and the situation of women in it, as in other gay organisations in the 1970s, was often fraught. However, Jill Posener's *Any Woman Can* (1975) soon followed. The play begins with Ginny's direct address: 'You are looking at a screaming lesbian . . . in seat D22, yes sir, right next to you' (15). Other members of the cast sit among the audience: a public lesbian theatre space is claimed. Nonetheless, Ginny has problems and most of them involve other women. At school, though oppressed by staff and pupils, she manages an affair, but the other girl backs off. Married women expect her to carry on secretly. She makes her way to a club, but the women there are scarcely less hung up; she is picked up by a super-stereotypical stone butch. She finds a partner who 'wants to be a woman', but doesn't want to become too settled (21). Observe that even this early play is not organised on feel-good principles (as is often alleged of lesbian and gay theatre). Posener focuses on awkward issues in the way women relate to sexual dissidence.

At the end of *Any Woman Can* three other women explain why one should not be open. The first lives with a woman but denies that she's gay; the second doesn't want to lose her job ('That's not being in the closet − that's common sense'); the third just wants to be normal ('I'm not ashamed of being a lesbian, of course, I just don't want anybody to know'). Ginny relates how by wearing a badge in the street she enabled a lonely and confused woman to approach her and talk with her. The play itself replicated this opportunity: 'I've never met another one before', many women said when they came up after the show (24–3).

Sweatshop was aspiring to revise, radically, the terms on which queer representation had occurred for most of the period addressed in this book. In Brighton, *Mister X* was presented at the Co-op Hall where the last (was it?) of the 42 Club revues had recently featured: this deliciously camp show, sponsored by an old-style private club and packed with local allusions, was followed directly, for many of the same audience members, by a Sweatshop occasion which demanded a new kind of political visibility. But how would these two approaches relate?

John Fraser, who joined the Gay Liberation Front at the London School of Economics in 1970, notes: 'There were screaming queens who had one particular idea of what being gay was about. There was another group of much straighter people who thought it was about something else . . . there seemed to be a lot of acrimony between the groups'.[18] Gay activists were divided over what they should do with the existing tradition of the effete leisure-class queer, and, concomitantly, with the theatre of Wilde, Maugham, Coward and Rattigan. One option was to reclaim and build up camp and drag – Bette Bourne formed the Bloolips to exploit the potential of 'gender-bending' or 'radical drag' at this time (their collaboration with Split Britches on *Belle Reprieve* is discussed in chapter 17). The other option was to repudiate most of that tradition as self-oppressed, misogynist and compromised by implication in class oppression, and to assert a more robust style of gayness. These alternatives were worked through in early Sweatshop productions.

As Time Goes By (1977) by Noël Greig and Drew Griffiths presents three moments: England in 1896, Berlin in 1929–34, and New York in 1969, each concluding with the closing down by the State of a rather unsatisfactory gay scene. In a male brothel just after the trials of Oscar Wilde, two boys act out for the gentleman patrons a 'Greek' scenario of nobleman and shepherd. However, the egalitarian pastoral ethos is belied by financial transactions. There is an alternative: one man is reading the socialist Edward Carpenter. When the exploitative attitude of the owner leads to the police closing the brothel, the gentlemen leave for France. They don't need to fight for sexual rights because they can afford to pay for them; otherwise the boys would be making it with each other instead. 'They'd be running off to set up house together. How dull for us. We'd only have each other' (28).

The bar owner in Berlin also scuttles without a struggle. 'And what of all the queens who've paid their way here? Paid for your ticket out of Germany?' 'I was running a club, not a welfare unit' (60). However, some of these men are striving to develop a new consciousness. One supports the Communists, another is working with Magnus Hirschfeld. 'Oh dear,' says Kurt, 'I can remember the time when all we ever did was sit around and natter about gowns' (44).

In the third section, in a bar in Christopher Street, a drag queen, the barman, a student, a businessman and a leather queen scarcely communicate (specially the leather queen, who says nothing at all, pointing to his glass and grunting when he wants another drink). Despite this alienation, these men resist the attempt of an undercover policeman to arrest the drag queen: we have arrived at the Stonewall riot.

As Time Goes By attempts not just a record of relations between the subculture and the State; it is revising gay ideas about gender. The drag artistes are treated respectfully throughout, but Hirschfeld's idea of women's minds in men's bodies is disputed by Hans: 'How can *you* have a woman's mind? You can't divorce your mind from everything else you are. It sounds like a woman's mind is something you can order from a warehouse. It's a dangerous idea.' 'Well, alright, a feminine mentality then, does *that* suit you?' Kurt responds; after all, queers do have wide hips. Some do, some don't, Hans retorts − and look how this kind of stereotyping is facilitating oppression of the Jews. In the third section the drag queen quotes from *A Streetcar Named Desire* as he hands out flowers to commemorate Judy Garland. It's crap that we loved her because 'she mirrored the anguish and loneliness of our own lives', he says: the most anguished and lonely people he has known are his parents. 'I loved her because no matter how they put her down, she survived' (62). Meanwhile the student is thinking about gender. He doesn't like gay friends speaking of him as 'she' and 'sister' − 'It was just like the kids at school, putting you down, calling you a woman.' But, he muses, his sister is the most interesting, involved and energetic person he knows − 'She and those women she hangs around with are really strong together.' He'd like to belong to a group like that (67). *As Time Goes By* works to reject misogyny and promote positive relations with women, while maintaining the drag traditions of gay men. This delicate balance, Kate Crutchley says, was the particular project of Griffiths; it was he, Julie Parker says, who insisted that Sweatshop should open up to women.[19] Drew Griffiths was murdered by a person or persons unknown in 1984 at the age of thirty-four.

The next main Sweatshop production, *The Dear Love of Comrades* (1979) by Noël Greig, explored the historical links between socialism and sexual dissidence in the person of Edward Carpenter. This led Sweatshop (now without Griffiths) into another kind of negotiation with femininity. Carpenter had contested the effeminate model of same-sex love that Ulrichs and Krafft-Ebing had proposed. He grants that there are 'extreme specimens', but those of 'the more normal type' possess 'thoroughly masculine powers of mind and body', and 'are often muscular and well-built'.[20] In *The Dear Love of Comrades* (the title is from Walt Whitman) everyone is manly; George Merril darns the socks, but it is explicitly denied that he is like a wife. He and Carpenter hang out the washing together, and anyway, we are told, working men used to do the washing until recently. There are no women characters, though Carpenter had argued for feminist causes and women such as Olive Schreiner figured in his circle, and some of his lovers had wives.

Whether to repudiate or appropriate effeminacy has proved a persistent gay dilemma. Consider the rise and decline of the 'masculine' *clone* look. Reviewing *Master Class* (1995), Terrence McNally's play about Maria Callas, Paul Taylor complains: 'The character may be played by a woman but, in this work, Callas is, to all intents and purposes, a gay man performing a diva routine'; she tosses out 'bitchy one-liners with frightening articulacy'. One might attribute these comments to the homophobic notion that gay writers can't write about women without making them honorary gay men. However, Steven Mathers, founder of the 'Callas Circle' fan club, writes in the *Gay Gazette*: 'She was a most assuredly glamorous creature within which there was an undeniable element of the drag queen, in her elegant dresses and slightly overdone eyeliner . . . echoing gay men's body consciousness, she completely reinvented herself'.[21] Blanche DuBois lives.

Martin Sherman's *Bent* (1979, Royal Court; Broadway, 1979), was inspired by the Berlin episode in *As Time Goes By* and intended for Sweatshop (Griffiths encouraged Sherman to seek a larger outlet). Max and Rudy may not be an ideal couple, but they complement each other rather well. Max seems the more casual, but he passes up an opportunity to escape from Nazi Germany because Rudy can't come too. This makes it the more excruciating when Max, in order to survive, is forced to deny all knowledge of Rudi as he is mutilated and killed. After this the betrayals become systematic: because queer prisoners are the worst treated at Dachau, Max behaves appallingly to get classified as Jewish, and again to get better conditions for his new friend, Horst. Since the guards are incensed by any affection between the men, it is a triumph when Max and Horst reach orgasm by talking in the three minutes when they have to stand still. 'We did it — fucking guards, fucking camp — we did it! They're not going to kill us. We made love. We were real. We were human' (58).

Bent has proved a significant exploration of our part in a great historic oppression, and of the conditions that may promote and thwart gay love. What I have always found unsettling, beyond those matters, is the interface with sado-masochism. Sherman does not try to evade the fact that some people find Nazi iconography sexy. Wolf, whom Max has picked up at the start, is not only garbed in leather and chains, such that Max calls him his 'own little storm-trooper' (12);

Wolf *is* a storm-trooper, a few notches down from Ernst Röhm. And when Max's verbal love-making becomes 'rough', which he finds 'exciting', Horst accuses: 'You're like them. You're like the guards. You're like the Gestapo. We stopped being gentle. I watched it, when we were on the outside. People made pain and called it love' (66–7). So Max does it gently. However, while this asserts the priority of loving kindness, it cannot displace entirely the excitement of being 'just a little rough'. How, then, does this relate to the overwhelming bulk of sadistic violence in the play, which is perpetrated by the Nazis? For many of us, the crucial difference is that their violence is not consensual; however, Sherman does not propose that distinction, but one of roughness versus gentleness. Furthermore, fantasies of non-consensual violence are important to many S/Mers, and while the sadistic behaviour of the SS officers in the play is depicted by Sherman because he wants to critique it, it may be available also for a sexually arousing reading. This is not, in principle, a problem; there are uses for pornography; anyone may enjoy cheap thrills. But they are not appropriate in the context of the historical atrocities evoked in *Bent*. The concept of the human — 'We made love. We were real. We were human' — is not sufficient to stabilise this difficulty because Nazis, after all, are human too. The point is not that Sherman has written a pornographic play, but that the inability of representation to control reception becomes especially troubling in relation to such themes.[22]

Women Together

The issues facing lesbians in the 1970s were distinctively complex. The women's movement in the USA launched a campaign for legislative reform over 'reproductive rights' (contraception and abortion); on this agenda lesbians and sexuality scarcely figured. Activists soon changed that. In a series of articles and speeches lesbian feminists defined lesbianism as the way for women to abrogate their dependence on men and male power. Some women embraced 'political lesbianism' as an alternative to the tiresome routines and misunderstandings with men — which feminism had been exacerbating. In what Eve Sedgwick refers to as 'a stunningly efficacious coup of feminist redefinition', lesbianism was transformed, 'in a predominant view, from a matter of female virilization to one of woman-identification'.[23]

This did not, immediately at least, address the scope and specificity of lesbian sexuality as such. Lesbianism was taken as standing for everything that was not male-dominated, and it became difficult actually to discuss it beyond that position. 'Women-loving-women meant gentler, non-possessive, non-competitive, non-violent, nurturing and egalitarian relationships', Lynne Segal says, and gave some women the confidence 'to make changes in their relationships with men'.[24] In this context, the wish of some lesbians to structure their relationships by analogy with traditional gender roles (butch/femme) was criticised as a residue of pre-feminist self-oppression. It remained for lesbian socialist feminists such as Elizabeth Wilson to assert (in 1974) that lesbian sex was not about retreating from or combating men, nor about marking out a healthy regime of female sexual practice. Lesbians had concerns of their own.[25]

Theatre became a notable site for explorations in feminist thought. The practice of group consciousness-raising and the maxim 'the personal is the political' meshed easily with the dominant dramatic tradition, which focuses on the interactions of individual characters while pointing beyond them to wider moral and political arguments. Theatre has always produced significant images of women; the task was to revise them, sometimes by reconceiving mythic figures, such as Cinderella, Demeter and Persephone, Lilith, Lear's daughters, Aunt Jemima. To accomplish this, women had to wrest a part of the control of theatre away from men. The fringe, off-off organisation of alternative theatre suggested how independent work might be done. Companies such as It's All Right to be a Woman in New York (founded in 1969) and Monstrous Regiment in Britain (from 1975) cultivated collective decision making as a way of avoiding masculine-type power hierarchies.[26]

Dedicated lesbian companies were founded with diverse policies in the USA in the 1970s. The Lavender Cellar in Minneapolis produced revues and coming-out dramas; the Red Dyke Theatre in Atlanta sought 'to entertain lesbians and celebrate their sexuality, *not* to educate straight people about lesbians and gay issues'; Medusa's Revenge of New York aimed to explore 'a homoesthetic sensibility' with women-only audiences (this meant boldly sexual work). However, the Lesbian-Feminist Theatre Collective of Pittsburgh set out to dispel 'myths about lesbians for straight audiences'.[27] The Front Room Theater Guild in Seattle in 1980 declared itself 'dedicated to the proposition that . . . all dykes need and deserve to see their lives represented on stage; that we best know what our lives are like and that we deserve an opportunity to portray the lives we live'.[28]

Jane Chambers' plays have been widely performed at Off-Broadway, regional and community theatres. *A Late Snow* (1974) brings together a group of women who manifest varying degrees of embarrassment and commitment in their lesbianism and their personal relations. Ellie, a college professor, doesn't want people to know about her sexuality, though her partner Quincey, a sparky young student, is keen to make a stand. Ellie's position is understandable; when she was young the lesbian was invisible – 'like a vampire: she looked in the mirror and there was no reflection' (308). Pat is Ellie's former partner and is trying to get her back; she is feisty but she drinks too much and likes to stir things up. Ellie wants to get Margo, a famous, reclusive writer, to come to teach at the university, and asks the other women to conceal their lesbianism lest it deter Margo. Ellie is outed through an amusing combination of inadvertence (from Quincey) and mischief (from Pat). However, Ellie's reticence is misplaced, for Margo is bisexual and ready for a new involvement. A fifth woman arrives: Peggy, on whom Ellie had a crush in her college days. Peggy is fed up with marriage and has a new best friend, but denies that she is a lesbian. Ellie brushes her aside and makes a new bid for passion and loyalty, and openness as well. Pat doesn't give up.

There is ample testimony to the success of *A Late Snow* in illuminating women's lives. When William M. Hoffman published it in 1979 it had been produced only once; Emily Sisley lists ten performances at various venues in the following twelve months.[29] This shrewd and entertaining play perhaps succeeded because it was traditional in form. Hoffman believed it to be unique as a realistic romantic drama about lesbians.[30] Also, it develops motifs that were already in circulation, in plays such as *The Killing of Sister George* and *Boys in the Band*. In *Last Summer at Bluefish Cove* (1982) Chambers brings a heterosexual woman into a lesbian summer resort. Again, the outcome is a reassuring empowering of women, as they assert their right to personal fulfilment.

In Britain lesbian-themed work was developed in feminist contexts and in dedicated companies and venues. During 1977 Gay Sweatshop split along gender lines, with artistic autonomy for each under the one administrative umbrella; they reintegrated in 1984. *Julie* by Catherine Kilcoyne (1985, Sweatshop) takes up the situation of one of the characters who frustrated Ginny in *Any Woman Can*. Julie finds sex with women beset with difficulties, but hates herself for being drawn back into relations with men, which always become exploitative – or perhaps she likes it that way? She wants 'Love for the sake of love. / Not love for the sake of power', she declares; she finds this with another woman. Yet that relationship gives her a kind of 'strength', making her 'powerful' (43–4). Julie finds that love with a woman has given her body and her pride back to her, but it is not easy to separate that from the kind of empowerment that she is trying to escape. The clear political and personal objectives of *Any Woman Can* give way to a more sombre and fragile awareness of identity and control.

Double Vision (1982), which was devised by Libby Mason and the Women's Theatre Group, who performed it, focuses through two characters the relationships between traditional lesbians and the new women's movement. Sparky is playing pool in a gay bar when she is approached by Chum, who is recruiting for a march to demand protection for women on the streets. 'I'll protect you', Sparky volunteers, challenging Chum to an arm-wrestling contest (32). Chum, though she has tried sleeping with a couple of woman friends, has a boyfriend, but she succumbs to Sparky's witty seduction. They move in together and experience a sequence of differences, deriving from temperament and educational background and illuminating points of political principle. In Brechtian manner, *Double Vision* invites the audience to ponder alternative futures for the relationship, and hence for women. (I discuss formal aspects of *Julie* and *Double Vision* in chapter 17.)

The consequences of lesbian identification are yet more intricate and sensitive for women of colour. Jackie Kay wrote *Chiaroscuro* (1986) for the Theatre of Black Women and they performed it at various fringe venues. To Opal's surprise, she and Beth are drawn to each other; they become lovers. Aisha, meanwhile, takes things carefully with the conservative Yomi; she introduces her to a feminist, all-women disco where she sees women kissing — 'And black women at that! I didn't think we produced them' (64). When the four of them dine together Aisha wants Beth to tone down the lesbian bit because Yomi doesn't know. But Beth is upset by Yomi saying she is 'half-caste' and drops a hint about Opal talking in her sleep. Eventually Opal tells Yomi, who reacts badly: 'Don't look at me like that! As if I'm the one that's saying something terrible to you. You're the lesbian.' Yomi realises that Aisha must be a lesbian too — 'What if I am?'. Eventually Yomi is moved to recall her mother talking about 'women she used to know in Nigeria who lived with their husbands but loved each other' (76–9).

A mirror and a photograph album run through the dialogue and action: these props help Beth and Opal to work out their identities, because each of them has been brought up in a milieu where their blackness was denied. This is a pressure on their relationships as well — they seek to mirror themselves in their partners, gaining from them the recognition that is withheld in the wider culture. 'When I first met you, you were so familiar, a dream I never expected to come true. Like seeing my own reflection. I used to feel that I was the only black lesbian in the world, you know' (65–6). Finally Yomi looks critically at herself in the mirror: she will try to change.[31]

A play by the Chicana writer, Cherríe Moraga, offers another array of attitudes to women loving women, corresponding to different experiences of race and culture. In *Giving Up the Ghost* (1989, Theatre Rhinoceros, San Francisco) we see Marisa alongside her childhood self, Corky, finding her Chicana, Catholic, family at odds with other children in a neighbourhood in the Los Angeles basin. Her lesbianism is continuous with her history as a tough tomboy, as well as being influenced by white US feminists. It corresponds also to Moraga's awareness of imperialist oppression. In *Loving in the War Years* she recalls the founding myth of Malintzin Tenepal, the indigenous woman who gave herself as translator, adviser and mistress to the invading Spaniard, Hernán Cortéz: 'In the effort not to feel fucked, I became the fucker, even with women.'[32]

Marisa forms a relationship with Amalia, who is Mexican and soft where Marisa is hard; Amalia is a generation older, has relations with men and has a son. She maintains her feeling for her male lover, Alejandro: 'I loved the way he had made México my home again'. She needs to return there to feel whole (19). It is Mexico, then, and more traditional ideas of gender relations, that thwart Marisa; yet her love for Amalia is bound up with her own 'nostalgia for the land she had never seen' (17). The action culminates in Amalia's fearful dream: she crouches in terror of thunder and lightning, realising that Marisa has 'gone against the code of our people'. Yet she does not respect this visionary indictment: 'It was merely that the taboo *could* be broken' (33). Mexican and Chicana cultures have to negotiate new kinds of relation with lesbian sexuality.

A proliferation of alternative venues has been the indispensable condition for lesbian and gay theatre in the 1980s and 1990s. In London, Oval House and the Drill Hall (under the direction of Julie Parker since 1981) have been consistently available.[33] *What's Wrong with Angry?* by Patrick Wilde, for instance, went from the Lost Theatre in Fulham to the Battersea Arts Centre and then to Oval House in 1993–94; it was filmed in 1999 as *Get Real*.

In New York, Peggy Shaw and Lois Weaver started the Women's One World festivals of mainly lesbian performance in 1980, and installed this work at the WOW Café in the East Village in 1982. WOW became the launching pad for Split Britches (Shaw, Weaver and Deb Margolin) and for Holly Hughes and Sarah Schulman, and has kept an open door for new material by women.[34] Cheryl Moch first presented there *Cinderella, The Real True Story* (1985; Drill Hall, 1987). In this light-hearted reworking of the fairy tale, Cinderella and the Princess discover their love for each other and, after marvellous adventures, persuade the King that they should marry. Such an unusually genial settlement with patriarchy is perhaps suitable for a Christmas show. In her note to the printed text Moch credits the opportunity afforded by Weaver and WOW: 'The emergence, in the last ten years or so, of lesbian plays can be traced to the emergence of lesbian, feminist and gay-controlled spaces and theatre groups as well as to the playwrights' (147). And it was at WOW, according to Kate Davy, that *The Lady Dick* (1985) by Holly Hughes 'liberated lesbian and feminist theater from the "good-girl syndrome"'. Hitherto lesbian writing, typically, had 'carried either a direct or a surreptitious request for acceptance'. Hughes' characters are 'bawdy, sinister and sinful, aggressive, sexy, and dangerous – no nurturing types'.[35]

In the early and mid-century, lesbian and gay representation was to be gleaned in the margins of mainstream plays; since the 1970s it has been situated in the margins, or fringes, of theatre institutions. In fact there are two main strands in alternative theatre, as it has developed since the 1960s: avant-gardism and minority representation. Both contribute to the idea that sexuality is a kind of special interest, and/or good for us. In chapter 17 I assess the consequences of this orientation for the class and educational composition of audiences, and the scope for queer drama in mainstream theatre. First we have to consider how theatre has dealt with HIV and AIDS.

16

AIDS: Crisis and Drama

A Play with no Protagonist

That gay men were falling sick mysteriously came to notice in New York in 1981 and then in other Western cities; the virus was identified in 1984. Activists complained that no one paid any attention. When Rock Hudson died in 1985, that changed; a wave of phobic hostility followed.

The epidemic, as well as making many of us fall sick and die, transformed the sense of who we are — in our own eyes and in the eyes of others. It threw into disarray the 1970s structures through which many gay men, especially in US cities, had accommodated themselves to a largely homophobic society: abundant sex in back-rooms and bath-houses, the cosy couple, the congenial occupation, special friends, distanced relatives. It is the world of *Tales of the City* (1978), the initial volume in Armistead Maupin's series. As the nature of AIDS became apparent, the baths closed, the couple came under unanticipated stress, colleagues and friends found they had other priorities, and back home was needed after all as a place to die.

HIV and AIDS reopened the whole question of the legitimacy of gayness: it still required justification, it still hurt. In his prologue to *The Destiny of Me* (1992) Larry Kramer admits what many had already inferred — that his own attitude to AIDS and the gay community was fuelled by misgivings about 'acceptance of one's own homosexuality' (xii). In Britain too, for Gerry in Andy Kirby's *Compromised Immunity* (1985, Gay Sweatshop) it is not only the virus that requires a strong immune system: 'It took me years to build up a resistance to the way people treated me as gay and now that's as compromised as my physical immunity' (61). For while gay men are by no means the only people

314

to be devastated by AIDS, they are the group whose identifying stigma — our way of doing sex — is specific to the transmission of the virus. This is why so many plays depict it as a triumph when a sick or positive person and his partner succeed in making love in the face of HIV. Thus they repel the accusation that the virus has demonstrated gay love to be wrong.

Already before the epidemic was fully registered, Eve Sedgwick saw the task as 'not so much to redefine "the homosexual", but to assume or resume some control over the uses and consequences of historically residual definitions'.[1] This subcultural work became more urgent as the opportunity for stigmatisation was seized by right-wing media and religious institutions. 'The emergency role of gay culture is clear', Gregory Woods writes: 'The notorious volatility and inaccuracy of written responses to AIDS — notably in the press and on toilet walls — have underscored, in the eyes of those whose communities have been affected, the need for a considered and considerate literature of the crisis.'[2] In this cultural work on AIDS, theatre has been special in that almost all the significant writing has been originated by people closely involved in the epidemic. Unlike most film and television, these plays do not focus on parents at the expense of gay people, underplay the importance of sex among gay men, or pretend that people with AIDS do not get very ill in very unpleasant ways. Theatre, being relatively informal and inexpensive, has afforded important subcultural resources.

For some writers, especially at the initial impact of the epidemic, the existentialist-absurdist vision of Samuel Beckett, Eugène Ionesco and Fernando Arrabal offered the obvious dramatic model. Already it had seemed sometimes that the all-male alternations of power, intimacy and desperation in *Waiting for Godot* and *Endgame* have queer resonances. The arbitrary irruption of AIDS seemed to confirm the hostile or indifferent universe evoked by absurdist writers.

Absurdist drama flourished in the 1950s, in the shadow of the prospect of nuclear annihilation; for metropolitan gay men, AIDS has constituted a threat of that dimension. Paul Sellig's *Terminal Bar* (1983) discovers what may be the last three people in New York. The radio is broadcasting the symptoms of HIV and groups of people all over the country are dying; all the mirrors have been broken because people can't bear to see the signs of their sickness. The streets are empty except for looters and nuns 'riding around the city in a yellow schoolbus drunk outa their habits an' firebombing the neighbourhood so it'll be sterile for the Last Judgment' (49). This is not far from *Endgame*.

Lanford Wilson's powerful play *A Poster of the Cosmos* (1988) dresses Tom all in white like the clown figures of absurdist writing and seats him at a table with a tape recorder (as in *Krapp's Last Tape* by Beckett); it is not easy to discern sequence in his speech. It transpires that there are realistic reasons for all this, but the play maintains a metaphysical level of inference in its culminating report of a drinking of blood — a communion whose deathly potential is a sign of great human love. The Cosmos of the title is a football team, but the audience may feel that the play has sketched a poster image of a ghastly universe.

Other plays are formally reminiscent of Beckett's *Play*. In *Jack* (1987) by David Greenspan the lines are distributed between three performers, who speak independently and sometimes simultaneously, and are only partly visible ('ideally the image is one of floating busts': 139). We piece together the story of Jack who killed himself while suffering AIDS-related illnesses, his mother, his lover and his lover's wife and girlfriend. *Zero Positive* (1987) by Harry Kondoleon collects a bizarre bunch of characters under the threat of death from the virus; at one point they are 'as still as Beckett's characters caught in urns' (226).

Robert Chesley in *(Wild) Person, Tense (Dog)* (1990) redeploys a Pinteresque aspect of absurdism. A sinister figure lurks — 'A live ghost. Standing outside, just outside that door' (127). As in Pinter's *The Room* and *A Slight Ache*, the stranger has a mysterious connection with Dog, the man inside. He enters; he is at an advanced stage of AIDS. He demands some kind of recognition from Dog. 'I AM YOU, DOG', he says, very intensely; 'I . . . am . . . your . . . ghost' (134, Chesley's pauses). He is Dog's past — they once had great sex together; his present — a shadow of his former self; and his future — the walking-dead that he too must expect to become.

In a collection of plays on the crisis, *The Way We Live Now* (1990), the introduction by Michael Feingold draws an epigraph from Beckett's *Endgame* ('you're on earth, there's no cure for that!'), and begins:

> Imagine a play with no protagonist. The action proceeds, some characters suffer unimaginably and die, others in their wake are left bereft, crazed, numb with shock. The performance goes on, lasting days, months, years. Uncounted numbers participate. The torment continues without explanation and without letup; alleviations are found, but no solutions. The end of the performance is not yet in sight. The main character is still invisible.[3]

The epidemic is, itself, an absurdist drama.

The Therapeutic Mode

Most plays featuring AIDS are less ambitious in form and theme: they aspire to represent the human reality of the epidemic. They hope thereby to draw the attention of the wider community to the emergency and, above all, to help gay people with the (inter)personal dilemmas of bereavement, stigma, loss of health, and impending death. The main orientation is toward individual therapy.

John Clum offers *As Is* (1985) by William M. Hoffman as 'the paradigmatic AIDS drama': its characters forge new understandings of the present and the past, living through 'personal revolutions'.[4] *As Is* transferred from the Circle Repertory Company to Broadway, won awards, and was filmed for television in 1986. Rich's lover, his brother, his friend Lily, and his business partner shrink from him when his AIDS diagnosis becomes known. He is penniless and no longer able to pick up men in bars (though such men are wittily mocked as pretty limited types anyway). Only Saul, an ex-lover, wants to stand by Rich. Meanwhile, numbers of their friends succumb; the scale of the epidemic is evoked through choric sequences in which multiple voices detail their experiences. However, Saul proves staunch and Lily and the brother rally round, once they become used to the idea. Dramatically, we are close to the mode of *The Boys in the Band*: the guys josh around, playing dangerously upon the parts that hurt in others because this is their own hurt too. The necessary move, then, is to love yourself to the point where you can open yourself to the love and support that others really want to give. Finally Rich is convinced that Saul will stand by him; 'I'll take you as is', Saul promises (58). They make love in the hospital bed.

A Quiet End (1986) by Robin Swados, which has been performed in Long Beach (California), London, Amsterdam, St Louis and Off-Broadway, discloses similar motifs. Max, Billy and Tony have been placed in an apartment by an AIDS welfare agency. Their interaction enables a therapeutic testing and consolation: they discover — indeed it has really always been there — a harmony and mutual respect in the fact of their sickness and death. Tony dies after a heart-to-heart with Billy, inspiring Billy to be open with his Midwestern family: 'He refused to hide from anyone. All I've *done* is hide' (204). Max will not be alone, however. His lover Jason — they have separated because of Max's cultivation of 'distance' — will not allow him to give himself up to 'a quiet end'. 'You're asking me to open up my heart all over again', Max says (209–10). Opening up to other people is the defining mark of a worthwhile life and a good death.

Safe Sex (1987) is a formally neat piece by Harvey Fierstein in which the steadiness of the two characters is figured by their balance on a see-saw. They have to reach a point of trust where they can continue with sexual relations together. In Fierstein's *On Tidy Endings* (1987) the partner and wife of a man who has died from AIDS fence over his memory until it is revealed that she too is HIV positive. Through opening up to each other, they gain in humility and respect. Even the young son is cajoled into admitting his love for his deceased father's partner. *Brave Hearts* (1991) by Canadian playwright Harry Rintoul has G.W. cruising Rafe for the entire action, only to back off at the last moment because he is experiencing opportunist infections. 'I don't want you hanging around, gettin' involved, and I don't need it − falling in love with you again. . . . Don't. Don't touch me' (268). However, Rafe won't take no for an answer; G.W. falls into his arms.

The therapeutic orientation of these plays is often explicit. Often five stages of trauma management are invoked: denial, anger, bargaining, depression, acceptance. The conversation between the men in *A Quiet End* is cut in with sessions with the therapist who has been assigned to them; after the death of Max, the play concludes with Jason sharing his experience with the analyst. So committed is Hoffman to therapy that he gives the first and last speeches of *As Is* not to gay men or people with AIDS, so as to signify how they may control their own lives, but to a Christian hospice worker. She channels Rich's experience into the five-stage therapy routine, and even appeals, albeit ruefully, to God.

Kirby's *Compromised Immunity* shows Gerry coming to terms with his condition partly through the ministrations of Peter, a nurse. In *Tell* (1991) by Victor Bumbalo the Visitor (male) is 'reminding' the Man in hospital by telling of a sexual encounter; the Nurse (female) gets in the way. But when the Visitor is out of town the Nurse reminds the Man by massaging him and recounting her own experience; so don't underestimate your supporters. Colin Thomas (another Canadian) has Jim addressing his therapy group, i.e. the audience, in *Flesh and Blood* (1991).

Although the person with AIDS is urged to trust his supporters, survival comes down finally, it is often suggested, to his own will to live. Larry Kramer in *The Normal Heart* (1985) has Ned accuse Felix, when he can't take food, of wanting to die (80). I am suspicious of this idea; it is bad enough being ill, without being told it is your own fault for not committing yourself to 'life'. In a key episode in *As Is* Rich asks Saul to collect pills so that he can take his own life when things get too bad. To my mind that is a reasonable proposal, but the play makes them both reject it on vaguely religious grounds: 'A phrase came to my head: "The Lord taketh and the Lord giveth"' (58).

In their determination to make their writing valuable for people involved with AIDS, dramatists and others can hardly avoid implying that there is a proper way to cope, and that people who take other approaches are doing it 'wrong'. In *Andre's Mother* (1988) by Terrence McNally the mourners for Andre are expected to 'let go' and release their balloons. But Andre's mother is reluctant, she has been 'almost anonymous in her remoteness'; she is not one to open up. This, the text implies, is bad. 'I wish I knew what you were thinking. I think it would help me', says Cal, Andre's lover. But she remains unresponsive; 'even now, after all this. I can't reach you. I'm beginning to feel your disapproval and it's making me ill', Cal accuses (192–3). Eventually, after Cal has given up on her, Andre's mother does release her balloon. At last, the text suggests, she is getting it right.

A well-intentioned orthodoxy is still an orthodoxy, as some playwrights indicate. 'Must one go through the five official stages?' Robin demands in Robert Patrick's *Pouf Positive* (1987). He substitutes his own: 'Flippancy, sentimentality, sarcasm, camp, and smut' (209). Thomas in *Flesh and Blood* allows us to see how well-meaning support may amount to coercion. 'People live because they want to live', Ralph declares when Jim tests positive. But it is Ralph, evidently, who needs to believe this: 'You better live. You better want to live, goddamit. 'Cause this isn't just your little life, alright? You're my other half' (292). In fact Jim partly resists Ralph's ministrations, insisting that it is his relationship with his younger brother that he wants to work on.

Thomas Yingling writes of 'what we must call a boom industry' in 'spiritual solutions' to AIDS, as exemplified in the best-selling books of Louise Hay. The probable cause of AIDS, Hay says, is 'Feeling defenseless and hopeless. Nobody cares. A strong belief in not being good enough. Denial of the self. Sexual guilt.' And the healing thought pattern to be adopted is: 'I am part of the Universal design. I am important and I am loved by Life itself. I am powerful and capable. I love and appreciate all of myself.'[5] McNally is on this track in *Love! Valour! Compassion!* (1994). 'We don't love one another because we don't love ourselves', Ramon says (54); he is destined for success as a dancer. The simplest kind of achievement for most of the men involves dressing up in tutus and dancing in public a piece from *Swan Lake*, in order to raise money for AIDS charities. Meanwhile, extremes of (in)ability to give oneself in love are marked out by the twin brothers John and James Jeckyll (Mr Hyde is implicit). John tries but can't change; 'No one mourned me. Not one tear was shed' (139).

But James, who is dying of AIDS, is granted a late romance. 'He's gorgeous and he's a saint', says Buzz, who is also sick (141). James, it seems, has 'the secret of unconditional love'; 'Only God is unconditional love' (124–5, 87).

Partners of positive-testing men also come under pressure to do the right thing. 'So what the fuck is the matter with me?' Louis exclaims in Tony Kushner's *Angels in America Part 1: Millennium Approaches* (1991), when he finds that he can't cope with Prior's condition. 'You can love someone and fail them. You can love someone and not be able to . . .' (36, 58, Kushner's pause). Louis eventually changes his mind, accomplishing a growth in personal maturity. The eponymous protagonist in Paul Rudnick's *Jeffrey* (1992) is too fearful to take as a lover a man who has tested positive, but his friends assert that he is under an obligation − to gayness and humanity − to reorient himself. He becomes a 'good' member of the community when he changes his stance. Of course the relations between positive- and negative-testing men need cultural work, but the answer does not lie in shaming nervous people.

Christopher Durang in *Laughing Wild* (1987) throws a caustic slant on the therapeutic mode. To enable him to 'see the positive', Man is attending a 'personality workshop' (171). He has note-cards to help him: 'I am the predominant source of my life. I release anger from my solar plexus. It is replaced by serenity and white light and joy and . . . serenity. Everything in my life works. Except the plumbing and career and relationships' (176, Durang's pause). So far from discovering God in himself, Man challenges the deity to justify his capricious disposition of suffering. So he hates homosexuals − and haemophiliacs and Haitians? 'Anything beginning with the letter H' (182).

Catharsis vs. Politics

It has been believed since Aristotle that profound dramatic experiences may induce catharsis − a spiritual purging − in the audience. This idea overlaps with the therapeutic treatments offered to people experiencing trauma, sickness and bereavement.

Many of the plays I have mentioned come with pronouncements by the writer about the personal truth of the action; the idea is to guarantee the authenticity of the situations and emotions. In one scene of *As Is* we get a sequence of names of people whose memorial services have occurred; the names correspond to those of the forty people to whose memory the playtext is dedicated. David Drake prints with his monologue *The Night Larry Kramer*

Kissed Me (1992) a glossary of the real-world people, places and organisations referred to. The monologue is a favoured form partly because it aspires to close the gap between the writer and the performance, alleging total sincerity. Clum calls the one-person show 'the ideal form for the age of identity politics'.[6]

As Brecht argued, cathartic plays, especially insofar as they invite identification with a leading 'character' and his (occasionally her) fate, tend to encourage individual adjustment to the system, rather than criticism of it and organisation against it. The five stages of therapy conclude with 'acceptance'. Catharsis, and the therapeutic mode, tend to obscure the need for political change, and for a collective approach to its pursuit.

For instance, difficulties in obtaining healthcare in the USA are noticed in therapeutic plays as they affect individuals. Rich in *As Is* finds that his insurance doesn't cover him: 'They're pulling a fast one' (30). Tony in *A Quiet End* has to wait for an ambulance while they check whether he is insured (201). Buzz in *Love! Valour! Compassion!* calls it 'not fair' that there are 'healthy people with healthy lovers in nice apartments with lots of health insurance' (131–2). However, in none of these instances is there any further consideration of the ideology and the business interests that make collective health provision appear unAmerican. Emma in Larry Kramer's *The Normal Heart* takes the point a bit further: 'Do you know this is the only country in the industrialised world besides South Africa that doesn't guarantee health care for everyone?' (8). Yet, here too, there is no follow-up analysis. Individual problems seem to require individual solutions, and there seems to be no place for the assessment of power structures and public policy.

As we move into the topic of AIDS and politics, the prominence of *The Normal Heart* makes it the text that has to be addressed. It traces the early years of the epidemic (1981–84), and the attempts of activists, especially Ned Weeks, to get the attention of gay men and support from the mayor of New York and the media. Meanwhile new cases are reported at the rate of thirty a week in the city, and lovers, friends and acquaintance die in dozens.

As commentators have pointed out, Ned's analysis is undermined by his inability to endorse gay men as they currently are.[7] He is obsessed with the approval of straight society - the mayor, the *New York Times*, his brother Ben. He colludes in the notion that straight-acting role models should spearhead the campaign, and agrees with Ben that gays shouldn't be pictured in leather and chains. He fails to notice that his movement is dominated by white and upper-middle-class men. He thinks we need to be justified by a list of historic culture heroes ('Proust, Henry James, Tchaikovsky, Cole Porter, Plato . . .': 76–7).

He doesn't want to be 'considered different', any more than the conservative Bruce. 'You've got to say it. I'm the same as you. Just say it. Say it!' he demands of his brother Ben (26, 37). He blames gays for promiscuity and for not forming pseudo-marriages: 'the gay leaders who created this sexual-liberation philosophy in the first place have been the death of us' (51; already in 1978 Kramer's novel *Faggots* was alleging that gay lifestyles were asking for trouble). When Ned 'marries' the dying Felix, the witnesses are Ben and Emma, the straight doctor. The play doesn't take the opportunity to announce the principles of safer sex, though by the time it was produced this was certainly the message that had to be communicated.

What passes for politics here, and in some other writing on AIDS, is little more than casting round for someone to blame. Dennis Altman has noted the dominance in US ideology of 'a particular moralistic view that depicts AIDS as a disease of modern decadence, for which both homosexuality and America itself can stand as convenient symbols'.[8] Reacting against this view has led much gay thinking on AIDS into a recriminatory stance, whereby culpability is turned back upon the system that blames us. Drake, in his introduction to *The Night Larry Kramer Kissed Me*, writes of the virus itself as 'the outgrowth of a hatred that informs the care of queer people's health. Active homophobia created AIDS' (xiv). This idea appears also in the first monologue in Michael Kearns' sequence *Intimacies/More Intimacies* (1989–90): 'We have been poisoned by something but not bodily fluids. We have been poisoned by hate, hate from moms and dads and uncles and aunts and priests and nuns and school systems and mayors and the Moral Fucking Majority and Miss Jesse Helms and Calvin Klein underwear and the Reagan Fucking Administration. Bodily fluids gave me life, honey. Hatred is what's killin' me' (241).

It may be that ideas such as Ned's were necessary to fuel Kramer's activism, inspiring him to found Gay Men's Health Crisis and ACT UP. Ned in *The Normal Heart* does challenge gay orthodoxy by calling on us to blame ourselves. He complains that activists pull their punches because they are afraid of being identified as gay, that wealthy and prominent gays do nothing to help the rest, and that gay men generally will not stop having sex while a remedy is discovered. But *The Normal Heart* blames the system rather than critiquing it − hence the obsession with the mayor and the president.

And hence the linking of AIDS to the Holocaust which was inflicted upon the Jewish people by the Nazis and their allies in the 1930s and 1940s. At least we can see who is to blame for that. But, as Stuart Marshall and Michael Sherry have argued, this is to substitute gesture for analysis.[9] The principled malignancy of Fascism is not the same as the casual indifference of governing elites; which, after all, is visited as a matter of course upon many other groups who are not strong enough to stand up against the system — the poor, the elderly, the sick, the unemployed, the homeless, racial minorities. Why should regimes that bomb civilian populations because of dislike for rulers have any qualms about leaving people with AIDS to suffer? That's not Fascism, it's President George Bush's 'new world order'. Certainly the system doesn't care whether gay men die prematurely and in pain, but if we produce enough political pressure it may have to be seen to be doing something. Activists are on the right track, therefore (whereas in a Fascist state they would not be tolerated).

The fact is, although the characters in the plays discussed here are outlaws in that they are gay, in other respects almost all of them are notably privileged — white, male, affluent, professional, metropolitan. (A Hispanic hospital worker has a small part in *As Is*, but none of the principals reflects that he too might be in a high-risk group.) These men have no tradition of political dissidence. They had not expected to need the State, and when they do they cannot quite believe that it is not on their side. In *Love! Valour! Compassion!* the men hear a gay demonstration being violently broken up — 'They've always hated us. It never ends, the fucking hatred' (107). But it is at a safe distance, in Seattle, on the television. When Mickey in *The Normal Heart* gives voice to suspicions which challenge US democratic ideology — suggesting that the virus may have originated as a military experiment — he is quickly declared to be having a breakdown and hustled out of the action (67–8). In 1995, in an interview with Lisa Power, Kramer says that lately he has been 'accepting and facing . . . that all these myths I have swallowed about humanity and America and "one voice can make a difference" — these things that we're all taught, that democracy works and all — turn out to be bullshit when you're gay or you have AIDS or are a member of a minority or whatever the reason'. 'That was a surprise?' Power asks.[10]

In his preface to *The Destiny of Me* (1992) Kramer wonders why he was so determined to get this play produced. 'For blame? For catharsis?' (xiii). Ultimately, Ned and Kramer, despite all the calls for action, remain within the therapeutic mode (they both talk a lot about their analysts). *The Normal Heart* works towards a very traditional closure, accomplished through the deathbed marriage of Felix and Ned, and the reconciliation with Ben. Thus the action seems complete, encouraging the cathartic inference that further action would be inappropriate. Despite its political pitch, *The Normal Heart* tends always to pose issues as (inter)personal dilemmas. We are offered as the moral lines through which W.H. Auden announced his retreat from socialism: 'the normal heart' in each of us craves 'Not universal love / But to be loved alone' (84). This proposition makes the failure of collective projects, such as the gay movement, appear inevitable.

Sue Ellis and Paul Heritage condemn the tendency of *The Normal Heart* 'to transcend its own political location by inducing an emotional overload in the audience'. They compare *We All Fall Down* (1986) by Principal Parts, a radical Swansea group, which is 'deliberately fragmentary and open-ended' and offers 'no conclusive ending'.[11] Some other dramatists draw attention to the constructedness of their own discourse and of the discourse of AIDS. Robin in Patrick's *Pouf Positive* undermines the conventional authority of the monologue when he issues instructions for his funeral: 'And I don't want you reading any of your crappy monologues, / Or mine.' He adds: 'If you have to do something, write me a funny AIDS play' (205, 212). Patrick confirms in his preface that this is the play we are in fact seeing, claiming a playful rather than an authentic self, and asserting his independence from therapeutic routines (xvii). In Guillermo Reyes' *Men on the Verge of a His-panic Breakdown* (1994) La Gitana's monologue is spoken largely in the third person while she dons her flamenco drag; as when the Pope is robed in Brecht's *Galileo*, we see her become her role. 'She is ready now to take her place among the immortals. "Bring me the castanets", she demands. "They'll cover some of the lesions on the hands!"' Tonight 'La Gitana *insists* — as her ancestors did — to perform until that final moment, that grand moment when the last breath passes through her ruby red lips' (421–2). Her race, her gender identity and her impending death are parts of her act.

I pursue in the next chapter the strategic issue of how far distancing stage techniques are more effective politically. In the remainder of this section I want to discuss three plays which place AIDS in a political context by standing back from the immediate experiential details of the epidemic.

Robert Chesley in *Night Sweat* (1984) shows gay men committing themselves to the Coup de Grâce Club, where it is arranged for them to die in the course of their ultimate sexual scenario, rather than endure the later stages of AIDS-related illnesses. We see Ratman and Bobin up against a monstrous opponent, card-players cutting the pack to see who will be murdered tonight, Lucia di Lammermoor killing herself. The tone thus far, as I read it, is grotesque but not sinister: we might think that we are witnessing the logical conclusion of the excesses of the 1970s scene, or that these men are making a creative response to impending sickness and death. However, the Club is not right for Richard, who finds himself unable to relinquish loving feelings — for Tom whom he meets there, and Allan his former lover. Allan accuses the Director of profiting from death: 'Well', he replies, 'some would say that's what capitalism is all about' (53).

The next scenario features the owner of a gay disco and bathhouse who is tortured into confessing to 'crimes against nature and humanity' — striving for 'the American Dream of Success' and becoming rich through corrupt business practices which have proved fatal to the gay patrons of his establishment. 'I sold you *all* down the river! Because you *deserve* to die, faggots! . . . I chose the money! 'Cause money is a bigger and harder dick than you've ever seen!' (56–7). The exploitation of gay men is part of the exploitation of capitalism.

As in therapeutic texts, Richard has to learn to accept love and opt for life. 'Live until the very *moment* you die!' Tom tells him. 'And make love! Make love in every possible, safe and sensible way! Enjoy it all, from the most delicate cruising to the heaviest S and M trips!' (66). This conclusion is saved from mawkishness by the fact that Richard is not required to choose between Allan and Tom as loving partners, and by the final unmitigated terror of (disco) Bunny in the face of death.

Chesley's *Jerker, or the Helping Hand* (1986) features the pleasures of phone sex; Bert and J.R. also talk intimately about other parts of their lives. Nor is this (just) a resort for the time of AIDS, when touching can be dangerous. We may infer that J.R. gets more sex through anonymity because he uses crutches after being wounded in the US attempt to occupy Vietnam. From his war experience he 'learned what "immoral" means. And that's why nobody but nobody tells me I'm immoral if I love a man' (99). Again, the trials of gay men and AIDS are placed in a wider context. In the concluding scenes J.R. leaves Bert messages of love, but he doesn't pick up the phone, for the reason we can all guess.

Paula Vogel indicates that her play *The Baltimore Waltz* (1990) is about a last journey to Europe which she and her brother thought of taking before his death from AIDS. But she constitutes the main action as a fantasy. Anna is diagnosed with ATD — Acquired Toilet Disease; elementary schoolteachers are specially at risk. Since you can't transmit it through sex, she sets off for an orgy in attractive European cities with her gay brother Carl, who hopes to find new treatments for her in Vienna. In fact, the slides of their trip reveal that they never got far from the Johns Hopkins Hospital and the urban desolation of Baltimore. Setting the action at a distance from the AIDS crisis enables Vogel to comment on some familiar tropes. For instance, in coming to terms with her illness Anna passes briskly through the recommended stages (denial, anger, bargaining, depression, acceptance) but makes two less compliant additions: hope and lust. A sense that researchers and drug companies are motivated by political and economic agendas is conveyed when the purveyor of a new drug turns out to be the unscrupulous Harry Lime played by Orson Welles in *The Third Man*, and the doctor exhibits the peculiarity of Dr Strangelove from Stanley Kubrick's ominous film — his right hand cannot prevent his left hand from groping for the urine he craves to drink. At the end it is Carl who is dead, but perhaps he and Anna can waltz off together, in fantasy.

British Aids

The reader may have noticed that almost all the plays I have discussed derive from the USA, with a couple from Canada. Ian Lucas remarks that British theatre 'has made a very poor response to the subject and challenge of AIDS. Mainstream theatre has largely ignored the "problem", heterosexualised the context in order to make it more "universal" (commercial), or allowed us the honour of viewing imported (mainly American) plays.'[12] He notes two main exceptions (his book came out in 1994): Andy Kirby's *Compromised Immunity*, which I have referred to, and *Anti Body* (1983) by Louise Kelley, produced by Consenting Adults in Public, which Lucas describes as a thoughtful and campaigning account of the consequences of a man's diagnosis. There are other instances, but not very many.

The point is partly that British lesbian and gay activists tend to locate themselves within a broad-left political awareness, and therefore are more likely to present the epidemic in a wider context, rather than in 'an AIDS play' as such. Noël Greig presents *Plague of Innocence* (1988, Sheffield), his play for schools, as a response to 'the terrible times we lived through in the eighties: the jingoism of the Falklands, the real fear of nuclear annihilation, police battalions attacking mining communities, the catastrophe of AIDS' (144). Then there was the Section 28 legislation (1988), which sought to place unique restrictions upon lesbian and gay cultural expression, marking a startling setback in what had seemed to be a gradual improvement in civil rights. Greig sets his play in a future police state in which the compulsory testing of (alleged) 'potential victims of HIV' has led to a general quarantine of dissidents and 'anyone / who didn't fit' (120–1).

The wider political context of the 1980s is evoked also in Neil Bartlett's *Vision of Love Revealed in Sleep* (1989), which was presented by Gloria, Bartlett's company. This play is shot through with the fear, shame and tenacity of what Bartlett recalls as 'a very specific time':

> The thing I remember most about that time is an unbelievable kind of daily hatred. You couldn't walk down the street or open a newspaper without flinching, because there would be some new graffito about AIDS – on the wall or as a headline in the best selling newspaper. . . . People that I loved were falling and I had to be ready to catch them; and the disasters of the past which I was attempting to rescue and recuperate were running parallel with disasters in the future.[13]

Bartlett's response is to reassert gay history and subculture by memorialising the Victorian painter Simeon Solomon and acclaiming the courage and initiative of drag artistes. Bette Bourne: 'You dress for hours, the whole thing's done by hand, you spend at least half an hour putting on your face and then you sit down and have a really good cry. You let yourself go' (*A Vision of Love*, 104).

Other plays focus on interpersonal relations but, with the exception of *Compromised Immunity*, tend to be distinctly thin on consolation, winning only a degree of therapeutic growth and acceptance, and only at considerable expense. Billy Lawrence's *The Show Must Go On* (1990, Brighton, revised as *You'll Never Walk Alone*, 1990) installs maximum aggression by setting a camp gay man and an angry and vengeful straight football supporter in adjacent beds in an AIDS hospice. However, the two men do move towards each other. *In One Take* (1994), one of John Roman Baker's plays for the AIDS Positive Underground Theatre of Brighton, finds Jake caring for his ex-lover, Thomas, but unable to resist bringing a new lover into the house. The rough, experienced and insecure Cal functions as a catalyst, sadistically forcing Jake to admit his repugnance from AIDS and from Thomas. Say 'you are disgusted by it, and by him', Cal demands (42); he torments Thomas by flaunting his control over Jake. Jake and Thomas reach a new under-standing, but Cal also is sick, probably with AIDS, and has no personal resources for dealing with it. Gay Sweatshop presented Carl Miller's *The Last Enemy* (1991), in which a group of individuals have to confront various forms of death – leukaemia, cancer and cot death as well as AIDS – and a dramatisation by Malcolm Sutherland of Dale Peck's violent and distressing novel, *Fucking Martin* (1994).

The most successful British play centred upon HIV and AIDS (at the time of writing) is Kevin Elyot's *My Night with Reg* (1994), which has been acclaimed for its humour and humanity by critics. It transferred from the Royal Court to the West End, and was filmed for BBC Television. The tone is set by the shy and nervous Guy: 'He won't look at pornography without a condom over his head.' He nurses an unspoken romantic attachment to an old college friend, John, and gets by on phone sex with a man who wants to be housetrained like a dog ('I do hear a lot of panting and he has been known to let out the occasional bark': 23). On holiday Guy gets assaulted by a man who uses no protection. John is wealthy and attractive and has no trouble finding partners, but he lacks the courage and integrity to tell Daniel, his best friend, that he's been having an affair with Reg, Daniel's partner. When Reg dies of AIDS-related illnesses, Bernie and Benny (who are already rocky as a couple) also admit to having slept secretly with him, and without taking precautions. So by the end everyone is either dead or in bad faith and very frightened; insofar as anyone begins to open up, it gets them nowhere. This may well be a purposefully unAmerican, unheroic version of AIDS — wry and understated, furtive and thwarted, class-conscious, and virtually without uplift.

The key reason for the relatively muted British theatrical response to HIV and AIDS is that the experience here has been different. This is a sensitive matter, but because I have written about it in *Gay and After* I deal briskly with it now.[14] We have heard in Britain with horror and fear of US men nursing lovers and a sequence of friends and attending a dozen funerals in fewer months. Canadian cities seem to be comparable. 'It's like a tidal wave, you know. Sometimes I wonder if there's going to be anybody left. You know my biggest fear? That I'm gonna be the last faggot' — so *Flesh and Blood* by Colin Thomas (290). But relatively few Britons have undergone such an ordeal; mainly those in sensitive occupations and with friends in North America. There is a different density in UK experience, chiefly because the initial transmission of HIV was slower and later. We had not developed, or been allowed to have, bath-houses and back-rooms, so knowledge about safer sex arrived in time to hinder the rate of infection. Edward King establishes this in his book, *Safety in Numbers*.[15] Several British friends have remarked to me, in a rather baffled manner, that they have suffered more personal losses from cancer than from AIDS.

Meanwhile, virtually all the US plays considered in this chapter have been performed in Britain, and some have appeared as films and on television. Jonathan Larson's musical *Rent* (1996) has brought into the West End the New

York (East Village) version of HIV and AIDS as comparable to tuberculosis in Puccini's *La Bohème*. As with so much of the metropolitan imagery of gayness — blue-jeans and T-shirts, short hair and moustaches — we have been getting our stories about AIDS from the USA. We have adopted candlelit vigils, quilting, buddying and photo-obituaries, none of which has much historic resonance in Britain. We have imagined that the US experience has been ours. We have not been writing AIDS drama because it has been done for us.

Except that it hasn't — the plays have not been about UK experience. This is dangerous. Because the fiction and drama of AIDS have drawn British gays vicariously and powerfully, into North American experience, we may be tempted to believe that we have passed through the crisis. Those of us who are older and uninfected may feel that it was not so hard to survive; those who are younger may regard it as over and done with. We may start to believe that it will be all right whatever we do, or if we relax just a bit. Such complacency is reinforced by protease inhibitors and other new treatments, which allow us to hope for indefinite remission. But they are difficult to manage, have nasty side effects and appear not to work for everyone. As the British epidemic continues — and it is continuing — we have few first-hand imaginative and intellectual resources to meet it.

17

Dissident Strategies

The larger part of this book has been concerned with the scope of theatre in the pre-Stonewall era — the period of ambiguity, discretion and innuendo. A key aspect of the argument has been that a lot more queerness was produced in theatre than has been properly registered, so some consideration of virtually all the relevant plays I have been able to uncover has seemed appropriate. After the mid-1970s the game changes entirely: indirection is hardly required, and there is a great burgeoning of material. At the same time, the level of theoretical debate becomes very much higher. In this chapter, therefore, I select symptomatic plays and institutional contexts, seeking to elucidate how the current options for theatre work were installed in the 1980s, and to comment on the continuing scope for those options at the turn of the century.

Realism and Camp

An enduring role for lesbian and gay writers is to establish and explore the reality of their lives. In the mid-1970s this produced a phase of social realist and agitprop playwriting in Britain, especially among women's companies. The publicity leaflet for the Gay Sweatshop production, *Care and Control* (1977), scripted by Michelene Wandor out of materials collected by the cast, explained that the play was drawn from the actual experiences of women who had to fight for custody of their children. The first act shows three marriages breaking up as the man pursues his own interests while the woman, with the support of the women's movement, discovers her own path in life and gives priority to her child. In the second act the three custody cases come to court, and in two of them the mother's lesbian partner is taken into account during the adjudication. Scenes between the women and between the women and their husbands are realistic, while officials read from authoritative sources or interrogate in a formal manner; slides of the women with their children are shown. The husbands are selfish and violent, and authority figures reveal blatant prejudice, so the atmosphere is generally rather grim. However, when Carol is asked whether she and Sue leave 'appliances' lying around the house, she replies, 'Well, we've got an electric toaster, but it's broken, so we use the grill' (106).

The goal, Wandor says, was 'showing hitherto suppressed lesbian experience as it really is'.[1] This goal remains pertinent. In *Supporting Roles* (1988, Oval House) Sandra Freeman brought into representation older women who were barely figuring in lesbian iconography — established couples who hardly thought of their lesbianism as exceptional any more.[2] It is a middle-aged, menopausal crisis that disturbs their equilibrium. In fact, as much as on their partners, these women depend on a network of lesbian friends — including Rick, a wise elderly woman. 'But we're not ordinary couples', she insists. 'Last thing I ever wanted, to be part of an ordinary couple' (74). In *Ladies of the Vale* (1988, Oval House) Freeman takes up the story of Eleanor Butler and Sarah Ponsonby, two upper-class Irish women who eloped together and set up house in the North Wales village of Llangollen. Freeman challenges any sentimental notion that a lesbian relationship was somehow simpler and more acceptable in 1800, both between the women and in their relations with the world.[3] They arouse suspicion, partly because of their imperious attitude toward the local people, partly because of 'the way they live together, the way they are together' (6). Such themes may resonate for queer couples who relocate to a rural setting.

Although *Supporting Roles* and *Ladies of the Vale* differ in style from *Care and Control*, they are alike in offering a version of social reality for the reader to identify with. Wandor notes that in *Care and Control* a 'sense of recognition from audiences was a consistent part of the response during the time we performed the play'; Freeman says that in *Supporting Roles* 'the appeal for recognition from the audience was strong'.[4] Thus, in terms of the quest for the 'right' artistic form which had dominated Marxist cultural theory in mid-century, both are closer to Georg Lukács' call for 'social realism' than to the distanced, denaturalised mode championed by Bertolt Brecht.

The political value of a Brechtian approach was re-argued by Colin MacCabe in the 1970s, mainly in relation to film, and by Catherine Belsey in relation to fiction.[5] If the most powerful strategy of ideology is making its dispositions appear natural, the theory runs, then the project of a dissident theatre must be to *de*naturalise, mainly by disrupting any prospect of realistic stage illusion. Audiences may be drawn in to the performance but they must also be distanced from it. What we perceive as reality must be presented not as the way things *are*, but as an ideological arrangement operating mainly in the interest of the prevailing power structure. Even the individual human subject must be *decentred* – shown to be contingent upon social organisation, rather than the source of truth and meaning. In Catherine Kilcoyne's *Julie* (discussed in chapter 15) the protagonist, under pressure from the demands of the people around her, produces alternative versions of her story. Also, while the published text shows her winning through to a promising lesbian relationship, we are told that the scenes may be played in different sequences. There is no single, necessary outcome to her predicament.

If this dissolution of the subject sounds postmodern, the difference is that a Brechtian approach looks for ways, not just to present a complex reality, but to change it (the most toxic slogan produced in the Thatcher–Reagan years was 'There is no alternative'). At the end of Brecht's *Good Person of Szechwan* – in which the subordination of the individual to the economic system is figured by a gender switch – the audience is invited to ponder diverse resolutions for the play: 'But what would you suggest? / What is your answer? Nothing's been arranged' (311). In *Double Vision* (discussed in chapter 15) Libby Mason and the Women's Theatre Group adapt this approach to the prospects for feminism. The action is placed by comments from a narrator, who offers three possible and plausible endings. Sparky and Chum may become different people, according to how they and other feminists pursue their political objectives. Brecht is invoked in a feminist theoretical context by Jill Dolan and Elin Diamond; Alisa Solomon argues against commentators who have believed that the deployment of gender in *The Good Person of Szechwan* depends on biological essentialism.[6]

Brechtian theory has obvious connections with the Foucauldian principle that sexualities are constructed rather than essential. The queer potential of this theory was seized on by Jonathan Dollimore, who in *Radical Tragedy* (1974) applied Brechtian concepts to Renaissance drama and credited *The Revenger's Tragedy* (1606) by Cyril Tourneur with 'black camp'. In an essay published in 1983 Dollimore described Orton's mode in *What the Butler Saw* as 'a kind of delinquent or black camp' which refuses 'the authentic self, the repressed human essence' and insists on 'the arbitrariness and narrowness of gender roles' – such that 'sexuality, like language, becomes decentred and therefore radically contingent'.[7] In another essay, Dollimore contrasts the strategies of Gide and Wilde. The former asserts the naturalness and authenticity of queer relations, seeking to reverse the usual notion of what is 'natural'. The latter, like Orton, validates the artificial, the non-natural, the insincere, so that we may see that sexual relations are not essentially thus or thus, but are contingent — founded in manners, convention, custom, ideology, power. There may be political value in both these strategies, Dollimore argues.[8]

As I said in chapter 14, I am not persuaded that *What the Butler Saw* is radical in the way Dollimore suggests. And in chapter 10 I queried David Savran's application of Brechtian concepts to Tennessee Williams. However we assess these cases, they do not disqualify the Brechtian argument in principle. The most acclaimed play in this vein is *Cloud Nine* (1979, Joint Stock), in which Caryl Churchill cross-dresses her characters in order to suggest the constructedness and malleability of their gendering. Probably this works; the success of *Cloud Nine* is due also to the shrewdness with which British imperialist relations are satirised, and to the charm with which its modern characters negotiate their choices. It is quite hard to see now where such optimism came from.

The project of using camp and drag to disturb the sex/gender system materialised in Off Off-Broadway theatre in the later 1960s in and around the Playhouse of the Ridiculous, with which John Vaccaro, Charles Ludlam and Ronald Tavel were associated (see chapter 15). Ronald Tavel's *Gorilla Queen* (1967) was an Off Off-Broadway success. Distancing devices include allusions to films such as David O. Selznick's *King Kong*; 'Gee, it's jist like i the movies. The "B" features' (204). Characters remark that they have seen the play before and know how it is going to end; and of course everyone knows about Queen Kong — 'It's printed in the program credits' (192). The decentring impetus behind the writing is made explicit: 'I am Clyde Batty, the *great* Clyde Batty, by Hollywood given the jurisdiction to corner, capture, and round up all — to cage, categorize, and define!' (227). Stable categories are what the play is designed to challenge: 'Male! man! female! king! queen! human! animal! ape! — what are these terms except expedient, comforting designations?' (195).

Batty's obsession with ordering is thwarted by the refusal of the action to settle to one level of reality, and by the perverse gendering of the performers. Mais Ouis is a very effeminate man, played by an actress; Taharahnugi White Woman is played by 'a brownskin male actor, ravishing in a tight white sarong and wig of long raven hair; bare footed with ankle bracelets, huge round falsies, thick lipstick, and long lashes' (185). Sister Carries, the witch doctor, is a male actor in a grass skirt and a nun's head-dress. A male actor plays Queen Kong also; his manner alternates between threatening and limp-wristed. These figures make sexual advances to each other indiscriminately and fervently. At one of the climaxes of the action (and climaxes are distributed wantonly), Taharah's sarong is pulled down and he is revealed as flat-chested, to the dismay of the others. He complains: 'What's wrong wit all you guys?! Ain't cha never seen a naked white woman before??!! . . . A figger ain't eferthink. A man who's really a man can appreciate a woman for her mental development, her culture, her talents, etc.' (236).

The final gestures of *Gorilla Queen* are a shotgun wedding of 'man and wife, or man and man, or ape and man, or queen and woman, or queen and man, or queen and queen, or ape and ape up and up'; a chorus inviting everyone in the theatre to 'bend right over'; and a refutation: 'Forget dem dirty-minded fakes: art ain't never 'bout life, but life *is* only 'bout art' (252–4).

Whether Brecht would have recognised a continuation of his kind of project in the Playhouse of the Ridiculous is a question; the line back has became pretty attenuated. But this is not a factor unique to lesbian and gay work: as 'Brechtian' principles have entered into the actual stage practice of new times, places and politics they have cross-fertilised with other modes – Artaudian attempts to lay bare the audience's (supposed) repressions, music hall, Sixties zaniness, television documentary.

Recently the idea of radical potential in camp and drag has derived new theoretical authority from Judith Butler's argument that all gender is 'performative – that is, constituting the identity it is purporting to be'. We do not act out the gender that we are; we become gendered persons through actions. 'In this sense, gender is always a doing, though not a doing by a subject who might be said to preexist the deed.'[9] Drag, then, may add a distinctive self-consciousness, drawing attention to the customary performance. 'In imitating gender, drag implicitly reveals the imitative structure of gender itself – as well as its contingency' (137). These arguments have helped to inspire the use of camp and drag in protest actions by ACT-UP, Lesbian Avengers and OutRage! Ian Lucas describes a demonstration outside Bow Street police station in London, where the officiousness of the police was rendered ridiculous by 'pretty policemen' in parody uniforms, feather boas and make-up, while the proximity of Covent Garden opera house and its customers made the event even more perversely theatrical.[10]

Camp and drag have been accused of misogyny, for instance by Carole-Anne Tyler.[11] This charge cannot simply be set aside. In *Gay and After* I write about Harvey Fierstein's *Torch Song Trilogy*, pointing out how, for the emotional and political survival of Arnold and gay men, Arnold has to have the best lines.[12] He has to prevail in the argument with his mother. And if he is to win Ed, it follows that Laurel, Ed's girlfriend, must lose him. Further: Arnold doesn't just take the man from Laurel, he takes 'the feminine'. He speaks in the manner of Bette Davis, Blanche DuBois and Mae West, and commandeers the torch-song stance of bravely suffering and waiting for his man; it is Arnold who has a son, to whom he is 'Ma'. His gay triumph is, almost inevitably, at the expense of women. I conclude that there is no magic wand for this; we just have to try very hard to get our subcultural myths to do what we want for us without damaging people we respect.

Kate Davy, having in mind work by Tavel and Ludlam, believes that 'male camp tends to reinscribe, rather than undermine, the dominant culture paradigms it appropriates for its farce and means to parody'. She contrasts lesbian cross-dressing at the WOW Cafe, where what is represented is simply lesbian butch/femme subculture: since the performers are not impersonating men there is no necessary reference to 'the heterosexual imperative'.[13] I don't think Tavel's *Gorilla Queen* is fairly comprised in Davy's accusation. Anyway, it must be doubtful how far butch/femme subculture can succeed in sidestepping 'the heterosexual imperative'. At the same time, Davy's belief that lesbian cross-dressers have not generally sought to ironise gender is supported by historical evidence, as Judith Halberstam shows.[14] In this light, Sue-Ellen Case's affirmative account of camp in relation to lesbian culture and performance art should perhaps be understood as highlighting a potential, in the current context of lesbian assertiveness, rather than a tradition.[15]

That cross-dressing can unsettle gender norms has been demonstrated, in my view, in the Cheek by Jowl production of *As You Like It* in 1991, in which other audience members confirmed my own sense of uncertainty, from moment to moment, as to whether I was watching a boy, a girl, a girl playing a boy, or a boy playing a girl playing a boy.[16] Such gender confusion was generated also in *Belle Reprieve* (1991), which Split Britches (Peggy Shaw and Lois Weaver) and the Bloolips (Bette Bourne and Paul Shaw) composed together as a response to the film of *Streetcar Named Desire*. The characters are listed as Mitch, 'a fairy disguised as a man', Stella, 'a woman disguised as a woman', Stanley, 'a butch lesbian' and Blanche, 'a man in a dress' (150). A persistent theme is whether they are plausible in their ostensible gender roles.

Blanche (Bette Bourne) finds Stanley (Peggy Shaw) over-insistent: 'His postures are not real, don't seem to be coming from a true place. He's a phoney.' Blanche adds: 'Only someone as skilled as I am at being a woman can pick up these subtle signs' (172–3).

Within this framework, *Belle Reprieve* can invoke realism as one of the available styles. 'I want to be in a real play!' Blanche demands. 'With real scenery! White telephones, French windows, a beginning, a middle and an end! . . . There isn't even a fucking drinks trolley. Agatha Christie was right' (178). OK, Stanley says, but this means the reality of heterosexism rather than the illusion of gender-bending.

STANLEY: If you want to play a woman, the woman in this play gets raped and goes crazy in the end.

BLANCHE: I don't want to get raped and go crazy. I just wanted to wear a nice frock, and look at the shit they've given me!

'Did you figure it out yet?' Stella asks the audience at the end: 'who's who, what's what, who gets what, where the toaster is plugged in?' (181–2).[17]

Commentators on lesbian performance art have conducted salutary studies of how denaturalising theories work with actual audiences. Davy remarks how Lisa Kron's *Paradykes Lost* (1988), at the WOW lesbian theatre space, was misread by non-lesbian reviewers: they were insufficiently familiar with the dynamics of butch/femme role-play. Taking another instance, Split Britches' production of Holly Hughes' *Dress Suits to Hire* (1987), Davy observes that 'the operations of theatrical representation are over-determined, foregrounded, and made visible, thereby undermining, paradoxically, the construction of *woman as body*'; the performance 'scrambles the signals, the processes of identification'.[18] This worked well, Davy believes, for an avant-garde (though heterosexual) audience at P.S. 122, 'an East Village venue for new, or nonmainstream, theatre, dance, music, and performance art' (153). However, at the University of Michigan, Ann Arbor, 'in a conventional theatre setting, in the legitimate (and legitimizing) institutional setting of a major university, the work's potential to subvert dominant ideology was seriously undermined' (166). Sue-Ellen Case, who had admired Split Britches' *Beauty and the Beast* (1982), also thought this: she saw the Michigan audience for *Dress Suits* being gleefully entertained, consuming and erasing the specificity of lesbian lives and desires.[19]

It is in the nature of the task, we need to remember, that our strategies will be precarious. A leading theme of this book has been the perseverance of

lesbian and gay people in carving out their subculture where they could. This
has meant (a) writers encoding queer nuances for those in the know; (b)
audiences reading in their own concerns, regardless of the ostensible tendency
of the text. If conventional theatre could not prevent us from doing this, we can
hardly expect that our own texts will be immune to misguided or hostile
readings. Indeed, it is axiomatic that no text or performance can secure its
reception.

Suppose a queer production redeploys a heterosexist stereotype − as, for
instance, Split Britches do in *Anniversary Waltz* (1990), where Shaw and
Weaver celebrate their ten-year partnership through images of 'romance and
familial relations'. Because these themes are not confined to lesbian sexuality,
the outcome may well be 'ultimately an assimilationist lesbian text' − that is
how it appeared to Jill Dolan, in Milwaukee, Wisconsin.[20] Lynda Hart saw
Anniversary Waltz at the University of Pennsylvania, where, despite dramatic
techniques which 'upset expectations of conventional narrativity, linearity, or
causality', a broadly progressive audience largely ignored the lesbian aspect.
'Numerous spectators commented on the familiar themes and wide-based
appeal of the performance'; there was 'an almost seamless repudiation of any
lesbian presence'. Probably, Hart suggests, this was a well-meaning, liberal
attempt to integrate lesbians as 'just like everyone else' − which, of course, is
incompatible with any project of subverting, or even calling attention to, the
sex/gender system and the position of lesbians in it.[21]

Liberal and subversive readings are not the only possibilities. A more
conservative audience might be grossly affronted at lesbian performers laying
claim to such 'normal' structures as 'romance and familial relations'. But then,
such people would not be likely to attend such a performance. These
arguments apply also to the 'gay family' in *Torch Song Trilogy*.

The entire idea of 'challenging the audience', which has been deployed by
liberal and radical theatre people for generations, needs reconsideration. As
Baz Kershaw, from his work in community theatre, avers: 'what may be
challenging to one audience/community may be innocuous to another'.[22] On
the one hand, there is the liberal audience that is already experienced at
questioning the system and is confirmed in its preconceptions by seeing
another decentring narrative. On the other, there is the conservative audience
that is so repelled by a thwarting of its expectations that it either walks out of
the theatre or brings to bear a battery of repudiating mechanisms (the play and
players are perverted, unChristian, ghettoising, etcetera). If one wants to make
challenging theatre, the task must be to devise a performance that is likely to

disconcert the people likely to attend, but only to the degree that they will be able to apprehend the challenge productively.

The snare with deconstructionist strategies — and it has haunted leftist drama since Brecht — is avant-gardism. Most queer work has occurred alongside other alternative theatre, in urban fringe venues and on the college and arts-centre touring circuit. Thus it shares with that other work its funding structure (precarious) and the lifestyle and working conditions of its practitioners (dedicated and ruinous). Like earlier institutional developments, such as the little theatre and the subsidised company, fringe groups have altered the mode of cultural production and created a new constituency. Their audiences tend to be well educated — they can handle 'difficult' work, and probably believe it does you good. They are not fazed by direct address, singing and dancing, doubling up of parts, bits of film, poetry, flashback, fantasy, and so on. The danger, indeed, is less that such experienced viewers will feel their conventional identities sliding away as they watch a denaturalising play, than that they will relax into a familiar, avant-gardist response, such that the very devices that are designed to disconcert them will reassure them and confirm their possession of cultural capital.

At the same time, that description does not account for the entire audience for fringe drama: some people are drawn to it because they do not find their lives represented elsewhere: black and unemployed people as well as sexual dissidents. Jay Prosser, endorsing the autobiographical performance of Kate Bornstein and other transsexual artists, stresses the importance of transgendered subjects speaking for themselves, telling their own stories.[23] Such audiences are not necessarily attuned to avant-garde techniques. When Gay Sweatshop toured *Entering Queens* by Phyllis Nagy and *Jack* by David Greenspan in 1992, some audiences (for instance a large audience in Brighton) were impatient with material that seemed excessively abstract and hard to comprehend. (*Jack* has three, apparently unconnected speakers, like Samuel Beckett's *Play*.) Nagy felt afterwards that she 'should have written something much simpler', instead of 'the best play that she could from an artistic point of view, which would challenge and extend all concerned'. She had not realised that 'Sweatshop's criteria were not, could not be, only artistic'.[24] I think that is a mistaken way to regard the matter. Her play was not addressed in a way that would challenge or extend that audience; the demanding 'artistic' project was to devise one that would.

Many commentators, while accepting the decentring argument in principle, are ready to grant that there is value in representing real (as it were) lesbians and gay men on stage. 'For theorists who would continue to write from within a lesbian position — if only provisionally, and if only one among many — the challenge becomes to reconstruct lesbian subject positions without reinstating essentialisms', Dolan writes.[25] For Lynda Hart the question is: 'How can performers like Split Britches hold in tension the *performative* nature of lesbian identity (the constructionist perspective) without erasing the material and historical reality of lesbian lives?'[26]

I conclude that it is a mistake to expect that there will be one, truly dissident, dramatic (or literary) form — social realist, Brechtian, camp, or otherwise. On the one hand, while Brechtian theory is probably right in principle, we have supposed too readily that to demonstrate instability in a dominant ideology is to demonstrate its weakness and vulnerability to subversion. On the other hand, while it is true that drama which draws audiences into emotional identification may not move them to action, or even to thought, realist plays can extend the experience of audiences and hence prompt political deliberation. The dissident potential of camp and drag has to be assessed not in the abstract, but in particular instances.

In her article 'Sexual Indifference and Lesbian Representation', Teresa de Lauretis assesses diverse modes through which 'lesbian writers and artists have sought variously to escape gender, to deny it, transcend it, or perform it in excess, and to inscribe the erotic in cryptic, allegorical, realistic, camp, or other modes of representation'.[27] None of these strategies emerges as the magical answer. The task is not to specify the one, true strategy, but to be flexible and cunning — as dominant ideologies are.

Into the Mainstream

A central concern of this book has been the oblique terms on which queer representation might occur in mainstream theatre — from *Richard of Bordeaux* through *The Children's Hour* and *The Mousetrap*, to *The Killing of Sister George* and *What the Butler Saw*. By the early 1980s it was possible to bring in from the fringe candid representations of sexual dissidence, so long as they did not much unsettle prevailing notions about gays. Hence, I think, the success of *A Chorus Line* (1975) by Marvin Hamlisch and Edward Kleban, with a gay chorus boy (only one); *The Dresser* (1980) by Ronald Harwood, where a good-natured camp man looks after a tyrannical theatre star; *Another Country* (1981) by Julian Mitchell, which revisits familiar public-school, spy-scandal territory; and *La Cage aux Folles* (1983) by Jerry Herman and Harvey Fierstein which, though it does humble the secretary of the 'Union for Moral Order', is not quite as far as one would wish from Charles Dyer's *Staircase* (1966; see chapter 14). All these shows were filmed.

Beginning in the late 1980s and accelerating in the 1990s, a distinct flurry of gay-themed work has changed the picture again. By 1994 the London press, provoked mainly by the cross-over success of Jonathan Harvey's *Beautiful Thing* (1993), was complaining about an alleged flood of gay plays. In fact explicitly straight plays remained overwhelmingly preponderant, as was demonstrated by Nicholas de Jongh, the out gay *Evening Standard* critic. 'If gay plays are possessed by sex – and not all are – it is because homosexuality remains stigmatised and penalised', de Jongh averred. Lest this seem too progressive, the *Standard* ran on the next day an article by veteran critic Milton Shulman, titled so as to mock our distress over AIDS: 'Stop the Plague of Pink Plays.'[28] However, the success of *Beautiful Thing* does suggest that the mainstream is changing. Harvey's play makes rather shrewdly the case for regarding seriously and sympathetically gay feelings among young people. For anxieties about 'the corruption of minors' are not necessarily homophobic – they may be founded in a proper wish to protect the vulnerable. *Beautiful Thing* enlists such emotions on behalf of gay youngsters by making Ste and Jamie subject to homophobic cruelty at school and in the family.

Of course, 'the mainstream' is not a straightforward term. Nowadays it includes regional and national subsidised companies, as well as the West End and Broadway. Terrence McNally in 1995 proudly announces an 'American . . . *national* theater – regional theaters are in the vanguard of producing the world premieres of our best playwrights'.[29] In its various manifestations, the mainstream has found that gay plays may now be profitable. And this, surely, is paradoxical. While Section 28 in Britain and restrictions on the National Endowment for the Arts in the USA have enabled reactionaries, exploiting a new wave of stigmatisation sanctioned by HIV and AIDS, to trammel queer cultural production in the public sector, the market has embraced our culture. Surging past the urgent admonitions of campaigning activists, business has seen an opportunity. Gay-themed shows, like gay wine bars, holidays, therapies, financial services, litigation and T-shirts, may make money. Several factors have been sanctioning this development. Despite an air of perpetual crisis, capitalism is expanding, exuberantly or desperately, into the most recalcitrant markets. The service sector thrives, for the time being, as manufacturing industry declines. Gays offer a fairly precise marketing niche, having a certain disposable income and a culture that is not very anxious about hedonism. Meanwhile, respect for traditional authorities and decencies has been weakening. If market forces are all that count, the money of gay men, and perhaps lesbians, is as good as anyone else's.[30]

More specifically, theatre is in financial difficulty at all levels. Lone performers on bare platforms thrive because they are very economical. Gay writing has succeeded partly because few other people have very pressing ideas about what to do on a stage.[31] One effect, Savran observes, is to consolidate theatre in its heartland, as a site for middle-class liberalism — which, after our earnest and vivid rights campaigning, includes queerness. 'In the 1990s, a play without a same-sex kiss may be entertainment, but it can hardly be considered a work of art. It now appears that the representation of (usually male) homosexual desire has become the privileged emblem of that endangered species, the serious Broadway drama.'[32]

Up to a point, these factors embrace lesbians as well, but lesbian-themed work is surely inhibited by continuing discrimination against women in theatre. A survey of companies funded by the Arts Council in 1994 found that only one in five of performed playwrights were women, only one in three held senior posts, and only 8 per cent of funding was controlled by them. The figures were virtually the same in a survey of 1985–86.[33] *Voyeurz*, a lesbian-themed musical by Michael Lewis and Peter Rafelson featuring nudity, was ill-received and ran for only eight weeks in London in 1996.

There is no simple recipe for gay mainstream success; as always, star performers and acclaimed presentations elsewhere are extremely helpful. Until recently one would have said that the treatment had to be upbeat and sentimental — like Fierstein's *Torch Song Trilogy*, Harvey's *Beautiful Thing*, and Paul Rudnick's *Jeffrey* (1992). Jonathan Larson's musical *Rent* (1996) is in this vein. However, Kevin Elyot's *My Night with Reg* (1994) thrived on pain and melancholy (see chapter 16), and Mark Ravenhill's *Shopping and Fucking* (1996) shows that a play can draw wide audiences if its publicity leaflet can quote John Peter pronouncing in the *Sunday Times* that it's 'barbarous, compassionate, shocking and callously witty'. Actually, most gay-themed mainstream plays have crossed over from the fringe. The audiences may cross over as well: lesbians and gay men who might have seen the play in a fringe venue join the mainstream audience.

These developments raise the prospect that the obscurity, indirection and dedicated work that have been traced through this book are now irrelevant.

We can emerge from subcultural milieux into the full light of . . . whatever is going to happen next. 'We won't die secret deaths anymore. The world only spins forward. We will be citizens. The time has come', Prior Walter proclaims at the end of Tony Kushner's *Angels in America Part 2: Perestroika* (1992: 99).

The defining concepts for the exploration of the relations between mainstream and subculture are company, venue, constituency and address. *Company* means the little theatre movement, the English Stage Company, Gay Sweatshop, alongside the great West End and Broadway producers. *Venue* means not just the place of performance, but its entire significance − where it is, how you get there, how much the tickets cost and how you buy them; and what it is like inside − the foyer space, the auditorium, the stage. By making the audience member comfortable or nervous, these factors set likely horizons for the experience of the play. 'There are elements in the language of the theatre beyond the text, even beyond the production, which are often more decisive, more central to one's experience of the event', John McGrath observes: 'notably the choice of venue, audience, performers, and the relationship between performer and audience'.[34] 'The same' play may be fringe at the Bush and mainstream at the Haymarket. In fact it will not be the same, because both the scale and audience expectations will be different. A production at the Royal National Theatre in London in 1992 helped Tony Kushner's *Angels in America Part 1: Millennium Approaches* toward classic ranking, but it seemed portentous there, whereas it might have seemed camp and fun in a fringe venue.

The experience of venue is not, of course, an individual matter. It is a major determinant in the construction of *constituency*: which groups feel at home here? Theatre people often say that they don't think about who is in the audience. If this is true, the outcome will be either confusion, or a default to the standard audience customarily associated with the company and/or venue. For it is not possible to use language without making some assumptions about the creatures that will decode it. Lesbian and gay companies that are explicit about their constituency are often accused of preaching to the converted. I still have difficulty taking this notion seriously enough to rebut it. Don't straight-oriented productions, overwhelmingly, do that? Mainstream culture ignores, hampers and vilifies gays and lesbians and then complains when we take halting steps toward getting together our own representations. In fact all the Sweatshop productions, through all the changes of personnel, have been controversial to substantial sectors of their audiences. They have been interventions; *Mister X* and *Any Woman Can* must have been been profoundly challenging for people who were uneasy about coming out. Further, establishing a constituency is a desirable prelude for a serious critical appraisal, which in a mainstream context may appear offensive — washing dirty linen in public.

Address is the other factor in constituency and it has the most subtle consequences. As the text is written and performed, whose knowledge, experience, beliefs and feelings are being appealed to, and, more important, taken for granted? Diverse audiences may attend, and may negotiate the play in their own ways. But some will feel themselves to be in focus, as the constituency that is being addressed, while others will feel marginal. These are familiar matters for members of sexual, racial and other minorities, who are either ignored or specially managed in all kinds of mainstream institutions.

Jimmie Chinn's *Straight and Narrow* (1987) instances mainstream address, though it took five years to come in from the fringe. 'A little theatre history was made in London last night', the *Evening Standard* declared in 1992. 'For just about the first time in a quarter of a century the West End theatre has dared present a mainstream comedy about homosexuality' (quoted on the back cover of the play). *Straight and Narrow* manifests mainstream address very clearly, for the action is mediated to the audience by Bob's narration:

> Jeff and I have been partners now for yonks, and this is our lounge — living-room — call it what you like. This is our couch, and our carpet; our tables and chairs, and these are my paintings — I mean I did them — good, aren't they? Actually, it's just like a real house, isn't it? Tell you the truth, we have a friend called Marion who was heard to whisper, 'they've got a double bed — just like a real couple!' (5)

This is tongue in cheek, but gay audience members don't need to be told that their houses and couples are real; the play is addressed, so to speak, to Marion and her husband.

Mainstream address tends to accompany mainstream ideas about gays. Bob is artistic and written to be played camp; Jeff fixes up the house and used to 'fancy a bit of straight' (21); he disturbs the relationship by spending time with a woman on holiday and wanting to have children. The way forward, gays might assume, is for Jeff and Bob to discuss whether children would actually be a good idea for them both, and how they might explore the possibilities with lesbian friends. However, it is taken for granted that Jeff's wish to have children is incompatible with Bob and him living together, and there is no reference to lesbian sexuality in the play. Eventually it is revealed that Jeff does have a daughter, though he doesn't know where she is; it is not suggested that they look for her.

Mainstream address is specially germane to *Straight and Narrow* because the theme is that Bob and Jeff are almost like a straight couple. This notion requires continuous insistence. 'I must say I'm surprised', says Arthur, Nona's husband. 'I thought things were different when you were bent.' But no. Lois is made to say, 'You men, you're all the bloody same. Just because you get fed up and fancy a change you think you can just sod off . . . then come home whenever it suits you and expect everything to be normal' (39–40). Conversely, Arthur, Bill's uncle and Bob's father are all said to be or have been somewhat gay.

Yet it is not hard to think of relevant differences that the play suppresses. Gay men have distinctive opportunities for casual sex if their relationship has become too uneventful; they experience AIDS as more than a reason for monogamy; they have gay friends, helplines and organisations to turn to when they have a problem. Bill's uncle probably knows something about all this because he 'goes on marches an' stuff like that', but he's mentioned only as an aberration (20). Finally, having divested Bob and Jeff of any gay distinctiveness, *Straight and Narrow* insinuates that they can never quite be 'normal' after all. Jeff's confession to Bob about how rewarding it felt to be going round with a woman − 'it gave me some sort of kick, pretending to be normal' − is acknowledged as hurtful but allowed to stand as only reasonable. 'We are normal . . . except . . .' (45, Chinn's pauses).

Not all cross-over plays have such intentions or make them so blatant. But mainstream address is bound to have thematic consequences. As Mary Remnant shows, Sarah Daniels' feminist work at fringe venues had been vilified by male critics (appointed by their newspapers to address a mainstream constituency) as a perverse assault on men − a 'cascade of bile' (Milton Shulman), a 'scream of outrage' (Irving Wardle).[35] So it was bold of the National Theatre to ask Daniels for a play on lesbian parenting, and of her to take on the project with that company in that venue. *Neaptide* (1986) is witty at the expense of both women and men, though male teachers in the school staffroom reveal a notable viciousness. A liberal case for Claire, the good (lesbian) mother, to be with her daughter is well made.

Daniels manages to suggest also, through a vein of mythic allusion, that women would be wise to have as little as they reasonably can to do with men. Persephone 'still had to visit her husband once a year', but 'neither husband nor child nor stranger would ever claim her as his own. Persephone belonged to her mother. That was Demeter's gift to herself' (this story is told by Claire to her daughter: 239). Women do better when they act together, *Neaptide* shows. The anxious teacher, the radical students and the discreet headteacher discover each other and amount eventually to a lesbian network; the mother, despite her conventional socialisation, finally rescues Claire with the help of another daughter. However there is a cost, in the representation of lesbian lives, for getting all that onto a National Theatre stage: Claire has no love scenes, no women partners, no evident attraction to other women. These are the conditions upon which a mainstream audience may be expected to agree that a lesbian mother may keep her child. Further, these emphases cut the play off from themes that might engage a lesbian audience, such as how your partner and your child get along together.[36]

As de Jongh said, there is no shortage of plays that assume a mainstream address in respect of sexuality. *M. Butterfly* (1988) by David Henry Hwang, which won a clutch of awards on Broadway, is an interesting instance. Plainly, the story of how a male French diplomat lived with a Chinese man for years while believing him to be a woman is open to diverse interpretations. According to Joyce Wadler, who interviewed the Frenchman at the centre of the original story, he did have queer liaisons at some points in his life.[37] However, Hwang's version resolutely writes out any suggestion that homosexuality might explain Gallimard's confusion. To the contrary, he displays a strongly heterosexist address, for instance when he says that 'while we men may want to kick Pinkerton [who exploits a Japanese woman in Puccini's *Madame Butterfly*], very few of us would pass up the opportunity to *be* Pinkerton' (42). We men all want to abuse women, this says; gay men are off the map. Of course, nothing can prevent the audience from supposing that this is latency - that Gallimard is really queer underneath. However, such an assumption, besides entailing a conservative notion of sexuality, would obstruct Hwang's point: that Song is able to seduce Gallimard because s/he plays to a favourite (Madame Butterfly) fantasy of the Westerner — 'The submissive Oriental woman and the cruel white man' (17). When, finally, Song presents himself as a man, Gallimard's secret yearning is not uncovered; on the contrary, he is repelled. So resolutely heterosexist is his mind-set that Song's masculinity and his own weakness prompt him to recast himself, finally, in the feminine, Butterfly role.

Certainly, there are topics which stir the imaginations of writers, performers and audiences, and which are not specific to sexual constituencies. Queer people join in explorations of them. However, my final thought is that the questions we have to sort out among ourselves are as momentous as those we share with the mainstream. There is still a role for subcultural work.

Subcultural Work

The 1994 London dispute about the alleged flood of gay plays was triggered by the transfer to the West End of *Beautiful Thing*. Charles Spencer in the *Daily Telegraph* welcomed Harvey's next play, *Babies* (1994), specifically because 'his plays are accessible to anyone who happens to be sitting in the audience'. They were not like 'some new dramas' that seem 'intent on making any heterosexual in the audience feel uncomfortable, if not downright unwelcome'.[38] That is the point: mainstreaming, by definition, ensures that, if anyone is to be uncomfortable, then it will not be heterosexuals.

Yet few theatre people these days are inclined to think of themselves as doing gay work. Paul Martin performed his *One-Man Crisis on the A46* (1998) at alternative venues: it tells of 'a young gay man and his struggle with inner demons'. But it's 'not just a gay play − I hate that phrase', Martin says. 'It's more universal than that.'[39] In *Gay and After* (chapter 8) I argue that honorific concepts such as 'art', 'literature', 'universal', 'tragic' and 'classic' are neither spontaneous nor innocent. They are bestowed by the gatekeepers of the cultural apparatus, and should be understood as tactics for conferring authority upon certain works in the service of certain ideological positions. Though sexual dissidents have not been excluded from these processes, they have been admitted only on limited terms. Lesbian and gay cultural workers would do well to claim space in which to explore questions that are − *inevitably* − ignored or manipulated elsewhere by others. It must be unwise to leave our concerns within the control of people who, we know, do not like us.

The rewards of addressing a subcultural constituency are spelt out by Simon Callow. When he was invited to appear in the Sweatshop production of Martin Sherman's *Passing By* (1975), he was 'deeply sceptical about the whole enterprise. Ghetto theatre, I said. What next? Plays by chartered accountants, about chartered accountants, for chartered accountants?' But when he read the play he was delighted. 'When had I ever seen any film or play about gay people, in which *homosexuality* was not the subject or the problem, as opposed to simply the condition of the protagonists?'[40] The address of *Passing By* is evident in what it assumes. Simon and Toby exchange glances in a cinema and are next seen in bed together. They would like to see more of each other, but have no convention as to who should forgo fulfilment in his career; they don't have to start swearing everlasting love just because they like each other and go to bed. This was how gay men were living. Audiences, in 1975, were deeply moved, Callow says:

> It was as if a secret that had been kept for too long were finally being told to people who knew it individually but had never seen it acknowledged. The quality of attention was transformed. It was their lives they were watching. . . . Now surely here, I thought, is an essence of theatre; and it's a political essence: the actors were acting, as it were, on behalf of the community; or a section of it, in this case.[41]

Only a few audience members today will experience such an epiphany. But feeling oneself to be addressed is still energising.

The point is not that lesbian or gay theatre may create that ever-elusive sense of gay community. De Lauretis rejects 'the presumption of a unified lesbian viewer/reader, gifted with undivided and non-contradictory subjectivity'; 'There is no universal lesbian spectator', Dolan says.[42] Certainly, lesbians and gay men manifest the divisions of class, gender, race, age and education that occur in the wider society. The task is not to imagine an exclusive group of like-minded people, but to build on the diverse strengths of our constituency, to enlarge it, and to politicise it.

It has proved difficult to sustain subcultural theatre financially – though by no means so difficult as it is to produce (say) lesbian and gay film. In the USA almost as much as in Britain, fringe drama developed in the 1970s on the assumption that it was entitled to support from some kind of arm's-length State body; under right-wing governments in the 1980s this became increasingly insecure. In the USA, where Karen Finley, John Fleck, Holly Hughes and Tim Miller were 'defunded' by the National Endowment for the Arts in 1990 after objections to the sexual nature of their work, Sarah Schulman observed that the overwhelming proportion of lesbian artists have never been funded. Further, they may be tempted to adjust their work to fit the preferences of committees, thus distorting their work and the culture of the lesbian community. 'In this manner, much of the development of lesbian arts is taken out of the hands of the audience and given instead to a small group of critics and administrators.'[43] In my view it would be better if we could avoid this grant dependency. Penny Casdagli, a Greek writer and performer working in Britain, argues for 'theatre made by lesbians, informed by their perspective

. . . and performed within their control. . . . The salient point is that its intentions and impetus are lesbian. It is *owned by* lesbians.'[44] Theatre doesn't have to be hugely expensive. Arguably, it forsakes its great privilege — actor–audience intimacy — when it competes with electronic media and goes spectacular.

In practice, there is no single, correct institutional answer; we have to exploit the openings that present themselves. The task is still, almost as in the time of Noël Coward, to improvise our subculture where we can, in opportunistic manner.

In London, at the time of writing, there are excellent, continuing prospects for the Drill Hall under the artistic direction of Julie Parker.[45] Neil Bartlett, although he resists the concept of subcultural work, has proved adroit at creating conditions for inventive productions by himself and others through his company Gloria, now at the Lyric, Hammersmith. And we can maintain a confident expectation of exciting work in England while Lois Weaver and Peggy Shaw choose to work here. In large part, though, we may have to reconcile ourselves to gleaning our culture in the margins of straight-oriented productions. If that is so, awareness of address will remain crucial for recognising and resisting mildly dismissive or subtly homophobic nuances.

Many lesbians and gay men regard the mainstream more positively. Consider William Hoffman's comments on *The Madness of Lady Bright* (1964) by Lanford Wilson (discussed in chapter 15). Hoffman is bothered that the protagonist is too limited: Leslie '*is* representative of one kind of male homosexual. But Wilson's queen transcends the stereotype and all of the clichés by being so *individually* effeminate. He stands for any aging person who cannot come to terms with the facts of death.'[46] Now, *The Madness of Lady Bright* may be enjoyed on those terms, though we might wonder who but a hustler-queen would consider himself or herself to be entering terminal old age at forty. But this play is not important because it is about 'any aging person', but because it dramatises the situation of some sexual dissidents. If Leslie 'transcends the stereotype', it is not by passing beyond it but by totally embodying it.

Michael Wilcox, who has edited five collections of gay plays, argues against theatre that makes gayness its main focus. This is partly because he wants to show how gays fit into everyday life, just like other people, but also because he wants a wider audience — 'not plays written by a minority for a minority'. Companies such as Sweatshop who prioritise 'politics' are in danger of smothering 'the more durable, dramatic instincts of most of the playwrights'.[47]

In his own play *Accounts* (1983, Traverse Theatre, Edinburgh) a mother and her two sons are struggling to run a farm after the death of their father. It emerges that one of the brothers is gay, but in the understated rural Scots Border idiom through which Wilcox presents them this is scarcely a matter for comment. He is also an excellent rugby player, hardly a gay stereotype: anyone may be gay. *Accounts*, like other plays by Wilcox (*Rents*, 1979; *Lent*, 1983), has been produced widely and has gained access to television, so the strategy works. Yet I feel that he is trying to talk his audiences into seeing homosexuality as unremarkable by depicting it like that. This too is a political project.

Bartlett holds that mainstream theatre has always been gay. After all, 'if you remove Wilde, Rattigan, Maugham, Coward, Osborne, Orton, and Novello from the post-1900 British theatre profession – from the money-earning profession of theatre – you're left with a pretty serious problem at the box office'.[48] This belief has inspired Bartlett to produce *The Letter* by Somerset Maugham, *Splendid's* (1948) by Jean Genet and *Cause Célèbre* by Terence Rattigan. His play *Night after Night* (1993) is about how 'gay people were there all the time, occupying a central place in the manufacture of all our nights out – stage managing, dressing, selling the tickets, directing, designing, composing and choreographing the most popular shows in town' – and especially the boys in the chorus (preface, 3).

> Of course there is a point of view
> That says of course there are a few
> But frankly that is nothing new
> And anyway we always knew. (23)

Sexual dissidence has infiltrated theatre of all kinds, and one outcome is a body of playtexts and a performing tradition that are still of extraordinary interest. This is the position that Bartlett and I share – and also that theatre has been a key site for the cultivation of gay, and to a considerable extent lesbian, identities. Yet this subculture was steeped in subterfuge and equivocation, such that it affords a record of humiliation, oppression and self-oppression, as much as a ground for celebration. Indeed, Bartlett acknowledges that his mainstream is a very particular selection from earlier work: 'it's not a tradition so much as a cluster of artistic flashpoints – points of aesthetic excess at which the mainstream becomes ripe for my evil purposes, for plucking'.[49]

Culture performs two main functions. First, it creates a sense of belonging. Many of us value our sense of national, regional and civic belonging, our racial or ethnic identity, our involvement in a world of work, our sense of shared political or religious commitment. To be disturbed in those allegiances is uncomfortable — though many people experience that, either because others stigmatise and reject them or because they bravely repudiate aspects of the dominant ideology. Queer people want all those kinds of belonging, but they also need validation of their sexualities and genders (straights need that too, but for them it is everywhere). Theatre, like other modes of cultural production, can help to fortify people who are under pressure.

Second, culture is where a group addresses contested aspects of its ideological formation. 'Faultlines', I have called them: faultline stories take up the awkward, undecided issues, the ones that require the most assiduous and continuous reworking. They hinge upon a fundamental, unresolved ideological complication that finds its way, willy-nilly, into writing, the presentation of plays, and so on.[50] There is nothing mysterious about this; producers and consumers of culture want it to be interesting, and that means, by definition, working at the faultlines. It doesn't require earnest problem dramas — though *Beautiful Thing* is a vivid, recent addition to that genre, as is Patrick Wilde's *What's Wrong with Angry?* (1993), which shows the confusion and distress of a boy who can find gayness only in public toilets, and was presented explicitly by its author as a contribution to the debate about the age of consent for gay men. Queer people share many concerns with other people, but we also have particular problems — matters of class, racial and intergenerational exploitation; of misogyny and sado-masochism; of HIV and AIDS; of bisexuality and transgender; of the global extension of metropolitan concepts of gayness. To some extent we find these evoked in mainstream and cross-over theatre, but hardly with the scope and precision that we require. We still need subcultural address — work that speaks to us on our own terms, as a constituency in our own venues. The plays about AIDS discussed in chapter 16 all started life as fringe, subcultural events.

In early chapters of this book, as we saw the modern concept of the homosexual emerging, theatre struggled to represent lesbians and queer men. Now, on the stage and in other media, everyone can see and hear versions of what lesbians and gays are like. It is no coincidence that this is the moment at which new topics in sexual dissidence are forcing their way into representation, opening out new concepts of identity. The cultural work that has enabled the consolidation of lesbian and gay identities now prompts awareness of further possibilities to be explored.

Kate Bornstein's *Hidden: A Gender*, first performed at the Theatre Rhinoceros, San Francisco, in 1989, assumes an audience that is comfortable with gayness. The challenge now is transgender. 'You look liberal enough. You wouldn't be here tonight if you weren't, am I right? Of course I'm right. We are well-fed, well-educated people.' Even for this audience, though, gender is a hot topic: 'because you want to relieve the nagging feeling that you're not quite a man, you're not quite a woman' (172–3). The play suggests that such anxieties might be those of people who experience themselves as assigned to the wrong sex, socially and physically – Herculine Barbin in the nineteenth century, and Kate, the contemporary protagonist.

Nor is it just a matter of reallocating misplaced individuals to alternative slots in the gender system (male to female, female to male). While transsexuals have sometimes experienced themselves as restored, by surgery, to their true gender, Bornstein, as Jay Prosser observes, instances a current tendency to refuse conventional categories.[51] 'I don't consider myself a man, and quite frequently I doubt that I'm a woman', Kate says at the end of *Hidden: A Gender*. Audiences will have strategies for dealing with such disturbances: 'I know what you're thinking. . . . Damned good point. In theory. / But that's got nothing to do with you and me.' Yet are we not 'a bit unsettled by all this?' Such a topic might not be contained within the performance space. 'You just come see me backstage' (222–3).

Other groups experience themselves as anomolous in the spaces that lesbians and gay men have created. Chay Yew's *Porcelain* (1992) investigates why a nice Chinese British boy, John Lee, might murder a man he loved in a public toilet. (Investigates literally: the play consists mainly of interviews conducted for a television programme, and between John and his criminal psychologist. We are shown a society of incessant scrutiny but no true concern.) John is always left standing by himself in clubs; white guys aren't into Orientals, or are trying to relive the old colonial days. Sex in toilets is the best way he can find of being wanted. However, the man he meets there, Will Hope, becomes violent and then abandons John. 'Told you from the start that I date women and I like to fool around with guys – you know, just to get off – but I'm not like that – like you', Will says (390). His favourite music is *Madame Butterfly*. John kills Will when he finds him cruising again; Madame Butterfly becomes Carmen. John's father disowns him.

Porcelain prompts two strains of thought. One is about how marginalised people may be driven to extreme behaviour in a racist society. The other is about John's readiness to collude in the love-lorn, Butterfly/Carmen stance. Sometimes he wishes he was white: 'I see pictures of handsome white guys hugging, kissing, holding hands in magazines like they were meant for each other. . . . Suddenly I'm that beautiful white guy everybody wants to make love to' (373). Chay Yew provokes, but doesn't pursue, reflections on the prospects for Asian men and women to cultivate a queer scene on their own terms. *Porcelain* has been presented at alternative venues in London and widely in the USA.

In *Why Is John Lennon Wearing a Skirt?* (1991, Traverse Theatre, Edinburgh) Claire Dowie performs a woman who couldn't understand what was happening when her girl friends began to make themselves feminine for boys (or for what boys are supposed to want) — 'There's something seriously wrong with me' (45). She could see that only men count. 'Sandie Shaw and Lulu, they don't speak, they can't speak, they can only sing and look pretty, look shyly at the camera and smile and wear dresses, pretty dresses and pretty smiles. But the Beatles speak, they're allowed to speak, they're listened to.' The speaker is 'only a tomboy, which is only second best, but at least it's higher than a fluffy pink little girl' (54). The women's movement looks promising, but they hate men and are into being female. 'And I said, "Doesn't anybody hate women? . . . Doesn't anybody just love what men do and want to do it too?"' No. She gets chatted up by a lesbian, but that's not right either: 'No, I'm a boy, you know' (59–60). In retrospect the resolution is obvious: she takes up with a gay man.

In a later piece, *Leaking from Every Orifice* (1993), first performed at a bisexual conference in Nottingham, Dowie or her persona conceives a child with the gay man (the condom breaks). Her decision to bear it provokes new negotiations with womanhood; negotiations which, Joelle Taylor remarks, lesbians have hesitated to undertake: 'It is as though she lives in terror, or at least persistent surprise, at her femaleness. . . . I don't believe that she and I are the only dykes whose bodies hide around corners and leap out at us during distracted moments. Usually once a month.'[52]

Mark Ravenhill's *Shopping and Fucking* represents the *ménage à trois* of Robbie, Lulu and Mark as unexceptional, but foundering because of Mark's substance abuse. He decides, as part of his cure, to avoid personal dependency; Gary is to be just a financial transaction, but his story of abuse by his stepfather draws Mark in after all. Gary, however, doesn't want love, he wants to be owned and hurt. So why not gratify him? 'When someone's paying, someone wants something and they're paying, then you do it. Nothing right. Nothing wrong. It's a deal', Gary says (83). Meanwhile Robbie and Lulu, trying to fend for themselves, fall into the clutches of the brutal, manipulative and sentimental drug dealer, Brian.

This play is challenging in different ways for different audiences, but for me it says something like: OK, so we didn't make it to the utopian vision of Gay Liberation (there is plenty of talk of utopia in *Shopping and Fucking*, but mostly from the maudlin Brian and from Robbie when he takes the Ecstasy tablets he is supposed to be selling). We have settled for the cosiness of the 1–2–1 (as the contact ads have it: most of the plays about AIDS discussed in chapter 16 offer that as the remaining affirmation); Robbie and Lulu belong together. But how is that interpersonal intimacy going to cope with the actualities of life without the security and stability of a job and an income? Again, we are learning to acknowledge and accommodate a range of S/M and fetishistic practices that previously would have been thought embarrassing, if not disgusting. For Robbie, Lulu and Mark, more or less anything goes. But does that mean we can have any experience that we can afford to pay for? For Brian it all comes down to money. 'The getting is cruel, is hard, but the having is civilization. Then we are civilized' (85). Robbie and Lulu don't quite manage to pay him off with cash from phone sex; they have to accept the money which Gary wants to pay them for assaulting him.

The urgency of coping with current pressures should not diminish our engagement with the main body of twentieth-century work discussed in this book, much of which retains considerable potential in the theatre today. Indeed, many of the preoccupations analysed in earlier chapters are still with us. In different forms, we still have to worry about the tactics of discretion and disclosure, the stigma and pride of gendering, the demands of diverse constituencies, the negotiation between assimilation and difference. The earlier plays may contribute to gay and lesbian history and tradition: we were always there. And they may refocus our dilemmas by filtering them through the assumptions of other times. Theatre has always thrived on such pressures. For queer people, in special ways, the drama on the stage is intimate with the dramas of our lives.

Notes

1 Introduction

1. D.J. West, *Homosexuality* (London: Duckworth, 1955), 21.
2. Richard Dyer, *White* (London: Routledge, 1997), xiii.
3. See Mel Steel, 'Pictures from a Familiar Past', *Pink Paper*, 19 June, 1998, 12.
4. Terry Castle, *Noël Coward and Radclyffe Hall* (New York: Columbia University Press, 1996).
5. Terry Castle, *The Apparitional Lesbian* (New York: Columbia University Press, 1993), 12.
6. Charles Duff, *The Lost Summer* (London: Nick Hern, 1995), 144.
7. Ben Jonson, *Poetaster* (1601), ed. Tom Cain (Manchester University Press, 1995, I.ii.15–17.
8. See Jeffrey Weeks, *Coming Out* (London: Quartet, 1977), 37; Regenia Gagnier, *Idylls of the Marketplace* (Aldershot: Scolar Press, 1987), 147.
9. Jocelyn Brooke, *Private View* (London: Robert Clark, 1989), 153.
10. Noël Langley, *There's a Porpoise Close Behind Us* (London: Methuen, 1939), 110–11.
11. National Lesbian and Gay Survey, *Proust, Cole Porter, Michelangelo, Marc Almond and Me* (London: Routledge, 1993), 83.
12. Frank Pearce, 'The British Press and the "Placing" of Male Homosexuality', in Stanley Cohen and Jock Young, eds, *The Manufacture of News*, 2nd edn (London: Constable, 1981), 308.
13. Rodney Garland, *The Heart in Exile* (1953; Brighton: Millivres Books, 1995), 188.
14. Richard Hauser, *The Homosexual Society* (London: Bodley Head, 1962), 100.
15. See Duff, *The Lost Summer*, 107.
16. Will Waspe, 'A World Suddenly Less Gay', *Spectator*, 31 March, 1973, 399–400.
17. Kaier Curtin, *We Can Always Call Them Bulgarians* (Boston: Alyson, 1987), 97.
18. Reprinted in Martin Duberman, ed., *About Time* (New York: Meridian, 1991), 220–3.
19. 'The Homosexual in America', *Time*, 21 January, 1966, 40–1.
20. Havelock Ellis and John Addington Symonds, *Sexual Inversion* (New York: Ayer Company, 1994), 123–4.
21. Quoted ibid., 124.
22. Kenneth Plummer, *Sexual Stigma* (London: Routledge, 1975), 176–7.
23. John Lahr, *Coward the Playwright* (London: Methuen, 1982), 5.
24. Otto Fenichel, *Collected Papers*, 2nd series (London: Routledge, 1955), 350.
25. Yoti Lane, *The Psychology of the Actor* (London: Secker, 1959, 50; quoted in Donald L. Loeffler, *An Analysis of the Treatment of the Homosexual Character in Dramas Produced in the New York Theatre from 1950 to 1968* (New York: Arno Press, 1975), 13.
26. Richard Green, *The 'Sissy Boy Syndrome' and the Development of Homosexuality* (New Haven: Yale University Press, 1987), 256–7.
27. Gordon Westwood, *A Minority* (London: Longmans, 1960), 166, 176. Westwood is a pseudonym of the sociologist Michael Schofield.
28. Martin Hoffman, *The Gay World* (New York: Basic Books, 1968), 72, quoted in Loeffler, *An Analysis of the Treatment of the Homosexual Character*, 111.
29. H. Montgomery Hyde, *The Other Love*

(London: Mayflower, 1972), 111–14.

30. Kevin Porter and Jeffrey Weeks, eds, *Between the Acts* (London: Routledge, 1991), 120, 26, 114. See also Rupert Croft-Cooke, *Feasting with Panthers* (London: Allen and Unwin, 1967), 264, 268, 270.

31. Peter Burton, *Parallel Lives* (London: Gay Men's Press, 1985), 28–9.

32. Kristina Straub, 'The Guilty Pleasures of Female Theatrical Cross-Dressing and the Autobiography of Charlotte Charke', in Julia Epstein and Kristina Straub, eds, *Body Guards* (New York: Routledge, 1991). See Emma Donoghue, *Passions Between Women* (London: Scarlet Press, 1993), 87–91

33. Marjorie Garber, *Vested Interests* (New York: Routledge, 1992), 37.

34. Ellis and Symonds, *Sexual Inversion*, 83-4.

35. Blair Niles, *Strange Brother* (London: Gay Men's Press, 1991), 1991.

36. Katharine Cockin, *Edith Craig (1869–1947)* (London: Cassell, 1998).

37. Michael Baker, *Our Three Selves* (London: Gay Men's Press, 1985), 170.

38. Castle, *Noël Coward and Radclyffe Hall*, 20–1, 24–5.

39. Hall Carpenter Archives and Lesbian Oral History Group, eds, *Inventing Ourselves* (London: Routledge, 1989), 11, 39, 61, 65–7.

40. Elizabeth Lapovsky Kennedy and Madeline D. Davis, *Boots of Leather, Slippers of Gold* (New York: Routledge, 1993), 37; see 43–4, 134–7.

41. Wolcott Gibbs, *Season in the Sun and Other Pleasures* (London: Heinemann, 1947), 201.

42. Quoted from the Lord Chamberlain's correspondence in Christine Fox, 'Conduct Unbecoming: Noël Coward, Censorship and the Fallacy of the Inconsequence', unpub. D.Phil. thesis, University of Sussex, 1996, 70.

43. Quoted ibid. 246.

44. Ivor Brown, *Shaw in His Time* (London: Nelson, 1965), 30.

45. Quoted in Richard Findlater, *Banned* (London: MacGibbon and Kee, 1967), 207–8.

46. John van Druten, 'Sex and Censorship in the Theatre', in Norman Haire, ed., *World League for Sexual Reform: Proceedings of the Third Congress (1929)* (London: Routledge, 1930), 319.

47. John van Druten, *Young Woodley: A Novel* (New York: John Day, 1929).

48. Findlater, *Banned*, 127, 176–7.

49. Brian Inglis, *The Spectator*, 13 April, 1956, 490; see also Findlater, *Banned*, 167.

50. See John Johnston, *The Lord Chamberlain's Blue Pencil* (London: Hodder and Stoughton, 1990); Fox, 'Conduct Unbecoming'; Dan Rebellato, *1956 and All That* (London: Routledge, 1999); Stephen Rooney, 'Literary Constructions of Male Homosexuality 1954–1969', unpub. D.Phil. thesis, University of Sussex, 1998.

51. West, *Homosexuality*, 121.

52. Rooney, 'Literary Constructions of Male Homosexuality', 147–8.

53. Andrew Rosenthal, *The Extra Man* (London: W.H. Allen, 1977), 138.

54. Noël Coward, *Three Plays* (London: Benn, 1925), v.

55. David A. Miller, *The Novel and the Police* (Berkeley: California University Press, 1988), 206; see Eve Kosofsky Sedgwick, *Epistemology of the Closet* (Hemel Hempstead: Harvester Wheatsheaf, 1991), ch.1.

56. D.A. Miller, 'Anal Rope', in Diana Fuss, ed., *Inside/Out* (New York: Routledge, 1991), 125.

57. Robin Wood, 'The Murderous Gays: Hitchcock's Homophobia', in Corey K. Creekmur and Alexander Doty, eds, *Out in Culture* (London: Cassell, 1995), 209–11.

58. IIIa, 64; on the referencing of Maugham's plays see my Note on Indexes and Citations.

59. Quoted in Michael Holroyd, *Lytton Strachey* (London: Book Club Associates, 1973), 357–8.

60. Sara Mills, 'Reading as/like a Feminist', in Mills, ed., *Gendering the Reader* (Hemel Hempstead: Harvester, 1994), 27, 29. See Judith Fetterley, *The Resisting Reader* (Bloomington and Indianapolis: University of Indiana Press, 1978).

61. Christine Gledhill, 'Pleasurable Negotiations', in E. Deidre Pribram, ed., *Female Spectators* (London: Verso, 1988), 67–8.

62. Wood, 'The Murderous Gays', 209–11.

63. Teresa de Lauretis, 'Sexual Indifference and Lesbian Representation', *Theatre Journal*, 40 (1988): 155–77, 169.

64. Richard Huggett, *Binkie Beaumont* (London: Hodder and Stoughton, 1989), 173–4. The actor was Bryan Coleman.

65. Emlyn Williams, *Emlyn* (London: Bodley Head, 1973), 280.

66. Desmond MacCarthy, *Drama* (London: Putnam, 1940), 287.

67. James Agate, *Red Letter Nights* (London: Cape, 1944), 310–11.

68. See Steven Connor, *Samuel Beckett* (Oxford: Blackwell, 1988), 185–201.

69. Sigmund Freud, *The Interpretation of Dreams*, trans. James Strachey (New York: Avon Books, 1970), 545.

70. Quoted in Curtin, *Bulgarians*, 57–8.

71. Bob Cant and Susan Hemmings, eds, *Radical Records* (London: Routledge, 1988), 15.

2 Society and its Others: Scandal

1. Kaier Curtin, *'We Can Always Call Them Bulgarians'* (Boston: Alyson, 1987), 16–17; Patricia Flanagan Behrendt, *Oscar Wilde* (London: Macmillan, 1991), 174; Linda Gertner Zatlin, *Aubrey Beardsley and Victorian Sexual Politics* (Oxford: Clarendon Press, 1990), 151; Joel Fineman, 'The Significance of Literature: *The Importance of Being Earnest*', *October*, 15 (1980), 79–90, 89.

2. Eric Partridge, *A Dictionary of Slang* (London: Routledge, 1937); 8th edn, ed. Paul Beale (London: Routledge, 1984); John S. Farmer, *Slang and Its Analogues* (1890–1904; London, Kraus, 1965).

3. John Ayto and John Simpson, *The Oxford Dictionary of Modern Slang* (Oxford University Press, 1992). See also William Green, 'Oscar Wilde and the Bunburys', *Modern Drama*, 21 (1978), 67–80; Neil Bartlett, *Who Was That Man?* (London: Serpent's Tail, 1988); Joseph Bristow, in Bristow, ed., *'The Importance of Being Earnest' and Related Writings* (London: Routledge, 1992), 16–19.

4. Alan Sinfield, *The Wilde Century* (London: Cassell, 1994). See Ed Cohen, *Talk on the Wilde Side* (Routledge: New York, 1993).

5. See Humphrey Carpenter, *Geniuses Together* (London: Unwin Hyman, 1987), 116–17.

6. Martin Green, *Children of the Sun* (London: Constable, 1977), 107, and see chs 4 and 5.

7. Michael Davidson, *The World, the Flesh and Myself* (London: Quartet, 1977), 148–9.

8. Jane Marcus, *Art and Anger* (Columbus: Ohio State University Press, 1988), 17.

9. Philip Hoare, *Wilde's Last Stand* (London: Duckworth, 1997), 171.

10. Paul Bailey, *An Immaculate Mistake* (London: Bloomsbury, 1990), 91, 93–4.

11. On the reception of the Sewells' *Oscar Wilde*, see Curtin, *Bulgarians*, 240–7.

12. Christopher Fitz-Simon, *The Boys* (London: Nick Hern, 1994), 239.

13. Neil Bartlett, programme note to Bartlett, *The Picture of Dorian Gray*, Lyric Theatre Hammersmith and Nottingham Playhouse (1994).

14. Eve Kosofsky Sedgwick, *Between Men* (New York: Columbia University Press, 1985), 93. See Ellen Moers, *The Dandy* (London: Secker, 1960).

15. Théophile Gautier, *Mademoiselle de Maupin*, trans. R.E. Powys Mathers (London: Folio Society, 1948), 140.

16. Behrendt, *Oscar Wilde*, 175–6.

17. Oscar Wilde, *The Picture of Dorian Gray*, ed. Isobel Murray (Oxford University Press, 1981), 36; and see 101-2.

18. Pat Moorman, reviewing a Royal Shakespeare Company production, *Brighton and Hove Leader*, 26 March, 1992, 26; Kerry Powell, *Oscar Wilde and the Theatre of the 1890s* (Cambridge University Press, 1990), 71.

19. H. Montgomery Hyde, *The Other Love* (London: Mayflower, 1972), 166–7; Regenia Gagnier, *Idylls of the Marketplace* (Aldershot: Scolar Press, 1987), 206.

20. C. Wright Mills, introduction to Thorstein Veblen, *The Theory of the Leisure Class* (New York: Mentor, 1953), xvi.

21. Beatrice Webb, *My Apprenticeship*, with introduction by Norman MacKenzie (Cambridge University Press, 1979), 50.

22. Leonora Davidoff, *The Best Circles* (London: Croom Helm, 1973), 32; see 62–3, 65–7. I draw a good deal upon Davidoff on this topic.

23. Geoffrey Best, *Mid-Victorian Britain 1851–75* (London: Fontana/Collins, 1979), 266.

24. Walter Bagehot, *The English Constitution* (1867; London: Collins, 1963), 121.

25. George Bernard Shaw, review of *The Ideal Husband*, in Shaw, *Our Theatres in the Nineties*, vol. 1 (London: Constable, 1932), 11.

26. Bagehot, *English Constitution*, 248.

27. Gagnier, *Idylls of the Marketplace*, 107–8.

28. George Augustus Sala, *London Up to Date* (London: Black, 1894), 50–5; quoted in Joseph Donohue, ed., *Oscar Wilde's 'The Importance of Being Earnest': A Reconstructive Critical Edition* (Gerrards Cross: Colin Smythe, 1995), 32.

29. Joel H. Kaplan and Sheila Stowell, *Theatre and Fashion* (Cambridge University Press, 1994), 11.

30. William A. Cohen, *Sex Scandal* (Durham, NC: Duke University Press, 1996), 17.

31. Hyde, *The Other Love*, 221.

32. Bartlett, *Who Was That Man?*, 93.

33. H. Montgomery Hyde, *The Trials of Oscar Wilde* (London: William Hodge, 1948), 12.

34. Oscar Wilde, *De Profundis*, ed. Vyvyan Holland (London: Methuen, 1949), 48–9.

35. William Butler Yeats, *Autobiographies* (London: Macmillan, 1961), 288–9.

36. Claude J. Summers, *Gay Fictions* (New York: Continuum, 1990), 31–2.

37. Quoted in Hyde, *The Other Love*, 173.

38. Ted Morgan, *Somerset Maugham* (London: Cape, 1980), 39–40. See Bryan Connon, *Somerset Maugham and the Maugham Dynasty* (London: Sinclair-Stevenson, 1997), 30–1, 45–7.

39. Sean O'Connor, *Straight Acting* (London: Cassell, 1998), 10.

40. IIb, 76; on the referencing of Maugham's plays see my Note on Indexes and Citations.

41. Quoted in Robert Calder, *Willie* (London: Heinemann, 1989), 236–7. See also O'Connor, *Straight Acting*, 82–4.

42. Quoted in Raymond Mander and Joe Mitchenson, *Theatrical Companion to Maugham* (London: Rockliff, 1955), 121.

43. Morgan, *Somerset Maugham*, 192.

44. Connon, *Somerset Maugham and the Maugham Dynasty*, 171.

45. Beverley Nichols, *A Case of Human Bondage* (London: Secker, 1966), 7.

46. In Bryan Connon, *Beverley Nichols: A Life* (London: Constable, 1991), 265–71, Connon supposes that the Haxton episode was Nichols' reassignment of the Wilson episode, but in Connon, *Somerset Maugham and the Maugham Dynasty*, 91–2, he accepts that both incidents happened.

47. See Alan Sinfield, *Gay and After* (London: Serpent's Tail, 1998), chs 4, 5.

48. Philip Hoare, *Noël Coward* (London: Mandarin, 1996), 290–1.

49. See Alan Sinfield, *Faultlines* (Berkeley: University of California Press; Oxford: Oxford University Press, 1992); see particularly 35–42, 45–51, 291–9.

3 Society and its Others: Bohemia

1. Samuel Hynes, *A War Imagined* (London: Bodley Head, 1990), 353–4.

2. Raymond Williams, *Culture* (Glasgow: Fontana, 1981), 74.

3. Raymond Williams, *The Politics of Modernism*, ed. Tony Pinkney (London: Verso, 1989), 45.

4. Williams, *Culture*, 78.

5. Colin Campbell, *The Romantic Ethic and the Spirit of Modern Consumerism* (Oxford: Blackwell, 1987), 195–6.

6. A.T. Fitzroy, *Despised and Rejected* (1918; London: Gay Men's Press, 1988), 234–5.

7. Quoted by Jonathan Cutbill in his introduction to Fitzroy, *Despised and Rejected*; no pagination in the introduction.

8. Lillian Faderman, *Odd Girls and Twilight Lovers* (New York: Penguin, 1992), 64–5.

9. John D'Emilio and Estelle B. Freedman, *Intimate Matters* (New York: Harper and Row, 1988), 228–9.

10. Leslie Fishbein, *Rebels in Bohemia* (Chapel Hill: University of North Carolina Press, 1982), 82–3.

11. Kevin J. Mumford, *Interzones: Black/White Sex Districts in Chicago and New York* (New York: Columbia University Press, 1997), 73 and 148, and ch.5.

12. Faderman, *Odd Girls*, 67–79.

13. Blair Niles, *Strange Brother* (London: Gay Men's Press, 1991), 152–4.

14. Elizabeth Wilson, *The Sphinx in the City* (London: Virago, 1991), 60–4, 75–8.

15. Faderman, *Odd Girls*, 64–5.

16. Henry F. May, *The End of American Innocence* (New York: Knopf, 1959), 307–10. See Faderman, *Odd Girls*, 81–92.

17. Joseph Allen Boone, *Libidinal Currents* (Chicago University Press, 1998), 209.

18. George Chauncey, *Gay New York* (New York: Basic Books, 1994), 229–30.

19. Andrew B. Harris, *Broadway Theatre* (London: Routledge, 1994), 11.

20. Gerald M. Berkowitz, *American Drama of the Twentieth Century* (London: Longman, 1992), 6.

21. The Arts Council of Great Britain, *The Theatre Today in England and Wales* (London: Arts Council, 1970), 52–3.

22. Sue-Ellen Case, *Feminism and Theatre* (London: Macmillan, 1988), 50–3.

23. See Maurice Marc LaBelle, *Alfred Jarry* (New York University Press, 1980), 33–5; Keith Beaumont, *Alfred Jarry* (Leicester University Press, 1984), 50–3.

24. Faderman, *Odd Girls*, 85–7.

25. Marjorie Housepian Dobkin, *The Making of a*

Feminist: Early Journals and Letters of M. Carey Thomas (Ohio: Kent State University Press, 1979), 86–7, quoted in Carroll Smith-Rosenberg, *Disorderly Conduct* (New York. Oxford University Press, 1986), 281.

26. Michael Baker, *Our Three Selves* (London: Gay Men's Press, 1985), 283.

27. Norman Marshall, *The Other Theatre* (London: John Lehmann, 1947), 122–3.

28. Katharine Cockin, *Edith Craig* (1869–1947) (London: Cassell, 1998), 154.

29. Harris, *Broadway Theatre*, 17.

30. Helen Deutsch and Stella Hanau, *The Provincetown: A Story of the Theatre* (New York: Farrar and Rinehart, 1931), 5.

31. Robert Károly Sarlós, *Jig Cook and the Provincetown Players* (Amherst: University of Massachusetts Press, 1982), 4.

32. Linda Fitzsimmons and Viv Gardner, eds, *New Woman Plays* (London: Methuen, 1991), ix–x.

33. Jill Davis, "'This be different" – the Lesbian Drama of Mrs Havelock Ellis', *Women: A Cultural Review*, 2 (1991), 134–48, 146. Lynda Hart calls attention to *The Mothers* and Rachel Crothers' *Criss Cross* (see ch.7 below) in her essay 'Canonizing Lesbians?' in June Schlueter, ed., *Modern American Drama: The Female Canon* (Madison, NJ: Fairleigh Dickinson University Press, 1990).

34. Jerrold Siegel, *Bohemian Paris* (New York: Viking, 1986), 11.

35. Leonora Davidoff, *The Best Circles* (London: Croom Helm, 1973), 78; see 76–80.

36. Philip Hoare, *Noël Coward* (London: Mandarin, 1996), 32–6.

37. Noël Coward, 'Me and the Girls', in Coward, *Pretty Polly Barlow and Other Stories* (London: Heinemann, 1964), 119.

38. Hoare, *Noël Coward*, 73.

39. Martin Green, *Children of the Sun* (London: Constable, 1977), 152.

40. Hynes, *A War Imagined*, 388–90.

41. Hoare, *Noël Coward*, 133.

42. Ibid., 133.

43. T.S. Eliot, *Selected Prose* (Harmondsworth: Penguin, 1963), 101–2. Arthur Hopkins 'produced the memorable Freudian *Hamlet* with John Barrymore in 1922': W. David Sievers, *Freud on Broadway* (1955; New York: Cooper Square, 1970), 47.

44. John Lucas, *The Radical Twenties* (Nottingham: Five Leaves Publications, 1997), 111–17.

45. James Agate, *Red Letter Nights* (London: Cape, 1944), 237.

46. II-1-3; on the referencing of plays quoted from typescript see my Note on Indexes and Citations.

47. Hoare, *Noël Coward*, 157.

48. Robert Graves and Alan Hodge, *The Long Week-End* (London: Faber and Faber, 1940), 124; see Green, *Children of the Sun*, chs 5, 6.

49. Cecil Beaton, *The Glass of Fashion* (London: Weidenfeld, 1954), 153–4.

50. Philip Hoare, *Wilde's Last Stand* (London: Duckworth, 1997), 29.

51. See Humphrey Carpenter, *Geniuses Together* (London: Unwin Hyman, 1987), 121–2.

52. Chauncey, *Gay New York*, 309.

53. Quoted in ibid., 235.

54. Reprinted in Martin Duberman, ed., *About Time* (New York: Meridian, 1991), 160–2.

55. Max Ewing, *Going Somewhere* (London: Cassell, 1933), 23.

56. Wyndham Lewis, *The Apes of God* (London: Nash and Grayson, [1932]), 119.

57. Noël Coward, *Three Plays* (London: Benn, 1925), x; Noël Coward, 'Mrs Worthington', in Coward, *The Lyrics* (London: Methuen, 1983), 200.

58. Kaier Curtin, *'We Can Always Call Them Bulgarians'* (Boston: Alyson, 1987) 137; see 68–102, 127–37.

59. Pamela Robertson, *Guilty Pleasures* (London: I.B. Tauris, 1996), 31; Lillian Schlissel, ed., *Three Plays by Mae West* (London: Nick Hern, 1997), 25.

60. James Agate, *The Contemporary Theatre, 1925* (London: Chapman and Hall, 1926).

61. See Charles Duff, *The Lost Summer* (London: Nick Hern, 1995), 148–56 and 167.

62. Williams, *Culture*, 77, 81.

63. Campbell, *The Romantic Ethic*, 196.

64. Fishbein, *Rebels in Bohemia*, 206.

65. Joel Pfister, *Staging Depth* (Chapel Hill: University of North Carolina Press, 1995), 76 and 73–8.

66. Douglas Goldring, *Odd Man Out* (London: Chapman and Hall, 1935), 227, 320.

4 Emergings

1. Quoted in Richard Findlater, *Banned* (London: MacGibbon and Kee, 1967), 141.

2. Elizabeth Lapovsky Kennedy and Madeline

D. Davis, *Boots of Leather, Slippers of Gold* (New York: Routledge, 1993).

3. Hall Carpenter Archives and Lesbian Oral History Group, eds., *Inventing Ourselves* (London: Routledge, 1989); Emily Hamer, *Britannia's Glory* (London: Cassell, 1996).

4. George Chauncey, *Gay New York* (New York: Basic Books, 1994).

5. T.W. Heyck, 'From Men of Letters to Intellectuals: the Transformation of Intellectual Life in Nineteenth-century England', *Journal of British Studies*, 20 (1980), 158–83.

6. N.G. Annan, 'The Intellectual Aristocracy', in J.H. Plumb, ed., *Studies in Social History* (London: Longmans, 1955).

7. H. Montgomery Hyde, *The Other Love* (London: Mayflower Books, 1972), 206–11; Jeffrey Weeks, *Coming Out* (London: Quartet, 1977), 107–11; Michael Baker, *Our Three Selves* (London: Gay Men's Press, 1985), 245–6.

8. Quoted in Hamer, *Britannia's Glory*, 102.

9. Samuel Hynes, *A War Imagined* (London: Bodley Head, 1990), 234; see Philip Hoare, *Wilde's Last Stand* (London: Duckworth, 1997), 188–9, 202–7, 227–31.

10. Quoted in Humphrey Carpenter, *The Brideshead Generation* (London: Weidenfeld, 1989), 80–1.

11. Louis MacNeice, *The Strings are False* (London: Faber and Faber, 1965), 94, 103.

12. Michael Darlow and Gillian Hodson, *Terence Rattigan* (London: Quartet, 1979), 40.

13. Weeks, *Coming Out*, 60–1.

14. Quoted in Hyde, *The Other Love*, 200.

15. Kenneth Lewes, *The Psychoanalytic Theory of Male Homosexuality* (London: Quartet, 1989), 59, 69–94. See Jonathan Dollimore, *Sexual Dissidence* (Oxford: Clarendon, 1991), ch.12; Alan Sinfield, *The Wilde Century* (London: Cassell, 1994), ch.7. Magnus Hirschfeld's *Homosexuality* (1914, 1920) was not translated, however.

16. A.G. Tansley, *The New Psychology and its Relation to Life*, revised and enlarged edn (London: Allen and Unwin, 1922), 275.

17. Joel Pfister, *Staging Depth* (Chapel Hill: University of North Carolina Press, 1995), 63–7.

18. A.A. Brill, *Psychoanalysis: Its Theories and Practical Application*, 2nd edn (Philadelphia and London: W.B. Saunders, 1918), 55.

19. Nathan G. Hale, *The Rise and Crisis of Psychoanalysis in the United States* (New York: Oxford University Press, 1995), 57–8. See Hynes, *A War Imagined*, 365–6.

20. Jonathan Dollimore, *Death, Desire and Loss in Western Culture* (London: Allen Lane, 1998), 280–1.

21. Hale, *The Rise and Crisis of Psychoanalysis in the United States*, 77; and chs 4 and 5. See also Leslie Fishbein, *Rebels in Bohemia* (Chapel Hill: University of North Carolina Press, 1982), 83–93. I discuss *Strange Interlude* in ch. 6.

22. IIIb, 285–7; on the referencing of Maugham's plays see my Note on Indexes and Citations.

23. Brian Masters, *The Life of E.F. Benson* (London: Chatto and Windus 1991), 214.

24. E.M. Forster, *Abinger Harvest* (1936; London: Arnold, 1940), 141.

25. Joseph Bristow, *Effeminate England* (Buckingham: Open University Press, 1995), 102.

26. Paul Delany, *D.H. Lawrence's Nightmare* (Hassocks: Harvester, 1979), 157–8, 167.

27. Quoted by Polly Devlin in her introduction to M.J. Farrell, *Devoted Ladies* (London: Virago, 1984), x.

28. Henry F. May, *The End of American Innocence* (New York: Knopf, 1959), 346.

29. Laurence Senelick, 'Lady and the Tramp: Drag Differentials in the Progressive Era', in Senelick, ed., *Gender in Performance* (Hanover, NH: University Press of New England, 1992), 37.

30. Harry M. Benshoff, *Monsters in the Closet: Homosexuality and the Horror Film* (Manchester University Press, 1997), 34.

31. Julian Symons, *The Thirties*, revised edn (London: Faber and Faber, 1975), 40.

32. Quoted in H. Montgomery Hyde, *The Trials of Oscar Wilde* (London: William Hodge, 1948), 359–60.

33. See Joseph Bristow, *Empire Boys* (London: HarperCollins, 1991), 86–7.

34. Michel Foucault, *The History of Sexuality, Volume I: An Introduction*, trans. Robert Hurley (New York: Vintage Books, 1978), 69.

35. Havelock Ellis and John Addington Symonds, *Sexual Inversion* (New York: Ayer Company, 1994), 141.

36. Douglas Goldring, *Odd Man Out* (London: Chapman and Hall, 1935), 36–7.

37. Martin Taylor, 'Introduction', in Taylor, ed., *Lads: Love Poetry of the Trenches* (London: Constable, 1989), 29.

38. John van Druten, *The Way to the Present* (London: Michael Joseph, 1938), 266.

39. Kaier Curtin, *We Can Always Call Them Bulgarians* (Boston: Alyson, 1987), 228.
40. See ibid., 229–34; Nicholas de Jongh, *Not in Front of the Audience* (London: Routledge, 1992), 45–7.
41. J.R. Ackerley, *My Father and Myself* (London: Bodley Head, 1968), 117.
42. Jeffrey Weeks, *Sex, Politics and Society*, 2nd edn (London: Longman, 1989), 155.
43. Ackerley, *My Father and Myself*, 117.
44. Quoted in Peter Parker, *Ackerley* (London: Constable, 1989), 98. Siefried Sassoon said the play was very like his own experience: ibid., 91.
45. Ibid., 90.
46. Quoted in Stephen Rooney, 'Literary Constructions of Male Homosexuality 1954–1969', unpub D.Phil. thesis, University of Sussex, 1998, 144.
47. Curtin, *Bulgarians*, 212–16.
48. Ackerley, *My Father and Myself*, 116; *Prisoners of War*, 107.
49. Curtin, *Bulgarians*, 215.
50. de Jongh, *Not in Front of the Audience*, 28–30.
51. Peter Burton, introduction to *The Prisoners of War*, in Michael Wilcox, ed., *Gay Plays*, vol. 3 (London: Methuen, 1988), 91.
52. Neville Braybrooke, ed., *The Letters of J.R. Ackerley* (London: Duckworth, 1975), 112–13.
53. T.C. Worsley, *Flannelled Fool* (London: Alan Ross, 1967), 74.
54. Lillian Faderman, *Odd Girls and Twilight Lovers* (New York: Penguin, 1992), 14–15.
55. Carroll Smith-Rosenberg, *Disorderly Conduct* (New York: Oxford University Press, 1986), 273–4.
56. Sheila Jeffreys, 'Does It Matter If They Did It?', in Lesbian History Group, *Not a Passing Phase* (London: Women's Press, 1989), 25–7.
57. Lillian Faderman, *The Scotch Verdict* (New York: Columbia University Press, 1993), 65; see 220–5.
58. Emma Donoghue, *Passions between Women* (London: Scarlett Press, 1993); Dell Richards, *Lesbian Lists* (Boston: Alyson, 1990).
59. Nina Rapi, '"That's Why You Are So Queer": The Representation of Lesbian Sexuality in the Theatre', in Lizz Gibbs, ed., *Daring to Dissent* (London: Cassell, 1994), 39–43.
60. Faderman, *Odd Girls*, 65; Donald L. Loeffler, *An Analysis of the Treatment of the Homosexual Character in Dramas Produced in the New York Theatre from 1950 to 1968* (New York: Arno Press, 1975), 16.

61. Curtin, *Bulgarians*, 167.
62. ibid., 165.
63. Faderman, *Scotch Verdict*, 281, 273.
64. Eric Bentley, *The Dramatic Event* (London: Dennis Dobson, 1956), 74.
65. Théophile Gautier, *Mademoiselle de Maupin*, trans. R.E. Powys Mathers (London: Folio Society, 1948), 222.

5 Noël Coward's Audiences

1. Sean O'Connor, *Straight Acting* (London: Cassell, 1998), 106. See Nicholas de Jongh, *Not in Front of the Audience* (London: Routledge, 1992); John M. Clum, *Acting Gay*, 2nd edn (New York: Columbia University Press, 1994); Donald L. Loeffler, *An Analysis of the Treatment of the Homosexual Character in Dramas Produced in the New York Theatre from 1950 to 1968* (New York: Arno Press, 1975); Kaier Curtin, *We Can Always Call Them Bulgarians* (Boston: Alyson, 1987).
2. John Lahr, *Coward the Playwright* (London: Methuen, 1982), 3, 66, 82, 121, 128.
3. Philip Hoare, *Noël Coward* (London: Mandarin, 1996), 245, 417.
4. Noël Coward, *The Lyrics* (London: Methuen, 1983), 226–7; Hoare, *Noël Coward*, 359; Adrian Wright in *Gay Times*, 197 (February, 1995), 14.
5. Cecil Beaton, *Self-Portrait with Friends* (London: Weidenfeld and Nicolson, 1979), 11–12, quoted in Hoare, *Noël Coward*, 201.
6. Hoare, *Noël Coward*, 268.
7. Ibid., 206.
8. Coward, *The Lyrics*, 213.
9. Eve Kosofsky Sedgwick, *Between Men: English Literature and Male Homosocial Desire* (New York: Columbia University Press, 1985), 1–5.
10. Jacqui Russell, *File on Coward* (London: Methuen, 1987), 53.
11. A.A. Brill, *Freud's Contribution to Psychiatry* (New York: Norton, 1944), 133; quoted by W. David Sievers, *Freud on Broadway* (1955; New York: Cooper Square, 1970), 217.
12. Lahr, *Coward the Playwright*, 83.
13. Harry M. Benshoff, *Monsters in the Closet* (Manchester University Press, 1997), 188.
14. Stephen Rooney, 'Literary Constructions of Male Homosexuality 1954–1969', unpub. D.Phil. thesis, University of Sussex, 1998, 226.

15. John van Druten, 'Sex and Censorship in the Theatre', in Norman Haire, ed., *World League for Sexual Reform: Proceedings of the Third Congress* (1929) (London: Routledge, 1930), 322.
16. *The Collected Plays of W. Somerset Maugham*, 3 vols, vol. 2 (London: Heinemann, 1931), Introduction, x–xii.
17. James Agate, *Red Letter Nights* (London: Cape, 1944), p.239.
18. George Chauncey, *Gay New York* (New York. Basic Books, 1994), 288.
19. Curtin, *Bulgarians*, 82; Clum, *Acting Gay*, 90.
20. Andy Medhurst, 'That Special Thrill: *Brief Encounter*, Homosexuality and Authorship', *Screen*, 32 (summer 1991), 197–208, 202, 204.
21. Hoare, *Noël Coward*, 140.
22. Ibid., 335, 313.
23. Benshoff, *Monsters in the Closet*, 85; see also 125.
24. See Jeffrey Weeks, *Coming Out* (London: Quartet, 1977), 156–8, 163–4; Alan Sinfield, *Literature, Politics and Culture in Postwar Britain*, 2nd edn (London: Athlone, 1997), ch.5.
25. Hoare, *Noël Coward*, 393.
26. Chauncey, *Gay New York*, 12–23.
27. Ronald R. Butters, 'Foreword', *South Atlantic Quarterly*, 88 (1989), 1–5, 2.
28. John Boswell, *Christianity, Social Tolerance and Homosexuality* (Chicago University Press, 1980), 43.
29. Donald Webster Cory, *The Homosexual in America* (1951; New York: Arno Press, 1975), 107–8.
30. Hoare, *Noël Coward*, 92–3.
31. See ibid., 206.
32. Curtin, *Bulgarians*, 170. In UK newspaper criticism of Coward 'gay' is used unselfconsciously in a general sense (Russell, *File on Coward*, 59, 61, 74, 76); also in *The Green Bay Tree* (1933), 78, 90.
33. Coward, *The Lyrics*, 109.
34. Ibid., 151.
35. Russell Davies, ed., *The Kenneth Williams Diaries* (London: HarperCollins, 1994), 8.
36. Peter Wildeblood, *Against the Law* (London: Weidenfeld and Nicolson, 1955), 23. Wildeblood goes on to use the word and record its use by others: 27, 105. See Weeks, *Coming Out*, 42, 190; Neil Bartlett, *Who Was That Man?* (London: Serpent's Tail, 1988), 89.
37. Colin Spencer, *Which of Us Two?* (London: Viking, 1990), 14.
38. D.J. West, *Homosexuality* (London: Duckworth, 1955), 28; Gordon Westwood, *A Minority* (London: Longmans, 1960), 207.
39. Stephen Jeffery-Poulter, *Peers, Queers and Commons* (London: Routledge, 1991), 69–70.
40. Kevin Porter and Jeffrey Weeks, eds, *Between the Acts* (London: Routledge, 1991), 38, 126.
41. Hall Carpenter Archives and Gay Men's Oral History Group, *Walking After Midnight* (London: Routledge, 1989), 44, 72.
42. See Peter Burton, *Among the Aliens* (Brighton: Millivres, 1995), 39–40.

6 Gay Men and Gender

1. Bryan Connon, *Beverley Nichols: a Life* (London: Constable, 1991), 39–40. I quote this instance in *The Wilde Century* (London: Cassell, 1994), but it is too apposite to omit here.
2. Ia, 115; on the referencing of Maugham's plays see my Note on Indexes and Citations.
3. Jonathan Weinberg, *Speaking for Vice* (New Haven: Yale University Press, 1993), 203.
4. Kaier Curtin, *We Can Always Call Them Bulgarians* (Boston: Alyson, 1987) 115–18.
5. Richard Findlater, *Banned* (London: MacGibbon and Kee, 1967), 142. See Curtin, *Bulgarians*, 176–88.
6. Quoted in John Johnston, *The Lord Chamberlain's Blue Pencil* (London: Hodder and Stoughton, 1990), 172–3.
7. Curtin, *Bulgarians*, 183.
8. Quoted from the Lord Chamberlain's correspondence in Christine Fox, 'Conduct Unbecoming: Noël Coward, Censorship and the Fallacy of the Inconsequence', unpub. D.Phil. thesis, University of Sussex, 1996, 245.
9. Curtin, *Bulgarians*, 183–7.
10. John M. Clum, *Acting Gay*, 2nd edn (New York: Columbia University Press, 1994), 99.
11. Quoted from a newspaper report in Curtin, *Bulgarians*, 136.
12. Quoted in Lillian Schlissel, ed., *Three Plays by Mae West* (London: Nick Hern, 1997), 240.
13. Marybeth Hamilton, '"I'm the Queen of the Bitches": Female Impersonation and Mae West's *Pleasure Man*', in Lesley Ferris, ed., *Crossing the Stage* (London: Routledge, 1993).
14. Laurence Senelick, 'Lady and the Tramp: Drag Differentials in the Progressive Era', in Senelick, ed., *Gender in Performance*

(Hanover, NH: University Press of New England, 1992); Sharon R. Ullman, *Sex Seen* (Berkeley: University of California Press, 1997), 45–61.

15. Allan Bérubé, *Coming Out Under Fire* (New York: Plume, 1991), 71–2.

16. Don Paulson with Roger Simpson, *An Evening at the Garden of Allah* (New York: Columbia University Press, 1996), 81. See Elizabeth Drorbaugh, 'Notes on Stormé De Larverié and the Jewel Box Revue', in Ferris, ed., *Crossing the Stage.*

17. Esther Newton found these distinctions largely in place in the 1960s: Newton, *Mother Camp*, 2nd edn (Chicago University Press, 1979).

18. George Chauncey, *Gay New York* (New York: Basic Books, 1994), 13.

19. Ibid., 100.

20. Quoted in Donald Webster Cory, *The Homosexual in America* (1951), with a retrospective foreword (New York: Arno Press, 1975), 188.

21. Gore Vidal, *The City and the Pillar*, revised edn (New York: Signet, 1965), 100.

22. Hall Carpenter Archives and Gay Men's Oral History Group, *Walking After Midnight* (London: Routledge, 1989), 87; see also 45, 50.

23. T.C. Worsley, *Flannelled Fool* (London: Alan Ross, 1967), 26.

24. Bryan Connon, *Somerset Maugham and the Maugham Dynasty* (London: Sinclair-Stevenson, 1997), 167.

25. See Sinfield, *The Wilde Century*, 109–17.

26. Quoted in Geoffrey Wansell, *Terence Rattigan* (London: Fourth Estate, 1995), 248.

27. Jeffrey Weeks, *Coming Out* (London: Quartet, 1977), 33–5.

28. Kate Millett, *Sexual Politics* (London: Hart-Davis, 1971), 349.

29. John van Druten, 'Sex and Censorship in the Theatre', in Norman Haire, ed., *World League for Sexual Reform: Proceedings of the Third Congress* (1929) (London: Routledge, 1930), 319. George Jean Nathan made a similar complaint in New York in 1945: see Curtin, *Bulgarians*, 252.

30. Quoted in Curtin, *Bulgarians*, 183–4.

31. Blair Niles, *Strange Brother* (London: Gay Men's Press, 1991), 156.

32. Curtin, *Bulgarians*, 252.

33. Neil Bartlett, *Who Was That Man?* (London: Serpent's Tail, 1988), 121–2.

34. See C. Tyler Carpenter and Edward H. Yeatts, *Stars without Garters* (San Francisco: Alamo Square Press, 1996), 25

35. Kevin Porter and Jeffrey Weeks, eds., *Between the Acts* (London: Routledge, 1991), 99.

36. Curtin, *Bulgarians*, 252.

37. Fidelis Morgan, ed., *The Years Between* (London: Virago, 1994), 325–6. However, other pieces were censored – see Morgan, 271–2, 320–2

38. Michael Flanders and Donald Swan, *At the Drop of a Hat*, quoted from the record (London: Parlophone PMC 1033, n.d.)

39. Alan Bennett, Peter Cook, Jonathan Miller and Dudley Moore, *The Complete Beyond the Fringe* (London: Methuen, 1987), 28–30.

7 Lesbians and Gender

1. Compton Mackenzie, *Extraordinary Women* (London: Secker, 1932), 134.

2. Frank Mort, *Dangerous Sexualities* (London: Routledge, 1987), 89; and 116–30. See Philippa Levine, *Victorian Feminism 1850–1900* (London: Hutchinson, 1987), 132–3.

3. Alan Bird, *The Plays of Oscar Wilde* (London, Vision Press, 1977), 128.

4. Patricia Flanagan Behrendt, *Oscar Wilde* (London: Macmillan, 1991), 152–3. Cf Rita Felski, 'The Counterdiscourse of the Feminine in Three Texts by Wilde, Huysmans and Sacher-Masoch', *PMLA*, 106 (1991), 1094–1105; Alan Sinfield, '"Effeminacy" and "Femininity": Sexual Politics in Wilde's Comedies', *Modern Drama*, Special Issue on Oscar Wilde, ed. J.H. Kaplan, 37 (1994), 34–52.

5. George Chauncey, Jr., 'From Sexual Inversion to Homosexuality: Medicine and the Changing Conceptualization of Female Deviance', *Salmagundi*, 58–9 (1982–83), 114–46, 144.

6. Sheila Jeffreys, *The Spinster and Her Enemies* (London: Pandora, 1985), 185.

7. See also Coward's 'Spinster's Song', from the revue *On with the Dance* (1925), in Noël Coward, *The Lyrics* (London: Methuen, 1983), 26.

8. IIa, 157; on the referencing of Maugham's plays see my Note on Indexes and Citations.

9. He is pictured in Raymond Mander and Joe Mitchenson, *Theatrical Companion to Maugham* (London: Rockliff, 1955), 85–6.

10. Ibid.,113.

11. W. David Sievers, *Freud on Broadway* (1955;

New York: Cooper Square, 1970), 70–1; Joel Pfister, *Staging Depth* (Chapel Hill: University of North Carolina Press, 1995), 198–201.

12. Sievers, *Freud on Broadway*, 91.

13. A.G. Tansley, *The New Psychology and Its Relation to Life*, revised and enlarged edn (London: Allen and Unwin, 1922), 276–7.

14. Clemence Dane, *Regiment of Women* (1917; London: Virago, 1995), 337.

15. Kaier Curtin, *Bulgarians*, 54.

16. Quoted in Richard Findlater, *Banned* (London: MacGibbon and Kee, 1967), 142.

17. Curtin, *Bulgarians*, 62; see 56–7.

18. Ibid., 53, 55.

19. See ibid., 105–12.

20. Quoted in ibid., 220.

21. Quoted in ibid., 220.

22. *Trio*, the novel, was published in New York by the Sun Dial Press in 1945; Jane Rule writes sympathetically of Dorothy Baker in *Lesbian Images* (New York: Doubleday, 1975).

23. Curtin, *Bulgarians*, 201.

24. Lillian Faderman, *Odd Girls and Twilight Lovers* (New York: Penguin, 1992), 34–5.

25. Carroll Smith-Rosenberg, *Disorderly Conduct* (New York: Oxford University Press, 1986), 278. See also Jeffreys, *The Spinster and Her Enemies*, chs 5, 6; Sally Munt, *Heroic Desire* (London: Cassell, 1998), ch.3.

26. Chauncey, 'From Sexual Inversion to Homosexuality', 125.

27. George Chauncey, Jr., 'Christian Brotherhood or Sexual Perversion', in Martin Duberman, Martha Vicinus and George Chauncey Jr., eds, *Hidden from History* (New York: New American Library, 1989).

28. Esther Newton, 'The Mythic Mannish Lesbian: Radclyffe Hall and the New Woman', in Duberman, et al., eds, *Hidden from History*, 283–4, 286.

29. Sonia Ruehl, 'Inverts and Experts: Radclyffe Hall and the Lesbian Identity', in Judith Newton and Deborah Rosenfelt, eds, *Feminist Criticism and Social Change* (New York: Methuen, 1985), 174.

30. Hall Carpenter Archives and Lesbian Oral History Group, eds, *Inventing Ourselves* (London: Routledge, 1989), 47–8.

31. Rule, *Lesbian Images*, 3–4.

32. Michael Baker, *Our Three Selves* (London: Gay Men's Press, 1985), 248.

33. Chauncey, 'From Sexual Inversion to Homosexuality', 128.

34. Ruehl, 'Inverts and Experts: Radclyffe Hall and the Lesbian Identity'.

35. Baker, *Our Three Selves*, 131–2.

36. Jay Prosser, *Second Skins* (New York: Columbia University Press, 1998), ch.4. See Faderman, *Odd Girls*, 4–5.

37. Jan McDonald, 'New Women in the New Drama', *New Theatre Quarterly*, 6, no.21 (February 1990), 31–42, 34; Declan Kiberd, *Men and Feminism in Modern Literature* (London: Macmillan, 1985), 61.

38. Jill Davis, 'The New Woman and the New Life', in Viv Gardner and Susan Rutherford, eds, *The New Woman and Her Sisters* (Hemel Hempstead: Harvester, 1992), 24–5.

39. Ibid., 30.

40. Faderman, *Odd Girls*, 42–3.

41. Eustace Chesser, *Odd Man Out* (London: Gollancz, 1959), 115.

42. Wyndham Lewis, *The Apes of God* (1930; London: Nash and Grayson, n.d.), 222.

43. Maurice Cranston, *Sartre* (Edinburgh: Oliver and Bell, 1962), 63.

8 Class Conscious

1 Kevin Porter and Jeffrey Weeks, eds, *Between the Acts* (London: Routledge, 1991), 74.

2 Ibid., 77.

3. See Raphael Samuel, Ewan MacColl and Stuart Cosgrave, *Theatres of the Left 1880–1935* (London: Routledge, 1985).

4. John Binnie, 'Unity Then and Now', *Gay Times*, 141 (June 1990), 29.

5. Howard Goorney, *The Theatre Workshop Story* (London: Methuen, 1981), 118. On other such 'Cockney improvisations' at Stratford East see John Russell Taylor, *Anger and After*, revised edn. (Harmondsworth: Penguin, 1963), 121–5.

6. Jeffrey Weeks, 'Discourse, Desire and Sexual Deviance: Some Problems in a History of Homosexuality', in Kenneth Plummer, ed., *The Making of the Modern Homosexual* (London: Hutchinson, 1981), 105. See Alan Sinfield, *The Wilde Century* (London: Cassell, 1994), ch.6.

7. Alan Sinfield, *Gay and After* (London: Serpent's Tail, 1998), 81 and chs 4, 5.

8. George Chauncey, *Gay New York* (New York: Basic Books, 1994), 118–21.

9. Rodney Garland, *The Heart in Exile*

(Brighton: Millivres, 1995), 179. Cf Leonore
Davidoff, 'Class and Gender in Victorian
England: The Diaries of Arthur J. Munby and
Hannah Cullwick', *Feminist Studies*, 5 (1979),
87–141.

10 Emlyn Williams, *Emlyn* (London: Bodley
Head, 1973), 323–4.

11. Ibid., 380.

12. Peter Burton, introduction to *The Green Bay
Tree*, in Michael Wilcox, ed., *Gay Plays*, vol.
1 (London: Methuen, 1984), 53–4.

13. Robin Maugham, *Somerset and all the
Maughams* (London: Longmans and
Heinemann, 1966), 201; Noël Coward, *Present
Indicative* (London: Heinemann, 1937), 250,
265; Philip Hoare, *Noël Coward* (London:
Mandarin, 1996), 272.

14. Williams, *Emlyn*, 364.

15. Quentin Crisp, *The Naked Civil Servant* (New
York: Plume, 1977), 203.

16. Geoffrey Wansell, *Terence Rattigan* (London:
Fourth Estate, 1995), 77–8; Michael Darlow
and Gillian Hodson, *Terence Rattigan*
(London: Quartet, 1979), 78–9. On Rattigan's
earlier play, *First Episode* (1933), about gay
life at Oxford, which was produced but not
published, see Wansell, ch.6.

17. Wansell, *Terence Rattigan*, 188–90; Bryan
Connon, *Somerset Maugham and the
Maugham Dynasty* (London: Sinclair-
Stevenson, 1997), 224.

18. Wansell, *Terence Rattigan*, 235, 253.

19. See T.C. Worsley, 'Terence Rattigan and His
Critics', *London Magazine*, new series, 4
(September 1964), 60–72. Other relevant stage
versions of Dumas *fils*' story include: Charles
Ludlam's cross-dressed *Camille* (1973; see ch.15
below); Harry Kondoleon's Off Off-Broadway
queering in *The Fairy Garden* (1982); Pam
Gems' attempt to reach through the stereotype
to the person in her Royal Shakespeare
Company and West End play, *Camille* (1984).

20. Wansell, *Terence Rattigan*, 293.

21. Kenneth Tynan, *A View of the English Stage*
(St Albans: Paladin, 1976), 221–2.

22. Alan Brien, *Spectator*, 16 May, 1958, 621–2. For
a complaint that Emlyn Williams wrote about
heterosexuals when his real theme was homosexual, see Kaier Curtin, *We Can Always Call
Them Bulgarians* (Boston: Alyson, 1987), 251.

23. Richard Huggett, *Binkie Beaumont* (London:
Hodder and Stoughton, 1989), 429–33;
Wansell, *Terence Rattigan*, 251–2.

24. Wansell, *Terence Rattigan*, 273–8; Darlow
and Hodson, *Terence Rattigan*, 227–8.

25. Wansell, *Terence Rattigan*, 258.

26. Tynan, *A View of the English Stage*, 147.

9 Queer Thrills

1. Peter Wildeblood, *Against the Law* (London:
Weidenfeld, 1955), 77, 26.

2. J.R. Ackerley, *My Father and Myself*
(London: Bodley Head, 1968), 120;
Wildeblood, *Against the Law*, 55.

3. Harry M. Benshoff, *Monsters in the Closet:
Homosexuality and the Horror Film*
(Manchester University Press, 1997), 4.

4. John van Druten, *Somebody Knows*, 14; J.B.
Priestley, *Dangerous Corner*, 393.

5. D.A. Miller, 'Anal *Rope*', in Diana Fuss, ed.,
Inside/Out (New York: Routledge, 1991),
121–4.

6. Sean French, *Patrick Hamilton* (London:
Faber and Faber, 1993), 202. See Robin
Wood, 'The Murderous Gays: Hitchcock's
Homophobia', in Corey K. Creekmur and
Alexander Doty, eds, *Out in Culture* (London:
Cassell, 1995), 211.

7. Keith Howes, *Broadcasting It* (London:
Cassell, 1993), 695.

8. French, *Patrick Hamilton*, 114.

9. James Agate, *Red Letter Nights* (London:
Cape, 1944), 257–8.

10. Michael Davidson, *The World, the Flesh and
Myself* (London: Quartet Books, 1977), 149.

11. William Stewart, *Cassell's Queer Companion*
(London: Cassell, 1995), 206; George
Chauncey, *Gay New York* (New York: Basic
Books, 1994), 15–16.

12. Ina Russell, ed., *Jeb and Dash* (Boston: Faber
and Faber, 1993), 14.

13. Oscar Wilde, *The Picture of Dorian Gray*, ed.
Isobel Murray (Oxford University Press,
1981), 149–52.

14. Alison Light, *Forever England* (London:
Routledge, 1991), 73; also 87–100.

15. Quoted in Christine Fox, 'Conduct
Unbecoming: Noël Coward, Censorship and
the Fallacy of the Inconsequence', unpub.
D.Phil. thesis, University of Sussex, 1996, 75.

16. Bryan Connon, *Somerset Maugham and the
Maugham Dynasty* (London: Sinclair-
Stevenson, 1997), 157.

17. W. David Sievers, *Freud on Broadway* (New

York: Cooper Square, 1970), 409.

18. Quoted by Lynda Hart, '"They Don't Even Look Like Maids Anymore": Wendy Kesselman's *My Sister in This House*', in Lynda Hart, ed., *Making a Spectacle* (Ann Arbor: University of Michigan Press, 1989), 132. Hart argues that Genet's version of the story derives from that of Jacques Lacan, who diagnosed the sisters as suffering from a paranoid disorder, *délires à deux* – 'insanity for two'.

19. Quoted in Fox, 'Conduct Unbecoming', appendix 1, 1 January 1952.

20. Martin Esslin, *Theatre of the Absurd*, enlarged edn (Harmondsworth: Penguin, 1968), 202–7.

21. Leo Bersani, *Homos* (Cambridge, MA: Harvard University Press, 1995), 173.

22. See Kaier Curtin, *We Can Always Call Them Bulgarians* (Boston: Alyson, 1987), ch.1; Alisa Solomon, *Re-Dressing the Canon* (London: Routledge, 1997), ch.4.

23. Curtin, *Bulgarians*, 258–63.

24. Russell Davies, ed., *The Kenneth Williams Diaries* (London: HarperCollins, 1994), 112.

25. Kenneth Tynan, *A View of the English Theatre* (St Albans: Paladin, 1976), 333.

26. Ibid., 334.

27. Martin Esslin, *The Peopled Wound* (London: Methuen, 1970), 129.

28. John M. Clum, *Acting Gay*, 2nd edn (New York: Columbia University Press, 1994), 113, and see 107–14.

29. Quoted in Jackie Forster, 'Frank Marcus and Sister George . . .', *Sappho*, 8, no. 3 (1980), 9–11.

30. Quoted in John Lahr, *Prick Up Your Ears* (Harmondsworth: Penguin, 1980), 178.

31. Ibid., 178.

32. Simon Shepherd, *Because We're Queers* (London: Gay Men's Press, 1989), 77.

10 Reading Tennessee Williams

1. Camille Paglia, *Sexual Personae* (New Haven: Yale University Press, 1990), 535–6; John Lahr, *Coward the Playwright* (London: Methuen, 1982), 66–8.

2. Molly Haskell, *From Reverence to Rape* (New York: Holt, Rinehart and Winston, 1973), 244, 248.

3. Peter Hall in 1979, quoted in Sean O'Connor, *Straight Acting* (London: Cassell, 1998), 174; and see 22–3.

4. Jack Babuscio, 'Camp and the Gay Sensibility', in Richard Dyer, ed., *Gays and Film* (London: British Film Institute, 1977), 53–5.

5. John M. Clum, *Acting Gay*, 2nd edn (New York: Columbia University Press, 1994), 150.

6. Mark Lilly, *Gay Men's Literature in the Twentieth Century* (London: Macmillan, 1993), 113.

7. Ian Lucas, *Impertinent Decorum* (London: Cassell, 1994), 91

8. Vidal, introduction to Tennessee Williams, *Collected Stories* (New York: Ballantyne, 1985), xxvi; Tennessee Williams, *Memoirs* (New York: Bantam, 1976), 164.

9. Williams in Winston Leyland, ed., *Gay Roots: Twenty Years of Gay Sunshine* (San Francisco: Gay Sunshine Press, 1991), 326.

10. Quoted in Jonathan Katz, *Gay American History* (New York: Avon Books, 1978), 155.

11. Williams, *Memoirs*, 62–3. See Gore Vidal, introduction to Williams, *Collected Stories*, xxvi.

12. Alan Sinfield, *The Wilde Century* (London: Cassell, 1994) and *Gay and After* (London: Serpent's Tail, 1998).

13. Stephen Maddison, 'Queer Sisters: Gay Male Culture, Women and Gender Dissent', unpub. D.Phil. thesis, University of Sussex, 1997, 229–30 and ch.1 (to be published as *Fags, Hags and Queer Sisters* [London: Macmillan, 2000]).

14. Simon Fraser, 'Visions of Love', interview with Neil Bartlett, *Rouge*, 8 (October–December 1991), 20–22, 21. See Alan Sinfield, '"The Moment of Submission": Neil Bartlett in Conversation', *Modern Drama*, 39 (1996), Special Issue on Lesbian/Gay/Queer Drama, ed. Hersh Zeifman, 211–21, 218–19.

15. Derek Jarman, *At Your Own Risk* (London: Hutchinson, 1992), 55.

16. Donald Spoto, *The Kindness of Strangers* (London: Bodley Head, 1985), 59; and see 15–20.

17. Lyle Leverich, *Tom* (New York: Crown, 1995), 224.

18. James T. Sears, *Growing Up Gay in the South* (New York: Harrington Park, 1991), 78, 91–3.

19. Harold Clurman, writing on the initial production, and in 1973; quoted in Signi Falk, *Tennessee Williams*, 2nd edn (Boston: Twayne, 1978), 60–1.

20. Sears, *Growing Up Gay*, 74.

21. Quoted in Brenda Murphy, *Tennessee Williams and Elia Kazan* (Cambridge University Press, 1992), 19.

22. John Gassner, *Theater at the Crossroads* (New York: Holt, Rinehart and Winston, 1960), 86.

23. Falk, *Tennessee Williams*, 159.

24. W. David Sievers, *Freud on Broadway* (New York: Cooper, 1970), 377, 379.

25. In Jordan Y. Miller, ed., *Twentieth Century Interpretations of 'A Streetcar Named Desire'* (Englewood Cliffs, NJ: Prentice-Hall, 1971), 33, 43; and see 28, 38.

26. John T. von Szeliski, 'The Tragedy of Sensitivity', ibid., 70.

27. David Bergman, *Gaiety Transfigured* (Madison: University of Wisconsin Press, 1991), 155.

28. Gene D. Phillips, *The Films of Tennessee Williams* (East Brunswick, NJ: Associated University Presses, 1980), 192, 196. On *Baby Doll*, see Spoto, *Kindness*, 209–11; David Savran, *Communists, Cowboys, and Queers* (Minneapolis: University of Minnesota Press, 1992), 120–1, 127–30.

29. Vidal, Introduction to Williams, *Collected Stories*, xxiv. See Savran, *Communists, Cowboys, and Queers*, 83–4.

30. See Savran, *Communists, Cowboys, and Queers*, 101.

31. Georges-Michel Sarotte, *Like a Brother, Like a Lover*, trans. Richard Miller (New York: Anchor/Doubleday, 1978), 119.

32. Williams, *Collected Stories*, 291.

33. Quoted in Leverich, *Tom*, 554.

34. Donald M. Kaplan, 'Homosexuality and American Theatre: a Psychoanalytic Comment', *Tulane Drama Review*, 9, no. 3 (1965), 25–55, 26.

35. *Tennessee Williams' Letters to Donald Windham, 1940–1965*, ed. Donald Windham (New York: Holt, Rinehart and Winston, 1977), 148.

36. *Cat on a Hot Tin Roof*, 168; Williams, *Memoirs*, 220–1; see 212–21. Cf Arnold Wesker, *The Birth of Shylock and the Death of Zero Mostel* (London: Quartet Books, 1997).

37. Williams, *Collected Stories*, xvi–xvii. On Hart Crane, see Thomas E. Yingling, *Hart Crane and the Homosexual Text* (Chicago University Press, 1990).

38. Williams, *Memoirs*, 16; see also Williams, *Collected Stories*, xvi–xvii.

39. Henry Abelove, 'Freud, Male Homosexuality, and the Americans', in Henry Abelove, Michèle Aina Barale and David M. Halperin, eds, *The Lesbian and Gay Studies Reader* (New York: Routledge, 1993), 386.

40. Spoto, *Kindness*, 215; Williams, *Memoirs*, 218–19.

41. Williams, *Memoirs*, 245; see 231–5, 238–9, 244–6, 297.

42. See ibid., 36, 53. On *The Glass Menagerie*, see Mark Lilly, 'Tennessee Williams', in Lilly, ed., *Lesbian and Gay Writing* (London: Macmillan, 1990).

43. Leslie Fiedler, *Love and Death in the American Novel* (New York: Stein and Day, 1966), 368, 12.

44. Allan Bérubé, *Coming Out Under Fire* (New York: Plume, 1991), 38, 186–93.

45. Quoted in Nicholas de Jongh, *Not in Front of the Audience* (London: Routledge, 1992), 77; see Clum, *Acting Gay*, 159–61, 346; Maria St Just, ed., *Five O'Clock Angel* (London: Deutsch, 1991), 108–10.

46. *Cat on a Hot Tin Roof*, 121. Williams said this was probably all Brick and Skipper ever did, 'and yet − his sexual nature was not innately "normal". . . . But Brick's overt sexual adjustment was, and must always remain, a heterosexual one': St Just, ed., *Five O'Clock Angel*, 110. See Clum, *Acting Gay*, 156–62.

47. Williams, in *The Theatre of Tennessee Williams*, vol. 3 (New York: New Directions, 1971), 168.

48. Murphy, *Tennessee Williams and Elia Kazan*, 103–7.

49. Phillips, *The Films of Tennessee Williams*, 144–7.

50. Maurice Yacowar, *Tennessee Williams and Film* (New York: Frederick Ungar, 1977), 43.

51. Ibid.

52. Quoted in Falk, *Tennessee Williams*, 106.

53. Marjorie Garber, *Vested Interests* (New York: Routledge, 1992), 112.

54. Savran, *Communists, Cowboys, and Queers*, 81, 145; see 89–99, 102–10. I discuss such theory in principle in ch.17.

55. Alisa Solomon, *Re-Dressing the Canon* (London: Routledge, 1997), 163.

56. Williams, *Memoirs*, 85–6; see also 118, 120, 142–3.

57. Spoto, *Kindness*, 210, 187; see also Marion Magid, 'The Innocence of Tennessee Williams', in Miller, ed., *Twentieth Century Interpretations*, 77.

58. Magid, 'The Innocence of Tennessee Williams', 73–4.

59. Miller, ed., *Twentieth Century Interpretations*, 6, 14.

60. Quoted ibid., 23–4, Kazan's emphases. See Murphy, *Tennessee Williams and Elia Kazan*, 37.

61. Quoted in Savran, *Communists, Cowboys, and Queers*, 79.
62. Stanley Kauffmann, *Persons of the Drama* (New York: Harper and Row, 1976), 152, 154.
63. Sacvan Bercovitch, *The American Jeremiad* (Madison: University of Wisconsin Press, 1978), 179–80, and ch.6.
64. Sievers, *Freud on Broadway*, 409–10.
65. Kaier Curtin, *'We Can Always Call Them Bulgarians'* (Boston: Alyson, 1987), 298.
66. I-1-14; on the referencing of plays quoted from typescript see my Note on Indexes and Citations.
67. See Curtin, *Bulgarians*, ch.16.
68. Leo Bersani, *Homos* (Cambridge, MA: Harvard University Press, 1995), 69.
69. David Savran, *Taking It Like a Man* (Princeton University Press, 1998), 244; *The Times*, 26 April 1999, 35.
70. For an interesting and persuasive case that the information given about Prior indicates Norman or Anglo-Norman stock, see Allen J. Frantzen, *Before the Closet* (Chicago University Press, 1998), 278–92. The point is important because Kushner seems to imagine Anglo-Saxons and other European peoples as unmixed and non migratory.
71. I, 68 refers to page 68 of *Angels in America Part 1: Millennium Approaches*. *Angels in America Part 2: Perestroika* is cited as II.
72. Kushner, quoted in Savran, *Taking It Like a Man*, 274, 357–8.

11 The All-American Family

1. W. David Sievers, *Freud on Broadway* (New York: Cooper, 1970), 217.
2. Allan Bérubé, *Coming Out Under Fire* (New York: Plume, 1991), 228, 127. See John D'Emilio, *Sexual Politics, Sexual Communities* (Chicago University Press, 1983), 23–33, 38–9.
3. Barry Feinberg and Ronald Kasrils, eds, *Bertrand Russell's America, vol. 2, 1945–1970* (London: Allen and Unwin, 1984), 359.
4. Donald Webster Cory, *The Homosexual in America* (1951; New York: Paperback Library Edition, 1963), ch.4; Bérubé, *Coming Out Under Fire*, ch.10; D'Emilio, *Sexual Politics*, ch.3; Lee Edelman, 'Tearooms and Sympathy, or, The Epistemology of the Water Closet', in Andrew Parker, Mary Russo, Doris Sommer

and Patricia Yaeger, eds, *Nationalisms and Sexualities* (New York: Routledge, 1992); Harry M. Benshoff, *Monsters in the Closet: Homosexuality and the Horror Film* (Manchester University Press, 1997), ch.3.
5. Quoted in Jonathan Katz, *Gay American History* (New York: Avon Books, 1978), 146, 148.
6. D'Emilio, *Sexual Politics*, 57–66, 75–87; the quotation is from 85.
7. John M. Clum, *Acting Gay*, 2nd edn (New York: Columbia University Press, 1994), 167–73.
8. William M. Hoffman, *Gay Plays* (New York: Avon Books, 1979), xxii; Michael Bronski, *Culture Clash* (Boston: South End Press, 1984), 117–18.
9. John van Druten, *The Widening Circle* (London: Heinemann, 1957), 108–11.
10. Bérubé, *Coming Out Under Fire*, 13–16, 33, 136–7, 142, 146–8, 159–60.
11. Sievers, *Freud on Broadway*; Donald L. Loeffler, *An Analysis of the Treatment of the Homosexual Character in Dramas Produced in the New York Theatre from 1950 to 1968* (New York: Arno Press, 1975), ch.3.
12. Quoted in Kenneth Lewes, *The Psychoanalytic Theory of Male Homosexuality* (London: Quartet, 1989), 136–7.
13. Sigmund Freud, *Standard Edition of the Complete Psychological Works*, ed. James Strachey, vol. 23 (London: Hogarth, 1964), 156.
14. Cory, *The Homosexual in America*, 30–1.
15. Norman Mailer, *Advertisements for Myself* (London: Panther, 1968), 193. See Jonathan Dollimore, *Sexual Dissidence* (Oxford: Clarendon, 1991), 46–7, 264–5.
16. Irving Bieber et al., *Homosexuality: a Psychoanalytical Study* (New York: Vintage Books, 1962), 18. See Lewes, *Psychoanalytic Theory*, ch.6 and 206–12.
17. Georges-Michel Sarotte, *Like a Brother, Like a Lover*, trans. Richard Miller (New York: Anchor/Doubleday, 1978), 31.
18. Dennis Welland, *Miller the Playwright* (London: Methuen, 1983), 74.
19. Clum, *Acting Gay*, 11–16.
20. Ibid., 146.
21. Eric Bentley, *The Dramatic Event* (New York: Horizon Press, 1954), 150–1.
22. Howard Taubman, 'Not What It Seems: Homosexual Motif Gets Heterosexual Disguise', quoted in Marilyn Stasio, ed.,

Broadway's Beautiful Losers (New York: Dell, 1972), 72.

23. George Rogers Taylor, ed., *The Turner Thesis*, 3rd edn (Lexington, MA: D.C. Heath, 1972), 14–56; see Henry Nash Smith, *Virgin Land* (Cambridge, MA: Harvard University Press, 1950).

24. William Carlos Williams, *In the American Grain* (New York: New Directions, 1956), 136–7.

25. Michael S. Sherry, *In the Shadow of War* (New Haven: Yale University Press, 1995), xi.

26. Godfrey Hodgson, *America in Our Time* (New York: Vintage Books, 1978), 468–70.

27. Erik H. Erikson, *Childhood and Society* (New York: Imago Publishing, 1950), 315.

28. Barbara Ehrenreich, *The Hearts of Men* (London: Pluto, 1983), 32–41, and ch.3. See Steven Cohan, 'The Spy in the Gray Flannel Suit: Gender Performance and the Representation of Masculinity in *North by Northwest*', in Andrew Perchuk and Helaine Posner, eds, *The Masculine Masquerade* (Cambridge, MA: MIT Press, 1995).

29. Herbert Marcuse, *Eros and Civilization* (1955; Boston: Beacon Press, 1974), 96–101.

30. See Jeffrey Weeks, *Sexuality and Its Discontents* (London: Routledge, 1985), 73; Henry Abelove, 'Freud, Male Homosexuality, and the Americans', in Henry Abelove, Michèle Aina Barale and David M. Halperin, eds, *The Lesbian and Gay Studies Reader* (New York: Routledge, 1993), 381; Dollimore, *Sexual Dissidence* (Oxford: Clarendon, 1991), 196–7.

31. Gustav Bychowski, 'The Ego of Homosexuals', *International Journal of Psychoanalysis*, 26 (1945), 114–27, 114, 125.

32. Lewes, *Psychoanalytic Theory*, 237.

33. Abram Kardiner, 'The Flight from Masculinity', in Hendrik M. Ruitenbeek, ed., *The Problem of Homosexuality in Modern Society* (New York: Dutton, 1963), 22, 27; Betty Friedan, *The Feminine Mystique* (London: Gollancz, 1965), 276.

34. Signi Falk, *Tennessee Williams*, 2nd edn (Boston: Twayne, 1978), 158. See Ehrenreich, *Hearts of Men*, ch.2.

35. Bieber et al., *Homosexuality*, 174, 187.

36. Sarotte, *Like a Brother*, 191, and ch.13.

37. David Savran, *Communists, Cowboys, and Queers* (Minneapolis: University of Minnesota Press, 1992), 41–2.

38. Michael Paul Rogin, '*Ronald Reagan': the Movie* (Berkeley: University of California Press, 1987), 241.

39. Erikson, *Childhood and Society*, 300. See Lucy Fischer, 'Mama's Boy: Filial Hysteria in *White Heat*', in Steven Cohan and Ina Rae Hark, eds, *Screening the Male* (London: Routledge, 1993).

40. Rogin, 'Ronald Reagan', 257.

41. Philip Wylie, *Generation of Vipers*, with a new preface (1942; London: Muller, 1955), 65–6; on Momism, see ch.11. Wylie became rabidly anti-Communist, but he opposed McCarthy.

42. Erikson, *Childhood and Society*, 301.

43. Bieber et al., *Homosexuality*, 79–80; see D'Emilio, *Sexual Politics*, 215–17.

44. Friedan, *The Feminine Mystique*, 273–6.

45. Gerry McCarthy, *Edward Albee* (London: Macmillan, 1987), 15, 66.

46. Richard Schechner, 'Who's Afraid of Edward Albee?' (1963), in C.W.E. Bigsby, ed., *Edward Albee, Twentieth Century Views* (Englewood Cliffs, NJ: Prentice-Hall, 1975), 63–4.

47. Tom F. Driver, 'What's the Matter with Edward Albee?', in Alan S. Downer, ed., *American Drama and Its Critics* (Chicago University Press, 1965), 242–3. See also Sarotte, *Like a Brother*, 137–49, and David van Leer, *The Queening of America* (New York: Routledge, 1995), 20–7.

48. See ch.10, and Alan Sinfield, *Cultural Politics – Queer Reading* (Philadelphia: University of Pennsylvania Press; London: Routledge, 1994), 9–20, 32–6.

49. Ralph F. Voss, *A Life of William Inge* (University of Kansas Press, 1989), 196.

50. Robert Brustein, *Seasons of Discontent* (London: Cape, 1966), 83–93. Brustein's case is accepted by Sarotte, *Like a Brother*, ch.9.

51. Clum, *Acting Gay*, 175–6. See Bronski, *Culture Clash*, 124–8; Kaier Curtin, *We Can Always Call Them Bulgarians* (Boston: Alyson, 1987), 320–6.

52. Brustein, *Seasons of Discontent*, 29. See Sarotte, *Like a Brother*, 134–6.

53. Philip Roth, 'The Play that Dare Not Speak Its Name', in Bigsby, ed., *Edward Albee*, 105 (see also 94–5).

54. Stanley Kauffmann, *Persons of the Drama* (New York: Harper and Row, 1976), 291–3. On Kauffmann's dismissal, see Merle Miller, *On Being Different* (New York: Random House, 1971), 49–50.

55. Bychowski, 'The Ego of Homosexuals', 117.
56. See Curtin, *Bulgarians*, 282. See also Hoffman, ed., *Gay Plays*, Introduction.
57. Curtin, *Bulgarians*, 266–79.
58. Nina Rapi, 'Lesbian Theatre', *Rouge*, 19 (Winter 1990–91), 19–21.
59. Sonya L. Jones, 'Introduction', in Jones, ed., *Gay and Lesbian Literature since World War II* (New York: Harrington Park, 1998), 2.
60. Valerie Taylor, 'Five Minority Groups in Relation to Contemporary Fiction', *The Ladder*, 5, no.4 (January 1961), 6–22, 17.
61. On the emergence of 'gay', see Ann Bannon, *I Am a Woman* (1959), in Bannon, *The Beebo Brinker Chronicles* (New York: Quality Paperback Book Club, 1995), 225–6, 233–4, 243.
62 Carol Ann Uszkurat, 'Mid Twentieth Century Lesbian Romance: Reception and Address', in Gabriele Griffin, ed., *Outwrite: Lesbianism and Popular Culture* (London: Pluto, 1993), 30; quoting Diane Hamer, '"I Am a Woman": Ann Bannon and the Writing of Lesbian Identity in the 1950s', in Mark Lilly, ed., *Lesbian and Gay Writing* (London: Macmillan, 1990), 51.
63. Jann Miller, 'The Children's Hour', *The Ladder*, 2, no.1 (October, 1957), 14.
64. Lillian Faderman, *Odd Girls and Twilight Lovers* (New York: Penguin, 1992), 186. On the Daughters of Bilitis see Faderman, 148–50, 190–4.
65. Florence Conrad, 'A Lesbian Looks at Tennessee Williams', *The Ladder*, 3, no. 8 (May 1959), 24.

12 The Problem of the Problem

1. Patrick Higgins, *Heterosexual Dictatorship* (London: Fourth Estate, 1996).
2. Kevin Porter and Jeffrey Weeks, eds, *Between the Acts* (London: Routledge, 1991), 112, 141.
3. H. Montgomery Hyde, *The Other Love* (London: Mayflower, 1972), 237; see Jeffrey Weeks, *Coming Out* (London: Quartet, 1977), ch.14.
4. Rupert Croft-Cooke, *The Life For Me* (London: Macmillan, 1952), 4–7, 241, 258.
5. Rupert Croft-Cooke, *The Verdict of You All* (London: Secker, 1955), 134; Peter Wildeblood, *Against the Law* (London: Weidenfeld, 1955), 26.
6. Porter and Weeks, eds, *Between the Acts*, 149.

See also Hall Carpenter Archives and Gay Men's Oral History Group, *Walking After Midnight* (London: Routledge, 1989), 35-6, 97–8.
7. Higgins, *Heterosexual Dictatorship*, 38–9.
8. Hyde, *The Other Love*, 238; see D.J. West, *Homosexuality* (London: Duckworth, 1955), xii, 43.
9. Richard Hauser, *The Homosexual Society* (London: Bodley Head, 1962), 11.
10. Gordon Westwood, *A Minority* (London: Longmans, 1960), 93, referring back to Westwood's *Society and the Homosexual* (London: Gollancz, 1952).
11. Antony Grey, *Speaking Out* (London: Cassell, 1997), 3, 71, 135.
12. *The Wolfenden Report* (1957; New York: Lancer Books, 1964), paragraphs 31, 186, 192–4.
13. David T. Evans, *Sexual Citizenship* (London: Routledge, 1993), 64 and ch.2.
14. David Bell, 'One-Handed Geographies: An Archaeology of Public Sex', in Gordon Brent Ingram, Anne-Marie Bouthillette and Yolanda Retter, eds, *Queers in Space* (Seattle: Bay Press, 1997), 86.
15. See Christopher Reed, 'Imminent Domain: Queer Space in the Built Environment', *Art Journal* (Winter 1996), 64–70.
16. Gregory Woods, *A History of Gay Literature* (New Haven and London: Yale University Press, 1998), 289.
17. Christine Fox, 'Conduct Unbecoming: Noël Coward, Censorship and the Fallacy of the Inconsequence', unpub. D.Phil. thesis, University of Sussex, 1996.
18. Richard Findlater, *Banned* (London: MacGibbon and Kee, 1967), 167 8.
19. Joan DeJean, *Fictions of Sappho 1546–1937* (Chicago University Press, 1989), 16.
20. John Johnston, *The Lord Chamberlain's Blue Pencil* (London: Hodder and Stoughton, 1990), 176. On the ambivalence of *Serious Charge* see Dan Rebellato, *1956 and All That* (London: Routledge, 1999), 170–2.
21. Ibid., 210.
22. Angus Wilson, 'Problems and Plays: The Theatre Faces the World: Morality', in Harold Hobson, ed., *International Theatre Journal*, 4 (1959), 184–9.
23. Roger Gellert, 'A Survey of the Treatment of the Homosexual in Some Plays', *Encore*, 8, no.1 (1961), 29–39, 29.
24. See John Hill, *Sex, Class and Realism* (London: British Film Institute, 1986).
25. See Higgins, *Heterosexual Dictatorship*, 97–8.

26. John M. Clum, *Acting Gay*, 2nd edn (New York: Columbia University Press, 1994), xvii.
27. Kaier Curtin, *We Can Always Call Them Bulgarians* (Boston: Alyson, 1987), 320–1; Jim Kepner, *Rough News, Daring Views* (New York: Harrington Park, 1998), 281. Kepner (199) notes revivals in New York in 1957 of *Oscar Wilde* (Stokes) and *The Captive* (Bourdet).
28. *Look on Tempests* (1960), in *Plays and Players*, 7, no.11 (August 1960), 24–30, 26.
29. Quoted in Stephen Rooney, 'Literary Constructions of Male Homosexuality 1954–1969', unpub. D.Phil. thesis, University of Sussex, 1998, 138.

13 Politics and Anger

1. Kenneth Tynan, *A View of the English Theatre* (St Albans: Paladin, 1976), 148.
2. John Russell Taylor, ed., *John Osborne, 'Look Back In Anger': A Casebook* (London: Macmillan, 1968), 37–9, 45.
3. Geoffrey Wansell, *Terence Rattigan* (London: Fourth Estate, 1995), 270; Taylor, ed., *John Osborne*, 49–50.
4. See Alan Sinfield, *Literature, Politics and Culture in Postwar Britain*, 2nd edn (London: Athlone, 1997), chs 11, 12.
5. Frank Parkin, *Middle Class Radicalism* (Manchester University Press, 1968), 43. The figures were 94 per cent in social classes 1–2, 87 per cent in classes 3–4 and 75 per cent in classes 5–7.
6. Michael Darlow and Gillian Hodson, *Terence Rattigan* (London: Quartet, 1979), 249–50.
7. Michelene Wandor, *Carry On Understudies* (London: Routledge, 1986), 144.
8. *New Statesman*, 31 October 1953, 508–9, 515–6.
9. Leslie A. Fiedler, 'The Un-Angry Young Men', *Encounter*, 10 (January 1958), 3–12.
10. See Arnold Wesker, *Chips with Everything* (London: Cape, 1962), 26, and Wesker, *Volume Three: Chips with Everything* [and other plays] (Harmondsworth: Penguin, 1980), 25.
11. Elizabeth Wilson, *Only Halfway to Paradise* (London: Tavistock, 1980), 104.
12. Patrick Higgins, *Heterosexual Dictatorship* (London: Fourth Estate, 1996), 297.
13. D.J. West, *Homosexuality* (London: Duckworth, 1955), xii.
14. Eustace Chesser, *Odd Man Out* (London: Gollancz, 1959), 93.
15. Quoted in Mary McIntosh, 'Class', in Andy Medhurst and Sally R. Munt, eds, *Lesbian and Gay Studies* (London: Cassell, 1997), 243.
16. Interview in Veronica Groocock, *Changing Our Lives* (London: Cassell, 1995), 138–9. Cf. Hall Carpenter Archives and Lesbian Oral History Group, eds, *Inventing Ourselves* (London: Routledge, 1989).
17. The reviews are quoted in Dan Rebellato, *1956 and All That* (London: Routledge, 1999), 208.
18. See Nicholas de Jongh, *Not in Front of the Audience* (London: Routledge, 1992), 108 and Charles Duff, *The Lost Summer* (London: Nick Hern Books, 1995), 107.
19. John Osborne, *A Better Class of Person* (London: Faber, 1981), 29.
20. Nicholas de Jongh, 'The Secret Gay Love of John Osborne', *Evening Standard*, 24 January, 1995, 12–13. See *Gay Times*, 198 (March 1995), 40–1.
21. Osborne, *A Better Class of Person*, 229.
22. Richard Findlater, *Banned* (London: MacGibbon and Kee, 1967), 188; Gordon Westwood, *A Minority* (London: Longmans, 1960), 141.
23. Osborne, *A Better Class of Person*, 244; John Osborne, *Almost a Gentleman* (London: Faber and Faber, 1991), 245.
24. See Higgins, *Heterosexual Dictatorship*, 307–21.
25. Westwood, *A Minority*, 150–1.
26. Chris Kirk and Ed Heath, *Men in Frocks* (London: Gay Men's Press, 1984), 13–28, 38–48.
27. Ibid., 56, 60, 83–5. For comparable occasions in the USA at this time, see Donald Webster Cory, *The Homosexual in America* (1951; New York: Paperback Library, 1963), ch.12; Esther Newton, *Mother Camp*, 2nd edn (Chicago University Press, 1979), 34–5, 120.
28. Rebellato, *1956 and All That*, 185–90.
29. B.A. Young, *Financial Times*, 1 July 1965, 22.
30. Osborne, *Almost a Gentleman*, 271; *West of Suez* (1971), 47.
31. Recent discussions include David T. Evans, *Sexual Citizenship* (London: Routledge, 1993); Leslie J. Moran, *The Homosexual(ity) of Law* (London: Routledge, 1996); Higgins, *Heterosexual Dictatorship*.
32. Findlater, *Banned*, 188, 179.

33. John Johnston, *The Lord Chamberlain's Blue Pencil* (London: Hodder and Stoughton, 1990), 190.
34. See Terry Browne, *Playwrights' Theatre* (London: Pitman, 1975), ch.4.
35. Johnston, *The Lord Chamberlain's Blue Pencil*, .251–2.

14 'The Sixties'

1. Elizabeth Wilson, *Only Halfway to Paradise* (London: Tavistock, 1980), 158.
2. Emily Hamer, *Britannia's Glory* (London: Cassell, 1996), 183.
3. Jackie Forster, 'Frank Marcus and Sister George . . .', *Sappho*, 8, no.3 (1980), 9–11. In an obituary for Jackie Marcus, Frank Marcus' wife, Forster indicates that she subsequently involved herself in lesbian circles, but *Sister George* had 'nothing to do with Jackie'. See The Other Jackie (Forster), 'Jackie Marcus', *Capital Gay*, 10 September 1993.
4. Jill Dolan, *Presence and Desire* (Ann Arbor: University of Michigan Press, 1993), 167.
5. See Sally R. Munt, ed., *Butch/Femme* (London: Cassell, 1998).
6. Quoted in Forster, 'Frank Marcus and Sister George'.
7. Eustace Chesser, *Odd Man Out* (London: Gollancz, 1959), 102–3.
8. Interview in Veronica Groocock, *Changing Our Lives* (London: Cassell, 1995), 138–9.
9. Forster, 'Frank Marcus and Sister George'.
10. The Other Jackie (Forster), 'Jackie Marcus'.
11. Susan Sontag, 'Notes on Camp', in *A Susan Sontag Reader* (New York: Vintage Books, 1983). See Moe Meyer, *The Politics and Poetics of Camp* (New York: Routledge, 1994).
12. Russell Davies, ed., *The Kenneth Williams Diaries* (London: HarperCollins, 1994), 324.
13. Quoted in Keith Howes, *Broadcasting It* (London: Cassell, 1993), 519.
14. Peter Burton, *Parallel Lives* (London: Gay Men's Press, 1985), 38–42.
15. Barry Took, *Laughter in the Air* (London: Robson Books, 1981), 153, and 146–55, Took's pauses. See Leslie J. Cox and Richard J. Fay, 'Gayspeak, the Linguistic Fringe: Bona Polari, Camp, Queerspeak, and Beyond', in Stephen Whittle, ed., *The Margins of the City* (Aldershot: Arena, 1994).
16. Ray Douglas Davies, 'Lola', quoted from the record (London: Pye 7N 17961, 1970).
17. See Richard Smith, *Other Voices* (London: Cassell, 1997).
18. See Martin Esslin, *Theatre of the Absurd* (1961), enlarged edn (Harmondsworth: Penguin, 1968), 64–6.
19. Quoted in Kaier Curtin, *We Can Always Call Them Bulgarians* (Boston: Alyson, 1987), 327.
20. See John Lahr, *Prick Up Your Ears* (Harmondsworth: Penguin, 1980), 206–7.
21. John Johnston, *The Lord Chamberlain's Blue Pencil* (London: Hodder and Stoughton, 1990), 202–3.
22. Joe Orton, *The Orton Diaries*, ed. John Lahr (London: Methuen, 1986), 127.
23. Johnston, *The Lord Chamberlain's Blue Pencil*, 199–200. Pinner's *Dickon*, about a man in his prime falling ill with cancer, had been received respectfully in 1966.
24. See Simon Shepherd, *Because We're Queers* (London: Gay Men's Press, 1989), 74–7.
25. Lahr, *Prick Up Your Ears*, 215.
26. Ibid., 236–8, 255–6. Also it had been revealed shortly before that rhino whips were in use in a Sheffield police station.
27. The Lord Chamberlain's changes are printed in Simon Trussler, ed., *New English Dramatists 13* (Harmondsworth: Penguin, 1968), 84.
28. Lahr, *Prick Up Your Ears*, 250–1; see Orton, *Diaries*, 112.
29. Simon Trussler, 'Farce', *Plays and Players* (June 1966), 72.
30. Orton, *Diaries*, 54.
31. Ibid., 249–50, 256. *Butler* was produced by Beaumont and Oscar Lewenstein at the Queen's Theatre in 1969.
32. Albert Hunt, 'What Joe Orton Saw', *New Society*, 17 April 1875, 148–50.
33. Trussler, 'Farce', 58, 72.
34. Shepherd, *Because We're Queers*, 96.
35. Orton, *Diaries*, 256–7. Stanley Baxter is quoted there as saying that the barracking started ten minutes after the start of the second act. I depend here upon a personal communication from Colin Spencer, author of *Spitting Image* (which I discuss shortly).
36. Lahr, *Prick Up Your Ears*, 249; see also 227, and Orton, *Diaries*, 75–6, 150.
37. Orton, *Diaries*, 91; Shepherd, *Because We're Queers*, 126. See also 26–8, 31, 56–8, 89, 97–8, 111; and Randall S. Nakayama, 'Domesticating Mr Orton', *Theatre Journal*, 45 (1993), 185–95.

38. Lahr, *Prick Up Your Ears*, 187, 189, 248.

39. John M. Clum, *Acting Gay*, 2nd edn (New York: Columbia University Press, 1994), 125–6, 133.

40. Jonathan Dollimore, 'The Dominant and the Deviant: A Violent Dialectic', *Critical Quarterly*, 28, nos 1–2 (1986), 179–92, 189. For this argument in principle, see ch.17 below.

41. Lahr, *Prick Up Your Ears*, 204.

42. Paul A. Robinson, *The Sexual Radicals* (London: Paladin, 1972), 15–16.

43. Charles Marowitz, 'Notes on the Theatre of Cruelty', in Charles Marowitz and Simon Trussler, eds, *Theatre at Work* (London: Methuen, 1967), 184.

44. Charles Rycroft, *Reich* (London: Fontana/Collins, 1971), 63. See Jonathan Dollimore, *Sexual Dissidence* (Oxford: Clarendon, 1991), 205–6.

45. Robinson, *Sexual Radicals*, 62.

46. See David Savran, *Taking It Like a Man* (Princeton University Press, 1998), 151.

47. Herbert Marcuse, *Eros and Civilization* (1955; Boston: Beacon, 1966), 49, 201. See Randall Halle, 'Between Marxism and Psychoanalysis: Antifascism and Antihomosexuality in the Frankfurt School', in Gert Hekma, Harry Oosterhuis and James Steakley, eds, *Gay Men and the Sexual History of the Political Left* (New York: Harrington Park, 1995).

48. See Eric Bentley, ed. *The Modern Theatre*, vol. 6 (Gloucester, MA: Peter Smith, 1974), 286; Johnston, *The Lord Chamberlain's Blue Pencil*, 176–7.

49. Alan Bates quoted in the *Evening Standard*, 4 July, 1975; Simon Gray quoted by Ronald Hayman in *The Times*, 26 July, 1975.

50. Germaine Greer, *The Female Eunuch* (1970; London: Paladin, 1971), 67–8. On this period see Lynne Segal, *Straight Sex* (London: Virago, 1994).

51. Wilson, *Only Halfway to Paradise*, 157–8.

52. Jane Rule, *Lesbian Images* (New York: Doubleday, 1975), 178–9.

53. Todd Gitlin, *The Sixties* (New York: Bantam Books, 1987), 213–14 and ch.8. See David Savran, *Communists, Cowboys, and Queers* (Minneapolis: University of Minnesota Press, 1992), 147–54.

54. See Werner Sollors, *Amiri Baraka/LeRoi Jones* (New York: Columbia University Press, 1978), 112.

55. Ibid., 111–14.

56. Ron Simmons, 'Some Thoughts on the Challenges Facing Black Gay Intellectuals', in Essex Hemphill, ed., *Brother to Brother* (Boston: Alyson, 1991), 217.

57. Eldridge Cleaver, *Soul on Ice* (London: Panther, 1970), 100; Huey Newton, 'A Letter from Huey to the Revolutionary Brothers and Sisters About the Women's Liberation and Gay Liberation Movements', in Mark Blasius and Shane Phelan, eds, *We Are Everywhere* (New York: Routledge, 1997), 404–6.

58. Martin Duberman, *Stonewall* (New York: Dutton, 1993); Lillian Faderman, *Odd Girls and Twilight Lovers* (New York: Penguin, 1992), 192–4.

59. Adrienne Rich, *Blood, Bread, and Poetry* (London: Virago, 1987), 120.

60. On GLF see Jeffrey Weeks, *Coming Out* (London: Quartet, 1977), ch.16.

61. See Michelene Wandor, *Carry On Understudies* (London: Routledge, 1986), 97, 194–8.

62. John Russell Taylor, review of *Spitting Image* in *Plays and Players*, 16 (November 1968), 64.

63. Michael Billington, *The Times*, 25 October, 1968, 8.

64. Nancy K. Miller, 'Emphasis Added: Plots and Plausibilities', in Elaine Showalter, ed., *The New Feminist Criticism* (London: Virago, 1986), 357, 352.

15 Subcultural Work

1. Kaier Curtin, *We Can Always Call Them Bulgarians* (Boston: Alyson, 1987), 320.

2. Robert Patrick, *Untold Decades* (New York: St Martin's Press, 1988), xiv.

3. See David Savran, *Taking It Like a Man* (Princeton University Press, 1998), ch.1; Juan A. Suárez, *Bike Boys, Drag Queens, and Superstars* (Bloomington and Indianapolis: University of Indiana Press, 1996), 126–40.

4. Werner Sollors, *Amiri Baraka/LeRoi Jones* (New York: Columbia University Press, 1978), 100–1.

5. Charles Marowitz, Introduction, in *Off-Broadway Plays, vol. 1* (Harmondsworth: Penguin, 1970), 9–10. See William M. Hoffman, ed., *Gay Plays* (New York: Avon Books, 1979), xxiii–xxix; Michael Bronski, *Culture Clash* (Boston: South End Press, 1984), 123–32.

6. 'The Homosexual in America', *Time*, 21 January, 1966, 40–1.

7. See Ruby Cohn, *New American Dramatists 1960–1990*, 2nd edn (London: Macmillan, 1991), 131–44.

8. Charles Ludlam, *Ridiculous Theatre: Scourge of Human Folly* (New York: Theatre Communications Group, 1992), 4, 42.

9. Ibid., 241.

10. Everett Quinton, '"Tootaloo Marguerite!"' in Nicholas John, ed., *Violetta and Her Sisters* (London: Faber and Faber, 1994), 151–3. See Alisa Solomon, *Re-Dressing the Canon* (London: Routledge, 1997), 144–54.

11. Theodore Shank, *American Alternative Theatre* (London: Macmillan, 1982), 54–5.

12. Curtin, *Bulgarians*, 328.

13. Merle Miller, *On Being Different* (New York. Random House, 1971), 51. See John M. Clum, *Acting Gay*, 2nd edn (New York: Columbia University Press, 1994), 253–9. *Boys in the Band* was first produced by Albee's production company, although Albee didn't like it: Philip C. Kolin, ed., *Conversations with Edward Albee* (Jackson: University of Mississippi Press, 1988), 200.

14. Robert Brustein, *Seasons of Discontent* (London: Cape, 1966), 83–93.

15. Peter Burton, 'American Schmaltz', *Gay Times*, 87 (November 1985), 70.

16. See Philip Osment, ed., *Gay Sweatshop: Four Plays and a Company* (London: Methuen, 1989), Introduction.

17. Gini Stevens, 'Dialogue with Maureen Duffy', *Lunch*, 9 (June 1972), 4–8, 7.

18. Hall Carpenter Archives and Gay Men's Oral History Group, *Walking After Midnight* (London: Routledge, 1989), 134–5.

19. Interview with Kate Crutchley and Julie Parker in Sandra Freeman, *Putting Your Daughters on the Stage* (London: Cassell, 1997), 26, 133.

20. Edward Carpenter, *Love's Coming of Age* (London: Swan Sonnenschein, 1906), 126–30.

21. Paul Taylor, 'The Drag of It All', *The Independent*, 8 May, 1997; Stephen Mathers, quoted in David Bret, *Maria Callas* (London: Robson, 1997), 93.

22. For a repudiation of some misgivings about *Bent* see Nicholas de Jongh, *Not in Front of the Audience* (London: Routledge, 1992), 145–56.

23. Eve Kosofsky Sedgwick, *Epistemology of the Closet* (Hemel Hempstead: Harvester Wheatsheaf, 1991), 84.

24. Lynne Segal, *Straight Sex* (London: Virago, 1994), 51–2. Segal draws upon Lillian Faderman, *Odd Girls and Twilight Lovers* (New York: Penguin, 1992), chs 8, 9. For another recent account, see Arlene Stein, *Sex and Sensibility* (Berkeley: University of California Press, 1997), 23–46.

25. See Segal, *Straight Sex*, 54–5.

26. On the development of this ethos, see Michelene Wandor, *Carry On Understudies* (London: Routledge, 1986), chs 1–4, and Charlotte Canning, *Feminist Theaters in the USA* (London: Routledge, 1996), ch.3.

27. Emily L. Sisley, 'Notes on Lesbian Theatre', in Carol Martin, ed., *A Sourcebook of Feminist Theatre and Performance* (London: Routledge, 1996), 54–5.

28. Quoted in Canning, *Feminist Theaters in the USA*, 116.

29. Sisley, 'Notes on Lesbian Theatre', 57. See Canning, *Feminist Theaters in the USA*, 194–6; Sue-Ellen Case, *Feminism and Theatre* (London: Macmillan, 1988), 77–9.

30. Hoffman, *Gay Plays*, xxxvii.

31. On *Chiaroscuro* see Mary Brewer, *Race, Sex, and Gender in Contemporary Women's Theatre* (Brighton: Sussex Academic Press, 1999), 133–40.

32. Cherríe Moraga, *Loving in the War Years* (Boston: South End Press, 1983), 125.

33. Freeman, *Putting Your Daughters on the Stage*, ch.8.

34. See Alisa Solomon, 'The WOW Cafe' in Martin, ed., *A Sourcebook of Feminist Theatre and Performance*; Sue-Ellen Case, ed., *Split Britches* (London: Routledge, 1996), 7–17.

35. Kate Davy, 'From *Lady Dick* to Ladylike: The Work of Holly Hughes', in Lynda Hart and Peggy Phelan, eds, *Acting Out* (Ann Arbor: University of Michigan Press, 1993), 57.

16 AIDS: Crisis and Drama

Note: David Román's valuable study, *Acts of Intervention: Performance, Gay Culture, and AIDS* (Bloomington and Indianapolis: Indiana University Press, 1988) arrived too late for me to use it in this chapter. Román is particularly strong on some things I have not been able to do so well: the circumstances of US productions, race and AIDS and, most profoundly, testing negative.

1. Eve Kosofsky Sedgwick, *Between Men* (New York: Columbia University Press, 1985), 90.

2. Gregory Woods, *A History of Gay Literature* (New Haven and London: Yale University Press, 1998), 361–2.

3. Michael Feingold, ed., *The Way We Live Now* (New York: Theater Communications Group, 1990), xi.

4. John M. Clum, *Acting Gay*, 2nd edn (New

York: Columbia University Press, 1994), 67–8.

5. Thomas Yingling, 'AIDS in America: Postmodern Governance, Identity, and Experience', in Diana Fuss, ed., *Inside/Out* (New York: Routledge, 1991), 303–4; Louise L. Hay, *You Can Heal Your Life* (Enfield, Middx: Eden Grove, 1988), 147.

6. John M. Clum, ed., *Staging Gay Lives* (Boulder, CO: Westview, 1996), 401.

7. See for instance David Bergman, *Gaiety Transfigured* (Madison: University of Wisconsin Press, 1991), ch.7.

8. Dennis Altman, *AIDS and the New Puritanism* (London: Pluto, 1986), 174–6.

9. See Stuart Marshall, 'The Contemporary Political Use of Gay History: The Third Reich', in Bad Object-Choices, eds, *How Do I Look?* (Seattle: Bay Press, 1991); Michael S. Sherry, 'The Language of War in AIDS Discourse', in Timothy F. Murphy and Suzanne Poirier, eds, *Writing AIDS* (New York: Columbia University Press, 1993).

10. 'Happy as Larry', Lisa Power interviewing Larry Kramer, *Gay Times*, 203 (August 1995), 49.

11. Sue Ellis and Paul Heritage, 'AIDS and the Cultural Response', in Simon Shepherd and Mick Wallis, eds, *Coming on Strong* (London: Unwin Hyman, 1989), 45, 48–9.

12. Ian Lucas, *Impertinent Decorum* (London: Cassell, 1994), 64.

13. '"The Moment of Submission": Neil Bartlett in Conversation', *Modern Drama*, Special Issue on Lesbian/Gay/Queer Drama, ed. Hersh Zeifman, 39 (1996), 211–21, 212–3.

14. Alan Sinfield, *Gay and After* (London: Serpent's Tail, 1998), ch.4. On the UK situation as distinctive, see also Philip Derbyshire, 'A Measure of Queer', *Critical Quarterly*, 36, no.1 (1994), 39–45, and Joshua Oppenheimer, 'Movements, Markets, and the Mainstream: Gay Activism and Assimilation in the Age of AIDS', in Joshua Oppenheimer and Helena Reckitt, eds, *Acting on AIDS* (London: Serpent's Tail and ICA, 1997).

15. Edward King, *Safety in Numbers* (London: Cassell, 1993), ch.1.

17 Dissident Strategies

1. Michelene Wandor, *Carry On Understudies* (London: Routledge, 1986), 56; also 61–4. On *Care and Control*, see Lizbeth Goodman, *Contemporary Feminist Theatres* (London:

Routledge, 1993), 76–8, 126–8.

2. See Sandra Freeman, *Putting Your Daughters on the Stage* (London: Cassell, 1997), 126–7, 173–4, 179–80.

3. See ibid., 128–9; and, for a historical account of the Ladies, Emma Donoghue, *Passions between Women* (London: Scarlet Press, 1993), 107, 129, 149–50.

4. Wandor, *Carry On Understudies*, 63; Freeman, *Putting Your Daughters on the Stage*, 173.

5. See Colin MacCabe, *Theoretical Essays* (Manchester University Press, 1985); Catherine Belsey, *Critical Practice* (London: Methuen, 1980). MacCabe's essays on this topic date from 1974.

6. Jill Dolan, *The Feminist Spectator as Critic* (Ann Arbor: University of Michigan Press, 1988), 106–15; Elin Diamond, 'Brechtian Theory/Feminist Theory: Toward a Gestic Feminist Criticism', *TDR: The Drama Review*, 32, no.1 (Spring 1988), 82–94; Alisa Solomon, *Re-Dressing the Canon* (London: Routledge, 1997), ch.3.

7. Jonathan Dollimore, 'The Challenge of Sexuality', in Alan Sinfield, ed., *Society and Literature 1945–1970* (London: Methuen, 1983), 78–80.

8. Jonathan Dollimore, *Radical Tragedy* (Brighton: Harvester, 1984), ch.9; Dollimore, 'Different Desires: Subjectivity and Transgression in Wilde and Gide', *Textual Practice*, 1 (1987), 48–67. Dollimore writes again on these topics in his book *Sexual Dissidence* (Oxford: Clarendon, 1991), ch.1 and 315–18. See also David Savran, *Communists, Cowboys, and Queers* (Minneapolis: University of Minnesota Press, 1992), 115–20, 159–61.

9. Judith Butler, *Gender Trouble* (New York: Routledge, 1990), 25.

10. Ian Lucas, *Impertinent Decorum* (London: Cassell, 1994), 112.

11. Carole-Anne Tyler, 'Boys Will Be Girls: The Politics of Gay Drag', in Diana Fuss, ed., *Inside/Out* (New York: Routledge, 1991). See Andy Medhurst, 'Camp', in Medhurst and Sally R. Munt, eds, *Lesbian and Gay Studies* (London: Cassell, 1997).

12. Alan Sinfield, *Gay and After* (London: Serpent's Tail, 1998), 107–11.

13. Kate Davy, 'Reading Past the Heterosexual Imperative', *TDR: The Drama Review*, 33 (1989), 153–70, 155. See further Davy,

'Fe/Male Impersonation: The Discourse of Camp', in Moe Meyer, ed., *The Politics and Poetics of Camp* (London: Routledge, 1994).

14. Judith Halberstam, 'Mackdaddy, Superfly, Rapper: Gender, Race, and Masculinity in the Drag King Scene', *Social Text*, 15, nos 3, 4 (Fall/Winter, 1997), 105–31, 115–7.

15. Sue-Ellen Case, 'Towards a Butch-Femme Aesthetic', in Henry Abelove, Michèle Aina Barale and David M. Halperin, eds, *The Lesbian and Gay Studies Reader* (New York: Routledge, 1993).

16. See Solomon, *Re-Dressing the Canon*, 21–7.

17. See Stephen Maddison, 'Queer Sisters: Gay Male Culture, Women and Gender Dissent', unpub. D.Phil. thesis, University of Sussex, 1997, 62–5 (to be published as *Fags, Hags and Queer Sisters* [London: Macmillan, 2000]).

18. Davy, 'Reading Past the Heterosexual Imperative', 158, 162.

19. Sue-Ellen Case's argument on *Dress Suits* is reported in Lynda Hart, 'Identity and Seduction: Lesbians in the Mainstream', in Lynda Hart and Peggy Phelan, eds, *Acting Out* (Ann Arbor: University of Michigan Press, 1993), 120.

20. Jill Dolan, *Presence and Desire* (Ann Arbor: University of Michigan Press, 1993), 192; see 159.

21. Hart, 'Identity and Seduction: Lesbians in the Mainstream', 121–22, 124.

22. Baz Kershaw, *The Politics of Performance* (London: Routledge, 1992), 33.

23. Jay Prosser, 'Transgender', in Medhurst and Munt, eds, *Lesbian and Gay Studies*, 317–18.

24. Interview with Phyllis Nagy, in Freeman, *Putting Your Daughters on the Stage*, 147–8.

25. Dolan, *Presence and Desire*, 160.

26. Hart, 'Identity and Seduction: Lesbians in the Mainstream', 127.

27. Teresa de Lauretis, 'Sexual Indifference and Lesbian Representation', in Abelove, et al., eds, *The Lesbian and Gay Studies Reader*, 144.

28. Nicholas de Jongh, 'The Love That Is Shouting Its Name', *Evening Standard*, 29 September, 1994; Milton Shulman, 'Stop the Plague of Pink Plays', *Evening Standard*, 30 September, 1994.

29. Terrence McNally, '*Love! Valour! Compassion!*' and '*A Perfect Ganesh*' (New York: Plume, 1995), ix.

30. See Sinfield, *Gay and After*, ch.9.

31. See John M. Clum, ed., *Staging Gay Lives* (Boulder, CO: Westview, 1996), xi–xiii.

32. David Savran, *Taking It Like a Man* (Princeton University Press, 1998), 277–8.

33. Jennie Long, 'What Share of the Cake Now? The Employment of Women in the English Theatre (1994)', in Lizbeth Goodman with Jane de Gay, ed., *The Routledge Reader in Gender and Performance* (London: Routledge, 1998).

34. John McGrath, *A Good Night Out* (London: Methuen, 1981), 7. See Mick Wallis and Simon Shepherd, *Studying Plays* (London: Arnold, 1998), 6.

35. Mary Remnant, ed., *Plays by Women*, vol. 6 (London: Methuen, 1987), Introduction.

36. See Freeman, *Putting Your Daughters on the Stage*, 168–9; Goodman, *Contemporary Feminist Theatres*, 128–31; Mary Brewer, *Race, Sex, and Gender in Contemporary Women's Theatre* (Brighton: Sussex Academic Press, 1999) ch.1; and, for a valuable comparison, Alison Lyssa's play *Pinball* (1981).

37. Joyce Wadler, *Liaison* (Harmondsworth: Penguin, 1993).

38. Charles Spencer, 'He Dares to Be Popular', *Daily Telegraph*, 21 September, 1994.

39. Paul Martin, quoted in the *Pink Paper*, 4 December, 1998, 47.

40. Simon Callow, *Being an Actor* (London: Penguin, 1985), 63.

41. Ibid., 64.

42. De Lauretis, 'Sexual Indifference and Lesbian Representation', 152; Dolan, *Presence and Desire*, 129.

43. Sarah Schulman, 'Is the NEA Good for Lesbian Art?', in Schulman, *My American History* (London: Cassell, 1995), 200.

44. Freeman, *Putting Your Daughters on the Stage*, 89.

45. Ibid., 133–5.

46. William M. Hoffman, ed., *Gay Plays* (New York: Avon Books, 1979), xxxvi.

47. Michael Wilcox, ed., *Gay Plays*, vol. 1 (London: Methuen, 1984), 6–8.

48. Alan Sinfield, '"The Moment of Submission": Neil Bartlett in Conversation', *Modern Drama*, 39 (1996), Special Issue on Lesbian/Gay/Queer Drama, ed. Hersh Zeifman, 211–21, 215.

49. Ibid., 218.

50. See Alan Sinfield, *Faultlines* (Berkeley: University of California Press; Oxford University Press, 1992), ch.2.

51. Jay Prosser, *Second Skins* (New York: Columbia University Press, 1998), 174.

52. Joelle Taylor, 'Deafening Smiles: Claire Dowie', *Glint*, 2, no.2 (summer 1994), 20–2.

Index of Plays

Plays are indexed here alphabetically by title; the date following the title (in brackets) is normally the date of first performance. Then the edition cited in the text is specified; and figures in bold type index references to the play in the text. Where a play is declared 'unpublished' that is, so far as I can ascertain. Playwrights appear alphabetically in the General Index.

Absolute Hell (1988) by Rodney Ackland. London: Oberon Books, 1994. **68**

Accounts (1983) by Wilcox. In Michael Wilcox, ed., *Gay Plays*, vol. 1. London: Methuen, 1984. **348–9**

Adventure Story (1949) by Terence Rattigan. In *The Collected Plays of Terence Rattigan*, vol. 2. London: Hamish Hamilton, 1953. **123–4**

Advise and Consent (1960) by Loring Mandel. New York: French, 1961. **210–11**

Afore Night Come (1962) by David Rudkin. In *New English Dramatists 7*. Harmondsworth: Penguin, 1963. **256, 265, 274**

After Haggerty (1970) by David Mercer. London: Methuen, 1970. **256**

Ah, Wilderness! (1933) by Eugene O'Neill. In O'Neill, *Ah, Wilderness!, The Hairy Ape, All God's Chillun Got Wings*. Harmondsworth: Penguin, 1960. **82, 117**

All God's Chillun Got Wings (1923) by Eugene O'Neill. In O'Neill, *Ah, Wilderness!, The Hairy Ape, All God's Chillun Got Wings*. Harmondsworth: Penguin, 1960. **146**

All My Sons (1947) by Arthur Miller. In Miller, *A View from the Bridge; All My Sons*. Harmondsworth: Penguin, 1961. **197, 220, 222–3**

American Dream (1933) by George O'Neil. New York: French, 1933. **208–9**

Index of Names and Topics